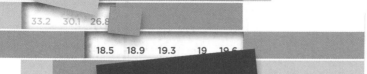

DATA AT WORK

Best practices for creating effective charts and
information graphics in Microsoft® Excel®

JORGE CAMÕES

DATA AT WORK
Best practices for creating effective charts and information graphics in Microsoft® Excel®

Jorge Camões

New Riders
Find us on the Web at www.newriders.com
New Riders is an imprint of Peachpit, a division of Pearson Education.
To report errors, please send a note to errata@peachpit.com

Acquisitions Editor: Nikki Echler McDonald
Production Editor: Kim Wimpsett
Development Editor: Dan Foster
Copy Editor: Jan Seymour
Proofreader: Scout Festa
Compositor: WolfsonDesign
Indexer: Karin Arrigoni
Cover and Interior Designer: Mimi Heft

ISBN 13: 9780134268637
ISBN 10: 0134268636

1 16

Printed and bound in the United States of America

To my family

Acknowledgments

I'd like to first thank Alberto Cairo. In non-English speaking countries, there are a few oases when it comes to publishing original data visualization books, but the landscape is basically a barren desert. I wanted to help change that, so I wrote the first manuscript of this book in my mother tongue, Portuguese. I then asked Alberto if he would read it.

Not only can Alberto read Portuguese, but we also share a similar view of what we think data visualization is all about, in spite of working in different areas. To make a long story short, he liked the book and introduced me to his acquisitions editor, Nikki McDonald, and so my data visualization journey took a turn. With the help of Nikki, my development editor Dan Foster, copy editor Jan Seymour, and production editor Kim Wimpsett, my poor manuscript became a real book. Alberto read several chapters of the English version and provided invaluable feedback.

Stephen Few also read a few chapters and saved me from myself once or twice, for which I am very appreciative.

If I know how to make a few charts that you can't find in the Excel charts library, that's because I learned it from, or was inspired by, Jon Peltier, the true Excel charts master. I'm deeply grateful to Jon for all the knowledge and generosity he shared with the community for well over 10 years.

Andreas Lipphardt's untimely death was the saddest moment along my data visualization journey. I wrote a few posts for his company's blog, and we talked often about working together in the future. I still wonder what would have happened if we had.

Finally, I thank my family. When I was more interested in writing this book than actually make a living, Teresa and the kids were very patient and supportive.

About the Author

Jorge Camões studied statistics and information management and has been consulting businesses on how to effectively use information visualizations since 2010, with clients in the top 25 pharma companies and major retailers. Prior to starting his consulting business, Camões worked for 10 years in the business intelligence department of the Portuguese subsidiary of Merck & Co. Camões runs the popular data visualization blog Excelcharts.com. He works from his home in Lisbon, Portugal.

Contents

3 Beyond Visual Perception — 62

4 Data Preparation — 79

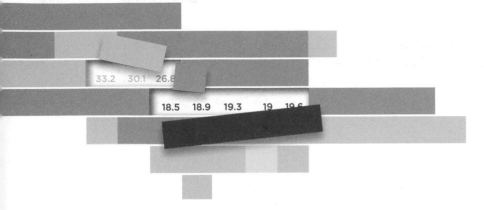

INTRODUCTION

No data point is an island,
Entire of itself,
Every data point is a piece of the continent,
A part of the pattern.

The venerable poet John Donne must be turning in his grave with this paraphrase of his beautiful meditation "No man is an island," but I couldn't find a better way to express the nature of data, which have a context and a web of relationships. The path to knowledge lies in discovering and making these relationships visible.

Social change and technological progress have made the world a more uncertain place. As another poet, Luís de Camões (not related), said, "Change doesn't change like it used to." In an effort to cope with uncertainty, we put technology at the service of mass data production and retrieval. This has been called by many names over the years. Today we call it "Big Data."

Acquiring and storing data has become the goal; the more data, the better. But are we missing the point? We no longer need *more* data if it's not accompanied by the right skills that turn it into truly *better* data. We need to consider how those who need the data will use it, and for what purpose. Otherwise, it's pointless to continue accumulating useless data, collecting digital dust in a forgotten folder on a hard disk. Waiting. Or, worse yet, making pie charts.

A Quantitative Change

Suppose that the data you work with is now updated daily rather than monthly, multiplying its total volume by 30. As Arthur C. Clark told us, **a quantitative change of this magnitude forces a qualitative change** in organizational culture, our attitude toward data, and data's role in decision making. Just imagine if the data allowed you to react to whatever is happening (rather than merely acknowledging what happened weeks ago) so that you become aware of its impact on all levels of the organization, beginning with how each person interprets their roles and tasks.

Only a planetary catastrophe would prevent the ever escalating volume of data. In the past, much of human experience was absent from our data monitoring systems, but it's now beginning to be quantified. In a few years, we'll reminisce affectionately over the complaints about information overload that we have today.

This is where data visualization begins. But beware. Data visualization is marketed today as the miracle cure that will open the doors to success, whatever its shape. We have enough experience to realize that in reality it's not always easy to distinguish between real usefulness and zealous marketing. After the initial excitement over the prospects of data visualization comes disillusionment, and after that the possibility of a balanced assessment. The key is to get to this point quickly, without disappointments and at a lower cost. This book is designed to help get you there.

A Language for Multiple Users

Data visualization helps us manage information. To make the most of this information, we must first accept the fact that "data visualization" does not exist *as a single entity.* Instead, think of it as a blanket term: It exists differently for each group of people who use it.

Visualization is like a language. Paraphrasing the Portuguese writer José Saramago, "There is no English; there are languages in English." For example, although people from the United States, Wales, and South Africa all speak English, they'd likely have some difficulty communicating because their versions of English are all so different, having changed from their common core over the years based on their geographical and social contexts.

Data visualization is a graphical language, used differently depending on the "speaker." A graphic designer, a statistician, or a manager starts from the same foundations of data visualization, but each has different goals, skills, and contexts, which are reflected in their different visualization choices.

A Wrong Model

Imagine that we all wish to write poetry. For the unfortunate not blessed with the gift of rhyming, the word processor offers some models that help with writing reports in the form of folk poetry. Seems absurd? Well, this is what happens with data visualization, too, when we look to spreadsheet chart templates to help overcome our weaknesses.

Graphic designers have made visualization the fashion phenomenon it is today— their poetry meant to be seen by large audiences and evidenced in data journalism, books, blogs, and social networks. Results vary between the brilliance of many visualizations in the *New York Times*, for instance, and the mediocrity of many infographics created by marketing departments as clickbait.

Meanwhile, millions of charts made with spreadsheets remain hidden within business organizations. The obscure, everyday users of office tools, unaware of better visualization models adapted to their contexts, mistakenly see the designers' work as a reference to imitate, often with catastrophic results. Peer pressure, the *this-is-what-the-client-wants*, vendor sales tactics, and a lack of training feed the illusion that there is beauty in bad poetry.

There is not. **The purpose of data visualization in organizations is not to make beautiful charts; it is to make** effective **charts.** And, as we shall see, if your charts are effective, they're also likely to be beautiful, even in aspects with strong associations to aesthetics, such as the use of color.

A Better Model

Visualizations crafted by graphic designers are often appealing, but in a business context we can't use the same model. At a time when graphic literacy in organizations is still low, we must evaluate this model's usefulness, beginning with four simple concepts:

- **Process.** Visual displays of information in business organizations and in the media have different goals and different production and consumption processes, which should not be mixed up.

- **Asymmetry.** Information asymmetry—whereby one party has more or better information than the other—is generally less evident within an organization than, say, between journalists and their readers. Graphical representations must adapt to this difference, adding detail in the former and finding the core message in the latter.

- **Model.** If you hire a data visualization expert, make sure she is aligned with your organization's specific interests or focus, because her data visualization model may prove incompatible with the organizational culture, daily work processes, available tools, and skill sets. It's almost impossible, for example, to convince an Excel user to learn a few lines of code, so this cannot be an expectation.

- **Technology.** Almost everything you need to understand about data visualization can be learned and practiced in a spreadsheet, which is an everyday tool people are familiar with.

Today, business organizations are encouraged to become more efficient and effective. Improving the return on investment (ROI) of their data should be a top priority. This is achieved by adhering to data visualization principles and best practices, and especially through a change of perspective, which has negligible costs, both in absolute financial terms and when compared to the results of past practices.

In fact, **many data visualization best practices are no different from the rules of etiquette**. A set of rules that is merely a ritualization of common sense is easy to understand, but must be internalized and practiced.

In short, data visualization in an organizational context has unique characteristics that must be identified and respected. The display of business data is not art, nor is it an image to attract attention in a newspaper, or a moment of leisure between more serious tasks. Business visualization is first and foremost an effective way to discover and communicate complex information, taking advantage of the noblest of our senses, sight, to support the organization's mission and goals.

Data Visualization for the Masses

I write a blog about data visualization (excelcharts.com), and over the years I have often been tempted to move away from the worksheet and devote myself to true visualization tools. This would be the normal path. But the spreadsheet is the only tool that the vast majority of us have access to in an organizational context, and getting data visualization to the average person must start from this contingency if we want to encourage learning and increase graphical literacy. Then, at some later point, people and organizations will assess whether the tool adequately satisfies their needs and can then make a natural and demanding transition to other applications. Or not.

This is therefore a book about data visualization for the masses—that is, for those who, with the support of a spreadsheet, use visual representations of data as an analytical and communications tool: students in their academic work, sellers in their sales analysis, product managers in planning their budgets, and managers in their performance assessments.

The Labor Market

Taking into account the economic circumstances of today, is it justified to invest in statistics, data analysis, and data visualization skills? As I mentioned, with the exception of a scenario of global catastrophe, it's difficult to imagine a future that does not involve an increase in the volume of data and the need to use it. In fact, these skills are becoming central to the vast universe of what we call "knowledge workers." Compared to other skills, these skills cut across more areas of activity, ensuring some competitive advantages in the labor market within the expected social, economic, and technological trends.

A study[1] by consultants McKinsey & Company on "Big Data" estimates that in 2018, in the United States alone, there will be a shortage of up to 190,000 people with high analytical skills, and a shortage of about 1.5 million managers and analysts with analytical skills to use data in the process of decision-making.

---

1   McKinsey & Company. Big data: The next frontier for innovation, competition, and productivity. 2011.

It's wise to read these reports with some skepticism, of course, considering their unknown agendas. Nevertheless, this study indicates the need for qualified human resources in this area, of which data visualization is an essential part.

My View of Data Visualization

I have on my desk a report that includes hundreds of charts, all of which are inefficient, ugly, and useless. There isn't a single chart *I* am proud of. And, yes, it was I who made them, many years ago, as one of my first professional tasks. Even more embarrassing is that I remember the report's commercial success.

I had not yet realized it, but working with data would become as normal for me as breathing. I didn't pay much attention to it at the time, until one day I stumbled upon a book: *The Visual Display of Quantitative Information*, by a certain Edward Tufte. For me, this was the Book of Revelation. In it, I discovered data visualization as a concept and as a field of study, and it was love at first sight.

Over the years, I realized that there are no universal rules and goals in this field. Subjectivity, personal aesthetic sensibilities, the task at hand, the profile of skills and interests, the audience—these all conspire to minimize things that we take for granted, such as the importance of effectiveness in the transmission of the message.

Within this relativism, the easy answer is to accept that anything goes. Throughout this book, you'll see examples of dead ends where this path sometimes takes us. But if we accept that there is no one-size-fits-all perspective, and that there are no universal rules, we still must seek a coherent theory for each group of practitioners and consumers.

My view of **data visualization is an exercise in everyday normality**: Simply give the eyes what they *need* to see, so that the visualization goals are met at minimal cost, in the same natural way we use vision to check whether we can cross a roadway.

To take advantage of vision, we must understand that there is no difference in nature between the physical landscape around us and the graphical landscape we create on a screen or on a sheet of paper.

Organization of the Book

This book follows a narrow path between theory that's too abstract to be useful for everyday tasks and practice that's too focused on a concrete task to help us understand the general rules. I tried to follow this path in every chapter, showing how theory applies in each example and how the specific task always has a theoretical framework that explains, justifies, and generalizes it. It's important to understand *why*, not just how.

To begin to understand data visualization, the first part of this book describes the context in which the action takes place: the characteristics of the human senses, the objects we use when making charts, the role of perception, how knowledge is acquired, and the many ways of defining data visualization.

In the second part of the book, we'll recognize that a chart is a visual argument, an answer to a question, and that the quality of this answer begins with the chart type you choose. Then, we'll format the chart. You'll see that the best chart formatting serves the content and is not distinguished from it, praising its qualities and reducing its flaws.

Throughout the book, we'll analyze data visualization in an organizational context, including good practices in data management, the Excel chart library, how to avoid bad software defaults, and how to use application flexibility to go beyond what the Excel library seems to offer.

The Limits of This Book

I wrote this book with a particular reader profile in mind: those who are not paid professionally for their aesthetic talents and artistic skills.

You might find this problematic, because designing a chart seems to require these skills. But I totally reject that. You need not be artistically talented to create effective charts.

I believe in increasing graphical literacy, and for that to happen we can help build a safety net of basic criteria for producing effective visual representations. I believe this will be useful at the professional level and will also contribute (marginally) to a more critical citizenship.

This book focuses on identifying the basic principles of data visualization for an organizational environment, as performed by individuals who have certain skills and who use a very specific tool: the spreadsheet. The intersection of these factors defines the main limits of this book:

- **Major visualization types.** In the first chapter, you'll see data visualization classified into three major groups: charts (we define "charts" in the first chapter), networks, and maps. Although they have some common principles, networks and maps are excluded from this book because they have a specific vocabulary that must be addressed in the proper context.

- **The chart.** A chart is just one part of the information communication within an organization, just like a single paragraph of a story. Since this is an introductory book, there will be a balance between this concept of the "graphical landscape" and the idea of a chart as the minimum unit of data visualization.

- **Excel.** The spreadsheet software I use now is Excel 2016, with which I made all the charts for this book. When it was necessary to refer to application features and capabilities, I tried to be as generic as possible in order to include other versions of Excel and even other spreadsheet programs.

- **Chart types.** Due to its flexibility, Excel allows us to go beyond its library. Throughout this book, you'll find many examples of this flexibility. But there are hard limits (charts that Excel just can't do) and soft limits (charts that would be so difficult to create and with such a low cost-benefit ratio that in practice we should not attempt to use them regularly). For Excel, networks and maps represent such exceptions.

- **Not a manual.** Although written with Excel users in mind, this book is not a manual of techniques, tips, and tricks.

- **No retouching.** It's important for me to ensure that the charts you'll find in this book are true to the original made in Excel, so they have not been retouched by additional software, even in the management of text elements, in which Excel is especially limited. However, for inclusion in the book with the highest possible quality, the charts were exported to PDF, which led to some minor changes that I have tried to minimize.

There's also a practical limitation regarding the data. I wanted to use real data, not some fake business indicators, but this poses problems of confidentiality and limited interest. To circumvent that, I used official statistics as a proxy for business data. Except for a few specialized contexts, we can use the same methodology and chart types. Both are in deep need of a more effective approach.

Break the Rules!

Data visualization is not a science; it is a crossroads at which certain scientific knowledge is used to justify and frame subjective choices. This doesn't mean that rules don't count. Rules exist and are effective when applied within the context for which they were designed.

You'll find many rules in this book—so many rules that the temptation to break them (intelligently) may be overwhelming. If this is your case, congratulations, that's the spirit. I myself could not resist and tried to test the limits and possible alternatives. I invite you to do the same.

Companion Website

As I said, this book is not a manual. It will not teach you how to make a chart in Excel. You won't find even a single formula.

That's why we set up a comprehensive companion website for the book:

- **dataatworkbook.com**

On the website, you'll find:

- All the relevant original charts in Excel files that you can download and play with. I've also included brief comments for each chart to help you learn how to make them. When you see the ⤳ icon, it means that the chart is available to download.

- Links to the original data sources and, when possible, a dynamic bookmark to the most recent data.

- Links to other content referenced in the book. You'll find icons sprinkled throughout the book that invite you to read a relevant paper, watch a video, go to a web page, and so on. When you see this icon ✇, it means that you'll find a link on the companion website.

I welcome your comments, suggestions, and change requests. I ask you to add them liberally on the website for the benefit of all.

I'll try to be aware of comments and suggestions made on social media and consumer reviews on major online book retailers and address them on the book's website, if needed.

Over time, I'll add original charts not published in the book as well as additional resources, so be sure to check in often.

You can find me on most social media, but I confess that Twitter is the only service I use regularly. I will tweet about new content, so if you follow me (@camoesjo) you won't miss it!

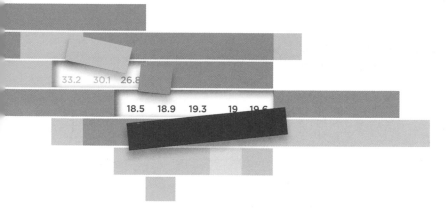

1

THE BUILDING BLOCKS OF DATA VISUALIZATION

Imagine you're in your living room reading a book. You look and see the TV, a fireplace, a few family pictures. A souvenir from a long-ago vacation draws your attention and makes you feel momentarily nostalgic. You shake off these feelings and return to your book.

In those fleeting moments, light reflected from the objects in the room entered your eyes and was converted into visual stimuli and sent to the brain. Your brain homed in on select stimuli to recognize and identify key objects (even that book over there partially covered by a newspaper) while ignoring others, and conjured up complicated feelings of wistful affection.

Now imagine that the book partially covered by the newspaper in our little scenario is a history of painting, inside of which you'll find a reproduction of René Magritte's *The Treachery of Images/This is not a pipe*.

Go to the
web page

Figure 1.1 Playing with representations of representations: *Ceci n'est pas Magritte,*
by Ben Heine © 2015.

Magritte's painting reminds us that the world and its representations are not the same. But there is something that the world and its representations share: the eye–brain system—the physiological system that converts light into visual stimuli and generates meaningful images (**Figure 1.1**).

Like the pipe in Magritte's painting, data visualization is a representation of the world. It isn't a representation of objects such as fireplaces, books, or pipes, but rather of abstract shapes—building blocks whose attributes of color, size, or position in space vary according to our design choices and according to the quantitative data upon which they're based. We manipulate these shapes to create charts, infographics, or "graphical landscapes" in general.

How do we translate a data table into visual objects? In the first chapters of this book, we'll analyze this connection and why it matters. We'll begin by transforming the building blocks into multiple chart types. Some charts will be more appealing and effective than others, though all will be useful to our study.

Data Sensing

Figure 1.2 represents the distribution of university students in Portugal[1] by areas of knowledge. Now, here's a question for you: Does this table have a flavor? Is it bitter, sweet, or sour?

TERTIARY STUDENTS IN PORTUGAL
Proportion by field of education (%)

Field	1998	2012
Teacher training and education science	11.9	5.7
Humanities and arts	8.4	9.5
Social sciences, business, and law	38.3	31.3
Science, mathematics, and computing	8.9	7.2
Engineering, manufacturing, and construction	18.9	21.9
Agriculture and veterinary	3.0	1.9
Health and welfare	6.9	15.9
Services	3.7	6.4
Unknown	0.0	0.1

Tertiary education: levels 5-6 of ISCED97
Source: Eurostat

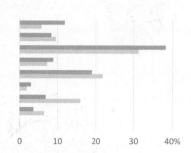

TERTIARY STUDENTS IN PORTUGAL
Proportion by field of education (%)

Figure 1.2 Student proportion by field of study.

Let me rephrase that to make it sound a little less bizarre: Would it be possible to use food to recreate this chart so that we could literally taste the difference in values? My limited cooking skills tell me that, yes, we could associate low values to a bitter taste and high values to sweet flavors and place them strategically on, say, a pizza. But although we could use other senses (such as hearing, smell, or touch) to make, well, sense of quantitative data, would we want to?

Not really. Vision is our most developed sense, and it accounts for a large proportion of all stimuli processed by the brain. In other words, the brain devotes more of its resources to processing visual data than any other sensory input, which explains why it's easier and more precise to use sight to read a chart than to use smell, taste, or touch.

Humans are visual animals. We are so aware of the power of the eye–brain system that when we imagine superior alien life forms, we usually envision creatures with big eyes and oversized brains, vanishing noses, invisible ears, and, most likely, a limited sense of taste and touch (**Figure 1.3**). These beings from planets in galaxies far, far away are closer to us than those blind creatures inhabiting the depths of the Earth's oceans.

Figure 1.3 Our vision of aliens: big eyes and big brains.

---

1 I'm using real data for this book, and my criterion for choosing a series is how interesting the variation is, not the reality it refers to. I would like to have chosen an obscure and rich Caribbean country with a sophisticated statistical system as my primary data source, so as to reap the benefits of real data with a fresh perspective not bound by a familiar reality. However, because I couldn't find such a source, I've struck a balance between data from the U.S. and the European Union.

Spatial Organization of Stimuli

Visual stimuli come from a finite space: the limits of our field of vision. Let's suppose **Figure 1.4** represents these limits. This detailed image allows us to choose several levels of analysis: We can start from a global view of a mountain landscape with a river, and then zoom in to a more detailed level where we notice a fallen tree trunk, several peaks, or perhaps recognize a species of tree.

Superimposing a coordinate system lets us reference points in the landscape: There's a fallen tree trunk in coordinates x_1y_1, a peak in x_2y_2, and so on. Each point, defined by a pair of coordinates, belongs at the same time to a single object (such as a tree trunk) and to an object within another object (for example, a tree within a tree line within a landscape). There are shapes and patterns with different levels of complexity.

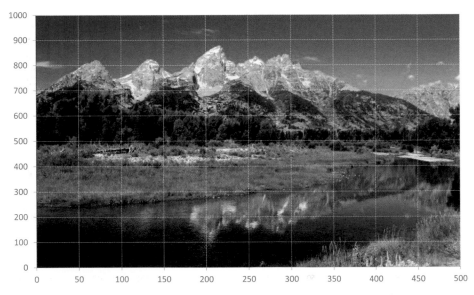

Figure 1.4 Grand Teton mountain.

But what if we use the coordinate system to *draw* the landscape?

This new picture (**Figure 1.5**) looks a lot like a simplified version of the previous one. We recognize the mountains and the river, but, as Magritte said, *this is not a pipe.* In fact, it's neither a landscape nor a pipe; it's a stacked area chart made in Excel. For all we know, it might represent the evolution of sales in some unknown market.

Just as we interpret a blue line in a photo as a river, we also seek recognizable patterns in a chart that allow us to read, understand, and act. Recognition of shapes and the attribution of meaning are similar in both images, in both *landscapes*. From this point of view, data visualization does nothing more than create graphical landscapes based on data tables.

If something distinguishes the two images, that something is our inability to create a graphical landscape as rich in stimuli and diversity in level of detail as the first image. Adding and managing meaningful details is one of the biggest challenges in data visualization.

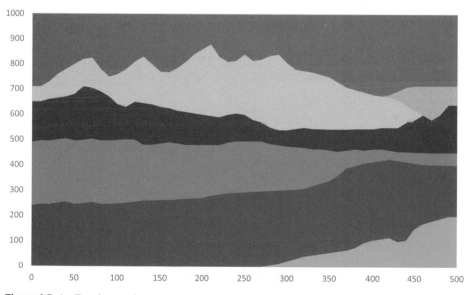

Figure 1.5 An Excel area chart.

Seeing Abstract Concepts

If a graphical landscape does not contain representations of real objects with physical shapes and instead represents abstract concepts only (such as the rate of inflation or population density), how can we make these concepts visible? The answer seems obvious now, but it was not so for many centuries: associating abstract concepts with geometric shapes whose characteristics vary according to the underlying data.

You may recall from school that there are four basic geometric primitives, distinguished by their number of dimensions: the *point* (dimensionless), the *line* (one dimension), the *area* or *plane* (two dimensions), and *volume* (three dimensions).

When we use the number of dimensions as the classification criterion of visual displays, we get four distinct groups: charts, networks, and maps, along with figurative visualizations as a special group. The table in **Figure 1.6** summarizes their essential characteristics.[2]

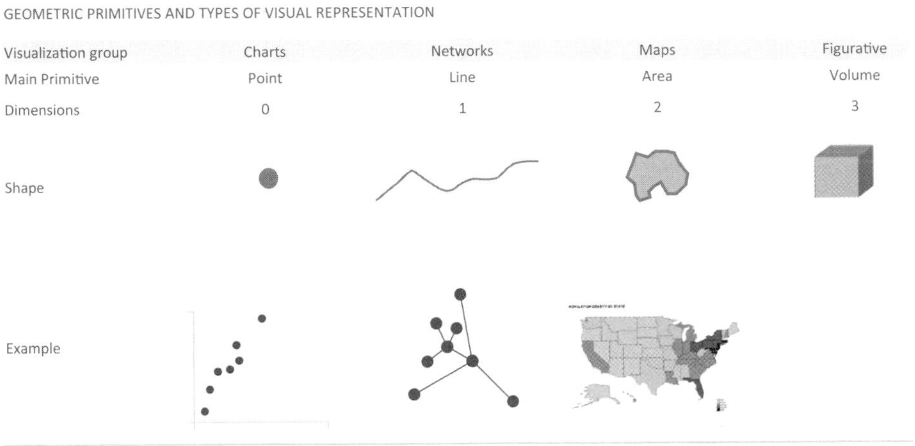

GEOMETRIC PRIMITIVES AND TYPES OF VISUAL REPRESENTATION

Visualization group	Charts	Networks	Maps	Figurative
Main Primitive	Point	Line	Area	Volume
Dimensions	0	1	2	3
Shape				
Example				

Figure 1.6 A summary of geometric primitives.

---

2 In other words, the minimum number of dimensions you need to represent an object. Although you can use an area (a slice of a pie chart) or a line (a bar in a bar chart), those are design choices, because all you need is a point. Likewise, the line is the minimum you need to represent a network, and points and areas can be used as design choices.

Charts

The primary geometric primitive used in charts is the *point*, represented in a 2D space through pairs of coordinates, horizontal (*x*) and vertical (*y*), with the origin in the lower-left corner (**Figure 1.7**). Values increase upward and to the right and decrease downward and to the left. When one of the coordinates is missing (or has a fixed value), the points are distributed along the opposite axis. You may need to adjust this description to fit the type of metric you're using: In a time series (**Figure 1.8**), the sequence goes from less recent (on the left) to more recent (on the right).

Note that the word *chart* can have several meanings and can include tables, maps, graphs, or network diagrams. *Graph* has a stricter definition of a visual representation of one or more variables, although it can be confused with a very specific field in mathematics called graph theory. "Graph" is the right word to use, I have no doubt. Unfortunately, 30 years ago Microsoft decided to use "charts" in Excel, and now it feels a little awkward to say "Excel graph" instead of "Excel chart." Since this book is aimed at Excel users, we'll use "chart" and define it as a visual object that you can find or derive from the Excel chart library.

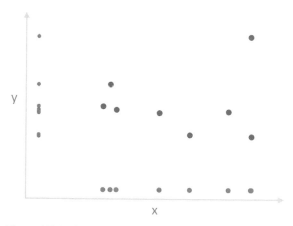

Figure 1.7 A chart is a set of data points plotted in a 2D plane.

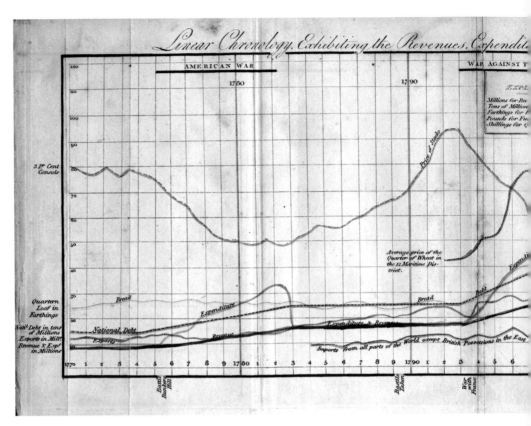

Figure 1.8 A line chart by William Playfair. Source: Wikimedia Commons.

In more abstract terms, a chart is the product of a process that transcribes a data table into pairs of coordinates and then applies design transformations that allow us to visualize them. We'll see what this means in a minute.

After transforming table values into data points and plotting them all on the plane, we'll get a cloud of data points where we get an accurate representation of their relative *distances*. This is the stepping stone for everything we'll do afterwards, because a lot of things start to happen when we see and compare distances between data points or between each of them and the axes. What will we do with this cloud? Essentially, we'll make it visible by, for example, using lines to connect data points and creating a line chart. These complementary primitives play a key role in the way we'll read the chart and how effective it will become.

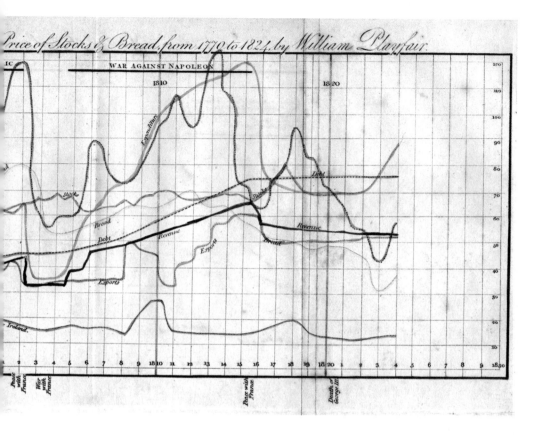

Networks

The line is the main geometric primitive for displaying networks (**Figure 1.9**) because it represents connections between data points. We still need to plot the data points in the 2D plane, but their coordinates are flexible and you can change them to better represent these relationships. Even though both points and lines are relevant when visualizing networks, observing relationships and detecting meaningful behavior (centrality, patterns, outliers) is our primary goal in network analysis.

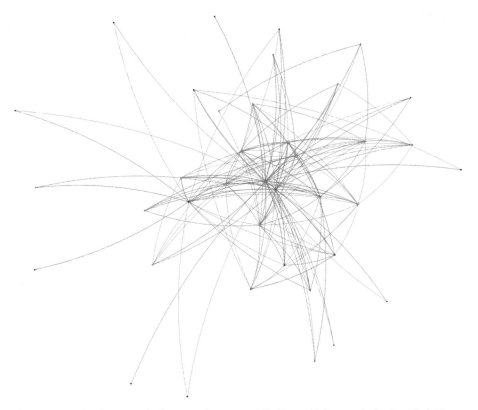

Figure 1.9 A simple network diagram of my recent Twitter activity, created using NodeXL, an Excel add-in for visualizing networks.

Go to the
web page

A classic example of network representation is the diagram of the London Tube, where geographic references to the world above are vague, and we measure distances by the number of tube stations rather than by miles.

Maps

Maps may use points and lines, but their use of area sets them apart from charts and networks. Maps are the most figurative form of visual display and the form we've been using the longest (**Figure 1.10**).

Figure 1.10 A map using points, lines, and area. Oahu, Hawaiian Islands. Source: Open Street Map.

Volume: Figurative Visualizations

Most visualizations take place in a 2D plane (a sheet of paper or a screen). There may come a time when immersive technologies allow us to navigate 3D data landscapes, but we're not there yet. And it isn't a technological issue only. It's also a perceptual one. In a 3D space, objects can be hidden behind other objects (occlusion). And our perception is not good at comparing sizes when distance from us is factored in: Is a particular car bigger than another, or is it simply nearer to us?

We can *fake* 3D, however. Scientific visualizations do it all the time to model physical objects, for example. Unfortunately, results are less than stellar when applied to abstract concepts. What we get are many pseudo-3D visualizations, where the third dimension is meaningless, irrelevant, and decorative. We'll discuss that later in the book.

So, we'll reserve volume not for 3D visualization but for representations of real-world objects or objects without a direct connection to a data table. You see these representations often in newspapers or magazines to show how an accident happened, for example. They work well, either alone or combined with other forms of visualization. We typically refer to them as *illustrations*, but this is too generic a term. I prefer to call them *figurative visualizations* because they depict a physical object or reality.

Visualization in Excel

Charts, networks, maps, and figurative visualizations share a common set of visual characteristics, but they're also different enough to make combining them all in a single tool almost impossible. Not surprisingly, charts are the major type of visualization offered by spreadsheets like Excel.

You can visualize basic networks and maps in Excel, but that requires a lot of work, buying add-ins, or both. And it never feels "natural" to the software, although this is starting to change with Excel 2016. That's why we'll focus almost exclusively on charts in this book, although you should always think of charts (as defined above) as a subset of all possible forms of data visualization.

Retinal Variables

We superimposed a grid over the photo of the mountain, and now the location of each point in the image can be defined by its distance to the horizontal and vertical axes. But what about depth? Can we change the position of the data point in the third dimension or, in the context of data visualization, the z axis? No, we can't, because we only have two dimensions in the image. But, what if we *pretend* that a third dimension exists and we can use it to our advantage? I'm not talking about holographic images or, even worse, pseudo-3D effects.

Imagine yourself flying over a mountain range (**Figure 1.11**). Using only indirect clues—the shades of blue in the sea, the brown earth, the green forests, and the white snow—you can estimate the relative altitude of the peaks below you. Maps have long copied this figurative scale to give us a sense of altitude on paper; the good news is that nothing prevents us from generalizing this pair (color, altitude) and going beyond a cartographic representation.

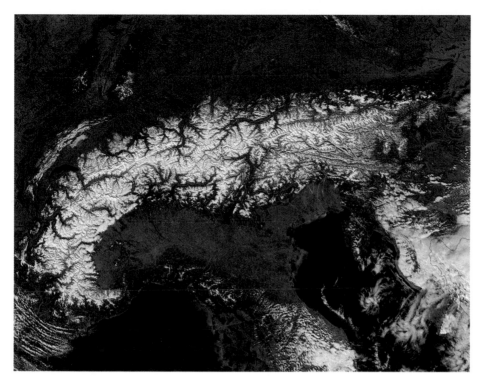

Figure 1.11 Satellite image of the Alps. Source: NASA.

This is the domain of what one of the founding fathers of data visualization, the French cartographer Jacques Bertin, called retinal variables: visual and positional characteristics of points, lines, and areas that we can use to manipulate graphical representations. Coordinates x,y define position, and instead of a z axis we have a z dimension where we display other visual features.

The table in **Figure 1.12** illustrates some of these variables. The first example, Position, uses only two variables: the position variables x and y. The example below that, Luminance, in reality contains at least four variables—position (x and y), luminance, and size—and it's possible to add more (multiple shapes, different directions). In practice, however, it's advisable to add no more than four variables to keep the charts readable.

VARIABLES OF THE IMAGE

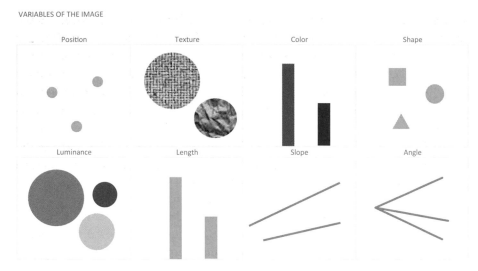

Figure 1.12 Some examples of retinal variables.

Note that retinal variables are not interchangeable. Their characteristics make them effective in representing certain data types and useless in representing others. Before seeing an example, remember a traditional classification of variables:

- **Quantitative.** These variables can, in theory, take any value in a range.

- **Qualitative.** These variables represent a limited number of categorical values that we can count. If these values have an implicit scale or order, we refer to them as *ordinal* variables (weekdays, for example); if there is no implicit ordering, we refer to them as *nominal* variables (gender, race, fruit names, cities).

As you can see in the table, variables such as position or size rank higher at representing quantitative data, albeit with different levels of accuracy. Texture and shape are better suited for representing nominal data, since they don't vary in range or allow for the perception of ordered data. (For example, in Figure 1.12, if textures encoded quantitative data, would you be able to tell which represent the highest value?) Color (hue) is used to encode nominal variables, but we often ask of it something it cannot give us accurately: an ordered representation of categories. Can you be sure these hues are ordered ▪▬▬▬▬▪ ?

Wouldn't it be better to use something like this ▬▬▬▬ ?

Several authors have, over time, suggested the addition of new variables to the original list. Jock D. Mackinlay is one of the authors who tried to make Bertin's list more comprehensive, while ranking each variable for its effectiveness at representing quantitative, ordinal, and nominal data types. In **Figure 1.13**, we see Mackinlay's list of variables, ordered by degree of effectiveness. Variable Position maintains its top place in the three lists, while Shape is useless to express quantitative or ordinal data and poorly represents nominal data. There's an exchange of positions in which the variables that best represent quantitative data are the worst at representing ordinal data, while, with a few exceptions, rankings are more stable between ordinal and nominal variables.

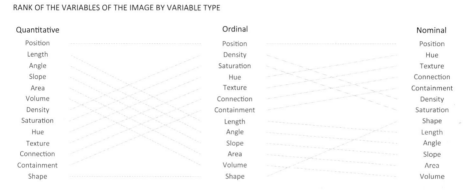

RANK OF THE VARIABLES OF THE IMAGE BY VARIABLE TYPE

Quantitative	Ordinal	Nominal
Position	Position	Position
Length	Density	Hue
Angle	Saturation	Texture
Slope	Hue	Connection
Area	Texture	Containment
Volume	Connection	Density
Density	Containment	Saturation
Saturation	Length	Shape
Hue	Angle	Length
Texture	Slope	Angle
Connection	Area	Slope
Containment	Volume	Area
Shape	Shape	Volume

Figure 1.13 Mackinlay's ranking of retinal variables.[3]

A third characteristic of retinal variables is their power to draw attention. This is a useful feature for managing data relevancy and is one of the largest contributors for communicating our interpretation, as opposed to the use of the default settings of the software. The manipulation of the characteristics of retinal variables to both emphasize and deemphasize has a technical dimension, but it needs to be framed in the context of a *visual rhetoric*.[4] We speak of visual rhetoric when, for example, we use the expression "lie with charts." Subjectivity in charts is inevitable, but throughout this book we'll seek ways to identify the fuzzy area where acceptable subjectivity ends and misleading visualization begins.

3 Adapted from Jock D. Mackinlay. "Automating the Design of Graphical Presentations of Relational Information." *ACM Transactions on Graphics*, Vol. 5, No. 2: 110–141, April 1986.

4 There is a long tradition of rhetoric as the art of persuasion through the spoken word. A visual rhetoric shares the same goals and uses many of the same strategies, but a significant amount of the message uses images instead of words. Simply put, we can *lie* to persuade (traditional rhetoric), and we can *lie with charts* to persuade (visual rhetoric).

From Concepts to Charts

As we've seen, to make a chart we need a data table, a two-dimensional plan with a coordinate system, one or more selected geometric primitives, and retinal variables.

Let's return to our table of student distribution and test these ingredients with two versions of the same chart (**Figure 1.14**). For simplicity's sake, we'll represent the year 2010 only, plotting the data points along the vertical axis. The coordinates for each data point take the form (2010,*y*). For example, the pair of coordinates for the Social Sciences is (2010; 31.8%). The highest value in the table also corresponds to the value furthest from the origin in the chart, and the relative distances between the points reflect the differences in the table: In this case, the distance of the point representing the Social Sciences (31.8%) is approximately two times the distance of the point representing Health (16.3%).

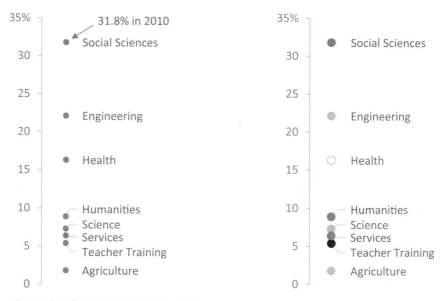

Figure 1.14 Plotting data along a single axis.

Although we're using a small table, the chart allows us to immediately grasp its content: Three areas stand out (Social Sciences, Engineering, and Health), followed by a tight group of four more areas, and one last point, Agriculture, with an almost residual value.

On the left chart, we keep dimensions x and z fixed, while dimension y varies. On the right, we added a new variable to the chart. This nominal variable groups knowledge areas (Social Sciences and Humanities, for example) using color or shades of gray. In other words, we color-coded the dots to add new information, varying the z dimension (in Bertin's definition).

The new information invites reading beyond simple comparisons. Depending on the goals, this can be seen either as an advantage (it adds complexity to the initial message) or as noise (more detail distracts from the essential). The red dot draws more attention than the other dots, influencing the way we read the chart and agreeing with the idea of a visual rhetoric.

The Proto-Chart

The point is the most important geometric primitive in a chart, and often the only one we need to be able to read the distances between them after visually transcribing the values in the data table. But we can add more objects to help us read and understand the chart: It would be difficult, for example, to analyze time series without the connecting lines in each series.

To understand how we get to each chart type, let's call the set of points plotted on the 2D plane a *proto-chart*. Imagine this proto-chart with no visible existence, nothing but data points coded within the computer's memory. The proto-chart becomes a visible chart when we apply geometric primitives, retinal variables, and supporting objects, like titles, axis labels, or grid lines.

Let's try an exercise where we apply a set of transformations to the same data to create various chart types, each of which will help us understand where the chart types come from (**Figure 1.15**).

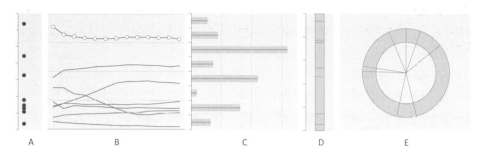

Figure 1.15 Multiple chart types for the same data.

- **Strip plot (A).** On the left, we have a strip plot (one variable, varying along an axis). This format most closely matches the proto-chart, with only a few identifying features added.

- **Line chart (B).** In the line chart, each data point gets its own pair of coordinates, based on value (vertical axis) and, in this dataset, time (horizontal axis). The line connects points in each time series, helping interpret the trend.

- **Bar chart (C).** This is nothing more than a chart in which the points are distributed along the vertical axis so that we can label them. A thick line (the bar) connects the point to the axis. We stop comparing distances and start comparing bar lengths. We'll discuss later why this is relevant.

- **Stacked bar chart (D).** To the vertical coordinate of a point, we add all coordinates of the previous points. Each bar connecting two points is usually color-coded so that we can identify it in the legend.

- **Donut charts and pie charts (E).** These are the result of transforming a stacked bar into a ring or a circle shape, although there are differences in the way we encode both charts.

This exercise confirms that we create a chart by applying a set of transformations to the original mapping of data points in the proto-chart. A chart type expresses a standardized set of transformations.

Chart Effectiveness

Even a small table can answer many questions, and there are a variety of chart types we can choose from to answer these questions. This means that we must define some sort of criteria to evaluate each chart's effectiveness.

One of the simplest ways is to check how well the chart meets certain require-ments—such as, does it offer good insights or can we interpret it at a glance? Let's test this.

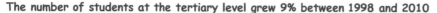

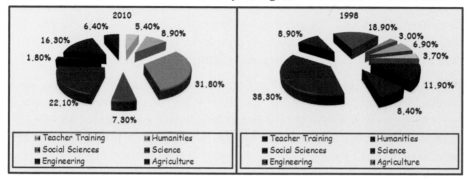

Figure 1.16. I call this the *Graphenstein*—a chart made of poor design choices I've collected from multiple real charts.

Figure 1.16 shows a common (and *ugly*) form of graphical representation. It's supposed to allow us to compare proportions between two years. Based on your reading, answer the following questions that anyone interested in the topic might ask:

▪ Which area of study grew the most?

▪ Which area of study decreased the most?

▪ How did Humanities behave?

▪ How many areas of study are increasing and how many are decreasing?

Difficult? Need more time? Believe it or not, these two pie charts contain the answers to all these questions.

But here's the contradictory thing about pie charts. A common argument in favor of pie charts is that reading the labels compensates for what really are our dif-ficulties in reading them accurately. As these charts show, this is not an argument in favor of pie charts; rather, it's an argument to the detriment of visualization. Shouldn't we be able to read the chart without deciphering all the labels? If we have to read both the labels and the chart, the chart becomes pointless, as labels should complement rather than entirely support it.

Obviously, this is an extreme example of a bad visual representation. Now multiply all the seconds spent trying to answer the questions by all readers of this book and the seconds turn into minutes, and the minutes into hours. If you're required to consume reports and presentations with charts as hideous and ineffective as these pie charts, you can only imagine the financial impact of all that wasted time and effort.

This is not, of course, the only possible representation of the data. We have to compare different displays to understand how chart type and chart design influence chart-reading effectiveness. Now try to answer the same questions using a new chart (**Figure 1.17**). I'm sure you'll be fascinated, just as one of my 10-year-old twins was, by how quickly and easily a problem went from *nearly impossible* to *dead simple* through a graphical representation.

This chart doesn't have glossy colors or special effects, and each option has a rational justification. As a result, the chart effectively answers all questions. Hard-to-spot variations in the pie charts are obvious here: Line slopes display changes clearly; and since we don't need to use color to identify each category, we can use it instead either to create groups that add another level of analysis or to make the chart easier to read.

HEALTH ATTRACTS MORE STUDENTS
Proportion of students at the tertiary level
by field of knowledge

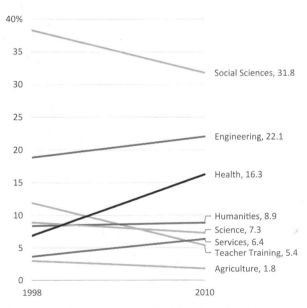

Figure 1.17 A better way to get insights from the data.

Poor chart choice and peculiar aesthetic options make the representation in Figure 1.16 useless, but the damage is even more extensive. Data acquisition, its preparation, chart design, and the time spent by the entire audience are costs that, although invisible for accounting purposes, are real and have no return. The absurdity is greater if we consider that the chart author would have taken longer "spicing it up" than making a good chart from the beginning.

This exercise shows how, with the same data table, you can create very different graphical representations resulting in extraordinarily different effectiveness. It's up to us to identify the goals and the answers that the task requires from us and look for the most appropriate visualization.

When you apply transformations to a proto-chart, you're exercising design options. The criteria for those transformations should be clear and aligned with the task and audience profile. As a rule of thumb, *the more design dimensions and the more transformations you apply, the less effective the chart becomes.*

Like many data visualization rules, you can always find a good exception: While an exploded, pseudo-3D pie chart and a treemap (**Figure 1.18**) are both heavily transformed, the transformations applied to make the pie chart are mostly gratuitous, whereas they have a clear purpose in a treemap.[5] If transformations respect the way human perception works and translate into a greater awareness and interest for the chart, the impact will be positive. Negative transformations and design options are generally due to the lack of awareness of those perceptual mechanisms—or to an excessive need to create what the organizational jargon calls "high-impact charts."

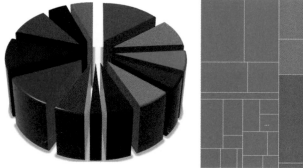
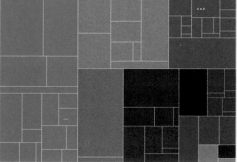

Figure 1.18 Multiple transformations can have a negative impact (pie chart) or a positive impact (treemap).

---

5   Like a pie chart, a treemap is used for a part-of-a-whole analysis, but because you have better control over the rectangle sizes than over slices, you can have many more data points. Unlike with traditional pie charts, you can arrange the data hierarchically. You can compare a rectangle to all data points or to its own branch. In most implementations, you can associate fill color with a continuous variable so that you can see, for example, a product's market share (rectangle size) and growth (rectangle fill color).

Anatomy of a Bad Chart

As you read this book, you'll gain a complete feel for what makes an effective chart. But for now, here's a partial list of significant errors specific to the sample pie charts you've just seen:

- **Title.** Summarizing the main findings in the chart title is a good idea, but here there is no relationship between the title and the content of the charts.

- **Font.** Not all fonts are suitable to a formal setting. If we try to escape the standard Arial or Times New Roman, a font like Comic Sans might seem like a solution. It's somewhat fun, unconventional, and appealing. But (as you can suspect from its name) it's more suitable for comics, children's books, and mom-and-pop stores. In other words, be aware that font choice can set the tone.

- **Chart type.** We'll see later why the pie chart is the wrong chart, but notice that if comparing slices in a pie is hard, it's even harder to compare them in multiple pies.

- **Time direction.** Convention tells us that time—as in the dates listed at the top of the two charts—flows from left to right, like our written text. Perhaps it's just a cultural thing, but if you want to break from this, first decide if there are clear advantages to compensate for the cognitive adjustment that you'll require from the reader.

- **3D effect.** The pseudo-3D effect is one of the deadly sins of data visualization.

- **Exploded slices.** When we want to emphasize an object, we make it different from those around it. This is the (doubtful) purpose of exploding pie slices, but it's destroyed when you do it for all slices, making the chart even more difficult to read.

- **Color differentiation.** With a single color, its range from lighter to darker must be great enough to allow for easy identification. In this case, differentiation is not great enough; not only are there too many tones, but they're harder to tell apart when seen in small samples, as in the legend.

- **Legends.** Replace legends with another form of identification whenever possible; contrary to popular belief, in pie charts they're never needed.

- **Frames.** Avoid frames. They create perceptual barriers and fill the chart with unnecessary clutter.

- **Clip art.** Annotating the chart, drawing attention, or explaining interesting details is a good practice. Inserting clip art does not fit into this practice and in this case emphasizes the infantile traits suggested by the font.

- **Number of slices.** In the chapter on pie charts, we'll discuss how many slices are acceptable in a pie. In this case, the number is excessive, making the comparison between them difficult.

- **Inconsistency.** Color sequence is reversed between the two charts. We must strive for consistency when representing the same entities over multiple charts.

- **Background.** The saturated yellow background is the main reason for the overstimulating effect, diverting attention from the data.

If you ask me for a phrase that describes the aesthetics of a good chart, I would likely choose *understated elegance*. The pie charts in Figure 1.16 are neither understated nor elegant. They are loutish and scream for attention, while saying little. The chart in Figure 1.17 is quieter and limits itself to conveying the message in a simple way, without distracting us with noise. Its aesthetics intend to be functional above all else, but the chart becomes an example of, as the visualization theorist Stephen Few put it, *elegance through simplicity*. That's the way for visualization to have a real and important role in knowledge-building processes and decision-making and not be limited to a decorative role with no benefit.

Throughout this book, not only will these perspectives become clearer, but also in the end you'll have the tools needed to apply the right way of understanding business visualization. For someone with the technical skills to make Excel charts, only a change of perspective (based on sound data visualization principles) is needed to be able to go from ineffective to effective.

Takeaways

- By associating values in a table to geometric primitives and variables of the image with their attributes, data visualization takes advantage of the eye–brain system to process abstract data.

- It all starts with the proto-chart, a transcription of the table values into pairs of coordinates.

- These pairs of coordinates map the data to a 2D plane, allowing us to start thinking in terms of distances instead of values.

- Depth, the third dimension in the physical world, is not used in data visualization.

- After mapping the table values, all transformations we apply to make the actual chart (retinal variables and attributes) depend on our design choices.

- What we call "chart types" are predefined sets of transformations, like connecting the data points to make a line chart.

- Chart effectiveness is not absolute. Among other factors, it depends on the task and on the audience profile.

- Our choices (like chart type or formatting options) can greatly influence chart effectiveness. Comparing multiple alternatives can help us to understand which ones work better for the specific task.

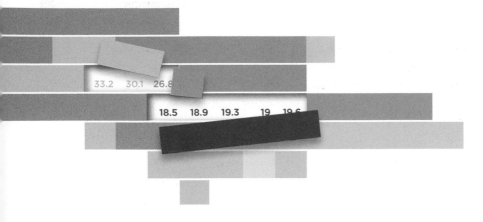

2

VISUAL PERCEPTION

A nice meal requires a little more than blending some random ingredients in a food processor. The same holds true in data visualization: The ability to manipulate geometric primitives and the retinal variables (as discussed in the previous chapter) is not enough to guarantee a "tasty" visual representation.

Throwing all the data into a chart and leaving software defaults unchanged is an unfortunate common practice—the visualization equivalent of cooking random ingredients with a food processor (you'll find an example later on in Figure 2.14).

There is more to data visualization than that, and if you want to follow the optimal path, then you're lucky, because the one you'll naturally follow is the path of least resistance. You may know this as the *principle of least effort*.

We can marvel at the brain's sheer processing power, but the way it manages (and often disguises) its finite resources is even more fascinating. Managing means allocating resources, defining priorities and goals, simplifying processes, selecting the right information to support decision-making, and getting results. The brain performs these functions to interpret ambiguities and environmental complexities.

Data visualization uses the image processing connection between the eyes and the brain (the eye–brain system, introduced in Chapter 1). We must understand the basics of how this system works in order to optimize our visual representations and conserve precious brain resources. We need more brain resources to recognize a tree that doesn't look like a tree or to compare two bars in a chart when the chart design makes them hard to compare. This is why it's important to design with the principle of least effort in mind. Many of the bad examples of data visualization are the result of disrespecting this principle. The pie charts from Chapter 1 offer a glaring example.

Everything in the complex eye–brain system influences the way we read visual representations. In this chapter, we'll discuss those things that *seem* more mechanical or objective: eye physiology, working memory, pre-attentive variables, and the Gestalt laws. Then, in the next chapter, we'll deal with the other side of the coin, the social dimension of the brain: prior experiences, social context, and culture. To start the discussion, let's first clarify the differences between perception and cognition and how they influence each other.

Perception and Cognition

Humans have a tremendous advantage over all other species: the ability to build and use *tools* to amplify our physical resources, protect ourselves, and make ourselves stronger. Human history is, largely, the history of discovering and using those tools.

In using these tools, however, the dilemma appears when we realize that our cognitive resources are finite and some intermediate tasks may use resources that we would instead prefer to allocate to higher-level tasks. If deciding whether you can buy a few copies of a data visualization book at a bookstore depends on calculating the total cost of the book and comparing that expense with your budget, then using a calculator (a tool) speeds up this task and gets you to the decision stage faster. It also allows you to allocate resources to more complex tasks, such as reading and evaluating the table of contents.

Cognitive Offloading

Calculator, fingers, pencil and paper, spreadsheets: When we use any of these *tools*, we offload some of the cognitive tasks with the assumption that this will benefit our overall cognitive processing.

Memory also aids cognitive offloading. As an example, quickly answer this question: Which multiplication product is higher, 7 × 8 or 6 × 9? Most adults memorized multiplication tables long ago and should have no problem answering this in a few seconds. Children, however, will take longer to answer because they haven't yet consolidated that memory and they must perform the calculations on the spot, perhaps using a tool. The memorization of elementary operations helps cognitive processing, which is one of the reasons we keep asking children to memorize multiplication tables.

Tools and memory are useful for removing those mental chores that small tasks impose on us, but have we done everything we can to avoid them in the first place? We know that a well-defined problem helps in solving it, and that applies to the way we represent data. When we replace letters and numbers with an equivalent visual translation, we transfer segments of our cognitive processes to our *visual perception*, minimizing cognitive costs. These cognitive differences between adults and children are much less significant if those values are presented visually (**Figure 2.1**), even if they're almost indistinguishable, and both adults and children would be faster at comparing two bars than at comparing multiplication products.

7 × 8

6 × 9

Figure 2.1
Performing cognitive calculations
is slower than comparing bars.

Each of these three types of cognitive offloading—using tools, memory, and visual perception—frees up cognitive resources. Data visualization deals with the last type, visual perception, and focuses on optimizing ways to transcribe data into equivalent visual objects that the brain can process more quickly.

A False Dichotomy

Suppose you can't remember where you parked your blue car in a huge parking lot. When you search for it, blue cars stand out more than red or white cars. Why is this?

We could view perception and cognition as a dichotomy, where perception corresponds to stimuli acquisition through the senses, while cognition processes those stimuli. However, one of the problems with this view is that we would need an extra-large, alien-sized brain to process all those stimuli. In fact, something already imposes a structure and a hierarchy of relevance to the stimuli, filtering out much of the world around us. We call that something *attention*. Attention will help you find your blue car and just about everything else in your life.

Our senses are not passive receptors of external stimuli. Senses act upon stimuli, making "selective perception" a redundant expression. Perception is always selective and is always a transformer of stimuli by definition. There is no one-way road to the brain. Perception and cognition are not a dichotomy.

Charts and Tables

Another false dichotomy is the one between charts and tables. Using one or the other is usually task-dependent, because they both have their own strengths and weaknesses. If it comes down to choosing one of them, think of the evaluation as a clinical trial. In clinical trials, a new treatment must be found more effective in the treatment group (the trial) than in the placebo group (the control). In data visualization, the quality and speed of the insights provided must be better with a chart (the trial) than with a table (the control); otherwise, the chart is useless and should be changed or deleted.

However, comparing charts and tables is a good starting point for understanding why perception is at the core of the visualization process. Forget those cases where the goal of reading a table is to get a precise value (for example, "When will the train arrive at the station?"), or where making all figures visible is a requirement, and focus instead on comparing multiple data points.

Here are two easy tasks for you: In the table at the left of **Figure 2.2**, find the top six importing countries and the top six exporting countries, and check whether they are the same. This shouldn't take long.

SHARE OF IMPORTS AND EXPORTS
Within the European Union (EU-28), by member state

Region	Imports	Exports
Belgium	7.8	8.5
Bulgaria	0.6	0.5
Czech Republic	3.1	3.7
Denmark	1.8	1.8
Germany	21.0	22.4
Estonia	0.4	0.3
Ireland	1.3	1.6
Greece	0.8	0.4
Spain	5.4	5.3
France	12.2	9.0
Croatia	0.4	0.2
Italy	7.1	7.4
Cyprus	0.1	0.0
Latvia	0.4	0.3
Lithuania	0.6	0.5
Luxembourg	0.6	0.4
Hungary	2.1	2.3
Malta	0.1	0.0
Netherlands	7.1	13.1
Austria	3.7	3.2
Poland	4.0	4.3
Portugal	1.5	1.2
Romania	1.5	1.3
Slovenia	0.6	0.7
Slovakia	1.6	1.9
Finland	1.4	1.1
Sweden	3.0	2.5
United Kingdom	9.6	6.2
EU-28	100.0	100.0

Source: Eurostat

Figure 2.2 Unlike charts, tables are slow to read, even with visual cues.

In the table, some of the figures we need have one more digit than others have, making them visually more salient and helping us to complete the tasks. This means that the perceptual mechanisms we use in visualization also help in reading the table.

When reading a table, most tasks remain at the cognitive level. That may not be a problem with a small table, but as the table grows our probability of missing even the most basic patterns or trends also grows.

Using the chart to the right in this figure to get the answers, on the other hand, is simpler, faster, and almost effortless. With the chart, we add a *data preprocessing system*, through which perception frees cognition from a large portion of elementary tasks, allowing us to focus on synthesis, integration, and interpretation.

Eye Physiology

Now let's move on to a bit of eye physiology so we gain a better understanding of how to design our visual representations.

Objects become visible when they emit light or when their surface reflects it. Light allows us to distinguish objects and recognize some of their properties. The eye is the organ we use to capture light stimuli. **Figure 2.3** shows the basic process.

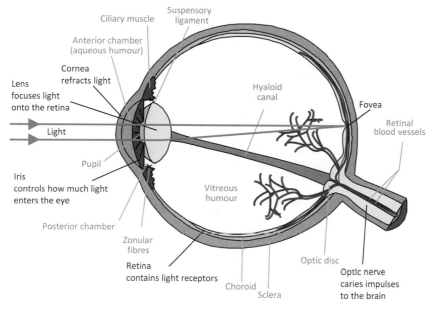

Figure 2.3 The eye captures light and converts it into electrochemical impulses.
Source: Wikicommons. Adapted from https://commons.wikimedia.org/wiki/
File:Schematic_diagram_of_the_human_eye_en.svg

The Retina

The retina is the photosensitive region of the eye that covers more than two-thirds of its inner surface. Refraction concentrates light in an 18° central arc of the retina, the *macula lutea*, where a transition from peripheral, low-resolution vision to central, high-resolution vision begins. We can define more concentric arcs, ending in the *umbo*, the very central point of the macula.

The horizontal axis of the chart in **Figure 2.4** represents the dimensions of these arcs with their approximate relative proportions. It also plots the distribution of photoreceptor cells in the retina in a 50° section to each side of the central point.

DENSITY OF PHOTORECEPTOR CELLS IN THE RETINA

Number of receptors per mm^2

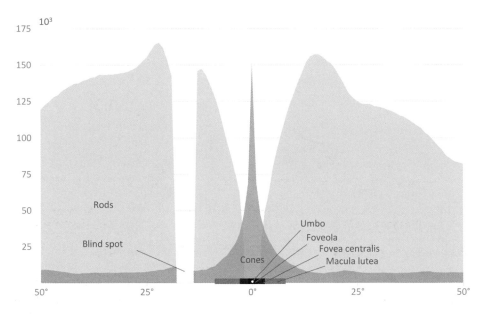

Figure 2.4 Photoreceptor cells are distributed along the retina.

The vertical axis represents the density of cells. It's obvious from the chart that these areas have significant differences in the type and concentration of photoreceptor cells.

Cones

The chart in Figure 2.4 shows the concentration of the two fundamental types of photoreceptor cells, the *cones* (6 to 7 million) and the *rods* (120 million). Rods are responsible for night vision and motion detection in the peripheral areas of the field of view. Since they have no significant role in data visualization, we won't discuss them here. Cones, the photoreceptor cells that we use in normal lighting conditions, have an opposite distribution. While their presence in the periphery is minimal, their density increases exponentially in the macula, peaking at the fovea, where their diameter is smaller, allowing for a higher resolution of the image.

There is also some functional specialization among cones, defined by their sensitivity to wavelengths at certain intervals and corresponding roughly to red, green, and blue. (The neuroscientist Stephen Kosslyn states that the correct colors are orangish-yellow, green, and violet.)[1]

---

1   Kosslyn, Stephen M. *Graph Design for the Eye and Mind*. New York: Oxford University Press, 2006.

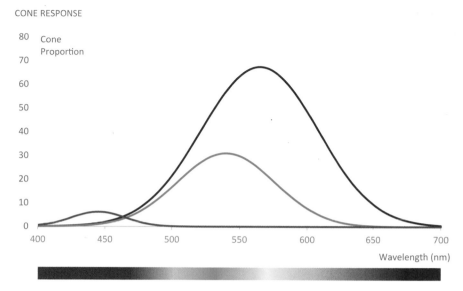

CONE RESPONSE

Figure 2.5 Cone response varies, depending on its sensitivity to wavelengths.

Cone sensitivity to red and green partly overlaps (**Figure 2.5**), which explains some of the vision issues associated with the processing of color. The inability to distinguish green from red is the most common form of color blindness, which affects up to 10 percent of men (but is almost residual in women).

Kosslyn notes that because the number of blue-sensitive cones is much smaller than the number of other cones, it justifies our inability to make subtle differentiations when using blue in text. In addition, blue-sensitive cones are placed deeper inside the retina, which can suggest a greater distance, generating some confusion when blue is superimposed on red (the opposite seems more "natural").

The Arc of Visual Acuity

The central point of the retina, where the number of cones peaks, is a small fraction of the total field of view. This leads to an equally narrow arc of visual acuity. Stretch your arms and join your thumbs and you'll have a good idea of the arc in the field of vision with maximum acuity (**Figure 2.6**). Our brain spends about half of its visual processing power on five percent of our field of vision.[2] No wonder it needs great management skills!

2　Ware, Colin. *Visual Thinking: for Design*. Burlington, MA: Morgan Kaufmann, 2008.

Now compare this with a digital photo. A high-resolution digital photo creates a large file because the increase in detail implies an increasing volume of information. However, while in a digital photo the resolution is constant, the image generated by the brain is dynamic and only a fraction is at maximum resolution. This reduces the brain's processing needs. The way the brain creates the image gives us the illusion of a perfect view of 180°, and it does this so perfectly that we are not aware of a hole in the image at the point that connects the eye and the optic nerve (the blind spot). We find that hole only if we search diligently for it.

Figure 2.6 This image gives (perhaps too generously) an approximate idea of how we see in reality.

Saccades

The periphery of our field of vision is available at low resolution, but we can convert it to high resolution on demand; we just have to change our attention through eye movements, called *saccades* or saccadic movements, from one point of fixation to the next.

Alfred Yarbus wrote one of the classic books on eye movement in 1965.[3] In a study, he asked a subject to look at an Ilya Repin painting (**Figure 2.7**) and answer several questions. In **Figure 2.8**, each ellipse represents the denser areas in terms of traces of eye movements while the subject was searching for some of the answers.

Even when there is no specific question, it's clear from the image that eyes don't wander randomly around the scene; they're attracted to salient features. Perhaps more interesting to data visualization is how the movements differ according to the task to perform. For example, notice how, when assessing people's age, gaze is focused on faces, while the assessment of how long the visitor was away also focuses on the same area but keeps moving from one face to the next to get an overall answer.

---

3   An English translation became available two years later: Yarbus, Alfred. *Eye Movements and Vision.* New York: Plenum Press, 1967.

Figure 2.7 Ilya Repin: *An Unexpected Visitor*, 1888. State Tretyakov Gallery, Moscow.

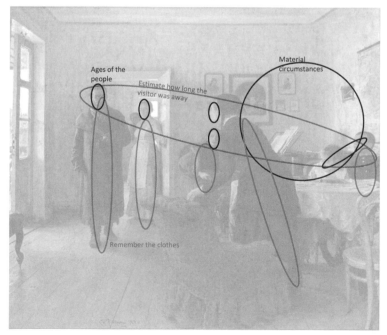

Figure 2.8 Attention is task-dependent, as shown by the recording of saccadic movements while the subject seeks answers.

In addition to the large number of eye movements, the experiment confirms that we focus our maximum visual acuity on the points of interest. Our experience and knowledge (but also prejudices and misconceptions) lead us to pre-select the points that seem most conducive for completing the task, which again demonstrates the link between perception and cognition.

Impact of Eye Physiology on Visualization

OK, Optometry 101 is over. Now, how can all that eye physiology be useful to our visualizations? Well, remembering the narrowness of maximum visual acuity can actually be very useful in planning visualizations. If we think of a chart as a unit of information, it's easy to understand that we should avoid saccades because of their disruptive effect on attention—that is, their requiring constant eye movement. As a rule, **between two informationally equivalent charts, the best one is the one that requires fewer saccades.**

There are several ways to reduce the number of saccadic movements, the first of which is to reduce chart size. Often a chart is much larger than necessary to convey its message. In a reduced size, there won't be room for all objects and you will need to prioritize them. Textures and pseudo-3D effects tend to increase image size without any benefits, so they're natural candidates for exclusion.

We should also redesign certain objects that seem indispensable. Using an imaginary internal monologue when reading each chart can help us understand this. In **Figure 2.9**, where the legend is outside the arc of visual acuity, the chart is ineffective for two reasons: It requires a split of attention and it forces working memory (see the section on working memory below) to enter into the interpretation, which disrupts the flow of the story. The chart reader's internal monologue might go like this:

The unemployment rates in the red and the orange countries are abysmal. Who are they? Let me check the legend... Ah, yes, Greece and Spain. And Portugal, where is it? It's the red, no, the green line. I should memorize them all. OK, what about those with lower rates? Ah, Germany and the U.S. They seem to have a similar trend in this decade.... Now I'm lost. Who's the red line, again?

The second chart (**Figure 2.10**) eliminates both issues by directly labeling the series, reducing the number of saccades and freeing the reader to interpret the chart. The internal monologue for this chart might be:

So over the last decade, the U.S. and Germany have a similar downward trend in unemployment, while the rate rose dramatically in Greece and Spain.

Note that placing the legend inside the arc of visual acuity would improve the chart, but you would still need a color-matching task between the legend and the lines in the chart. Removing the legend altogether and directly labeling the lines is the most effective option.

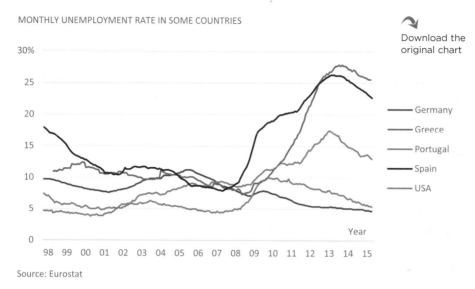

Figure 2.9 This chart forces a split of attention, a color-matching task, and the use of working memory.

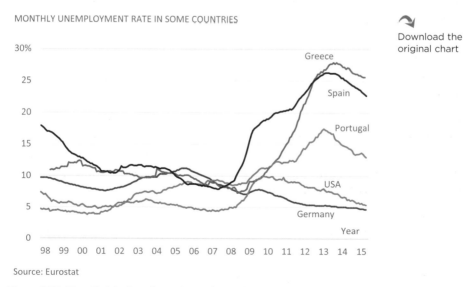

Figure 2.10 Directly labeling the series reduces the number of saccades and removes the color-matching task.

Pre-Attentive Processing

Contrary to what our sensorial experience tells us, visual stimuli processing is extremely fast, but it's not instantaneous; there is a progression in the construction of the image which becomes increasingly complex. Some basic features, like shape, color, or size, are processed at a faster speed. This is known as pre-attentive processing. It's as if your brain drew a quick sketch of your surroundings so that you could decide what your attention would turn to, or, as Colin Ware writes, "pre-attentive processing determines what visual objects are offered up to our attention and easy to find in the next fixation."[4]

Think of how you see a table and a line chart. Both are made of lines—lines that draw numbers in a table and lines that encode the data in the chart—and both are pre-attentively processed. In a table, pre-attentive processing allows us to recognize the overall shape as a table and a particular shape as the number 8, for example, but it still takes a lot of work when we actually start paying attention. There is not much we can infer about a table's content with pre-attentive processing alone. On the contrary, when you start paying conscious attention to a chart, much of the work is already done because the underlying data are transcribed into shapes that are processed pre-attentively.

Salience

Pre-attentive processing is a really, really good reason to make extensive use of data visualization. But I suspect you're already buying into this idea, so why bother even discussing it? It doesn't seem like something that you can act upon on a daily basis.

It turns out that there's a really cool feature that we can manipulate when making charts: *salience.* It's no accident that we use expressions such as "eye-catching" or "pops out" or even "blindingly obvious." For some reason, objects or features of objects often stand out from their surroundings in a way that draws our attention. Check these randomly colored squares:

---

4 Ware, Colin. *Information Visualization: Perception for Design.* Third Edition. Burlington, MA: Morgan Kaufmann, 2012.

None of the squares deserve special attention because none of them have an attribute that makes them stand out. Now compare this to the row below. Our eyes are drawn to the orange square, and even if you try to fixate on the first one on the left, that special orange square still requires your attention:

■ ■ ■ ■ ■ ■ ■ ■ ■ ■ ■ ■ ■ ■ ■ ■ ■ ■ **■** ■ ■

A high level of contrast to the background or to other objects that makes an object stand out is an extremely useful characteristic of the pre-attentive processing. It can occur naturally in the data themselves (when we visualize a time series and there is a sudden change in a trend, for example) or when we design the chart in a way that makes a series pop out.

As **Figure 2.11** shows, we could use many other attributes to get similar results. Note that although in the last row no color stands out, the row as a whole stands out when considering the entire image.

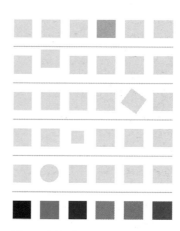

Figure 2.11 You can achieve salience using many attributes.

Impact of Pre-Attentive Processing and Salience on Visualization

If you've ever tried to find Waldo (the character of the children's book *Where's Waldo?*), you know how frustrating it is not to have a salient feature that helps you find the boy among dozens of other heterogeneous and distracting characters. That's why managing the salience level of an object greatly simplifies reading, giving the brain a hierarchical structure of stimuli relevance. This matches our narrative that establishes the brain as a manager, not a mere processor of raw data.

Look at the three versions of the chart in **Figure 2.12**. In the first version, the series of interest appears clearly differentiated from a uniform background. We focus on the evolution of that red series, while other series exist as a backdrop. This would fit the scenario of a manager who is evaluating a sales rep. The manager doesn't need, or want, to identify the other team members, but rather only to compare her performance against theirs.

Download the
original chart

SALIENCE IN PRE-ATTENTIVE PROCESSING

Color   None   Line thickness

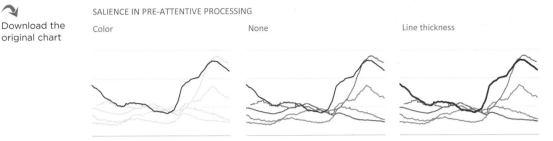

Figure 2.12 Salience in practice.

In the second version, in the middle, we assume a neutral position, giving equal weight to all the series. The reduction in contrast eliminates salience. The message is now a comparison of equals (although, in this case, since this is an example and you see all versions simultaneously, you'll be influenced by the red series on both sides). This now fits a second scenario in which someone in a meeting with their team shares a chart with them, comparing the performance of each territory.

In the last version, on the right, contrast returns with line thickness, and salience works again, though less pronounced. The message focuses again on the thicker red series, but in a different context—*primus inter pares*, first among equals. This represents a third scenario in which someone is meeting other managers and is showing them how their product's market share changed over time and how it compares to other major competitors.

No version is better than another if each is designed deliberately. Each version represents a point of view. A measure of the quality of the visualization is its ability to communicate our perspective faithfully.

In the chart in **Figure 2.13**, the growth in health insurance expenditure is doubly emphasized—by color contrast to the remaining variables and by the changing luminance that underlines the trend after 2010.

Another use of salience in these charts is that which makes data-encoding objects as a whole stand out, as opposed to supporting objects such as the grid lines, which are almost invisible.

When we opt for a "dump-all" strategy and use every bit of data that we can, the result is a spaghetti chart. Behind this strategy is often the fear of not being able to answer an unexpected question and therefore straying from the key message. This is a variant of "loss aversion," which makes us prefer avoiding losses to making gains. Because of loss aversion, it is only with great effort that we can draw any conclusions from such a spaghetti chart, yet it comforts us to know that it contains all the data, displayed with equal weight and with no editorial dimension in design or data selection.

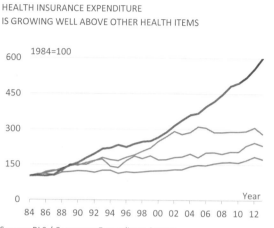

HEALTH INSURANCE EXPENDITURE
IS GROWING WELL ABOVE OTHER HEALTH ITEMS

Source: BLS / Consumer Expenditure Survey

Figure 2.13 Salience draws your attention to the thicker, colored line.

Download the original chart

Depending on our data, we don't always have to use salience in its extreme, or else we'll risk looking too bossy ("This is how you *must* read the chart"). In **Figure 2.14**, the left chart redraws the previous one. The way health insurance grows provides enough salience to make it pop out, and we can ease up, allowing the remaining series to be more than context. There is, however, a world of difference between this chart and the one on the right, which is a colorful and useless spaghetti tangle.

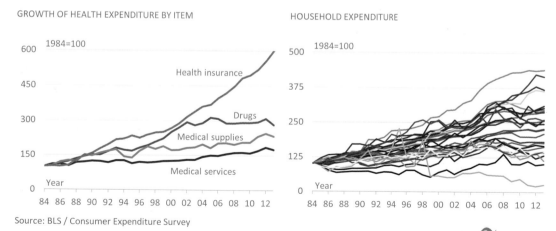

GROWTH OF HEALTH EXPENDITURE BY ITEM

HOUSEHOLD EXPENDITURE

Source: BLS / Consumer Expenditure Survey

Figure 2.14 From soft pop-out to spaghetti galore.

Download the original chart

Salience is a powerful tool that we should use with caution, because it risks either resulting in an overly dichotomous message or excessively emphasizing a single aspect of a heterogeneous reality. However, the amount of salience that you should take advantage of is something you should determine with careful forethought, as this defines your design. If the question forces polarity, the chart should do the same.

It makes sense that, when striving for communication effectiveness, chart design should be congruent with the questions you're trying to answer. Making a chart is an attempt to evaluate the relevance of the data. This exercise must be done by the author, not by the tool. Design a chart according to your own priorities. **A chart must be honest, but it is never neutral.**

Working Memory

If you've rehearsed a phone number repeatedly while trying to find a way to write it down and, in a moment of distraction, forgot it, it means that you've had conscious contact with working memory, the memory area where we keep chunks of information for immediate use. This information is then stored in long-term memory or eliminated and replaced by the next chunk.[5]

This experience with a phone number exemplifies two essential characteristics of working memory: its *limited storage capacity* and its *volatility*. Current studies suggest that three is the average number of objects that can be stored in working memory at any moment. This low limit, combined with pressure from outside to add new information, makes working memory very volatile. Blocking new information entry by rehearsing existing information is an effective method for reducing volatility, but it comes at a cost, making it hard to complete tasks that require its availability (try reading while rehearsing a phone number).

However, the capacity of working memory is flexible regarding the type and size of the objects that it can store. To see this in practice, memorize the following sequence, digit by digit:

1-4-9-2-1-9-1-4-1-9-3-9-1-9-6-9

---

5   In his seminal 1955 paper "The Magical Number Seven, Plus or Minus Two: Some Limits on Our Capacity for Processing Information" in *Psychological Review*, Vol. 101, No. 2: 343–352, George A. Miller uses the term "chunk" (whose size and nature are diffuse) to distinguish from "bit," which has a more precise meaning.

Not an easy task, I presume. With phone numbers, a strategy that helps memorization is to create groups of three digits. Let's try it out:

149-219-141-939-196-9

Hmm...not really helpful. Let's try again, this time with four digits:

1492-1914-1939-1969

Assuming that you know some of the most important dates in human history, you may think that memorizing 16 digits isn't that hard after all! We just moved from a sequence in which each digit is a unit of information to a sequence with four information units with four digits each. We now perceive four individual units, which memory recognizes as meaningful dates.

Various techniques are helpful for reducing information units. Some are universal (010101010101 = 6 × 01); others rely on the long-term memories shared by a large group of people (it would be harder to memorize historical dates of a little-known country); and others are personal (imagine that 27, 17, 13, 06 are the birthdays of each person in your family).

Whether used to store a few facts for your next exam or in complex systems by participants in memory championships, mnemonics is based on this principle of reducing the number of units of information to memorize, increasing complexity of each one, and connecting to objects stored in long-term memory.

Impact of Working Memory on Visualization

Excessive use of working memory brings information flow to a halt, preventing other brain processes from completing. A good visual representation should therefore include a cognitive resources conservation strategy via perceptual preprocessing.

We've seen that the narrow arc of visual acuity might leave out a chart's legend, forcing us to use memory or to move our eyes back and forth to find that legend. Labeling a series eliminates the need for working memory, making chart reading more effective.

In **Figure 2.15**, the visualization saves working memory by not using any form of identification in each series, assuming that all readers know the color code: broccoli is green, carrots are orange, and eggplants are purple. Of course, you should only risk doing something like this if you're sure that it's universal knowledge and beyond any reasonable doubt. Even then, some degree of redundancy is useful (the color-blind might not be able to distinguish colors).

Managing working memory usage must be a constant concern, but this is not limited only to the elimination of legends. In a document, you should position each image close to the text to which it relates to avoid the reader having to keep flipping pages back and forth to relate the two messages.

In a presentation, when we expect the audience to compare two charts, we should place them on the same slide rather than on multiple slides. How many times have you heard an audience ask the presenter to flip the slides back and forth repeatedly so that they can make a comparison?

Encoding inconsistencies also require the use of memory. Multiple charts representing the same entity with different color codes require a renewed effort from the audience that we can avoid by ensuring consistency between the charts.

Download the
original chart

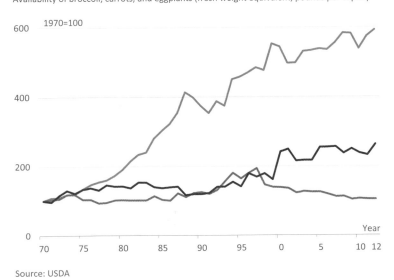

BAD NEWS FOR KIDS: BROCCOLI'S POPULARITY STILL GROWING STRONG

Availability of broccoli, carrots, and eggplants (fresh weight equivalent, pounds per capita)

Source: USDA

Figure 2.15 How far can we go to conserve working memory?

Gestalt Laws

If you take a close look at **Figure 2.16**, you'll notice that the Triangulum constellation (inset, upper left) is an outlier that accurately describes the location of three stars. Everything else seems kind of weird, at least for us. Try to find the Musca (Fly) constellation.[6] If you don't understand how, in someone's eyes, those stars turned into a fly, you're not alone, but you'll agree that because they're so close they form a group distinct from the rest.

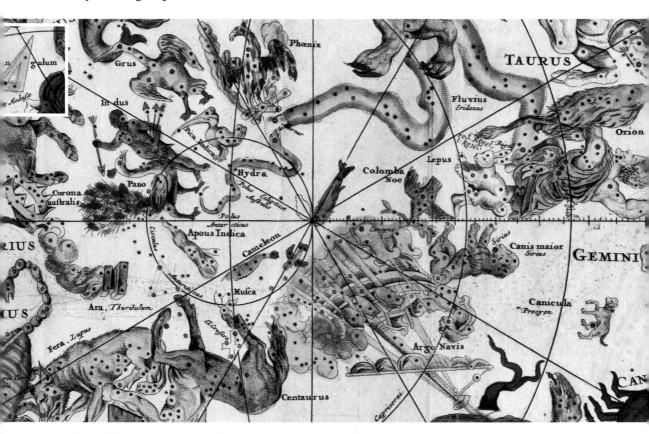

Figure 2.16 *Planisphærium cœleste* (detail). Celestial map from the 17th century, by the Dutch cartographer Frederik de Wit. Source: Wikicommons.

---

6 Hint: It's a small one, near Centaurus, at the bottom of the central circle, and reads like "Mufca."

Traditional constellation naming enjoys a historical legitimacy; names are the natural product of their authors' cultural and social circumstances. Try going outside on a starry night and let your eyes and your mind wander. Slowly, you'll begin to see groups of stars that remind you of the Mercedes logo, a shopping cart, or perhaps a fish. I can assure you that your constellations are as valid as the Musca. If, instead of stars, you stare at a set of randomly generated dots, you'll also discover some familiar shapes.

Our eye–brain system is always making constellations—that is, gathering points and giving meaning to the whole. It's the unavoidable tendency to search for simple shapes, since simple shapes are easier to process and consume fewer resources. This, again, is the thread for this chapter, but this time we have a name for it: *Prägnanz.*

Prägnanz, or "good form," is the unifying idea of Gestalt laws, or laws of grouping, summarized in the well-known sentence "The whole is greater than the sum of its parts" (and simpler too).

Form simplification means simplifying relationships among the components of the whole, emphasizing the whole and reducing the relevance of individual components by standardizing and generalizing relationships. This results in an increased weight of useful information (signal) against useless information (noise). (Interestingly, we could see the numbers used in the working memory example as the result of the search for good form.)

What shape do you see in **Figure 2.17**? If you answered "a circle," that's normal. In fact, it's just a few dashes that the brain connects to simplify the shape. While we can argue that these dashes are more similar to a circle than a few stars are to a fly, essentially it is the same process.

Figure 2.17 Is this a circle or a bunch of dashes cleverly placed?

Now try to describe the shapes (A) in **Figure 2.18**. Our natural tendency is to describe them as two partially overlapping circles (B). Of course, nothing prevents reality to be (C), but then the shapes become more complex: Just compare the number of words you need to describe (B) versus (C).

Grouping and simplification of form are core ideas in data visualization, and it all starts with the distances we perceive after mapping points on the proto-chart. We see points near each other as a group.

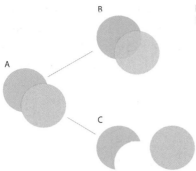

Figure 2.18 What is behind the orange circle? Is there actually anything there?

Let's look at some types of grouping without worrying about the implicit laws. Here is a basic display of the data points:

To create a chart, we must impose a minimum reading grid. We know from the data that there are two different series, so this is the first differentiation to make:

Our experience tells us that this distribution is compatible with a line chart, so connecting points of each series seems to be the obvious grouping:

Using lines to connect points is stronger than grouping them by color, and we can prove this if we change the connections. Introducing a vertical connection weakens horizontal reading and forces grouping and the reading of each pair of points:

In **Figure 2.19**, several Gestalt laws are at play. The chart relates Gross Domestic Product (GDP) per capita at purchasing power parity to the proportion of people who completed secondary or higher levels of education over the years 2002–2013.

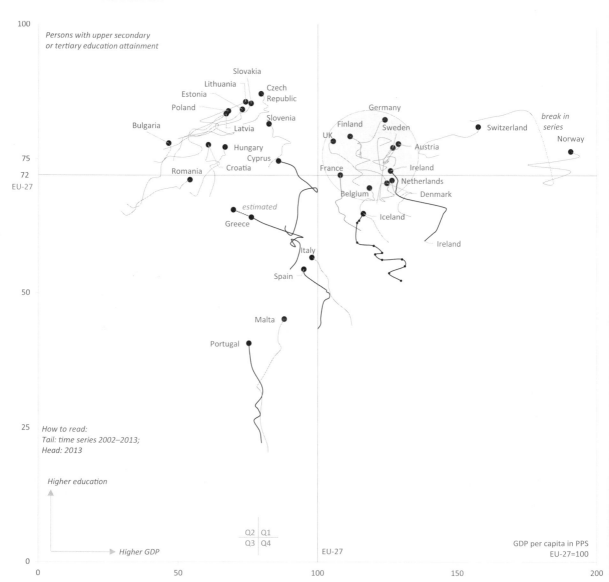

EDUCATION VS. GDP IN EUROPE 2002–2013

Source: Eurostat (data for Greece in 2013 not available; estimated from trend)

Figure 2.19 Gestalt laws in a scatter plot.

Download the
original chart

The chart is divided into four quadrants, defined by the EU-27 value for each variable. It's clear that there are three groups of countries: the Western European countries (high GDP, high education levels), the countries of Eastern Europe (low GDP, high education levels), and the Mediterranean countries (low GDP, and low education levels).

Law of Proximity

■ ■ ■   ■ ■ ■

Waldo Tobler's first law of geography states that "Everything is related to everything, but near things are more related than distant things." This is well suited to the law of proximity, according to which we see objects close to each other as a group and we assume they share the same characteristics.

Figure 2.20 Law of proximity.

That's something we do often when we read a scatter plot. In the chart, we easily recognize as a group most of the points in quadrant Q2. When we identify the points, that recognition is strengthened; with the exception of Cyprus, it's a group of countries of Eastern Europe (**Figure 2.20**). This is one of the most common laws used to read scatter plots, although we can find several others on the same chart.

Law of Similarity

■ ■ ▲ ■ ■ ■ ▲

We understand objects that share a common feature—such as color, size, or shape—as similar. In the chart, the red tail groups several countries, even if they are far apart. These are the countries hit hardest by the financial and sovereign debt crises (**Figure 2.21**).

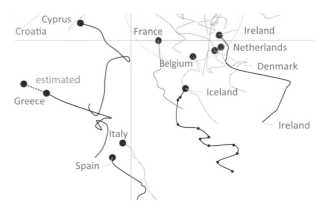

Figure 2.21 Law of similarity.

The law of similarity is particularly useful for grouping categories. In **Figure 2.22**, the colors of the first pie chart were chosen randomly and we see 12 independent slices, while in the second pie chart we see two segmented groups, blues and red-yellows, or cool and warm colors.

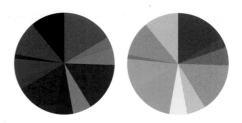

Figure 2.22 Random color coding versus taking advantage of the law of similarity.

Law of Segregation

The law of segregation tells us that objects within a closed shape are seen as a group. A frame around objects (charts or legends, for example) has this function, but it's also useful for adding visual annotations.

Figure 2.23 Segregation is one of the strongest Gestalt laws.

The ellipse and circle drawn around countries reinforce their status as a coherent group, even if some of them don't belong to the same quadrant and don't meet one of the criteria (**Figure 2.23**). This shows the grouping power of this law, so it's important that the criteria are clear and some level of redundancy is recognized (combining this law with the law of proximity, for example).

Law of Connectivity

The law of connectivity tells us that objects connected to other objects tend to be seen as a group. In the chart detail (**Figure 2.24**), the line connections between the data points (the "tails") allow us to read each of them as a group.

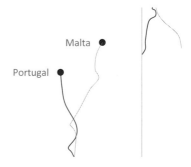

Figure 2.24 Law of connectivity.

The law of connectivity is the basis of the line chart (**Figure 2.25**) and is of such importance that it's not the individual points but rather the links between them that are the most relevant in reading the chart.

GREENHOUSE GAS EMISSIONS FROM TRANSPORT IN THE EU

Download the original chart

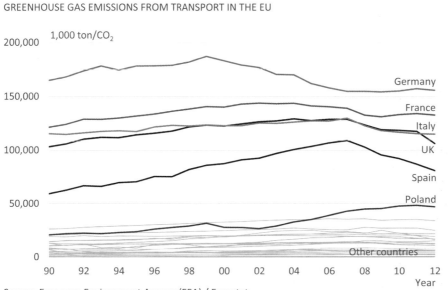

Source: European Environment Agency (EEA) / Eurostat

Figure 2.25 Law of connectivity in practice.

Law of Common Fate

The law of common fate tells us that objects moving in the same direction are seen as a group. In an animated chart, the animation helps you find patterns in the data, and in this sense movement is taken literally. A good example is Hans Rosling's first TED conference, "The best stats you've ever seen."

Watch the video

Law of Closure

The law of closure tells us that we tend to complete forms. Examples are dashed lines that we see as solid, axes lines that allow us to avoid frames around the chart, or the connection we make between missing values. We come up with a smooth connection that best fits the existing values. This may not match the actual data, so we need to exercise some caution in its assessment. **Figure 2.26** exemplifies this.

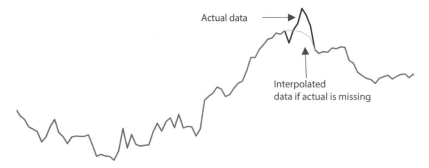

Actual data

Interpolated
data if actual is missing

Figure 2.26 When some data are missing, we tend to make smooth transitions between data points.

Law of Figure/Ground

We tend to see closed objects, objects seen as a unit, or objects that look smaller as the object that stands out from the amorphous background. A clear definition of what is figure and what is ground helps focus attention on the relevant objects. In this classic optical illusion, the figure may be either a vessel or two profiles (**Figure 2.27**).

In a chart, the visual encoding of the data is the figure, and any additional elements are their support (the ground). Our design choices must ensure that this differentiation is clear.

Figure 2.27
Figure versus ground:
"Rubin's vase."

Compare the two versions of the chart in **Figure 2.28**. In the version on the left, the grid lines are so noisy that they compete with the data for the leading role. In the chart on the right, they remain visible but work quietly, helping the reading and emphasizing the role of the data.

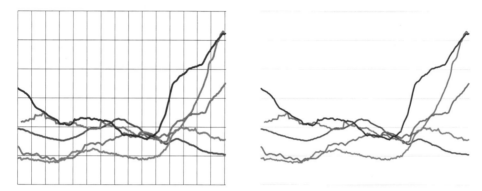

Figure 2.28 Lines in jail versus lines in the open.

Law of Continuity

The law of continuity states that we interpret images so as not to generate abrupt transitions or otherwise create images that are more complex.

Values hidden behind others in a 3D chart provide a good example. Because we can't see them, we can arbitrarily fill in the missing elements to complete a pattern. It's also the case of time series, in which we assume that data points in the future will be a smooth continuation of the past (**Figure 2.29**). Recall, for example, that back in 2007, everyone thought home prices would never go down.

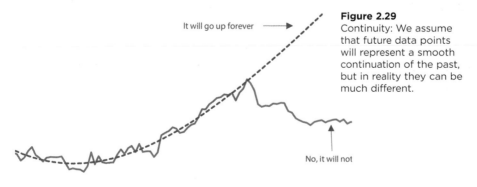

It will go up forever ⟶

Figure 2.29 Continuity: We assume that future data points will represent a smooth continuation of the past, but in reality they can be much different.

No, it will not

In a line chart, those series with a similar slope (that is, they appear to follow the same direction) are understood as belonging to the same group. In Figure 2.28, we divide the series into two groups: those with a downward trend and those with an upward trend. Also, the trend toward the upper right of many of the Q1 countries in Figure 2.19 helps us see them as a group.

Impact of Gestalt Laws on Visualization

The above examples reinforce the idea that the Gestalt laws are manifestations of a more general concept of "good form." In some cases, like the law of proximity, they're clear and well defined. In other cases, they don't appear to be more than subtle variations of the same concept. This explains, in part, the multitude of new laws that were suggested over the years and appended to the original list.

Whatever image you use, the brain works tirelessly to simplify it. Although our power to control the images of the world around us is small, this power is much stronger for images we create. We should exercise this power consciously as we suggest how to read an image.

We should use the mechanisms of Gestalt sparingly in chart making—just enough to make explicit groupings, depending on the aggregation power of each law (**Figure 2.30**). For example, the law of segregation is stronger than the law of connectivity,[7] and the law of connectivity is stronger than the law of proximity. Implicit groupings are sufficient to define a legend, making a frame unnecessary. In most cases, the chart itself does not need a frame because it's easily perceived as a unit. In the line chart, on the contrary, the laws of proximity and similarity are insufficient, and that's why a line connecting data points is needed.

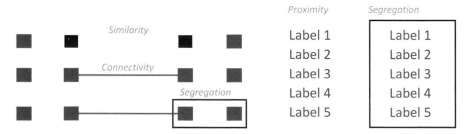

Figure 2.30 Comparing the strength of some Gestalt laws.

---

7   Assuming a fair comparison—that is, connecting and segregating lines are identical and there is no foreground/background relationship—a thick red connecting line in the foreground will surely make the law of connectivity stronger than a thin gray line in the background.

Sometimes grouping is dependent on the message in a more explicit way. Using the law of segregation to make it clear that all the countries of Eastern Europe have a similar profile may be useful in the communication context.

In data visualization, the Gestalt laws probably have the broadest impact on how we design our visual representations.

The Limits of Perception

How sure can you be that one person is taller than another? If they stand side by side, I'd say you could be quite certain in most cases. What about weight? That's trickier, right? The weight difference between two people must be significant for you to be sure that one person is heavier than another. This seems so natural that we don't question why. But...well, *why*? Why can we more easily discern height differences than weight differences?

Simply put, it's because human perception is imperfect—imbalanced in some cases, unable to resolve conflicts in ambiguous situations, and coming up with absurd answers in yet other cases. Many data visualization experts have studied these imperfections, trying to describe them, quantify them, and find remedies or alternatives because they have a direct impact on how we read a chart.

Precision varies for each retinal variable. A simple glance allows us to acknowledge that while comparing two adjacent columns is very accurate, comparing angles or areas is not as easy. In 1984, William Cleveland and Robert McGill studied how precise our perception is when reading retinal variables. The authors defined a set of encodings associated to elementary perception tasks we perform before any task of a cognitive nature, such as reading scales or legends.

According to this empirical study, we can order the retinal variables by degree of precision in performing elementary tasks. **Figure 2.31** shows examples of these tasks, ordered by degree of accuracy, according to the study.[8]

---

8 Cleveland, William S. and Robert McGill. "Graphical Perception: Theory, Experimentation, and Application to the Development of Graphical Methods." *Journal of the American Statistical Association*, Vol. 79, No. 387: 531–554, 1984. There are minor differences between the paper and the book. This list follows the book: Cleveland, William S. *The Elements of Graphing Data*. New Jersey: Hobart Press, 1994.

Read the paper

RANK OF SOME RETINAL VARIABLES
By level of accuracy

Figure 2.31
Elementary tasks ranked
by accuracy.

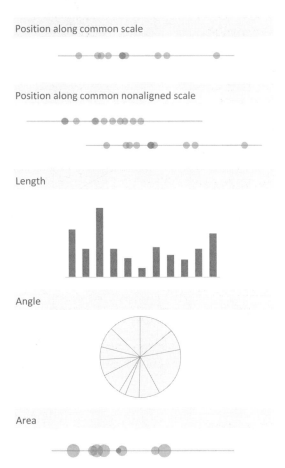

Position along common scale

Position along common nonaligned scale

Length

Angle

Area

We must not rush to conclude that we should always select the encoding that ensures a maximum degree of precision, which in practice would result in the exclusive use of dot charts, since those represent the example of "position in a common scale."

This is still a landmark study in data visualization, and it provides a good starting point for becoming aware of the differences in accuracy of the retinal variables. However, experimental studies in this field are faced with the problem of, on the one hand, obtaining generalizable results and, on the other hand, ensuring that the results are not contaminated by uncontrolled variables.

Some authors[9] noted that the Cleveland study does not take into account the specific task (among other factors). The type of reading that the task requires can influence the ordering. In **Figure 2.32**, there are minor differences between some values, but they're always visible in the bar chart. In the pie chart, they're almost indistinguishable. This is consistent with Cleveland's results. However, if you want to know the proportion of each value in the whole, the pie chart is more effective because, unlike with the bar chart, you don't need to refer to the scale (the whole is

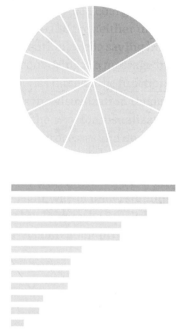

Figure 2.32 Pie chart versus bar chart.

already there). Later, we'll discuss whether it's relevant to use questions about proportions at all, but this example shows that the effectiveness of each chart type is often task-dependent.

Why We Need Grid Lines and Reference Lines: Weber's Law

Being aware of the limits of our perception helps us not only to choose a display that respects these limits, but also to find devices that minimize them.

Here is a concrete example: It's easier to detect the difference in length between two lines of six and seven inches each than it is to detect the difference between two lines of 20 and 21 inches each, even though the absolute difference is the same. This is an example of Weber's law, which postulates that *the minimum perceptible difference between two stimuli is proportional to the magnitude of the stimuli.*

---

9 Simkin, David and Hastie, Reid. "An Information-Processing Analysis of Graph Perception." *Journal of the American Statistical Association*, Vol. 82, No. 398: 454–465, 1987.

Cleveland uses two pairs of bars to illustrate the law from a different viewpoint, in comparing height (**Figure 2.33**). Because the bars are not aligned, determining whether they have the same height is not easy. In the first group, nothing in the picture helps us to compare them. In the second version, we added two gray rectangles of the same height. Now it's easy to see that the second bar is taller, because the section we have to compare is much smaller.

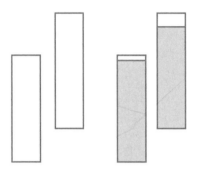

Figure 2.33 Weber's law: Shorter heights are easier to compare, as are shorter lengths.

In a laboratory setting, the comparison of two adjacent and aligned bars is very accurate, but in a real-world scenario, when using a chart with multiple bars, the comparisons are not made solely between adjacent bars but instead among all bars, and accuracy decreases when comparing bars spread apart from one another. When we add grid lines, they work like the gray rectangles of the previous image, reducing the sections to compare.

As a reaction against the excessive weight of grid lines, people sometimes go full minimalist and eliminate them. Rather, in addition to justifying the existence of grid lines, Weber's law also justifies the inclusion of reference lines. In **Figure 2.34**, the mean value of the EU is used as a reference line, making it easier to compare it to the various countries, a great improvement over using an additional (reference) column.

Being Aware of Distortions: Stevens' Power Law

In **Figure 2.35**, each bar displays the percentage of population at risk of poverty and social exclusion. In Italy, this risk is significantly lower than in Bulgaria, and this seems very clear when comparing the bars. The bubbles encode the same data, but in this case, the values seem much closer because we have a tendency to measure the diameter of the bubbles instead of their area.

PEOPLE AT RISK OF POVERTY OR SOCIAL EXCLUSION

Percentage of total population in 2013

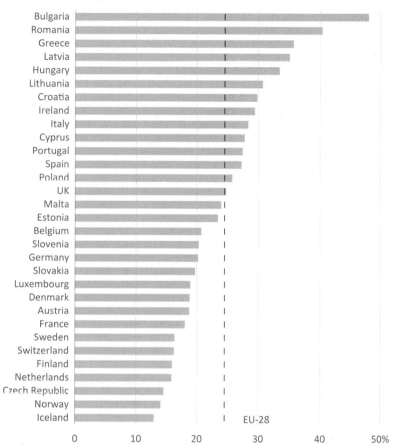

Source: Eurostat

Figure 2.34 Weber's law in practice. A reference line makes comparisons easier.

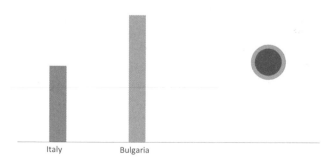

Figure 2.35 Stevens' power law. Real and perceived sizes are similar for the bars, but smaller areas appear larger in the bubble chart.

Stevens' power law, which establishes *a relationship between the magnitude of a physical stimulus and the perception of its intensity*, explains this effect. According to Cleveland, in the case of bars, the ratio of the magnitude and perception approaches 1—that is, real and perceived sizes are similar. The ratio for areas lies between 0.6 and 0.9, which means that smaller areas appear to be larger, while larger areas seem smaller, explaining the distortion when reading the bubble chart.

Context and Optical Illusions

Optical illusions show how the context and the interaction of objects lead us to a wrong assessment of their properties. The brain's pursuit of "good form" is not always successful. We sometimes generate absurd images or create images that are not there from shapes that cannot be grouped. **Figure 2.36** is the so-called Kanizsa's Triangle, wherein we see a white triangle supported by three circles over another triangle. None of these objects exist as such, beginning with the white triangle. (This phenomenon is called "reification," through which the brain identifies contours where they do not exist.)

Before the widespread use of color, it was common to use patterns to identify multiple series in a chart. Some combinations of patterns (most of them, actually) are annoying, because they generate a moiré effect (**Figure 2.37**), a flicker that gives movement to objects and changes their shape.

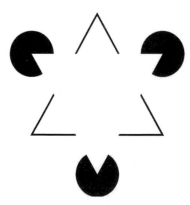

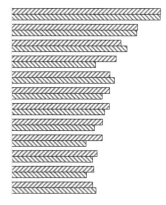

Figure 2.36 Kanizsa's Triangle. We generate images from shapes that don't exist.

Figure 2.37 Some combinations of patterns create a moiré effect.

It doesn't take much to guess that pseudo-3D charts are the epitome of optical illusions in data visualization. We'll get back to this idea more than once in this book, including in the section on lying with charts.

Impact of the Limits of Perception on Visualization

Ensuring that true differences among and relationships between data points are respected when displaying them visually is central to data visualization. However, our perception is imperfect, and in many cases, an accurate evaluation may be hard to achieve. Our first duty is to find solutions to minimize reading errors. We can do this by using grid lines, reference lines, and other graphic devices or by adjusting the type of analysis to use the most accurate retinal variables. However, as noted by critics of Cleveland's study, precision is not an absolute value. We must assess precision in terms of the concrete task and the level of familiarity with the proposed chart type.

For every rule in data visualization, there is a scenario where that rule should be broken. This means that choosing the best chart or the best design is always a trade-off between several conflicting goals. Our imperfect perception means that data visualization has a larger subjective dimension than a data table. Sometimes we only need this subjective, impressionist dimension and other times we need to translate it into hard figures. Striving for accuracy is important, but it's more important to provide those insights that only a visual display can reveal.

Few people would disagree if I said that it's necessary to have a good grasp of the data in order to make better charts. And although the need for a basic under-standing of human perception may be less obvious, it's not less necessary. If the knowledge is not there, it will likely be replaced by something else—probably some worthless templates. Trust me; you don't want *that*.

To fill the vacuum, I strongly advise you to read Colin Ware's books. Much of what you read in this chapter was my rather short interpretation of his work. You may want to start with *Visual Thinking for Design*. If you want to read a perspective closer to data visualization (and also heavily influenced by Ware), then check out Stephen Few's *Show Me the Numbers*.

To know more about the limits of perception and the work of William Cleveland, let me suggest his book *The Elements of Graphing Data*.

Takeaways

- Understanding how perception and the eye–brain system work affects data visualization in multiple ways, making your displays more effective while saving and optimizing cognitive resources.

- We have a small arc of visual acuity that forces us to constantly move our eyes from one point of fixation to the next (the saccadic movement). Designing a visualization should minimize the need for this movement.

- We read some features of objects, like color, shape, or size, before others, just like we make quick sketches before drawing an image in more detail. This is called pre-attentive processing, and it's one of the reasons why visualization can be so effective at processing data.

- We can take more advantage of pre-attentive processing by making key objects more salient (giving them higher contrast to other objects or to the background), creating a hierarchy of relevance.

- Working memory is another component that we should manage carefully. We should remove unnecessary steps for reading a chart or for comparing charts or objects. We should replace a legend by direct labeling, not place two charts on different slides that are to be compared, and we should leave the short storage capacity of our working memory for more complex chunks of information.

- The idea of "good form" that is easy to process and requires fewer resources can help structure a visualization, whether it contains one or multiple charts and other objects. Use the Gestalt laws to group objects that should be seen as a group by the audience.

- Human visual perception is not perfect and can actually be misleading in many situations. In data visualization, these situations can be altogether avoided by using the right chart or the right format for the task or by rejecting pseudo-3D effects. In other cases, we can minimize distortion or improve precision when comparing two objects far apart by using grid lines.

The eye-brain system is so essential to human beings that we can't confine it to the narrow limits of the individual; therefore, you can consider this chapter and the next as a single unit. Understanding how human perception works at the personal level helps us explain the formation of culture and the ability to live in society and, when left unchecked, the origin of preconceived ideas, prejudices, and stereotypes.

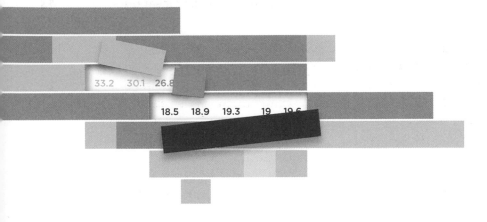

3

BEYOND VISUAL PERCEPTION

As you can imagine, the details behind what we've just covered in the previous chapter are infinitely complex; we've only scratched the surface of how perception affects data visualization. But even the little we do know so far is enough to stop us from making obvious mistakes. So let's continue by looking at the social and cultural aspects of visual representation.

After learning about the *mechanics* of perception, we'll agree that it's inevitable that a single red spot on a black-and-white photo will catch our attention; and we find it impossible to store 50 objects in working memory. Does this mean that, since humans share a similar physiology, the way we react to stimuli or manage information is predictable or, even worse, mechanical?

The answer is no, of course. (As the father of twins, I experience this firsthand, every single day. My twins are anything but predictable!) As we saw in the previous chapter, perception is not limited to receiving external stimuli and processing those stimuli as they are presented. The process depends on the unique characteristics and environment of each individual at a given time. (Reflect on the famous words of Spanish philosopher José Ortega y Gasset: "I am I and my circumstances.") We'll discuss these social and individual contexts in this chapter. We'll also examine the contexts that affect how an individual produces and consumes information: the person and her history, the society and culture she belongs to, and the organizational microcosm where she works.

Favoring "good form" and a reduction of ambiguity extends beyond the individual brain and into the social organization. That is why a set of social roles and mores exists in each community for self-regulation in pursuit of "good *social* form." The information analyst must always have these rules in mind when presenting data because they're associated with expected behaviors. Breaking the rules incurs a cost (mental and otherwise).

Social Prägnanz

Human societies perpetually search for a balance between unity and diversity—"unity without uniformity and diversity without fragmentation"—with the goal to create a certain stability. But our tendency for diversity is contradicted by the rules of social relationships, shared vision, language, and community symbols that together support unity.

Rules generate behavioral expectations and visions. When I take the role of "father," society expects that socialization has taught me the rules, and that I will act in accordance with those rules from the moment I assume that role (when I become a father).

The same happens in communication, where the rules of a language are rigid enough to allow sharing the code and establishing communication. When I write "chart," I use some signs of a pre-established set of symbols that we call the "alphabet," whose sound equivalents are known. I refer to a specific object (defined or clarified by the context, if necessary), distinguished from any other object. But these rules are still flexible enough to allow for a personal style in my communication.

Our search for stability makes relationships among individuals within the ecosystem less complex and ambiguous, and lowers processing costs, our goal here. In this process, we generalize and create low-resolution concepts to keep mental costs down and cope with all the information around us. However, these generalizations, such as "You men/women are so..." or "All Americans are...," generate perverse side effects such as sexism, racism, and so on. As such, the data are no longer sufficient to characterize an entity or person—whom for all relevant purposes ceases to exist and is replaced by an extreme generalized version of the group—and leads to greater instability, exactly what mental cost reduction is seeking to avoid.

The positive side to this, however, is that the boundaries between unity and diversity—and the individual and the social—are more fluid than we think. The brain, being the entity that manages our interaction with the environment, projects parts of its mechanisms in what we might call "social *prägnanz*." Recall in Chapter 2 we discussed prägnanz—the unifying principle of Gestalt laws that means the pursuit of the "good form" that minimizes the need for cognitive resources. If we export this concept to the social level, it means that "good social form" simplifies social relationships. Social prägnanz is then composed of conventions and rules that vary between the implicit and symbolic (the use of colors, for example) and the explicit and formal (the laws), conditioning and formatting the whole process of perception, including visual stimuli processing by the brain.

Since change is essentially the search for a new balance, it must encompass this idea of social prägnanz. Change leads to increased levels of ambiguity and complexity and may generate resistance, particularly when it challenges core knowledge, beliefs, or past practices. So when is change acceptable for establishing new rules and ideas?

Breaking the Rules

Rules and social conventions create a uniform and predictable background. When one person breaks the rules, it adds mental processing costs to the people it affects. It's like being a tourist in a different culture. At the same time, it generates something akin to salience in pre-attentive processing, to which we are naturally drawn: A change in circumstances is the basis of any good story that attracts our attention. But if there are multiple and simultaneous changes, they become hard to reconcile.

It isn't difficult to find an example in which perceptual and social dimensions intertwine. Imagine someone dressed in bright red at a funeral, where everyone else wears dark colors. This would be salient with respect to a uniform color context. But beyond the chromatic effect, there is also a symbolic dimension due to the breaking of the social rule that censors red at funerals. Naturally, we'll want to know who that rule breaker is, what kind of relationship she had with the deceased, and why she dresses that way in that environment.

In a young field like data visualization, questioning established ideas is a condition of growth, and we shouldn't be afraid of breaking the rules. Breaking the rules in data visualization has two very different meanings. The first is a vendor-sponsored rule breaking, those baseless practices suggested by some software applications (including Excel), of which the epitome is the pseudo-3D pie chart. They go against what we currently know about human visual perception and undermine data visualization effectiveness. Throughout this book, we'll fight against these baseless practices and implicit rules.

The second meaning is *test-breaking* cultural, perceptual, and visualization rules, and seeing how that may affect how we read graphic representations. We'll see that breaking the rules often has more costs than benefits, but sometimes, after an initial awkwardness, breaking the rules may prove very useful.

The Tragedy of the Commons

How do you attract attention and keep an audience interested? If you want to find a serious divide in the data visualization community, this seemingly innocent question will serve you quite well. On one hand, a designer gets so excited after hearing that his data visualization must "attract attention" that he runs back to his computer and fails to follow through with the "keep the audience interested" part. On the other end of the spectrum, you get Edward Tufte's famous quote: "If the statistics are boring, then you've got the wrong numbers."

Think of this in terms of the well-known "tragedy of the commons." The rational self-interest of each member of a group (sheep herders, for example) when using a common resource (the commons, or pasture) can work against the interest of the group as a whole, if it results in exploiting the resource beyond its sustainable level. In other words, what is good for the individual is not necessarily so for the group.

In this case, attention is the commons, a finite and, these days, valuable resource. Imagine graphic designers as herders, taking their portfolio to graze in this common pasture. (This also applies to heavy users of special effects in Excel and PowerPoint.) Attracting attention is easy (salience in pre-attentive processing will help), especially for someone with a modicum of artistic talent. But while it may seem rational from an individual point of view, if everyone kept creating highly unusual images just to attract attention, we'd soon deplete this resource and pollute the visual landscape by creating a strongly heterogeneous background, making contrast harder to create and ruining salience for everyone. Add to this that we now have online access to automatic infographics generators; the audience may decide these objects require more attention than they're willing to spare.

The pie charts in **Figure 3.1** provide an example at the chart level. The pie on the left attracts attention to the first slice. Then it's as if the other slices get envious and want more attention too. So the competition gets fierce and, in the end, everyone loses. The overall effect is that of a useless increase in noise and processing costs and a reduced attention pool.

Figure 3.1 Pie charts: from acceptable to wretched.

One of my pet peeves is the expression "a memorable and professional look" that many vendors use to describe the charts made by their applications. Well, the best of these charts are usually "memorable" for the wrong reasons (overly emphasizing design and eye-candy), and the "professional look" usually means that they included some irrelevant effects that happen to be missing in Excel or PowerPoint.

Think of memory as a non-renewable resource that you'll want to keep using at a sustainable level. In an organizational environment, you don't need to make memorable charts. If you wish to do so (from time to time), you must first look within the data for the reason why your chart should be memorable.

In the example in **Figure 3.2**, the memorable dimension of the chart is the exponential growth of unemployment in Greece. The author broke a rule by defining a fictitious border, forcing the series line to go beyond the frame and thereby emphasizing the drama that is already there (the word "skyrocketing" also made the point). Again, this is something that you should do at a sustainable level (meaning rarely), and only if the data justifies it.

Although a keen-eyed reader could criticize this chart because the exponential growth is fueled in part by its (hidden) real aspect ratio, not the one defined by the visible border, this is balanced out by the series for the entire European Union (EU-28) that acts as a reference. Always a good practice, but even more valuable when breaking a rule: Add more series to make relative comparisons possible.

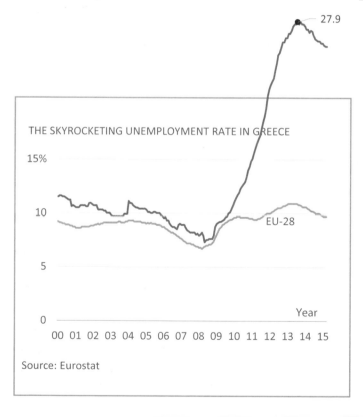

Figure 3.2
Framing a story without distorting it.

Download the original chart

Color Symbolism

Say it quickly: "She sells seashells by the seashore." Tongue twisters are usually correct but hard-to-articulate sentences requiring deep concentration. The chart in **Figure 3.3** is, by comparison, a visual version of a tongue twister (an eye twister, perhaps?). It displays the availability of three vegetables: carrots, broccoli, and eggplant.

Do you feel comfortable reading the chart? I don't, because the strong association between vegetables and color is broken. Usually, carrots are not green, broccoli is not purple, and eggplant is not orange.[1] Also, having to read the legend when the lazy designer (that would be me) could make things much easier is annoying. Things can get bad if you mess up traditional symbolic uses: pink and blue for the wrong genders, red and blue for the wrong political parties, faulty team colors, and so on.[2]

Playing with color symbolism is rarely justified and has no advantages over the long run, because in most cases long-standing color associations are unlikely to change in the short to medium term. Country flags rarely change, Coca-Cola is likely to remain red, and women will not be wearing bright red dresses to funerals any time soon.

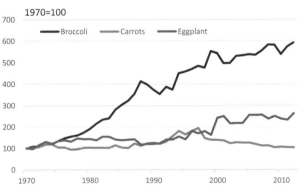

Download the
original chart

BAD NEWS FOR KIDS: BROCCOLI'S POPULARITY STILL GROWING
Food availability (fresh weight equivalent, pounds per capita)

Figure 3.3 Disrespecting expected colors annoys the reader, as does an unnecessary legend.

Source: USDA/ERS

---

1   This can be seen as a variation of the Stroop effect.

2   By the way, if you want to fight prejudice (for example by not using pink for female, if you think of it that way), don't simply opt to reverse color coding; it generates the same sterile confusion of the chart in Figure 3.3. Instead, choose colors that have no symbolic meaning in that context.

Representing Time

The way we represent time (and think about it) in the Western world is common across society. Time flows from left (older) to right (newer). In the left-hand chart of **Figure 3.4**, I've removed all labeling. Assuming a "normal" left-to-right time flow, you'll likely conclude that both series are trending down. In reality you'd be wrong. The version on the right with its labels shows that the opposite is true; there is an upward trend in both series.

In this particular example, the reader could suspect that the chart goes against convention because a downward trend in broadband Internet connection is unlikely. In cases where there are no expectations, this alert sign may not be present and the chart will lead us to draw opposite conclusions to what the data tell us. So there is a real danger that the reader won't be able to make correct perception-based conclusions (in this case, values decreasing when read from left to right) until after the cognitive task of reading the horizontal axis (the values are increasing). This is a capital sin in data visualization, and you should try to avoid it at all costs: **In a chart, cognitive tasks complement perceptual tasks and should never correct them.** Heck, what's the point of making quick-to-read charts if your audience can't trust them? If "trust but verify" should be your audiences' motto, it's your job to make sure the "trust" part is not missing.

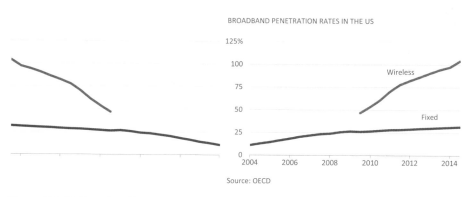

Download the original chart

Figure 3.4 Making time flow to the left can mislead the audience.

Axis Folding

Conventions tell us that the *y* values move away from the origin continuously, sometimes in two opposite directions (up and down, positive and negative). The horizon chart in **Figure 3.5** breaks these conventions of continuity and direction of the *y*-axis. It shows by how much the unemployment rate in West Virginia

MONTHLY UNEMPLOYMENT IN WEST VIRGINIA JANUARY 1976 — MAY 2015: DIFFERENCE TO NATIONAL RATE

Figure 3.5 This horizon chart unconventionally folds the *y*-axis.

diverged from the national average over the years. Red tones mean that the rate is higher, while blue tones mean the rate is lower. The larger the gap, the darker the tone.[3] In other words, both the positive and negative values of the y-axis fold over themselves, and color and shade become the means of differentiation.

It's OK if you don't find the chart easy to understand. Take your time to overcome the initial strangeness because it really pays off. The horizon chart is one of the best examples of effective rule breaking. It minimizes unused real estate, allowing for a much higher density of data points compared to traditional techniques.

Don't Make Me Think!

There can be several reasons why someone breaks the rules, whether from ignorance, malice, or the sincere desire to find a more effective way to explore the data or communicate the results. Whatever the reason, breaking the rules frustrates the audience's expectations and will incur a cost. Sometimes you might consider this an investment, while often it is nothing more than waste.

In *Don't Make Me Think! A Common Sense Approach to Web Usability*, Steve Krug's well-known book on interface design, he shows that the user must first understand that a certain object on a screen is a button and that its use then triggers a set of predictable actions. In data visualization, the way a chart is read should be so obvious to the reader that it becomes almost invisible; the reader can focus on what the chart says and not on its design. It should also be predictable in the sense outlined previously: There must be a consistency between perception and cognition.

I asked you above to spend some time getting familiar with the horizon chart. You may point out that this contradicts the idea that a chart should be obvious, and rightly so. But sometimes we need to introduce more complex charts and improve literacy; otherwise we'll be using Big Data to make pie charts. In other words, if you have a complex dataset (which doesn't necessarily mean big), you don't want to oversimplify it because of a lack of skills. After a chart type becomes obvious, we should be allowed but not required to think about its design.

3   We'll discuss this chart type in more detail in Chapter 13, where you can see the full chart with all the states.

Steve Krug doesn't want you to stop thinking. Instead he's saying that a well-designed interface frees cognitive resources so that tasks are executed more efficiently. This is what we've been discussing since the beginning of the book: Perception frees us of basic tasks of data analysis if we have the right chart and the right design. If Krug's book had a more explicit title, it might be *Don't Make Me Think, So That I Can Think.*

Literacy and Experience

Both human perception and culture influence the way we read visual representations, but we don't define an individual by the physiology of the brain and the rules of the social whole. Context, knowledge, emotions, experiences, and memories contribute to a personal and unpredictable interpretation.

Graphic Literacy

If an audience can't read a particular type of chart, it becomes as useless as speaking in an unfamiliar foreign language. "Know your audience" is a mantra you can apply to all types of communication, and data visualization is no different. Communicating effectively without dumbing down your message is always a challenge. You don't want your audience glued to the dictionary, looking up words it doesn't understand, but some unfamiliar terms may prove necessary to ensure that your message is not corrupted, so they should be introduced and explained.

Tailoring the message to the audience should not be synonymous with accepting its prejudices, routines, and the usual ways of doing things. Many of what we believe to be good data visualization principles are opposite to what is practiced within organizations. When presenting a chart type the audience is unfamiliar with, or when breaking a rule, the author must argue for its advantages. Annotating the chart, showing how to read it, drawing attention to key points, and making direct comparisons with alternative representations will help the audience feel safer in their reading and possible adoption of the new chart.

An Unknown Chart: The Bamboo Chart

The strip plot in **Figure 3.6** compares the risk of poverty and social exclusion in the European Union, highlighting one of the richest countries (Norway) and one of the poorest (Bulgaria).

What if we want to go deeper and compare socio-demographic groups? A bar chart, like the one in **Figure 3.7**, offers a solution. It compares the same countries again and, because of the background references, there is a little improvement over the simple point-to-point comparisons we usually get from a bar chart. The problem with this bar chart is that we are no longer able to see the countries in the context of the EU.

The easiest solution is to use both charts, where the strip plot adds context and the bar chart adds detail. This may not be enough if we want to say something like "a male living alone in the UK has a higher risk than the average risk in Greece."

Is it possible to combine both perspectives? Let's see. In **Figure 3.8**, each vertical line represents a country, so it's similar to the strip plot. The lines for Norway and Bulgaria are selected. I named this a "bamboo chart," where the vertical lines are the canes and the horizontal lines are the leaves. Each leaf shows by how much each group departs from the national average. In both countries, men have a little lower risk of poverty than women, the gap being higher in Bulgaria. In many countries, there is no gap, so we can assume gender is not a significant risk factor.

Now let's check if the level of income affects the risk. **Figure 3.9** shows that there is a huge impact (obviously!), but it's not identical in both countries. In Bulgaria, if you're in the first quintile of income (the lowest income group), the risk is absolute (100%), while in Norway, the risk is "only" over 60%. As you can see, in Bulgaria income influences risk much more than in Norway. It's also interesting to note that only the top income quintile in Bulgaria enjoys a risk similar to the national level in Norway.

There are many more groups and countries, so this analysis could go on and on. Your natural reaction (for the second time this chapter) may be of some strangeness, skepticism, or even resistance, either to this or to any other new chart. This is one of the reasons why many media do not publish more charts that are complex. A lack of knowledge and familiarity combined with a short attention span make the chart difficult to comprehend and increases the likelihood that readers will ignore it.

When you encounter a new chart type that goes beyond mere decoration, spend some time studying it, and try to imagine what the data would look like in a chart type you're familiar with. Then decide whether the new chart adds enough value to your data visualization resource kit.

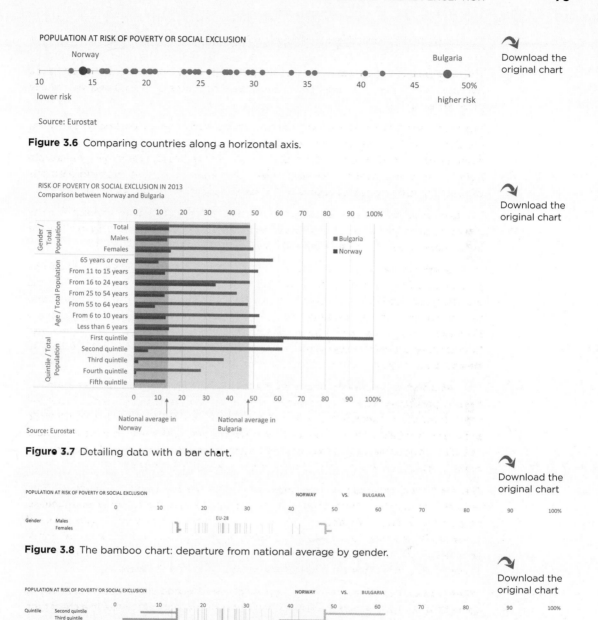

POPULATION AT RISK OF POVERTY OR SOCIAL EXCLUSION

Norway   Bulgaria

10   15   20   25   30   35   40   45   50%

lower risk   higher risk

Source: Eurostat

Figure 3.6 Comparing countries along a horizontal axis.

RISK OF POVERTY OR SOCIAL EXCLUSION IN 2013
Comparison between Norway and Bulgaria

0   10   20   30   40   50   60   70   80   90   100%

Gender / Total Population
  Total
  Males
  Females

  ■ Bulgaria
  ■ Norway

Age / Total Population
  65 years or over
  From 11 to 15 years
  From 16 to 24 years
  From 25 to 54 years
  From 55 to 64 years
  From 6 to 10 years
  Less than 6 years

Quintile / Total Population
  First quintile
  Second quintile
  Third quintile
  Fourth quintile
  Fifth quintile

0   10   20   30   40   50   60   70   80   90   100%

National average in   National average in
Norway   Bulgaria

Source: Eurostat

Figure 3.7 Detailing data with a bar chart.

POPULATION AT RISK OF POVERTY OR SOCIAL EXCLUSION   NORWAY   VS.   BULGARIA

0   10   20   30   40   50   60   70   80   90   100%

Gender   Males   EU-28
          Females

Figure 3.8 The bamboo chart: departure from national average by gender.

POPULATION AT RISK OF POVERTY OR SOCIAL EXCLUSION   NORWAY   VS.   BULGARIA

0   10   20   30   40   50   60   70   80   90   100%

Quintile   Second quintile
            Third quintile
            Fourth quintile
            Fifth quintile

Figure 3.9 The bamboo chart: departure from national average by income level.
(Find the complete chart on the companion website.)

But even the best-case scenario is likely to meet resistance. The more the previous chart type was integrated into the organization's workflow, the more disruptive the new proposed chart becomes. Think of the population pyramid, for example. It's a symbol of population studies, and everyone in the field knows how it should be read and what each population profile means. It is also a bad chart, so any changes should be made in small steps. Displaying males and females on the same side of the axis or using lines instead of bars would improve it without much disruption.

Familiarity with the Subject

The visual representation of invariant data points—or the opposite, data points that vary randomly—is irrelevant. **To be useful, a visualization must display variability that makes sense to the audience.** Even if an observer detects a pattern, it only makes sense if there is a contextual knowledge that allows for its interpretation.

Unlike the bamboo chart, the chart in **Figure 3.10** is well known. Everyone recognizes an electrocardiogram and is able to detect those very clear patterns. The problem is that these patterns are meaningless if you don't have a medical background to determine whether these are the typical patterns of a healthy heart. In an extreme case, not only is the interpretation of the patterns impossible, but the patterns themselves are invisible to those who lack the knowledge to detect them (such as with a nonprofessional trying to interpret a chest X-ray).

This example shows an important limitation of data visualization that we often forget: A new chart type might allow us to process more information, but we must be provided with context or prior knowledge in order to make it meaningful. An effective chart is a piece of a jigsaw puzzle whose place is known or guessed: We know that the piece will help us understand a problem and we know its general location (the section of the problem it covers), and the moment we interlock it with the other pieces, its full meaning is finally revealed.

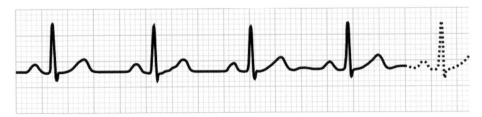

Figure 3.10 It's easy to see patterns in an electrocardiogram, but you need professional knowledge to interpret them.

Information Asymmetry

This relates to the very useful concept of "information asymmetry." This means that there is a knowledge gap between, for example, the producer and the consumer. Suppose the producer exploits this gap to claim health benefits of consuming its products based on some pseudo-scientific evidence. Most consumers can detect this *sound of science*, but because they lack the contextual knowledge, they can't actually fully understand the meaning of the message and tend to accept it because it's "scientific evidence."

There will always be strong information asymmetry between people or social groups simply because we can't all be specialists in everything. We need someone to bridge the gap *on demand*—for example, *today* I'm interested in earthquakes and want someone to explain to me how the "Modified Mercalli Intensity Scale" works in a way that, like a piece of the jigsaw puzzle, interlocks with my previous knowledge. I don't have to remind you of how brilliant Carl Sagan was at explaining the cosmos for us. Journalists also bridge this gap, translating complex issues into something the layperson can understand.

Visuals can be very helpful in this translation. Keeping with the jigsaw puzzle image, they replace the missing piece with a simpler one, with flexible anchor points that make it easier to interlock with the existing pieces. A specialist reading an unemployment rate of 13.8 percent realizes the implications, while the nonprofessional lacks this sensibility. However, if a chart shows how the rate evolved over time, a comparison to other countries, and what is normal and what goes beyond normal, the chart does not make the nonprofessional an expert, but it creates the basic anchor points that he uses to understand the information.

Inside an organization, information asymmetry is much lower and, in each area, people are basically on the same page. Visuals are useful for data exploration, communicating findings, and, hopefully, supporting decisions and not so much to fill deep knowledge gaps.

Organizational Contexts

While culture and social rules provide a generic behavior framework, the professional organizations we belong to tend to be more normative and explicit on the output they expect from us, and peer pressure is more palpable. Being a popular activity in organizations, data visualization reflects its internal culture and the many factors shaping it.

Wrong Messages from the Top

We often take for granted that charts, due to their ability to show relationships between data points, are superior to tables when the task requires such an approach. The choice seems obvious, so if someone from top management prefers a good data table, that will cause some uproar among data visualization enthusiasts. But instead of a sermon on the virtues of data visualization, let's think a bit about the possible reasons for using a table when it doesn't seem the right choice.

In senior positions, many of the hard data patterns are already internalized, so there can be multiple ways of dealing with new data. A popular stereotype, only partially confirmed by my own experience, says that senior managers prefer to use tables and they devalue charts as tools of knowledge acquisition and decision support, feeding the perspective of charts as merely illustrative and decorative items.

They may prefer tables because they are accustomed to them, or because it's easier to go along with a vendor's sales pitch and bad application defaults. In the end, they will always rely on hard figures to make decisions.

I'd like to suggest that people using tables for decision support are less aware of the patterns in the data (which are already internalized) and are more interested in a fluctuation band against which they compare the new data. This means that as long as my market share doesn't vary more than 1 percent, there are better ways to spend my time than staring at a bunch of charts. This is an interesting technique for data reduction and it's the result of a mature and consolidated knowledge. It's also very efficient in decision-making, as it helps in looking beyond short-term fluctuations. However, in a constantly and rapidly changing environment, this approach is less sensitive to unexpected but significant changes. Returning to the unemployment rate in Greece, for more than 10 years we could safely say that the rate would fluctuate around 10 percent. Then suddenly, it skyrocketed to almost 30 percent (**Figure 3.11**). *We're not in Kansas anymore.*

Unfortunately, when top managers don't use visuals for relevant tasks, this often translates into bad formal organizational guidelines. If, for example, you must use slide templates that allocate much of the slide real estate to branding, leaving only a tiny rectangle for actual content, you know that the guidelines and process standardization rules have really gone overboard.

Many of my clients are local branches of multinational corporations. This means that their reporting must comply with headquarter guidelines. Much of the time, the local client and I feel handcuffed by guidelines that impose a set of bad practices worldwide, but occasionally a local report is recognized as "best practice" and starts moving toward corporate adoption.

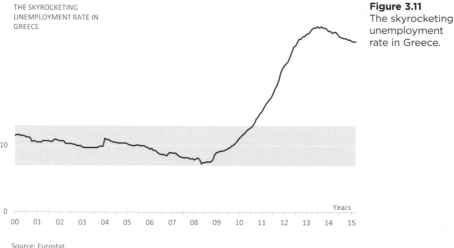

THE SKYROCKETING
UNEMPLOYMENT RATE IN
GREECE

Figure 3.11
The skyrocketing
unemployment
rate in Greece.

Download the
original chart

Source: Eurostat

Charts confirming what these managers already know (or sense) reinforce their predisposition, so the right strategy must be finding "pain points" through visualizations that show relevant but unexpected patterns and complex relationships that are not acquired by reading a table.

Impression Management

An organization is a complex ecosystem made of standard practices and culture, peer pressure, tension between technical and social skills, and strong competition for scarce resources in a collaborative context necessary for the pursuit of the organization's mission and goals.

In a context of low graphic literacy, poorly designed software defaults, and a focus on impression management,[4] data visualization has a great capacity to provide the "wow factor." If managers favor eye-candy, this will yield catastrophic results, where a string of pseudo-3D charts and special effects in PowerPoint can significantly reduce the return on investment on the data.

Of course, the impact of PowerPoint's canned special effects will fade away with their constant use, resulting in the search for more unique and spectacular stimuli, which will further degrade the message: The pie becomes a 3D pie, the 3D pie becomes an exploded 3D pie, and the exploded 3D pie becomes an exploded 3D pie with flying slices.

---

4 Impression management is the conscious effort by individuals to adapt their public image to their goals and to control other people's perceptions about them.

Market research companies (who could otherwise contribute toward visualizations of their own data that are more effective and thus generate a higher return for their clients) tend to replicate this situation—the logic being "that's what the client wants."

This vicious cycle of overstimulation that feeds upon itself (and reinforces the idea that charts are entertaining but ultimately useless in the decision-making process) is difficult to break with a perspective that emphasizes the content and manages the inflow of visual stimuli according to the needs of the message. Overstimulation is like a drug, and withdrawal is not easy.

Takeaways

- Rules exist for a reason—to make things easier. But unlike dogmas, rules are meant to be broken and improved.

- Don't be afraid of testing a new way of displaying your data if you believe it adds value over traditional chart types, but think of it as a new word. You must define it, show examples of how to use it, and advocate its advantages over previous concepts.

- Make an effort to assess which social conventions to respect and which conventions to challenge with alternative visualizations that deliver meaningful results.

- Design your charts for effectiveness, not memorability. Use business visualization to get answers *now*, not for being remembered next year.

- Recognize the diversity of skills, knowledge, and experience of the audience, and ensure that the graphical representation provides the right context so that each individual can correctly interpret the message from the knowledge they already have.

- At the organizational level, some inhibiting factors may prevent the development of better data visualization practices. Managers are the key. They should make an effort to ingrain data visualization principles and best practices into organizational culture. A good starting point is to become aware of how software defaults are important and how you can change them to meet your priorities.

4

DATA PREPARATION

Jacques Bertin defines his semiology of graphics as a "visual transcription of a data table." In a perfect world, this table materializes in front of us when we need it, ready to use. In everyday reality, however, things involve more sweat and less magic. People coined the expression "data janitor" for a reason.

In a data visualization project, data extraction costs and data preparation are often overlooked, either by management that doesn't understand the level of detail required or by data analysts making overly optimistic assumptions. This translates into many hours of data cleansing that most people don't see. If not taken into account, these labor-intensive tasks can consume several times the resources available for a project, whether it's a simple chart for an upcoming meeting or an organization-wide project.

Brilliant visualizations cannot redeem bad data, either in content or in structure. Many spreadsheet users are not familiar with well-structured data, and that's one more reason to discuss data preparation.

We can summarize all preparation work on the data table, regarding both structure and content, by the acronym ETL, for *Extract, Transform, and Load*. ETL is just as applicable to your Excel files as it is to large, formal systems.

This chapter is not strictly about data visualization. If the tables you need actually materialize in front of you, ready to use, if you know how to structure the tables to take advantage of pivot tables, and if you organize sheets in your workbook by content type, it's probably safe to skip this chapter. In a more sophisticated organization, most of the issues discussed here are not relevant, and most of the data comes from internal systems. However, many people still struggle with these basic issues, so if you're in this category, read on.

Problems with the Data

Let's split data problems into two broad categories: 1) **structure without content**, and 2) **content without structure**. The first category affects our data in particular; the second is common in data we get from other sources.

Structure without Content

Even if you've never seen a table for which multiple users can enter data (such as a table for telemarketing operators), you can imagine how much garbage data is collected: incomplete ZIP codes, multiple abbreviations for the same entity, misspellings, logical inconsistencies...you name it.

It's challenging to define good data validation rules without forcing exclusions: What happens when a few ZIP codes are missing from a lookup table? Suppose, though, that you can maintain a table with a minimum number of errors. **Figure 4.1** represents an example of such a table. To make things more interesting, try linking this table to a second table containing other personal data (**Figure 4.2**). First, you'll have to split the field Name into Name and Surname, to be able to join both tables. Now, is John Doe in the first table the same person referred to as John F. Doe in the second table? The solution in these cases is to have common fields in both tables that are not subject to different interpretations (social security or driver's license numbers are good candidates). If there are no safe common fields, you'll need to allocate additional resources to determine whether it's the same person. Multiply this process by thousands of records and you have a problem on your hands that, if not anticipated, would generate serious time and resource management issues.

ID	Name	Surname	Address	City	Zip Code	State
1000	John	Doe	S Main St	Torrington	CT 06790	Connecticut
1001	Mary	Poppins	SW 11th St	Lowton	OK 73501	Oklahoma

Figure 4.1 A table with names and addresses.

ID	Name	Gender	Age	Height	Weight	Marital Status	Children	Occupation
1001	Mary T. Poppins	Female	34	5.38	182	Married	4	Librarian
1000	John F. Doe	Male	82	6.17	138	Widower	2	Retired

Figure 4.2 A table with socio-demographic characteristics. To get a better feel for structure without content, imagine that there are many more rows (records) and many entry errors in them.

A few other special cases also belong to the category of structure without content. One of the most common is a break in a time series, whereby you still get the same measure (an unemployment rate, for example), but changes in methodologies, concepts, technologies, or regional administrative boundaries make comparisons meaningless. Or, at least, comparisons must be carried out with extra care—the same care you should use when comparing countries that use different ways of measuring the same reality. For example, infant mortality rate depends on how a country defines "live birth." Because the definition is not the same across countries, this may affect country rankings in international comparisons.[1]

Content without Structure

Suppose you're a data provider, perhaps at the U.S. Census Bureau or at a small public relations company. The moment you release the data, you cease controlling it. You don't know how people will read and *reuse* the data. They may want to cross-check it if they suspect that the data is not telling the whole story. Or they will misunderstand the concepts. Whatever they do, first they must have access to the data in a format they can use.

Providers often make it hard to use the data beyond the format in which they released it; they're often unaware of this issue or focus on the end user and forget the data professional, who probably needs a more specific format.

---

1 MacDorman, Marian F. and Matthews, T.J. "Behind International Rankings of Infant Mortality: How the United States Compares with Europe." *NCHS Data Brief*, No. 23, November 2009.

Go to the web page

Data providers should then ask themselves two simple questions: How many data reuse issues are we causing by releasing the data in this format? Is this reuse friction level acceptable for our data dissemination goals?[2] Typical answers are, respectively, "a lot" and "no." The end result is that data reuse friction levels can range from none (rare), to mildly annoying, to a source of a barrage of unprintable curses.

Go to the web page

Let me give you an unfair example. Suppose you want to know the military budget as a percentage of GDP in each country. There are several sources, but you could start with the CIA's website publication *The World Factbook*. Country profiles in the *Factbook* contain several sections and subsections.

Figure 4.3 displays the Military section for the United Kingdom. You can manually open this section and copy the data you need for each country, or you could use a scraping tool that automates the process. If you're unable to automate the process, you'll have a few long and boring days ahead of you. Because the data are not displayed the way you need it, time and resource costs will increase since you'll have to structure it first.

Figure 4.3
UK Military data in the *The World Factbook* from the CIA.

Transportation :: UNITED KINGDOM	+

Military :: UNITED KINGDOM	–

Military branches:

Army, Royal Navy (includes Royal Marines), Royal Air Force (2013)

Military service age and obligation:

16-33 years of age (officers 17-28) for voluntary military service (with parental consent under 18); no conscription; women serve in military services, but are excluded from ground combat positions and some naval postings; must be citizen of the UK, Commonwealth, or Republic of Ireland; reservists serve a minimum of 3 years, to age 45 or 55; 17 years 6 months of age for voluntary military service by Nepalese citizens in the Brigade of Gurkhas; 16-34 years of age for voluntary military service by Papua New Guinean citizens (2012)

Manpower available for military service:

males age 16-49: 14,856,917

females age 16-49: 14,307,316 (2010 est.)

Manpower fit for military service:

males age 16-49: 12,255,452

females age 16-49: 11,779,679 (2010 est.)

Manpower reaching militarily significant age annually:

male: 383,989

female: 365,491 (2010 est.)

Military expenditures:

2.49% of GDP (2012)

2.48% of GDP (2011)

2.49% of GDP (2010)

country comparison to the world: 28

Transnational Issues :: UNITED KINGDOM	+

---

2   I'm not implying they do it on purpose; they may not be able to reduce friction due to technological reasons.

I said this is an unfair example because the *Factbook* actually allows us to jump between the country profile level and the list level. At the bottom of the page on the website, you'll see "country comparison to the world: 28." If you click the number 28, you'll get a list of all countries sorted by military expenditures as a percentage of GDP. Then you can choose a country from that list and return to the profile view. This nice feature is still quite rare, unfortunately.

These two broad categories of structure without content and content without structure try to make sense of the variety of issues when using data presented in an unfriendly format. Hadley Wickham brilliantly captured the difference between well-structured and poorly structured data in an excellent article[3] in which he quotes the first paragraph of Leo Tolstoy's *Anna Karenina*: "Happy families are all alike; every unhappy family is unhappy in its own way." The "happy family" dataset is structured according to some rules that make it similar to other "happy families," while **there is a virtually infinite number of ways to create an unhappy dataset**.

What Does "Well-Structured Data" Mean, Anyway?

The acronym GIGO (*garbage in, garbage out*) summarizes the issues we deal with every day: Results and insights depend on data quality. We can handle data critically (being aware of the "garbage" and factoring it in to the evaluation of results) or uncritically ("if the data has been subject to extensive processing by the computer, it can't be wrong").

Data integrity becomes essential when the volume of data increases and we need to update, filter, and aggregate it, and use data as a basis for derivative calculations. A clean, consistent, and well-structured table means lower update and maintenance costs and more flexibility to multiply the perspectives from which we can analyze the data.

This may not be good news for the user accustomed to the loose spreadsheet environment, where storage, presentation, intermediate calculations, and parameters often share the same sheet. Let's start untangling this mess with a concrete example.

---

3 Wickham, Hadley. "Tidy Data." *Journal of Statistical Software*, Vol. 59, No. 10, August 2014.

The first step toward improving data structures is understanding that storing data and presenting data are two very different things. You should never use storage and presentation features together in a single worksheet. Share your source table if requested, of course, but otherwise bury it deep down in a data-only sheet. If you have a well-structured table, you'll never have to touch it again, except when using a client like a pivot table or when adding a variable. **In Excel, tables are for storing data, and pivot tables are for analyzing and presenting data.**

A Helping Hand: Pivot Tables

Ah, pivot tables! Pivot tables are great at many levels. They can even serve as a litmus test for checking how well a table is structured. If every single cross-tabulation is done easily and you don't have to change the pivot table following an update, you can be reasonably sure that you have a well-structured table.

Figure 4.4 shows a sample of one of the output formats for the Consumer Expenditure Survey. Assuming we know the meaning of the Series ID, this is the typical manner of *presenting* the data, with time periods in columns and entities in rows.

Consumer Expenditure Survey
Years: 1984 to 2013

Series ID	1984	1985	1986	1987	1988	1989	1990	1991	1992	1993
CXU080110LB0101M	35	30	30	28	28	33	30	31	28	30
CXU080110LB0102M	26	24	24	23	23	24	23	26	23	24
CXU080110LB0103M	36	29	28	29	28	32	30	34	27	33
CXU080110LB0104M	37	32	34	28	28	32	29	29	29	31
CXU080110LB0105M	38	33	34	30	30	36	35	35	29	32
CXU080110LB0106M	43	35	32	33	30	37	33	34	35	33
CXU080110LB01A1M	36	31	30	28	28	32	30	32	28	31
CXU080110LB01A2M	34	29	27	28	27	35	29	28	26	29
CXU190904LB0101M	30	29	31	31	30	33	35	42	43	46

Figure 4.4 Sample output from the Consumer Expenditure Survey (Bureau of Labor Statistics).

Go to the
web page

Think of the table as a cross tabulation (Series ID × Year) that must be uncrossed so that we can use it. Unlike other output formats from the Bureau of Labor Statistics, you can get all the data you need in a single table, and it's very easy to reverse it to the right format, resulting in the table you see in **Figure 4.5**.

Series ID	Year	Value
CXU080110LB0101M	1984	35
CXU080110LB0101M	1985	30
CXU080110LB0101M	1986	30
CXU080110LB0101M	1987	28
CXU080110LB0101M	1988	28
CXU080110LB0101M	1989	33
CXU080110LB0101M	1990	30
CXU080110LB0101M	1991	31
CXU080110LB0101M	1992	28
CXU080110LB0101M	1993	30

Figure 4.5 Un-pivoting the data table.

Series ID contains multiple variables, so we must parse it and look for the descriptive text for each code. **Figure 4.6** shows how the final table will look.

Category	Item	Quintile	Year	Value
Food Total	Eggs	Lowest 20	2012	39
Food Total	Eggs	Lowest 20	2013	40
Food Total	Eggs	Second 20	2012	47
Food Total	Eggs	Second 20	2013	52
Food Total	Eggs	Third 20	2012	49
Food Total	Eggs	Third 20	2013	56
Food Total	Eggs	Fourth 20	2012	59
Food Total	Eggs	Fourth 20	2013	59
Food Total	Eggs	Highest 20	2012	71
Food Total	Eggs	Highest 20	2013	76

Figure 4.6 A few rows of the final data table.

Creating dynamic charts in Excel requires knowledge of advanced formulas, but often we only need them because the data table is not properly structured. **Figure 4.7** shows a simple dynamic chart (not a pivot chart) that you can create without a single formula. It displays the proportion of food expenditure away from home, over the years, for the selected income quintile. Select a different quintile and the chart will update.

From Figure 4.6 we can see that **a well-structured table is essentially a list of observations and their characteristics** (category and item, income quintile, and time) **and the associated measure** (expenditure). In a pivot table, measures are usually placed in the Values area, while characteristics go into the Rows, Columns, or Filters areas.

Category	Food Total
Quintile	Highest 20

Percentage	Items		
		Food at	Food away from
Year	Food	home	home
1984	100%	53%	47%
1985	100%	52%	48%
1986	100%	51%	49%
1987	100%	50%	50%
1988	100%	51%	49%
1989	100%	49%	51%
1990	100%	49%	51%
1991	100%	55%	45%
1992	100%	55%	45%

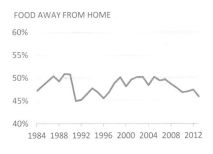

Figure 4.7 A dynamic chart using a pivot table.

In a well-structured table that can be easily used as a pivot table source, the content of each column must be understood as a group (years, quintiles), and the values in each measure should be comparable (expenditure in dollars in a column and expenditure units in a second column).

Reality can get more complicated, and so will the structure. Suppose you get expenditure by gender. Ideally, you'd add a new column ("Gender") with two values (Male, Female). But if they are averages instead of totals, you can't aggregate them, and, in this case, you have to add them as measures.

Extracting the Data

You successfully complete the first stage in the ETL process when you access a file that you can edit and manipulate. When you get a text file, you may need to open it in a text editor (such as the free Notepad++ for Windows) to solve multiple small issues with Search and Replace. Do your computer's regional settings and the text share the same symbols for decimal places and thousands separators? (Some may use periods while others use commas.) Are there any strange characters? Can they be removed?

Extraction can be a very long and rocky journey, so let's start with a smooth example first, again from the Bureau of Labor Statistics. I'm looking for the monthly unemployment rate, at the state level, for a period of several years. **Figure 4.8** shows a sample of the output. There are several output options, including an Excel file, but for now we'll work with a tab-delimited text file. I'm getting the data for each state, which means that I'll have to consolidate them into a single table, removing all unwanted text.

THE WAY YOU PASTE DATA CHANGES THE OUTPUT

Scenario 1: Direct paste from web page to Excel

Scenario 2: From web page to Notepad+ and from Notepad+ to Excel

Series Id:	LASST010000000000003

Seasonally Adjusted
Area: Alabama
Area Type: Statewide
Measure: unemployment rate
State/Region/Division: Alabama

Series Id:	LASST010000000000003

Seasonally Adjusted
Area: Alabama
Area Type: Statewide
Measure: unemployment rate
State/Region/Division: Alabama

Series ID	Year	Period	Value
LASST010000000000003	2010	M01	11.7
LASST010000000000003	2010	M02	11.6
LASST010000000000003	2010	M03	11.3
LASST010000000000003	2010	M04	10.8
LASST010000000000003	2010	M05	10.4
LASST010000000000003	2010	M06	10.1
LASST010000000000003	2010	M07	10.0
LASST010000000000003	2010	M08	9.9
LASST010000000000003	2010	M09	10.0
LASST010000000000003	2010	M10	10.1
LASST010000000000003	2010	M11	10.2
LASST010000000000003	2010	M12	10.3

Series ID	Year Period	Value
LASST010000000000003	2010 M01	11.7
LASST010000000000003	2010 M02	11.6
LASST010000000000003	2010 M03	11.3
LASST010000000000003	2010 M04	10.8
LASST010000000000003	2010 M05	10.4
LASST010000000000003	2010 M06	10.1
LASST010000000000003	2010 M07	10
LASST010000000000003	2010 M08	9.9
LASST010000000000003	2010 M09	10
LASST010000000000003	2010 M10	10.1
LASST010000000000003	2010 M11	10.2
LASST010000000000003	2010 M12	10.3

Figure 4.8 Pasting data into Excel, from a web page and from a text editor.

Figure 4.8 explains why you should have a text editor between a web page and the spreadsheet. Scenario 1, on the left, shows the result of a direct paste from the web page, while scenario 2 shows what happens when you paste to Notepad++ first: Excel recognizes the tab character and automatically parses the text.

As with the example on expenditure, we'll have to find what the Series ID codes mean. You may want to split the Series ID codes into multiple columns using the Text to Column function in Excel. Also, create a real date from the Year and Period columns.

When extracting data from other public sources, you may run into some limits imposed by the organization. The United Nations Population Division doesn't allow you to select more than five variables or countries in each query (**Figure 4.9**). Other organizations impose limitations at the cell level. The Eurostat limits each query to 750,000 cells. Depending on how high the limit is or how detailed are the data you need, you may have to run multiple queries to get all the data and then merge the results into a single file.

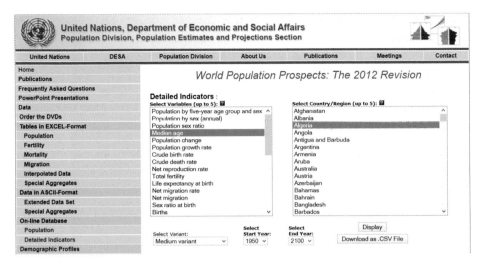

Figure 4.9 Extracting data from the UN Population Division.

The PDF Plague

With more or less pain, the chance of getting a text file from official statistical offices is high. Other data providers, such as professional associations, may have other, more restrictive policies regarding data dissemination.

Many years ago, I needed to get data on the various types of electricity consumption (high voltage, low voltage, domestic, industrial, public roads, and so on) at a very detailed regional level. The data were available only in large sheets of paper, where someone had elegantly *handwritten* all these thousands of values. It was an admirable job, almost worthy of a Charles Dickens novel. It also had an unanticipated cost, because my organization had to purchase a copy of all those sheets and hire someone to enter the data manually.

Today, no sane organization would share its data in this format. With all the technology we have in our hands, that would be ridiculous, right? Well, not so fast. Let's abstract for a moment from the technology and focus on the goal: getting a few thousand values into an editable table. Now tell me: What difference does it make if we have handwritten numbers on a sheet of paper or a PDF file with such a twisted formatting that the cost of extracting the data is higher than entering them by hand? Actually, there is a difference: I found those handwritten sheets only once, while I keep stumbling upon data tables in PDF files, to my despair and exasperation.

If you're a data provider, you have a degree of control over your data when you share them in a PDF. You might persuade some people not to use the data in a way different than you intend. This is not wrong if you have a strong reason to do it, but it will anger your users, even if that's not your plan. Again, make sure that the way you share your data is aligned with your goals. In addition to presenting your data the way you want people to see it by default, provide a link to the raw data. That way everyone is happy.

If you're a user of internal data, you might assume that you'll never have to extract data from PDF files. But, sooner or later, you will. And there will not be a quick fix. You may be able to open simple and well-behaved PDFs in Word 2013 or 2016, so there's no harm if you try that first. If that doesn't work, try copying the data from the PDF and pasting it into the text editor (such as Notepad++), and then from the text editor into Excel. Then you can try an additional application, such as the free tool Tabula, to extract the data into CSV or XLS files. None of the solutions will be entirely satisfactory, but the cost of editing the table should be lower than manual data entry.

Go to the web page

"Can It Export to Excel?"

Internal business intelligence (BI) systems should allow you full control over the content you want to extract and how you want to extract it. Unfortunately, that's not always the case. Let me paint a grim and somewhat exaggerated picture here.

First, you have to solve a *communications* problem. You, the business user, and the IT people apparently don't speak the same language: They don't understand why a market share above 100 percent is not possible, and you don't understand that they must have a rule for each of your beloved exceptions. So when you get the data from IT, crosscheck it to make sure you've got the right data.

Second, there is a *political* problem. The data you want and the way you want it may not fit into the current formal corporate policies regarding access privileges, data security, or data dissemination. You can also be caught in a power struggle between IT and other areas, and they may start dragging their feet to avoid granting you access to the data.

Finally, there may be *technical* issues. The eternal question "Can it export to Excel?" forced BI vendors to make this option available. After so many years, I think they still hate it, judging from the output files I have to deal with. If the application can export data to CSV or Excel, there's hardly a reason to create unfriendly table structures that force the user to take additional steps to clean the data. This means extra work for you, but if in every update the format is wrong but consistent, you might use a macro to correct it and solve the problem.

Cleansing Data

I'll assume that you survived the previous stage of the ETL process and you're now the proud owner of a nice-looking table. But the smile will vanish from your face if you now find a record of a *123-year-old* new mom living in a city called *Cincinatti, TX.*

The second stage of ETL, transformation, deals with data manipulation, but the first transformation, data cleansing, is so important and specific that it deserves to be promoted to its own step. Data cleansing suggests, of course, that the data is dirty. Data is dirty because it contains typos or inconsistencies or fails in some way to meet a standard.

All this "dirt" must be cleansed before any serious analysis can take place, and again a pivot table can be very handy for this purpose. If you count every category in a field, you'd soon find only one reference to Cincinatti, TX, while there are many references to Cincinnati, OH. So, you'll probably need to change that record because the city name is misspelled and associated with the wrong state. And what about the 123-year old new mom? Check the age range. She's probably only 23. Please note the word "probably"; **just because a value seems strange, that doesn't mean it's not real.** Be sure to cross-check against a lookup table and against other fields for logical inconsistencies, and don't forget to have a log that includes all your edits.

Transforming Data

One of the benefits of making data cleansing an autonomous step is that now transformation can focus on adapting the dataset to the goals of the analysis. If you're using a spreadsheet, you're now moving from the cell level to the column level where you add, remove, or change variables. Here are a few examples of possible data transformations:

◼ **Encoding:** If a column includes answers to an open question (where there are no predefined answers), you must add one or more columns to categorize those answers. For example, if you asked people to name three of their preferred movie actors, you'd have to parse the answer and code every one of the names.

◼ **Aggregation:** The level of detail may be excessive for the purposes of analysis, and we'll need to aggregate the data at a higher level. Our 23-year-old new mom can belong to a larger category (for example, ages 20–24), or data at the daily level can hide a pattern that can only be spotted at the week level.

Read the
blog post

◼ **Derived data:** If we're studying obesity and have weight and height data, we can calculate Body Mass Index (BMI) and add it as a new variable.

◼ **Removal:** Changes in project scope may make some of the observations irrelevant, or some variables may only be needed to calculate derived data (like BMI above). Keep in the dataset only the data you need.

◼ **Standardization:** If we need to link our new table to other tables in our system, some standardization may be needed, including changes in table structure and in labeling (for example, M/F instead of Male/Female).

Loading the Data Table

The last stage of the ETL process occurs when the data becomes usable. This can take many forms, such as uploading the file to a system such as a new table, appending the file to an existing table such as an update, or, in Excel, simply changing the data format from a range to a table. In recent Excel versions, you can also add the file to the data model.

Data Management in Excel

It's hard to find a tool that, like Excel, combines power, flexibility, and ease of use for some basic tasks when compared to other similar tools. The problem is that Excel training often focuses too much on the tool and leaves out task-specific aspects.

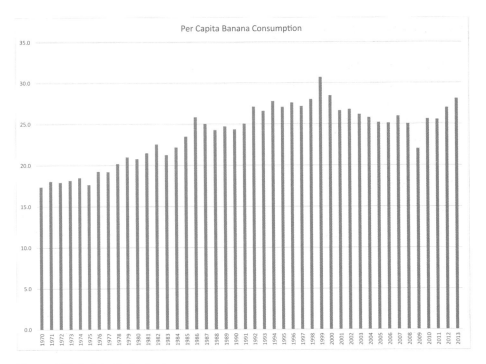

Figure 4.10 A default chart when pressing F11.

For example, take chart making. Knowing how to "make charts in Excel" and knowing how to "make charts" are two different creatures. Give a monkey a banana every time it presses F11, and you get a (very low-paid) Excel chart maker (**Figure 4.10**).

The same happens with the data. Unlike database applications, Excel does not impose any kind of structure, and because users lack the right training, they believe that this is the natural way to manage their data. Sure, people in IT make data structure a top priority, but they don't really understand business needs, do they?

Many organizations can gain much if there's a greater mutual understanding of IT and user roles. Users must obtain a minimum level of literacy with data structures. They must see how structuring the loose spreadsheet environment maximizes the power of functions and formulas that take advantage of that environment (pivot tables and lookup formulas, for example). This simplifies chart making, adds interaction, and reduces updating and maintenance costs. IT personnel and data users may sometimes have a conflicting relationship, but a greater proximity and understanding may help them all realize that users are not always a danger to system security, and IT is not always unaware of business needs.

Organizing the Workbook

The number of worksheets in an Excel file is virtually unlimited, and, surprisingly, we can use all we want without incurring extra costs. Hence, an Excel file that has some level of complexity must be organized in a way that clearly separates the results (charts, tables), intermediate calculations, parameters, and data tables in different, specialized sheets.

Links Outside of Excel

An IT-managed BI system in an Excel-centric organization risks becoming a dual BI system in which users get the data from the formal system, but all the actual analysis is done in Excel. This can quickly get out of control, with isolated file archipelagos in each computer, and impossible-to-reconcile data.

You can't eradicate Excel as a BI tool unless you uninstall it. The organization should have a better understanding of why users keep using Excel. If the formal BI model can't address those needs, it should provide direct access to data in a safe and controlled manner, which again requires a closer relationship between users and IT.

The ideal scenario is to create one or more tables that closely match the user's needs, connected to her workbook and from where she can refresh data.

Formulas

When one of the papers that shaped recent economic policy worldwide[4] draws conclusions based on faulty Excel formulas, and when news of millions of dollars being lost due to spreadsheet errors is common, the least we can do is to assume that a formula is a potential threat. With all other things equal, using fewer formulas makes a spreadsheet simpler to maintain, improves performance, and produces fewer errors.

Calculations with a database query are faster and errors are often easier to spot (you get to the needle-in-a-haystack frustration level much faster in Excel than when using database queries). You can connect your workbook to a query in an external database that performs all the calculations before feeding the data into the spreadsheet. And there are many other ways to avoid formulas, such as

---

4   Reinhart, Carmen M. and Kenneth S. Rogoff. "Growth in a Time of Debt." *American Economic Review: Papers and Proceedings*, Vol. 100, No. 2: 573-578, 2010.

Go to the
web page

using pivot tables instead of aggregate formulas or using a data model instead of lookups. Array formulas and calculations in tables are also safer and faster. Finally, named ranges are your friends; use them extensively.

So, as a mantra, you should think, "Avoid Excel formulas." This seems to contradict the very nature of the application, but when you avoid formulas, your workbook becomes safer and more solid. Note that the point is not to turn your workbook into a formula-free zone (that's almost impossible) but to think about better alternatives. Also, you should infer from the techniques suggested above that "avoid formulas" doesn't equal "hardcode data" (entering a value instead of a formula).

Cycles of Production and Analysis

There is a major difference between business visualization and media infographics.[5] Unlike most infographics, which aren't updated after they're published, business visualizations usually include a set of representations that remain useful from cycle to cycle and cut across the organization. Charts on market share and growth are updated for each cycle. They are seen at various levels of regional detail and are common to the multiple markets in which the organization operates.

Think of business charts as the three Rs of ecology:

- They should be *reused* across multiple markets.

- They should be *recycled* by updating the data.

- Their number should be *reduced*, making business visualization more cost-effective at multiple levels.

This does not cover all the data visualization needs in an organization, and you may use many charts only once, but try to evaluate whether a chart has the potential to be used more than once. If the answer is "yes," you should evaluate whether it makes sense to spend extra resources to prepare it for repurposing (by adding interaction or creating a database query, for example).

This is just a small part of the many things that relates to data management in Excel. If it were possible to synthesize this management in a single word, that word would be "structure." Recent Excel versions have introduced new features that suggest more investment in the data structure (including tables, data models, Power Pivot, slicers, PowerBI, and so on). This, in turn, allows you to manage a growing volume of data more effectively.

Go to the
web page

5   Check the work of one of my preferred designers, Adolfo Arranz, at Visualoop to make the concept of differences at several levels crystal clear.

Takeaways

- Data preparation is possibly the least thankful part of any data visualization process because it is slow, invisible, and undervalued. If you don't have access to a properly formatted table, assume that you'll spend much more time than anticipated preparing it.

- Pivot tables can help you structure your data tables.

- Although you can paste a few numbers to make a quick chart, the data source for more permanent charts should reside outside of Excel, and preferably be connected to a database query.

- Bring data into Excel as close as possible to its final format to avoid manipulating data inside Excel.

- Assume that formulas are a thread to data integrity, and avoid them whenever possible.

- Structure your workbook so that each sheet has a single purpose.

5

DATA VISUALIZATION

In Chapter 2, we imagined buying a data visualization book at a bookstore. But where was it shelved? Under Statistics? Graphic Design? Management Methods? Or Journalism, perhaps?

In theory, we could find a data visualization book on any of those shelves, and only the details of the actual book could help us choose the right shelf. However, you might have a preferred view of visualization that says a lot about your perspective. If you think visualization is simply graphic design with data, or even data art, you'll disagree with someone else who believes visualization is nothing more than visual statistics. If you think eye-candy is needed to attract attention, this will be contrary to someone who believes attention comes naturally only when reason guides both data display and design options.

Data visualization cuts across various fields of knowledge and attracts practitioners from varied backgrounds, who pursue different goals, use multiple tools, have different sensibilities and styles, and push their own practices and agenda as the standard way of working with data. Data journalism, graphic design, and business visualization are some of the largest groups, although the latter receives less media exposure.

That's why coming up with a one-size-fits-all definition of data visualization is not an easy (or even desirable) task. A better approach is to start from a minimalist concept and then add whatever characteristics make it group-specific. The core concept should include visualization as a tool, visualization as a transcript of abstract data into visual representations, and the roles of perception and context.

Data visualization is exploration and discovery, and it's also communication. Many of the differences among its practitioners reside exactly in the way their visual representations impact their communication.

From Patterns to Points

Figure 5.1 shows the three ways we read data points in a chart and how they become a type of data visualization. When there is nothing in our chart but dots (as in a scatter plot), our natural tendency is to group them. We already know that this is an effect of the Gestalt laws, and we know that grouping happens even with a random variation. We also know that, when we devalue individual data points in favor of a pattern (or, using a more generic term, a *shape*), the pattern becomes the basic unit of information.

Shapes   Points   Outliers

Figure 5.1 Three ways to read data points.

The ability to see meaningful shapes in the data represents the highest level of data visualization, because it represents the highest level of data integration and a richer graphical landscape. Line charts and scatter plots are frequently used for this **shape visualization**.

Because of the chosen chart type and the data itself, we may not be able to reduce points to shapes, but we can compare, rank, and evaluate them and get relevant insights. This is **point visualization**, the most common type of data visualization, which is offered by bar charts or pie charts.

From time to time, we find our perception unable to fit some data points into a pattern, or we find the points too far away from what we believe to be within the normal range. This is **outlier visualization**, which can be useful in many tasks, such as systems or sales monitoring. These perceptual outliers don't have to be statistically significant to attract our attention, and we should check whether there is a reason for their unusual variation, but statistics can help us quantify their *outlierness* and decide what to do with them.

In theory, we should choose shape visualization over point visualization, but in practice, the right choice is task-dependent and data-dependent, and these concepts often overlap and coexist in a single chart. For the same time-series, we may want to use a line chart or a bar chart. The former allows us to see the overall shape, while the latter is better suited for pairwise comparisons. We may have a good reason to choose one chart type over another, but because the task is often ill-defined, we sometimes end up comparing answers and then selecting the question to match.

We'll see that the distinction between shapes, points, and outliers plays a key role in our classification of chart types. Meanwhile, more important than identifying the type of visualization is making sure that the selected display fulfills its role in saving us from expending too many cognitive resources while allowing us to obtain the right insights quickly.

It's important to understand that, **contrary to a common misconception, "quickly" doesn't mean "in a split second" or even "at a glance."** Do you read a city map with a single glance? Or do you take a few minutes to understand the shape of the city, locate the landmarks, and find the best way to the hotel? The same applies to a complex visualization. Even if it's well-designed, it can take a few minutes to read and explore. **It's how quickly you get to the insights that counts, not the absolute time you spend familiarizing yourself with the lay of the chart.**

Shape Visualization

Perceptually grouping data points presented in a 2D space is the first step in the process of assigning meaning to a visual representation. That process continues when we encode the data points and add legends, titles, and other supporting objects.

We may realize right from the start that not all data points are made equal: Some are unique, others seem to be nothing more than random variation, and yet others are positioned so close together that we could generalize them—that is, replace them with fewer data points without losing relevant information while saving resources.

A shape is a form of generalization. If we can't spot shapes in our data, perhaps we have the wrong data or we're looking at it the wrong way. (You won't find meaningful patterns in every single dataset, but don't assume there isn't one before you try multiple perspectives.) More than anything else in visualization, data shapes trigger Eureka! moments. However, they can also trigger moments of illusory knowledge, like when we see an almost perfect, but spurious, correlation between two variables and start wondering if one causes the other. Some examples of bad causality are funny (margarine consumption increases divorce rate), while others are dangerous (vaccines cause autism).

Shapes leave a distinct trace in official statistics. An interesting place to look for these shapes is within the subcategories of the consumer price index (CPI), where they'll appear as regularities.

The chart in **Figure 5.2** compares the monthly all-items CPI of Greece to the U.S. The overall trend is similar and pretty much overlaps for a very large period, but two major events in the U.S.—the 9/11 attacks and the bankruptcy of Lehman Brothers—are clearly seen. However, let's focus on something else: the uncommon cyclic pattern in the Greek index.

WITH SOME HICCUPS, SIMILAR CPI IN GREECE AND THE U.S.

All-items monthly consumer price indexes comparison Greece/U.S.

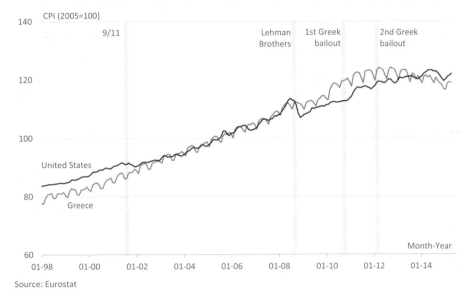

Figure 5.2 Consumer price indexes in Greece and the U.S.

THE IMPACT OF SALES DISCOUNTS OF CLOTHING AND FOOTWEAR
IS MUCH STRONGER IN GREECE THAN IN THE U.S.

Monthly CPI for clothing and footwear: comparison Greece/U.S.

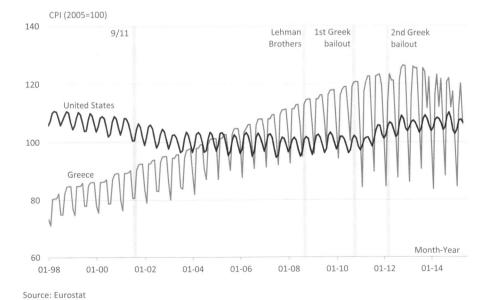

Figure 5.3 How discount sales influence CPI.

It doesn't take long to find the culprit. In many countries, the impact of sales discounts on clothing and footwear can be spotted in the CPI twice a year. In the U.S., these months are January and July, while in Greece they are February and August. The chart in **Figure 5.3** shows that sales discounts for clothing and footwear go much deeper in Greece than in the U.S., which could partly explain why the cyclic pattern is visible in the overall index. I suspect that's not the only reason, however. Because Greece is poorer, prices of basic items may weigh more in the Greek index than they do in the U.S. index. That would explain why there is so much overlap in both Greek indexes, while in the U.S. they look independent from each other.

Another example, also from the CPI in Greece, is in hair styling. The chart in **Figure 5.4** shows the evolution of the consumer price index in the category "Hairdressing salons and personal grooming establishments." The first patterns we spot on the left are those double peaks in the hairdressing category index (corresponding to festive periods in the months of December and April) until Greece's entry into the eurozone. The index was well below the all-items index, and after these peaks, prices returned to their normal level in the following month. Upon joining the euro, they no longer stand out as much—not because they did not exist, but because the other months rose to the level of the all-items index. Then, after the first bailout, the category index decouples from the general index and starts declining, without the peaks of the "old days."

RISE AND FALL OF HAIRDRESSERS IN GREECE
Monthly CPI of hairdressing salons and personal grooming establishments

Download the
original chart

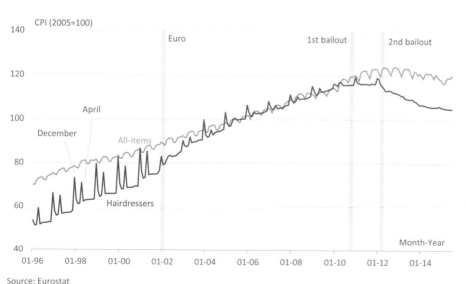

Source: Eurostat

Figure 5.4 The sad story of hairdressers in Greece.

WOMEN EARN LESS THAN MEN IN ALL EUROPEAN UNION COUNTRIES
Mean monthly earnings in euros, by sex and country, log scales

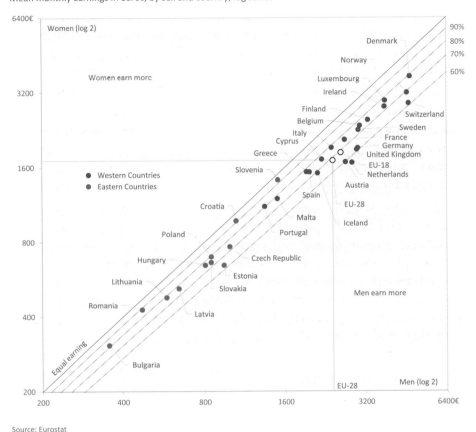

Source: Eurostat

Figure 5.5 Women consistently earn less than men in European countries.

The chart in **Figure 5.5** shows a strong relationship between two variables: mean earnings and gender. In an equal-earnings scenario, all the data points would be located along the line between the green and the orange triangles. If a data point falls below that line, it means that men earn more than women. As we can see, women earn consistently less than men in all countries. So, in this case the story is not about an almost perfect correlation between two variables but rather the gap between a reference and reality.

This chart was inspired by another, published by the *New York Times* comparing occupations, and the results are similar. Since the point in both charts is to compare gaps between men and women, and not between countries or occupations, our chart makes this more explicit by using a log scale[1] in both axes, which makes it easier to see where each country stands. I used different colors for Western and Eastern countries. While an expected pattern emerges (mean earnings are lower in Eastern countries), that is not what we are looking for. We shouldn't even consider it, since comparisons of absolute values are harder using log scales. Eastern countries do seem to perform slightly better than Western countries regarding the earnings gap, however, with three of them around or above 90 percent.

The scatter plot from Chapter 2, comparing GDP and education, allows for a third type of shape visualization. In that case, we didn't find a linear relationship between the two variables. Instead, we found three relatively homogeneous groups: Western European countries (high GDP, high education), Eastern European countries (low GDP, high education), and Mediterranean countries (low GDP, low education).

A different shape results from animating a chart. In many cases, animation shows change over time. At any given time, we can see a shape that results from a relationship between two variables, like the one in Figure 5.5. Now, suppose that the income gap between men and women was much deeper 50 years ago and that we have data for all those years. Playing the animation, we would see the data points moving up in most of the countries, meaning that the gap was closing. This is the second shape that only time can show. For a good example of this hidden shape, watch Hans Rosling's 2006 TED Talk.

Watch the video

Point Visualization

A chart facilitates the perception of distances between data points in a series. When plotted along a single axis, their distances are easy to grasp. When we use a different chart type, like a bar chart, sorting the data points by their quantitative dimension is a necessary first step.

Other analyses are possible, but when comparing points we tend to focus on the top and the bottom of the range, perform pairwise comparisons, and compare a data point to a reference value. In **Figure 5.6** we may want to check in which European countries it is safer to drive, at the top, and in which countries driving seems more dangerous, at the bottom. The Nordic countries, often grouped so close together statistically, are relatively spread apart from each other.

---

1   We use log scales in data visualization to improve chart resolution (when a large range prevents the details from being seen at the bottom of the range) or to compare rates of change. We'll discuss log scales in Chapter 8.

Download the
original chart

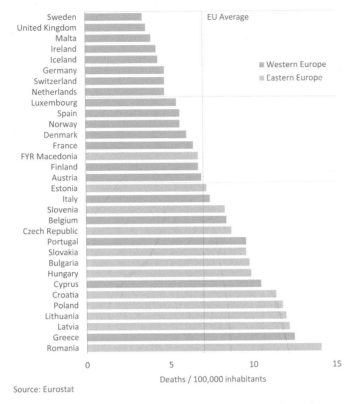

DEATHS IN TRANSPORT ACCIDENTS
Standardised death rate per 100,000 inhabitants

Source: Eurostat

Figure 5.6 Sorting data points for easier comparison. Countries are
sorted in ascending order because we are focusing on *safer* countries.

Note that the chart got more interesting because we were able to slip in a pattern:
Encoding basic geography in bar colors makes it clear that, in general, driving is
safer in Western Europe than it is in Eastern Europe.

Outlier Visualization

We can use visualization to support the validation and assessment of data quality because the genesis of an outlier may be in the data collection stage or from
incorrect data entry. In most cases, however, the outlier is a legitimate value that
appears again in other variables. Whatever the case, **an outlier should always
be examined and explained.**

The interest in an abnormal change in prices goes far beyond the economy. In **Figure 5.7**, the consumer price index in the "Utility (piped) gas service" category for the South Urban Area of the U.S. is clearly influenced by recurring disasters in that region, such as hurricanes and oil spills, which leave their fingerprints in the form of outliers.

There are several statistical formulas for determining outliers (see Chapter 10). To the brain, an outlier is just a data point that does not fit in the group, like the three spikes in Figure 5.7. It lies outside of the shape where most data points reside. If included, the outlier would create an overly complex shape. In a cost–benefit analysis, it seems more advantageous to disregard the outlier. On the other hand, its positional salience gets it more attention than any other point.

In Figure 5.7, prices remained flat for the last decade of the 20th century and steadily increased in the first decade of the 21th century. Understanding this could be useful, but we barely notice it because the spikes get most of our attention.

CONSUMER PRICE INDEX OF UTILITY (PIPED) GAS SERVICE
U.S. South Urban Area, All Urban Consumers

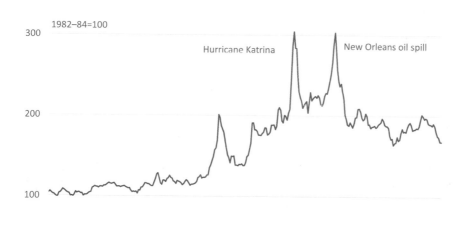

Source: Bureau of Labor Statistics

Figure 5.7 Some events can influence statistics as outliers.

Data Visualization Tasks

Many tasks in our daily routine can be supported by some kind of visual data analysis, and they are closely related to the questions we ask the data, as we'll see in the next chapter. At their core, these tasks have one of the visualization types:

- Searching for patterns and trends in univariate or multivariate data analysis.
- Searching for relationships in bivariate or multivariate data analysis.
- Ordering and ranking data points.
- Monitoring variation to detect data points that lie outside a fluctuation band or that show some other kind of strange behavior.

In a new project, it's natural to start with a simple descriptive analysis, comparing points and ranking them for each variable. Eventually, we'll start spotting patterns, either when analyzing single variables or when analyzing relationships among multiple variables. With this new knowledge, we create a monitoring system that draws our attention to any significant variations. This is just an example of how to articulate these tasks. In practice, the nature of the project may require a different sequence.

The Construction of Knowledge

Knowledge is a construction based on establishing relationships between facts and their interpretations. You can derive knowledge from everyday life (encoded in aphorisms and popular sayings), the supernatural and the religious (cosmogonies, for example), or from the scientific method. While aphorisms and religion tend to be closed systems with little room for change, the scientific method assumes that knowledge is a never-ending cumulative process that is always subject to revisions. Each of these constructions has their validation and evaluation criteria and their guardians (the old man, the priest, the scientist).

Establishing a relationship between two facts creates a new and more complex entity, which can be combined with other complex entities, thus repeating the cycle. This sequence has an implicit knowledge hierarchy, where each step adds a new level of complexity. This is known as the DIKW Pyramid: *Data* are combined to create *Information*, which results in *Knowledge*, integrated by *Wisdom*. A visualization pyramid wouldn't be much different, starting also with the data and ending with complex patterns that equate to knowledge.

We can also find this hierarchy in the types of answers a chart should be able to provide, according to Jacques Bertin: elementary, intermediate, and global. At the elementary level, the chart answers questions like "How much did we sell in March?" or "In which month did we have the most sales?" At this level, the chart is functionally equivalent to a table, and most charts can answer these questions. The intermediate level focuses on a subset of the data and answers questions like "What happened with the monthly sales of product X in 2015?" In the third level, a chart should be able to provide global answers such as "Are we gaining market share?" but also let the reader find answers to the elementary and intermediate questions.

Now let's look at the DIKW Pyramid sequence in more detail.

Data

A data point is a simple observation: the population density in region x, the number of births per year in country y, the interest rate on day z, and so on. One of the mantras of journalism is "Facts are sacred." But they are also useless. They are sacred because they're basic building blocks for the construction of knowledge, and they cannot be manipulated, changed, or deleted just because they do not conform to the theory or our worldview. But without context, the data are useless, because by themselves they are incomplete. Data are like the pieces of a disassembled jigsaw puzzle (**Figure 5.8**).

Figure 5.8
Data: a jigsaw
puzzle in disarray.

Information

We move up to the information level when we establish relationships between facts. This creates a new whole that, as the Gestalt laws teach us, is more than the sum of its parts. By juxtaposition, association, and comparison, we start finding patterns that were previously hidden in the scattered data. Our jigsaw puzzle begins to take shape (**Figure 5.9**). We have several sets of assembled parts, but the connection between them and their position in the jigsaw puzzle as a whole is not yet clear. Previously, we had an unconnected set of data. Now, we have unconnected sets of information.

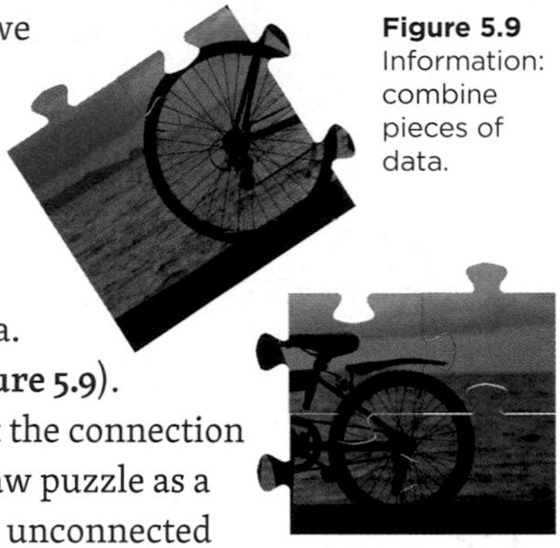

Figure 5.9 Information: combine pieces of data.

Knowledge

When we realize the place of each set of information in a context that generates a more complex object, we create knowledge. This is endless by nature, not only because there is potential for creating higher-level objects but also because (unlike jigsaw puzzles) it's always possible to find new ways of combining objects that take us to alternative paths (**Figure 5.10**).

Figure 5.10 Knowledge: start making sense of things.

Figure 5.11 Wisdom: see the whole picture.

Wisdom

Advancement in the knowledge hierarchy is not done by abstract entities; it's made by human beings with their memories, experiences, and personalities in a given context. But if the first three levels of the DIKW Pyramid belong to the realm of the scientific method—an approach based on observation and the accumulation of more complex patterns—wisdom is more of a "cultural melting pot" of a qualitative nature.

Wisdom is defined by the understanding of interactions and an integrated view, enabling action, and understanding the mechanisms and indirect results of the action beyond the field of study (**Figure 5.11**). When, in his acceptance speech of the Nobel Prize in Literature, José Saramago said that "The wisest man I ever knew...could not read or write," it is this understanding that he refers to, which is not necessarily associated with knowledge of complex scientific objects.

Defining Data Visualization

We can combine the idea of the brain as a stimuli manager constantly searching for the "good form" and disliking ambiguity with the task types we saw earlier. This helps us **define data visualization as a tool that, by applying perceptual mechanisms to the visual representation of abstract quantitative data, facilitates the search for relevant shapes, order, or exceptions.**

We can fit a statistical study or the work of a data artist in this deliberately minimal definition. Some definitions are more restrictive, such as the one professed by Stephen Few, where the goals of informing and aiding understanding belong to the core concept of data visualization:

> *There are as many definitions of data visualization as there are definers, but at the root of this term that has been around for many years is the goal that data be visualized in a way that leads to understanding. Whatever else it does, it must inform. If we accept this as fundamental to the definition of data visualization, we can judge the merits of any example above all else on how clearly, thoroughly, and accurately it enlightens.*

Read the
blog post

That's the spirit of this book, of course, but it is not the only possibility. We must think of data visualization as a generic field where several (combinations of) perspectives, processes, technologies, and objectives (not forgetting the subjective component of personal style) can coexist. In this sense, data art, infographics, and business visualization are branches of data visualization.

We can't define a set of strict criteria that may be applied to all types of visualization. That would be like trying to establish the same rules for a novel, a poem, or an essay. A visualization can be published in a media outlet or in a scientific paper and have different communication goals. It can be static or interactive; it can be used for analysis and discovery or for communication. The authors can have contradictory views on the role of design. Just because we don't agree on the path or on the goal, that doesn't mean that one visualization is valid and another is not.

This book deals almost exclusively with visualizing data in an organizational environment, which makes it easier to come up with a consistent narrative on what data visualization is all about. This also helps avoid combining multiple narratives, like assuming that a cool infographic we saw in the newspaper is the right visualization template to apply to the data in our organization.

Each player in data visualization has the responsibility of adding his personal complement to the basic definition. In business visualization, this differentiation is the emphasis on the functional characteristics. Everything is subordinated to drawing recognizable and relevant objects in the graphical landscape that communicate effectively, and inform and support the decision-making process in the organization. The desire to create a memorable chart through design is common and acceptable in other visualization perspectives but is less urgent in an organization.

Languages, Stories, and Landscapes

Data visualization is a language. Jacques Bertin makes this clear in the title of his book: *Semiology of Graphics*. Another author, Leland Wilkinson, sought to translate into concrete rules this semiology, writing another important visualization book, *The Grammar of Graphics*.

If data visualization is to replace or complement other forms of communication, it must have qualities other than some overlap with formal linguistics. These qualities are related to the creation of a unified message, based on a sequence (a visual narrative) or on the exploration of a graphical landscape.

Data journalism is one of the strongest trends in journalism² today. Adding charts or other visuals to a news piece isn't new, but now visualizations are moving from a supporting role to center stage, and changing their nature along the way. They're becoming interactive and more open to alternative discovery paths.

Data stories are a subset of the much broader concept (or buzzword) of storytelling. Marketers are jumping onto this bandwagon, so we should be careful how we create our own data stories and how we buy theirs.. Stories, or narratives, are useful in data visualization because they force us to recognize the limited value of a single chart in a complex environment. Stories also force us to recognize the need for a better integration of our displays, as we move away from strings of siloed charts.

---

2   For a deeper discussion, check out Segel, Edward and Jeffrey Heer. "Narrative Visualization: Telling Stories with Data." *IEEE Transactions in Visualization and Computer Graphics*, Vol. 16, No. 2: 1139-1148, 2010.

 Get the PDF

Today, narratives are often designed to be consumed from the small screens of smartphones, one tiny and digestible piece of information after the next.[3] This is fine for news consumption, but it becomes an issue if overly used in business visualization. Business visualization needs the time integration that a narrative provides, but it will be much more effective if it lets the user check a large amount of information at a glance. That means a space integration that only graphical landscapes can provide. And it means larger screens.

A few years ago, I spent a weekend with my kids listening to traditional storytellers. Often, they ended their story with the words "Now you know." Now you know why the poor girl became a princess. Now you know how the hunters caught the wolf. Now you know how the boy ended up in the witch's cauldron. And guess what? We did know! So now it's time to put your own storyteller hat on and try this: As a prefix to your chart title, add "Now you know why/how/where/who..." If the complete sentence makes sense, then you have a good chart title (and you can remove the temporary prefix). Then make sure the chart itself fulfills that promise.

Graphical Literacy

Graphical literacy, or graphicacy, is the ability to read and understand a document where the message is expressed visually, such as with charts, maps, or network diagrams.

When both the individual and the organizational level of graphical literacy are low, the organization might use many pie charts, pseudo-3D effects, and Excel defaults, with no one thinking this is a problem. Over time, that level of graphical literacy might rise only modestly, and likely due only to improved Excel skills. But I'm an optimist, and I like to imagine that a few well-placed epiphanies will turn this linear trend into an s-shaped curve. Here are three of them that will shape the learning curve:

- **Epiphany #1: The seed.** This is when the learning curve starts bending up. It is the symbolic moment when someone becomes aware that the power of data visualization goes far beyond illustrating numbers or competing for the most spectacular canned effect. This doesn't mean people start making

---

3 Hannah Fairfield, senior graphics editor at the *New York Times,* discusses this in a Tapestry 2015 keynote.

great charts full of insights, however. It means people start recognizing the problems and are willing to learn. It's when they start thinking, "This pseudo-3D bar chart looks silly."

■ **Epiphany #2: Relationships.** Typically, a new product has an initial low market share but grows fast. At some point, the product has a high market share and slow growth. I've lost count of the times I've watched people trying to demonstrate this behavior with two bar charts when a scatter plot makes it obvious. This epiphany marks the moment when we move from a merely descriptive attitude to an attempt to understand how the data are related.

■ **Epiphany #3: Holistic.** The third epiphany is understanding visualization not as a mere set of siloed charts prepared in a more or less coherent succession, but as a construction in which the individual chart is diluted in a web of relationships with other objects and other charts.

Graphical Landscapes

Don't think of the holistic epiphany as some kind of ethereal, incense-burning, new-agey aesthetic. It just means that if we want to communicate visually, we first must be in control of the message (how we send it, that is, not how it's received). This editorial dimension that we talked about can be exercised from the choice of data to legend placement. But the editorial dimension must go beyond the single chart and be able to integrate multiple charts and other visual objects into a coherent message, like paragraphs of a complex story. Let's look at some of these "wholes."

Profiling

Profiling is the display of multiple identically formatted and juxtaposed small charts, each displaying some entity's profile. A significant part of the knowledge gained from reading these charts comes from the observation of the whole rather than from the individual charts. This is why we should consider this construction a single chart. Because the charts are placed in a grid, they represent a more structured level of a graphic landscape. In the next chapter I suggest a new chart classification, where profiling appears as one of the categories.

FERTILITY RATE IN EUROPEAN COUNTRIES BY AGE GROUP 15–44

Variation 2002–2012

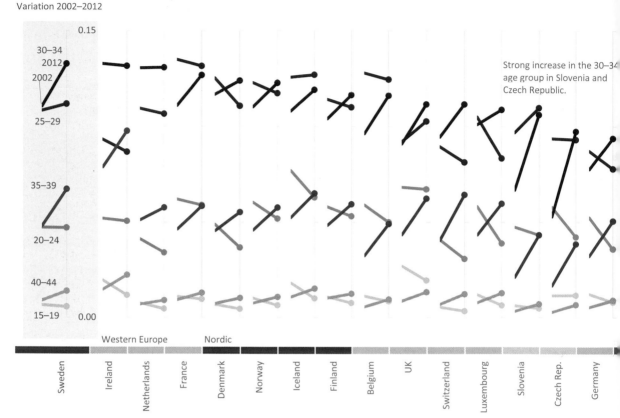

Source: Eurostat

Figure 5.12 An example of profiling using panels.

In **Figure 5.12**, profiling is used to compare how fertility rates changed between 2002 and 2012 in six age groups, creating a profile for several European countries.

Dashboards

According to Stephen Few, "[a] dashboard is a visual display of the most important information needed to achieve one or more objectives, consolidated and arranged on a single screen so the information can be monitored at a glance."[4]

---

4 Few, Stephen. *Information Dashboard Design: Displaying data for at-a-glance monitoring*. Burlingame, CA: Analytics Press, 2013. If you want to learn more about dashboard design, this should be your primary reference.

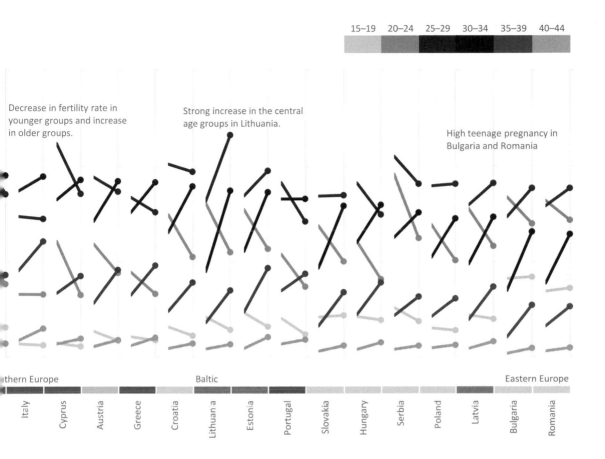

15–19 20–24 25–29 30–34 35–39 40–44

Decrease in fertility rate in younger groups and increase in older groups.

Strong increase in the central age groups in Lithuania.

High teenage pregnancy in Bulgaria and Romania

thern Europe   Baltic   Eastern Europe

Italy · Cyprus · Austria · Greece · Croatia · Lithuania · Estonia · Portugal · Slovakia · Hungary · Serbia · Poland · Latvia · Bulgaria · Romania

Unlike profiling charts, dashboards don't need to have a visual structure imposed at the outset, which substantially increases the freedom of their construction. However, they do have constraints: Because they're used for monitoring, their design tends to emphasize the goal of calling attention to outliers and other abnormal variations from the reference point.

I made the example in **Figure 5.13** for my course on Excel dashboards. The aim of the course is mainly to explore some Excel techniques for managing the data and adding some level of interaction (such as the choice of region, country, and year). In this case, I deliberately attempted to hide Excel. I sacrificed more effective design options in favor of a presentation with more aesthetic appeal, without breaking the boundaries of common sense.

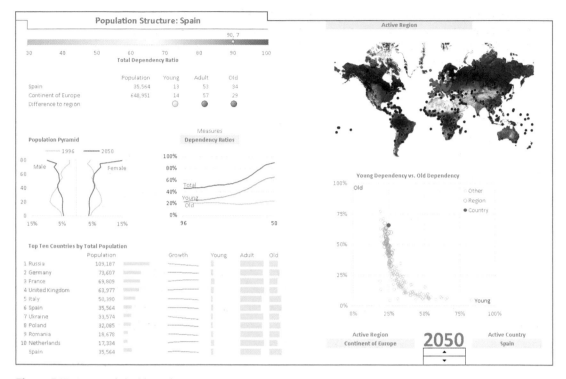

Figure 5.13 An Excel dashboard.

This dashboard invites exploration of the image without an explicit reading sequence. The placement of the graphic objects in the picture is not random: The main indicators are placed at the top left because that's where we start reading.

Infographics

Go to the
web page

Visually, the infographic is the loosest form of a graphic landscape. It is also the most confusing concept in visualization, as it's open to multiple definitions and interpretations. Asked about what makes a "cool" infographic, Alberto Cairo replies that:

[T]o be truly 'cool', an infographic needs to be honest, truthful, deep, and elegant. It can be fun, too, but it needs first to respect the intelligence of its potential readers, and be designed not just to entertain them, but to enlighten them. A bunch of out-of-context numbers or grossly simplistic charts surrounded by pictograms or illustrations is never a 'cool' infographic.

There is a very good reason for the last sentence in Cairo's answer. Ever since people found that infographics have a positive impact in web page ranks (making them appear higher in search engine results), marketing departments began producing infographics. But in most cases, these "infographics" are nothing more than junk visuals, using false or misleading data. Google seems to be reducing their relevance in recent updates of its algorithm, but they're still popping up. And now these "infographics" are no longer created; they're made with automated tools, generating profound indignation and justified irritation of visualization practitioners.

As a consumer, when reading a marketing infographic, you should always check for junk visuals, low data density, and dubious claims. As a data worker, you should recognize that an infographic is a media product that doesn't belong to a business environment (because of the lack of design skills, the wrong tools, and information asymmetry, as we discussed previously).

If you want to know more about infographics, you can browse a well-curated selection at Visualoop and the site of the Malofiej Awards that take place in March every year in Pamplona, Spain.

Go to the
web page

No entry-level book on data visualization is complete without a reproduction of the best-known infographic ever: the march of Napoleon's troops during the Russia campaign, by civil engineer Charles Joseph Minard (**Figure 5.14**). It shows the advance of Napoleon's troops toward Moscow (in brown) and their retreat (in black). The line width encodes the number of troops. Also represented are rivers and temperatures. Napoleon's troops were decimated by the Russians' scorched-earth strategy, which blocked supplies on the way to Moscow and river crossings during the winter when retreating.

Go to the
web page

Figure 5.14
The march of
Napoleon's
troops during
the Russia
campaign, by
Charles Joseph
Minard.

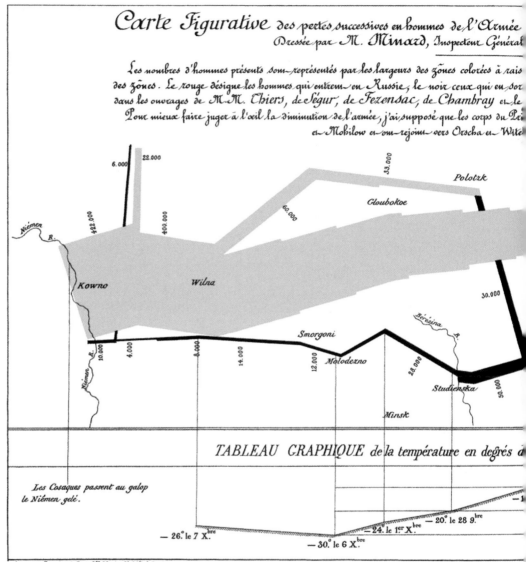

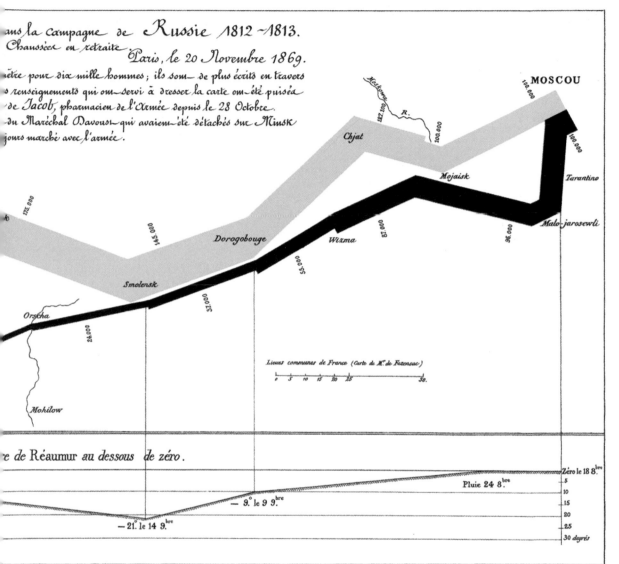

ms la Campagne de *Russie 1812 ~1813*.

Chaussée en retraite *Paris, le 20 Novembre 1869*.

ètre pour dix mille hommes; ils som—de plus écrits en travers
s renseignements qui om—servi à dresser la carte om—été puisés
de Jacob, pharmacien de l'Armée depuis le 28 Octobre.
du Maréchal Davoust qui avaient—été détachés sur Minsk
jours marché avec l'armée.

MOSCOU

Moskova R.

100.000

100.000

100.000

Chjat

175.000

145.000

Dorogobouge

Mejaisk

Tarantino

Wizma

87.000

96.000

Malo-jarosewli

55.000

Smolensk

37.000

Orscha

24.000

Lieues communes de France (Carte de Mr de Fezensac).

0 5 10 15 20 25   50.

Mohilow

re de Réaumur au dessous de zéro.

Zéro le 18 8.bre

Pluie 24 8.bre   5

— 9.° le 9 9.bre   10

                          15

                          20

— 21.° le 14 9.bre   25

                          30 *degrés*

Imp. Lith. Regnier et Dourdet.

A Crossroad of Knowledge

Data visualization is a tool and, like any other tool, requires a mixture of knowledge and skills to be used effectively. We already discussed a few of these: the role of perception and the eye–brain system, culture and social laws, and data preparation and management. Let's add a few more.

Statistics

You can't use a box plot (see Chapter 10) without understanding what "median" and "quantile" mean. You can't use a scatter plot without understanding correlation. These are but two of many examples where traditional statistics and data visualization are deeply intertwined, and the more you understand, the better. Even basic familiarity with concepts from descriptive statistics can make your visual analyses more robust, and at the same time, this knowledge increases the number of perspectives you can have with the data.

Design

Design is present in all stages of graphic representation. As an inevitability, it's tempting to consider design and artistic talent as basic necessary skills. They are indeed useful when the goal is to design infographics or when we move to an artistic environment. But this is not so in business visualization.

The design skills we need are of a functional nature and are aimed primarily at translating the rules of perception, which are much less subjective than aesthetics. It is possible to make a chart formally correct and at the same time aesthetically unpleasant because of, for example, the choice of colors. But the functional color tasks and rules of color harmony allow us, as we'll see, not only to reduce unfortunate choices but also to strengthen this component of functional design.

Applications

Core competencies in data visualization are application-agnostic. The way we apply them is not. All software applications have obvious functional differences, but they also have what Edward Tufte called a "**cognitive style**": the information flow model, the default settings, the way they make some tasks easier or harder.

Forcing applications to do what we want is often possible, but the cost is much higher than simply accepting the application's "suggestions." **The right application is therefore the one that imposes minimum resistance to specific tasks we need to accomplish**.

Knowing what we want to do, knowing that it can be done with the application we are using, and not being able to do it because we lack the skills is a particularly frustrating experience. One key skill in data visualization is, therefore, to make the application invisible—that is, to focus on the task and on the goals to be achieved and not on looking for the way to do it.

Content and Context

If you consider general principles and best practices of chart making, a data visualization expert may be able to create a perfect chart, and yet that "perfect" chart may be completely useless in the business context in which it is supposed to be applied. Meanwhile, a less than stellar chart may deliver the exact insights the organization needs. The difference, obviously, is in how well you know the organization and its data. Even a seemingly innocuous concept like market share can be challenging. Is it calculated in dollars or in units? Are there multiple definitions of "market"?

You can hire a data visualization expert to improve graphic literacy in your organization. If in the first day she can make more useful charts than the organization is used to, then there is something wrong with the organization's visualization practices, and hiring her was a real smart move.

Data Visualization in Excel

Excel is a spreadsheet tool. Excel is *not* a database, and Excel is *not* a specialized data visualization application. We should point this out from time to time, because Excel is often compared negatively to specialized applications, and that's unfair.

That said, it is also necessary to remember that most business charts are made in Excel, making Microsoft the leader in business visualization. Even so, Microsoft never took advantage of this to improve the graphic literacy of its huge user base. It always chose another short-term path, more defined by the sales department than by the principles and good practices increasingly accepted in data visualization.

A major change in Excel's chart engine took place in Excel 2007. Stephen Few pointedly said that this was an "opportunity missed":

> *Microsoft has the opportunity to make a stand for excellence, but either lacks the courage, doesn't understand what works themselves, or doesn't care. Regardless of the reason, it's the customers who will suffer.*

And he expressed a similar level of frustration with Excel 2010. Microsoft decided to fight its competition mostly through the cosmetics of visualization, with little or no substance added to the software. Things get better with Excel 2016, however.

Go to the web page

Go to the web page

The Good

The greatest advantages of Excel over other tools for quantitative analysis are, obviously, its familiarity and ubiquity. Everyone who works with quantitative data in an organization knows the basics of using spreadsheets, even if they use open-source spreadsheet software instead of Excel.

With Excel, you'll experience a few annoying compatibility issues when using different versions, but you'll be able to share files both within and outside of your organization. Employing Excel as the Swiss Army knife for all things data makes life easier for everyone, from human resources (training) to IT (infrastructure management) to users (standard computer skills).

New users can easily understand Excel basics, while its flexibility and the existence of a programming language allow advanced users to go far beyond Excel's typical uses and overcome some of its major limitations.

In the Excel-dependent environment in which numerous organizations find themselves, Excel is the right choice for learning data visualization because, in spite of its shortcomings, more than with any other tool you can focus on visualization itself rather than the tool (assuming the presence of some basic Excel skills).

While Excel was always the informal leader in Business Intelligence, Microsoft is paying more attention to it with Excel 2016, adding more powerful tools (Power BI) and expanding the chart library.

The Bad

If we start using Excel as a visualization tool, we'll soon notice that its tiny chart library (**Figure 5.15**) and many useless formatting options make it a tool better suited for communication than for visual data analysis—and especially the type of communication that prefers stylistic effects over communication effectiveness.

EXCEL 2016 CHART LIBRARY

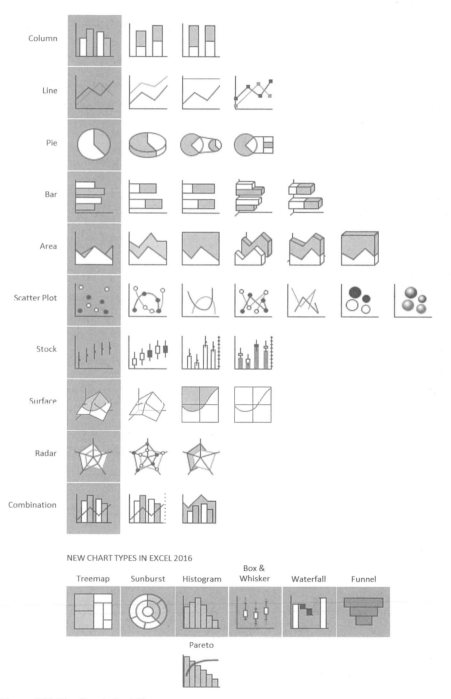

Figure 5.15 The Excel chart library.

Excel is a spreadsheet tool that includes some functionality to make a few in-dependent charts (independent from each other, that is). Excel is better suited for passive consumption than for active visual exploration. An active visual exploration does not entail simply making successive charts, but rather making dynamic charts that allow for visual filtering, tabulating, and grouping of data.

For example, pivot tables are great for data exploration, but if you want to explore visually through pivot charts, your options are very limited: Some charts, like scatter plots and all the new ones in Excel 2016, are not supported, and some of the functionalities available in regular charts are also missing.

Take profiling, the chart category proposed in the next chapter. In practice, with a real data visualization tool (such as Tableau, or R if you prefer a programming language), it's just a matter of dragging-and-dropping or adding a few lines of code, and the software will make all the charts for you. With Excel, you have to make a chart for each profile you want to compare; and as you create each chart, you have to point them to the correct range.[5]

If you're lucky and your chart is simple enough, some of the new features in recent versions of Excel (such as slicers) may reduce the workload. However, user interaction is still highly dependent on programming or formulas, which shifts the focus from data analysis to formula construction. In other words, it shifts our focus from the task to the tool, which we do not want.

The new chart types in Excel 2016 (treemap, sunburst, histogram, Pareto, box and whisker, waterfall) are welcome but greatly overdue additions. The Excel chart library is still surprisingly small, while the number of cosmetic options is unsurprisingly large. This significantly limits the type of display available to most users, while advanced users who know how to overcome these limitations have to question whether the costs justify the benefits.

The Ugly

I'd like to learn more about how Microsoft selects focus group participants, and specifically their age. Don't get me wrong, I *like* the construction blocks in **Figure 5.16**. I just don't understand how it can be, with only a few slight changes, one of the predefined chart styles.

---

5   Although you can't do this with an out-of-the-box Excel installation, you now can do it in Power BI.

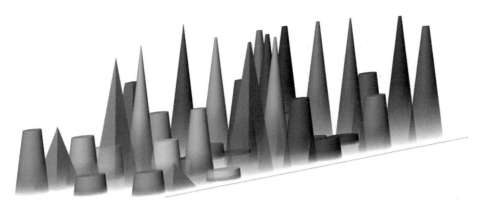

Figure 5.16 A creative chart style that looks like something "in a kingdom far, far away…"

You may argue that, if I want a flexible application, being able to make charts like this comes with the territory, and you would be partially right. The problem is not so much about flexibility, it's about defaults and suggested styles. Empirical studies prove what everyday practice tells us: **Most people don't change software application defaults**, and if they do, they tend to use a predefined alternative.

Unlike Excel users, graphic designers believe this is a capital sin because they value some level of artistic uniqueness. For Excel users, though, the matter belongs (again) to the editorial dimension and the need to make charts more effective. It's OK if Excel does not apply color tones to group data, use thickness to emphasize a series, or differentiate between signal and noise. That's our job. But default options are so imposing that not changing them means that the author was either careless or didn't know enough about the content to make such decisions.

Beyond the Excel Chart Library

In a series of posts right after I started blogging, I wanted to share my experience of replicating in Crystal Xcelsius (now renamed to SAP BusinessObjects Dashboards) a dashboard made in Excel. That experience was an utter disaster. Crystal Xcelsius didn't allow even basic changes that I took for granted in Excel.

Read the
blog post

Micromanaging formatting options at the data point level is essential for getting the results you want, and in Excel you can do pretty much anything. If things get really tough, you can even resort to programming. Most of the time, however, you won't have to go that far. Here are some simple paths to follow if you want to go beyond the library:

- Think of objects beyond their literal use.
- A dummy series is your friend.
- Use combination charts.

Line charts, bar charts, or box and whiskers are some of the many chart types you can make using a scatter plot. Remember the bamboo chart in Chapter 3? That was just a scatter plot. You don't have to write a single line of code to make charts like these.

Go to the
web page

Playing with the objects in Excel's chart library is fun and we can learn a lot, not only about Excel but also about data visualization. When playing with a scatter plot, you may become aware, for example, that a line chart is nothing more than a special case of a scatter plot. If you want to know more about going beyond the library, you must read and follow Jon Peltier's blog, as Peltier is the true Excel chart master.

The problem with going beyond Excel's library is its cost–benefit ratio. It's interesting to know that you can make a complex chart in Excel, but if that means that you must spend hours and hours formatting the chart, placing the data in special cells, or adding dummy data, you'll have to make sure the results are worth it. Maybe it's time for you to move on and find a tool that better suits your needs, by either following the Microsoft path (Power BI) or moving into a new direction (such as Tableau or QlikView).

The Lollipop Chart

Figure 5.17 shows an example of a chart type that you won't find in the Excel chart library. People call this a lollipop chart because, well, data points look like lollipops. Take a moment and try to guess how I made this chart.

This is actually a bubble chart. In a bubble chart, you can encode the horizontal and vertical positions and also the size of the bubble. We only have one series (GDP), which defines the position of the bubbles along the horizontal axis. The vertical position is added with the help of a dummy series: a series that places the bubbles along the vertical axis at regular intervals, like in a bar chart.

As you remember, answers in surveys always have an error margin. For example, if you get a value of 35, the real value in the universe may vary between 33 and 37. You visualize this interval with error bars, and Excel has an option to add them. In this case, since we don't have to use error bars for their regular purpose, we can use them creatively, like making sticks for the lollipops.

Bubble sizes don't change, so you might think using a scatter plot instead would be better. Problem is, with scatter plots you don't have much control over labeling the data points, so you wouldn't be able to identify the countries in the chart.

Finally, I split the data into two series, one with positive values and one with negative values. This allowed me to choose whether I wanted to place the labels to the left or to the right of the vertical axis.

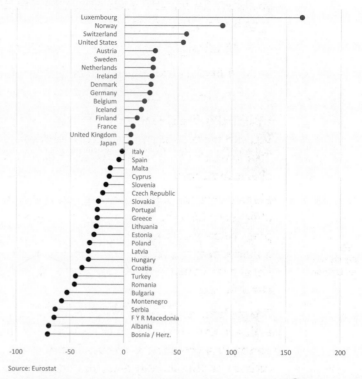

Figure 5.17 From bubble chart to lollipops

Download the original chart

Don't Make Excel Charts

You don't want your audience to think, "That's an Excel chart" or, even worse, "Are we paying for Excel 2003 charts?" **You want your audience to see the data, not the tool.** A good starting point is to select a different color palette, but Excel also offers many other formatting options that you can change from their default settings. (For example, you can set gap width in bar charts to 100 percent or reduce the number of grid lines.) If you're skeptical about how far you can go, let me ask you this: Do you think Excel could render a reasonable copy of an 18th century chart?

Few among the data visualization experts would disagree that William Playfair's *The Commercial and Political Atlas*, published in 1786, marks the beginning of the modern era of data visualization. Playfair created several of the chart types we use today. A well-known chart from his book displays the trade balance between England, on the one side, and Denmark and Norway, on the other (**Figure 5.18**). Note how well-annotated the chart is, with direct labeling instead of adding a legend, and fill colors encoding the positive or negative trade balance. This makes the chart very easy to read, and a good example even today.

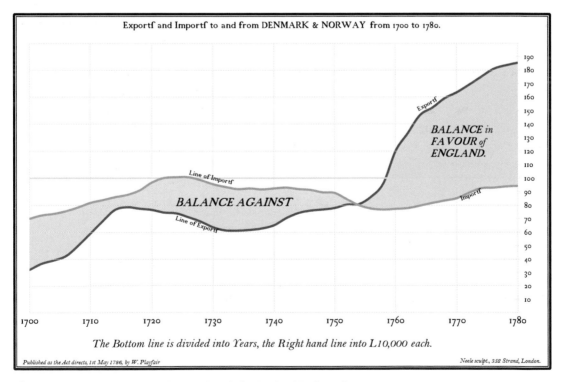

Figure 5.18 Balance of trade for England in the 18th century.

Download the
original chart

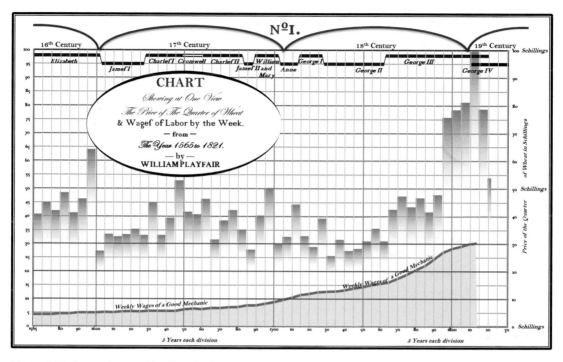

Figure 5.19 A complex combination chart.

Here is a more complex example. Several years after his *Atlas*, in 1822, Playfair published one of his most famous charts, comparing "weekly wages of a good mechanic" to "price of a quarter of wheat" (**Figure 5.19**). At the top, he plotted the monarchy reigns to add some context. Today it's unacceptable to compare two variables using a double vertical axis,[6] and we would get better insights with a different chart or a different metric, but trying to find a relationship between two variables and adding context is still, almost 200 years later, a novel idea.

Now is the moment when I should ask you to turn the page and check how Excel would handle these charts. The truth is, I have been counting on you not to scrutinize them too closely. If you do, you'll soon discover that these are not reproductions of the original images, but rather charts that I made from scratch in Excel. Yes, these are Excel charts. Not bad at hiding their nature, are they? To be honest, when I started making them I was convinced that they would always look like Excel charts, but, as you can see, they don't.

---

6 We'll discuss dual-axis charts in Chapter 14.

Figure 5.20 offers a different example. The dashboard lets the user select a year and study the network of Walmart stores in the United States, including the total population in the catchment area of each store. The map is a scatter plot of all counties in continental U.S. The most interesting part in this project is in the data themselves (how to define the catchment area and how to measure distances between the store and the population).

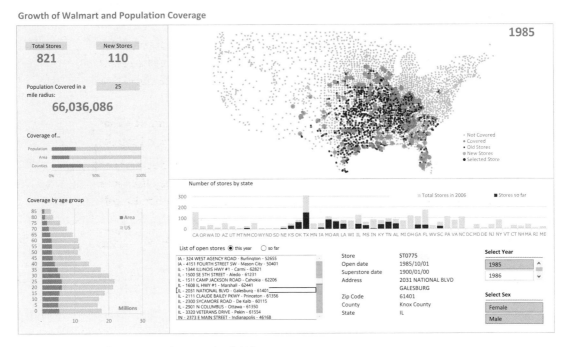

Figure 5.20 The growth of Walmart.

Takeaways

- You'll use data visualization to find, manage, and communicate shapes, order, and exceptions in the data.

- Business visualization favors a functional approach to data visualization where our main goal is to understand the data, and our weapon of choice is designing for effectiveness.

- Data integration leads us to information and knowledge. Adding data, finding relationships, using more sophisticated charts, going beyond siloed charts and designing graphical landscapes, or creating a visual narrative will help us climb the knowledge ladder.

- Excel can fulfill much of the data visualization needs in an organizational context because you can go beyond its library of pre-defined chart types.

- Being able to make a complex chart in Excel can be interesting as a proof of a concept but may not be the best resource allocation strategy. At some point you may need to change to a more efficient tool. If you need a full data exploration environment, you need to look elsewhere.

- When making charts in Excel, replace the default palette and change other default options to avoid the "Excel chart" look.

- Select a chart that you like and try to render it in Excel.

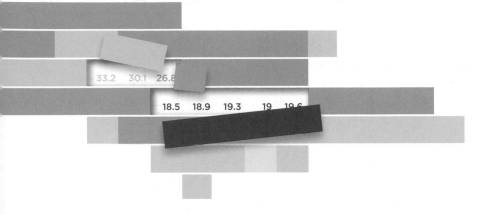

6

DATA DISCOVERY, ANALYSIS, AND COMMUNICATION

In the 1980s, change really started to accelerate, so that by the early 21st century, the simple and easy-to-understand bipolar world of the Cold War had been replaced by a foggy multipolar world of newspeak and fluid military and political alliances. Other well-defined polarities started to crack too. Technology blurred the divide between producers and consumers, TV networks and their audience, and mainframes and dumb terminals. Our world has become increasingly complex.

More complexity implies more variation, and more variation implies the need for more data, as any sampling methods handbook will tell you. However, at some point just adding more data will not be enough. We'll need better data, better tools, and better processes. Knowledge will be built, not only from reading someone else's report, but also from interacting with data using the right tools—blurring the divide between data exploration and data communication.

We saw how relevant, yet overlooked, data preparation is. We are at the point now where we need to get the data ready, not just to start making charts one after another but to start the second stage of the data visualization process: After thinking *about* the data, it's time to think *with* the data.

Where to Start?

The more knowledgeable you are about the data, the more linear the visualization process tends to be. If you have in your hands a new data table you know nothing about, the sequence will be much less linear, and often you'll be forced to return to earlier stages to ask new questions, search for new data, or change priorities.

This, of course, is rooted in the unpredictable nature of discovery. Subjecting data discovery to a structured process can make it happen (by eliminating dead ends) or prevent it from happening (by overly focusing on known paths).

In practice, data exploration is often an unruly process, and it should be, to some extent. Earlier, we saw how our brain becomes really good at processing routine tasks while becoming less able to respond to unexpected changes. Including some unstructured exploration in our analysis and looking at the data from unusual perspectives will often lead us nowhere, but doing so quite possibly could result in findings that would go unnoticed otherwise.

Between an overly structured process, where we seek only those data relationships that have already been found in the past and a chaotic and unproductive approach that has us walking in circles, we must find methodologies that allow us to uncover new insights without forcing the data to tell what is not there.

The Visual Information-Seeking Mantra

According to the population census of 2010, about 20 percent of the U.S. population is less than 15 years old, and 13 percent are more than 64 years old. These are facts, nothing more. To make them meaningful, we must compare them to something else. Compared to most European countries, the U.S. population is young; therefore, making a comparison to other places is a possible path. The U.S. population is also getting older, with all those baby boomers entering retirement age; comparing the present to the past is a second possible path.

Let's follow the path of comparing places, but only within the U.S. The top left scatter plot in **Figure 6.1** displays the percentages of both age groups at the county level. The vertical and horizontal lines mark the national averages for both series. Half of the counties in each series are within the range defined by the red lines. All the counties within the rectangle defined by the black horizontal and vertical reference lines have a higher percentage of adult population (15–64 years old).

There are a few things worth noting in this chart. We now know what kind of variation we should expect for the older age group and the younger age group, and where they're more concentrated. Because the ranges in both axes are the same, we can see that variation in the older population is higher. Also, we can infer that larger counties tend to have fewer elderly (65+ years old) than smaller counties, because there are more counties above the national average, while the national average of the younger population appears closer to the center.

The problem with data visualization when compared to, say, a data table is that we keep craving more. Questions keep popping up: Do all states have similar profiles? How about those counties with a much higher percentage of adult population—do they have anything more in common? Some questions can be answered simply by highlighting the counties belonging to each state. Let's do this for Florida (top right chart). It's clear that the population in Florida is older, both because it has a higher percentage of elderly people and a lower percentage of young people.

Again, new questions emerge: Does the group of counties at the bottom of the distribution share other characteristics, such as geographic proximity? What is happening with that outlier county at the top left with such a high percentage of elderly? I was so curious that I visited the county website and the single human face I saw on that site was of a young girl, probably the only child in the county (just kidding, of course).

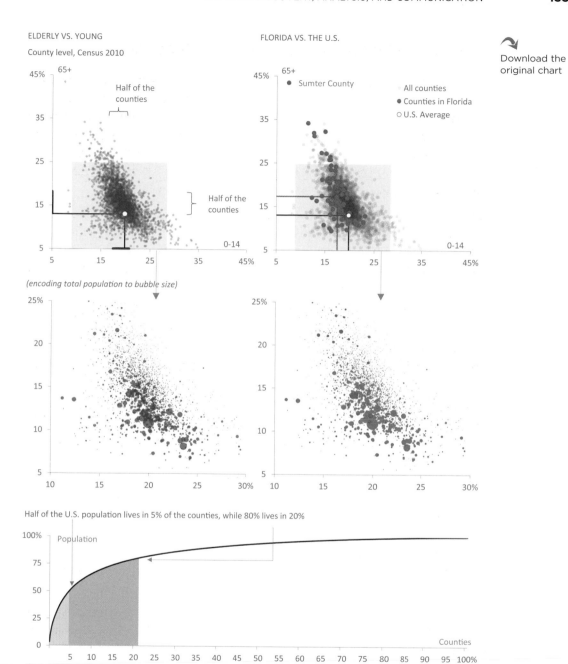

Figure 6.1 U.S. population at the county level.

The population in some of these counties is larger than the population of many countries, while other counties have only a few families and everyone knows each other. We already suspect that some of the larger counties have a younger age structure than the national average, but this portrait can be misleading. Let's focus on the darker area to improve resolution. The bubble charts confirm our suspicion: Some very large counties are close to the national average for the younger group but are below average for the older group. There is also a lot of dust (very small counties). This raises new questions again. Apparently, there is a strong concentration in a few counties. Can we measure that?

Yes, we can. The bottom chart shows that half of the U.S. population lives in only 5 percent of the counties, while 80 percent of the population lives in 20 percent of the counties. It can't get more Pareto than that (we'll get to the Pareto principle, also known as the 80/20 rule, in Chapter 10).

And we could go on and on. Without noticing, we moved our focus from age structures to county sizes to population concentrations. Data visualization can get slippery at times. Speaking of slippery, Alaska has the lowest percentage of elderly, while Washington, D.C., has the highest percentage of adult population, but we'd need to check that using small multiples (we'll get back to small multiples in Chapter 13).

You'll see what I've done here. I started by evaluating distribution shapes, and then I filtered the data using a variable (state) that could lead to more insights. Finally, I focused on specific details.

This scenario, in which we start from a bird's-eye view and progressively filter out and zoom in on details, fits what Ben Shneiderman calls the Visual Information-Seeking Mantra[1]:

Overview first, zoom and filter, then details on demand.

Don't overlook the overview. Even if it seems too generic, it's essential to establish an anchor point (which, as we shall see later in the book, can also have an emotional character) that structures the following analysis. It's not just a point where you start drilling down. For example, a national sales manager may want to know how much sales incentives are being paid and then filter by region or product, while a regional sales manager may want to start by checking how much is being paid to each member of her team.

---

1   Shneiderman, Ben. "The Eyes Have It: A Task by Data Type Taxonomy for Information Visualizations." *IEEE Symposium on Visual Languages*, 1996.

Focus plus Context

Although we should have a clear path that structures our analysis (when we want it to be structured), that doesn't mean that we need multiple charts or an interactive chart. Often, a single chart is all we need. **Figure 6.2** shows how much ahead of most other European countries the Nordic countries are when comparing share of energy from renewable sources. Albeit oversimplified, this is an example of focus plus context, in which a clear distinction is made between an entity that gets the focus of our attention and the remaining entities that provide context. Of course, a context entity may become a focus entity if we choose to switch.

NORDIC COUNTRIES AHEAD IN SHARE OF
ENERGY FROM RENEWABLE SOURCES

Download the
original chart

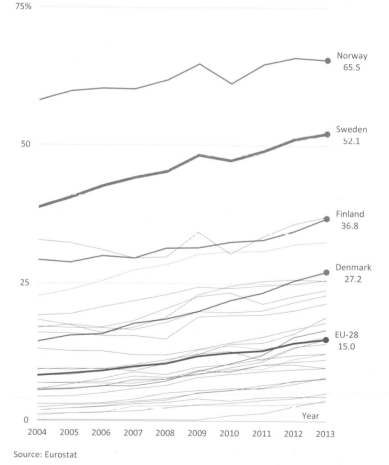

Source: Eurostat

Figure 6.2 Focus plus context.

The focus-plus-context approach not only nicely complements Shneiderman's mantra but also solves a recurring problem: the spaghetti chart. We have a reasonable concept of "spaghetti chart" (it's useful to display flows), but we often use it in a derisive manner when referring to some charts (especially line charts) where the series are so intertwined that you can read nothing from them. If you have numerous series and try to color-code them all, that's what you'll get. Figure 6.2 was a serious candidate for becoming a spaghetti chart, but that was avoided thanks to the focus-plus-context approach.

Asking Questions

The most pragmatic way of beginning the data visualization process is with a question, and then making a chart that answers that question. Sounds easy enough, doesn't it? But then try asking, "Why are our sales falling?" in a meeting. Before getting to the answers, other people at the meeting might ask you to clarify what you mean by "our," "sales," and "falling."

Ask people working in market research to tell you their horror stories about clients who come up with their own questions. It's terrifying, I assure you. Any question is subject to interpretation, whose variation should be minimized by a simple, clear, and accurate formulation. The way you interrogate the data is far more similar to the way you design a question for a survey than the way you ask a friend a question. That's why I advise you to browse the section on questionnaire design in a good market research handbook. You'll find many interesting tips. Not everything will be relevant to data visualization, but it'll help you understand charts as visual answers and it'll help you avoid many common pitfalls.

Begin with generic questions and gradually look for more detail, as in Shneiderman's mantra. Don't worry if your initial questions seem too obvious. You can dispose of some of them, but you'll need others to establish a common knowledge base with your audience. The data itself will suggest more questions, and comparing the new ones with the initial ones will be interesting (and enlightening).

The questions we ask tell a lot about us: what we know, what we don't know, and even what we think we know (which may be prejudices or misconceptions). The questions will also first gravitate toward descriptive, single-variable analysis before asking about relationships between variables, whose nature and relevancy is not clear at this stage.

A Classification of Questions

Certain charts are better suited to answer certain questions than others, but you should take this relationship as a broad principle. Subtle changes in the question and in the chart design can impact the results. Having a clear goal in mind and knowing what type of visualization could be more effective can help us reduce the range of options of chart types and design choices.

When defining a question, you should first make sure it can be answered by quantitative analysis. You should avoid questions like "What's the meaning of life?" or "Does he/she love me?" Answerable questions usually fall into one of these categories:

Order. Questions that emphasize comparison and sorting of individual points: Is my product selling more or less than the leading competitor?

Composition. Questions that assess the weight of each value in the whole, represented by absolute or relative values: What's my current market share?

Distribution. Questions about the location of data points along an axis: What's my customer's age profile (that is, how are customers distributed by age)?

Evolution. Questions that emphasize change over time: Is my product gaining market share?

Relationship. Questions that ask for relationships between two or more variables: Are marketing events influencing sales?

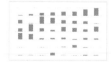
Profiling. Questions that help define a profile: What are the characteristics of my clients in New York and California?

Exceptions. Questions that search for data points outside a normal range: What was the daily product defect rate in the last month?

Order, composition, and distribution questions are typical of an early stage in the analysis. Evolution and, especially, relationship and profiling suggest a search for shapes in the data that already have implicit prior knowledge. In the next chapter, we'll see how these categories are the basis for the classification of charts and how they intersect with the type of task at hand.

One of the advantages of categorizing questions is that we become more aware of the multiple points of view that we can have on the data. Some of the answers to these questions will arouse curiosity and make you want to know more details, like an in-depth exploration of the market share in the age group of 25–34 years of our model X1 on the West Coast, for example. The average market share in the total population may hide significant variations by age group or at a regional level, so it's useful to deepen the analysis and detail the differences to a reference value. This in-depth analysis seeks meaningful variations within each of the perspectives.

If you want even more questions, imagine presenting the results and asking for feedback from a product manager, salesperson, or consultant. Choose real people, and, if possible, choose the challenging, difficult-to-please type.

You can also simply add, remove, or change something in the questions: What happens if you add a spatial dimension (such as a continent, nation, state, or region)? How about adding a time dimension? What if you use other metrics and other ratios? How about integrating other context variables (such as macroeconomic variables)?

Selecting and Collecting the Data

When you start analyzing the data, you'll discover how relevant your first questions are. You'll discover the questions you missed and the new questions they force you to ask. Finding new and more complex questions is a clear sign that you're learning and better understanding reality.

Let's return to the classical distinction between primary data (the data we collect specifically to answer our questions) and secondary data (the data collected for other purposes and which we can use, such as official statistics). If you want to know what a customer thinks of your product compared to a competitor's product, or how he would respond to a new offer, it's very likely that the data don't exist. You need a market research study.

However, if you want to estimate the size of the market based on some demographic indicators, it's likely that you'll be able to get that data through an official statistics office. When choosing secondary data, consider the obvious fact that the data was not collected with your needs in mind. Still, the primary and secondary data can be combined (quantifying the universe with primary data and using it to design a sample, for example).

The chapter on data preparation should have also prepared you for a few surprises you'll encounter when you start collecting the data. Take Eurostat, the European statistical office that coordinates and compiles statistics from each country within the European Union. After browsing the Eurostat site for a few minutes, you'll find data collected in some countries but not in others, differences in the length of time series for the same variable, and several non-simultaneous breaks in time series.

All this affects the way we analyze the data and communicate our findings. Missing data will cripple some analyses. Short time series or multiple breaks in series may prevent analyzing change over time, thus excluding line charts. Or the relationship between two variables may prove weaker than expected, changing the analysis and excluding scatter plots.

When using secondary data, you need to assess its quality and usefulness (again, a good desk research handbook can help you). Here are a few questions you should ask:

- Is it a reliable source?
- Is there a hidden agenda behind its publication?
- Can you use the concepts? For example, if you want to study "food consumption," is it OK to use the USDA's "food availability" data instead? They say it's a good proxy to actual food consumption for which there is no data.

Go to the web page

- How was the data collected? Via phone or Internet survey? Collected by legal obligations?
- Is it a sample, like in a survey, or is it data from the whole population, like in a census? (If it's a sample, you must ensure that your audience realizes that results will fluctuate within a statistical error margin.)
- When was the data collected? Data from population censuses show heavy trends that are slow to change, and the main results can be used for years with some confidence, whereas political polling during an election campaign is valid for only a few days.
- If the data represent a time series, are there any breaks?

Searching for Patterns

In old cartoon movies, a simple kick to the ground would trigger a gushing oil geyser. Real oil exploration is, of course, more complex and literally deeper. When we simply kick our data (that is, when we carelessly make a chart without thinking much about it), we may actually find some significant insights.

This does not mean that our deeper drilling is over—quite the contrary. What it really means is that if we can find some patterns effortlessly (perhaps the patterns we were expecting to find), it's likely that we'll find even more patterns as well as patterns that are more interesting. So those surface insights may be a sign of a deeper structure that we should investigate.

The opposite is also true. If all we get is a seemingly random variation, maybe we should take a closer look or change our vantage point. Reality tends to include a layer of randomness over a layer of regularity, where the thickness of each one depends on the reality itself and the way we look at it. This effort to bring out what the data has to say is well summarized by Jacques Bertin: "It is the internal mobility of the image that characterizes modern charts. A chart is no longer drawn once and forever; it is built and rebuilt (manipulated) until all the relationships that are hidden in it have been observed."[2]

Or we can follow Ronald Coase and put it ironically: "If you torture the data long enough, it will confess to anything."[3] As long as you don't lie or attempt to mislead, this is probably the one place in real life where you *should* inflict as much pain as possible, and then decide whether the confessions are useful and true to the data.

In a spreadsheet, the first kick to the data may take the form of sorting and conditional formatting, as exemplified by the graphical table in **Figure 6.3**. We can read this table top to bottom and find the usual split between Western and Eastern Europe. We can also read it from top left to bottom right and find that the tendency to improve energy intensity is clear in virtually all countries during more than a decade.

Exploring new data visually is like waking up in a place we do not know. Of the many new things that surround us, some fit with ease with our expectations, but others require a greater effort to understand, especially when they contradict our expectations.

---

2   Bertin, J. *Graphics and Graphic Information-Processing*. Berlin; New York: de Gruyter, 1981.

3   Coase, Ronald H. *Essays on Economics and Economists*. Chicago: University of Chicago Press, 1995.

ENERGY INTENSITY OF THE ECONOMY
Gross inland consumption of energy divided by GDP (kg of oil equivalent per 1000 EUR)

Download the
original chart

Geo / Time	2002	2003	2004	2005	2006	2007	2008	2009	2010	2011	2012	2013
EU (28 countries)	168	169	167	164	159	152	151	149	152	144	143	142
Ireland	107	100	99	94	91	88	89	90	93	83	83	82
Denmark	101	105	100	94	98	94	91	93	97	89	86	87
United Kingdom	135	132	129	125	120	112	111	111	112	103	106	103
Norway	112	119	112	111	110	109	127	125	135	111	114	126
Italy	126	131	130	131	126	123	122	121	123	121	120	117
Austria	133	139	139	140	136	129	128	126	132	125	124	124
Germany	157	156	156	154	153	140	140	139	140	129	129	131
Luxembourg	148	154	164	159	149	137	138	138	142	137	134	128
Spain	158	159	161	159	153	149	144	137	137	135	137	129
France	164	165	163	161	155	150	151	149	151	143	143	143
Sweden	190	180	179	171	159	154	154	150	157	149	148	144
Netherlands	159	163	162	159	150	150	149	150	158	145	149	150
Portugal	175	172	175	178	167	163	159	161	153	151	148	151
Greece	173	168	163	163	155	150	151	150	148	154	165	151
Malta	174	190	196	197	181	184	177	164	167	164	171	144
Cyprus	200	212	191	187	186	185	188	186	179	175	168	154
Belgium	197	204	199	195	186	178	183	181	191	177	167	173
Finland	244	253	244	219	229	216	207	213	226	212	208	206
Croatia	261	265	255	247	236	235	224	231	232	232	226	220
Slovenia	267	263	259	255	241	226	231	228	231	231	228	226
Turkey	240	239	226	218	225	231	227	238	233			
Hungary	330	324	307	311	298	291	286	290	294	282	269	257
Lithuania	529	499	475	415	378	375	363	390	307	299	292	266
Poland	409	408	387	377	373	349	336	319	327	314	298	295
Latvia	411	405	382	355	332	310	306	357	371	334	329	311
Slovakia	575	547	513	494	453	388	376	362	369	349	329	337
Czech Republic	472	476	466	431	414	391	371	364	374	354	356	354
Romania	573	568	516	491	471	442	410	387	395	394	379	335
Montenegro				598	605	549	553	463	522	488	474	
FYR Macedonia	590	626	588	572	566	554	523	494	494	522	503	454
Estonia	559	571	551	502	445	465	460	491	546	505	478	513
Bulgaria	963	942	866	849	824	760	712	661	669	706	670	611
Serbia	918	933	919	774	796	746	727	686	696	712	649	653

Low intensity	Medium intensity	High intensity

Data source: Eurostat

Figure 6.3 Using conditional formatting to kick the data.

Figure 6.4 offers another opportunity to kick the data. This chart displays the estimated and projected U.S. population between 1950 and 2100. Population projections like this are based on scenarios that take into account statistics on mortality rate, migration, fertility, and so on. The "medium variant" is the most likely projection.

Download the
original chart

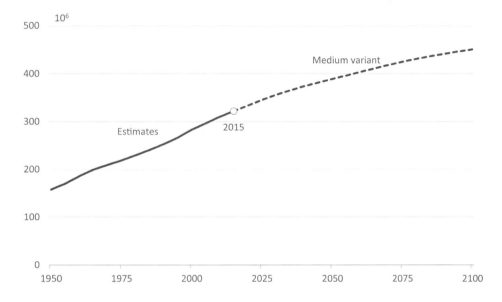

ESTIMATES AND PROJECTIONS FOR THE U.S. POPULATION

Source: United Nations Population Division, 2015 Projections

Figure 6.4 A boring line chart.

Boring, right? There is nothing very new and interesting here. Instead of absolute values, some well-known ratios in population studies such as dependency ratios may prove more useful. Let me define them first:

- **Young dependency ratio.** The ratio between the young population (0–14 years old) and the adult population (15–64 years old).

- **Old dependency ratio.** The ratio between the old population (65+ years old) and the adult population (15–64 years old).

- **Total dependency ratio.** A simple arithmetic sum of young and old dependency ratios.

The analysis of dependency ratios is important because it tells us about the burden placed on the adult (working) population to support social security, health, or public education. The higher the ratio, the heavier the burden.

If we plot these dependency ratios, the chart becomes much more interesting (**Figure 6.5**). See the hump in the total dependency ratio to the left? It's very similar to the one found in the young dependency ratio. If you guessed that this hump represents the baby boomers, you're correct. And if you guessed that they'll show up again 65 years later in the old dependency ratio, you're right again.

ESTIMATES AND PROJECTIONS FOR DEPENDENCY RATIOS FOR THE U.S. POPULATION

Download the
original chart

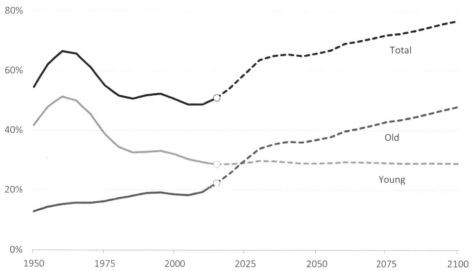

Source: United Nations Population Division, 2015 Projections

Figure 6.5 A more interesting line chart.

Now, you may not have noticed, but the flat young dependency ratio is very interesting. It is actually the key to the projection model.

To make it more obvious, let's do something a little different and plot young dependency against old dependency, and, instead of a single variant, let's also plot the low variant (lower fertility rate) and high variant (higher fertility rate).

Now, in **Figure 6.6**, it's clear that after the baby boom ended, the U.S. population started getting older. At first, the proportion of young relative to the adult population kept shrinking, while the old population remained relatively stable. Then, suddenly the baby boomers began entering retirement age and the trend bent up and slightly to the left, meaning that the population is now getting old mainly because there are more elderly people but also because the proportion of young is also reducing.

Figure 6.6 Making projection models more explicit.

Download the
original chart

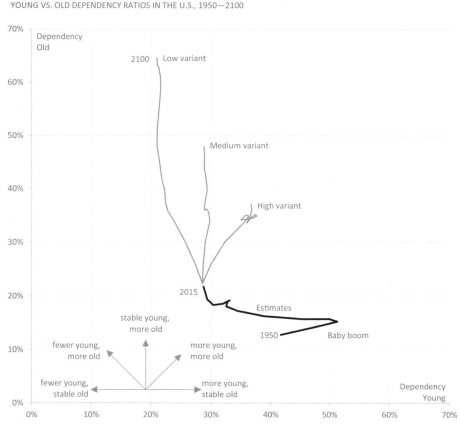

YOUNG VS. OLD DEPENDENCY RATIOS IN THE U.S., 1950—2100

Source: United Nations Population Division, 2015 Estimates and Projections

In a few years' time, these dependency ratios will probably be found between the low and the high variants. The low variant tells us that the proportion of young will keep diminishing, albeit slowly, while the proportion of elderly skyrockets. If the fertility rate remains stable at current levels, so will the young dependency ratio.

The old dependency ratio will keep climbing, but at a slower rate, according to the medium variant. The high variant shows that, in the unlikely event of Americans rediscovering the pleasures of parenthood, the old dependency ratio would still grow but at a much slower rate, while the young dependency ratio would invert the trend until both ratios plateau at around 35 percent.

The three charts are important. While the first one may look too obvious and boring, it frames the discussion (unlike in some European countries, the U.S. population is still growing). When we want to go beyond this first kick, we can follow a more data-centered path, such as calculating ratios (Figure 6.5), or a more visualization-centered path, such as using other chart types (Figure 6.6). Both paths are worth exploring.

Setting Priorities

The project example at the end of this chapter discusses the subject of live births from an unusual perspective. Perspective guides our research, defines priorities when retrieving and analyzing the data, and emphasizes certain aspects in the data while devaluing others. We should allow our perspective to float and adapt to the knowledge we have acquired until a final evaluation of priorities and relevance takes place.

Grouping charts according to a theme and in sequence with the message and putting them all on the same sheet or slide helps you find the thread of the message (even if the charts are separated again later).

Making multiple individual charts is like jotting down unstructured thoughts on pieces of paper. At some point, you will start to repeat some thoughts and forget others. Joining these charts in sequence and trying to form a coherent sentence from their titles will help you focus on your priorities. **Resist the temptation to make charts that try to respond to too many questions.** Be aware also that, by making something interesting, you're not actually hiding or demoting what is relevant.

You know that you should not use pseudo-3D effects on your charts, but this doesn't mean that they have to be entirely flat. Not all objects on a chart have the same importance, and its design should reflect that. So how do we make charts, as Tufte says, "to escape flatland"?[4] We already have an answer to this question: by apply-

---

4 Tufte, Edward. *Envisioning Information*. Cheshire, CT: Graphics Press, 1990. I'm using the expression in a different context. While Tufte focuses on data of a multivariate nature, I'm using it to show how design can define multiple reading levels.

ing editorial judgment on data relevancy and by making sure the design follows along—taking advantage of salience in pre-attentive processing, for example.

Several charts in this book can exemplify this. Take Figure 6.2: It's easy to detect a "primary" level (Sweden), a "relevant others" level (other Nordic countries), and an "everyone else" level (all other countries). You can apply this method to countries, products, or categories:

- **Primary.** The entity I'm most interested in. It requires my permanent attention.

- **Significant others.** My major competitors, countries I use as a reference, or complementary categories.

- **Everyone else.** You may consider leaving all other series visible if they don't add too much overhead (forcing you to enlarge the chart, for example). These series should be muted, allowing the reader to see the context without adding background noise.

Reporting Results

The previous stages will leave a trail of a multitude of charts, spreadsheets, and data files. We certainly learned a lot along the way. Now it's time to craft a message that is consistent, genuine, and preferably interesting for our audience.

Traditionally, some chart types, such as pie charts, are seen as more communication-oriented, while others, like scatter plots, are more suitable for data analysis and exploration. You'll need to simplify and remove detail to make the underlying structure more apparent, but **associating a certain chart type with communication or exploration is not helpful, unless you're actively seeking to dumb down your message**. This has relevant implications.

Clarification

The first of these implications is the further clarification of what we have learned, particularly as to how the various pieces fit together: What are the key points and how do they relate to each other? What are the details that facilitate the understanding of the whole? What details belong in the background and what should be emphasized?

The Human Dimension

Clarification can also provide a human perspective of the scale we're using. For example, especially after the financial crisis of 2008, we began to trivialize large sums of money without actually having any real awareness of what these values meant. What does 18 trillion dollars of U.S. public debt mean? It means around $56,000 per citizen, regardless of age. The real median household annual income in the U.S. was very close to that in 2014, at around $54,000. How much of that is my family paying?

See the
PDF report

There are many ways of adding a human dimension to statistics, all of which compare some abstraction to a concrete fact people are familiar with. Data don't have to be abstract just because they happen to be huge: The Dollar Street project, by the Gapminder Foundation, shows how income levels translate into the kinds of homes people live in. Hopefully, with familiarity come emotions, and emotions stimulate interest.

Go to the
web page

Figure 6.7 Gapminder's first version of Dollar Street.

The Design

You can make dozens, even hundreds, of charts during the exploration stages. Many you'll immediately delete because they don't make sense, are irrelevant, or are redundant. Some will be useful to learn more about the data. You'll add, remove, or split series, and play with scales. They're all for your personal consumption, so you won't care much about their format.

Then there are the charts that you'll actually use in your communication. Because things are so familiar and obvious to you now, it's easy to overlook the need to make everything very explicit, from the overall message to the formatting options and added value of each chart. This is a dangerous moment. It's the moment when you evaluate how you'll attract your audience's attention and how much effort you'll need to apply. Depending on your audience, one of these hooks should work:

- **WITFM (What's In There For Me)**. The data, or part of it, is about "me" (the audience) or about things I'm deeply interested in: my product, my country, my stock options.

- **The data have it all**. There is something so compelling about the data that not much effort is needed. Remember the skyrocketing unemployment in Greece? That's a good example.

- **Reason and emotion.** You capture the audience's attention with an emotional hook, but your visuals remain very clean and rational. You'll find an example in Figure 14.5 in Chapter 14.

- **Reason is the only reason.** People will naturally pay attention because their job or their task compels them to do so. You reward them by making the charts as effective as possible.

- **Clown nose.** Perhaps you don't have much to say, but vivid colors and moving parts will make people look.

We'll discuss design in more detail in Chapter 14.

Project: Monthly Births

In most developed countries, a larger proportion of elderly people combined with fewer births creates a scenario defined by many as a demographic time bomb. In some cases, it's already increasing social security and health costs.

For this project, we'll look at a tiny section of the whole issue: *how the proportion of monthly births changed over time.*

In Western societies, the number of births has fallen dramatically since the 1960s. The widespread access to contraceptives (the pill) has given couples more family planning ability and freedom to choose when they want to have children, while the role of women has also changed on many levels (including sexuality and the labor market).

Beyond the drop in birth rate, is this family planning capability also reflected in the monthly distribution of births during the year, which changed from a "natural" distribution to a planned distribution? This becomes our original question, from which it's easy to derive other questions, such as whether regional patterns exist or whether these patterns have evolved in the same way over time.

Defining the Problem

Let's define the scope of the project, starting with the timeframe we plan to study. These are long-term trends that need many years to become visible in the data. If we want to select a date that, more than any other, symbolizes the changes in sexuality in Western societies, then 1967 is the perfect starting point; it was the "Summer of Love," and just a few months earlier, on April 7, the pill was on the cover of *Time* magazine.

Statistical production varies from country to country, so we shouldn't be overly optimistic about obtaining data for the most recent years for all countries. With this in mind, 2012 seems to be a reasonable target as the ending point of our time series. Even if we do find meaningful trends, they will not be synchronous across all countries. Forty-five years' worth of monthly data may give us some legroom to spot them.

Should we include all countries, or should we impose a minimum monthly births threshold to reduce the risks of random variation? We should probably wait and see. We don't really know the data yet, so we shouldn't assume that variation is high in small countries, and we may be able to minimize it with a simple smoothing technique, such as a 3-year moving average.

Collecting the Data

What's the most effective way of collecting the data? Visiting each and every nation's statistical office's website doesn't seem the best resource allocation strategy. The nature of the data leads us to believe there must be international aggregators, so finding those should be our starting point.

After some quick research, we do find two likely candidates: the United Nations and Eurostat. Apparently selecting the UN is a no-brainer, since it publishes data for the entire world rather than only for European countries as Eurostat does.

Comparing a few UN and Eurostat live birth values picked randomly shows that their values are identical, although the time series in the Eurostat is slightly longer (it starts earlier and has more recent data). Keep in mind this isn't a good enough reason to limit our project to Europe, however, since it would be interesting to compare more heterogeneous realities.

Assessing Data Availability

The values may be identical, but what about missing values? Are there any? Instead of browsing the tables and comparing them, this is a good time to start visualizing the data. Not the values themselves, but rather a test to measure data quality. Specifically, we want to know how many months include data values, per country and per year. If there are fewer than 12 for any country and any year, then values are missing. We can accept some years with one or two missing months, but as a starting point, we can't accept more than six missing values.

The table in **Figure 6.8** shows the results after combining both sources. It is a pivot table where we applied conditional formatting according to the rules above. Blue means a complete year, orange contains between one and five missing values, and gray contain six or more missing values. No data was reported at all for the remaining cases. Each row represents a country, and each column represents a year. The countries are ordered by the number of available months.

The table is too large to display row and column headers, but we don't need them to see that the picture is not pretty. It's clear that most countries don't have enough data, and we can spot gaps even in countries that collect the data in a consistent and sustained way. Setting a timeframe between 1967 and 2012 turns out to be unrealistic. Only since 1973 does this collection of data become more systematic, following a United Nations recommendation (I verified that after noticing that several countries started to make the data available in that year).

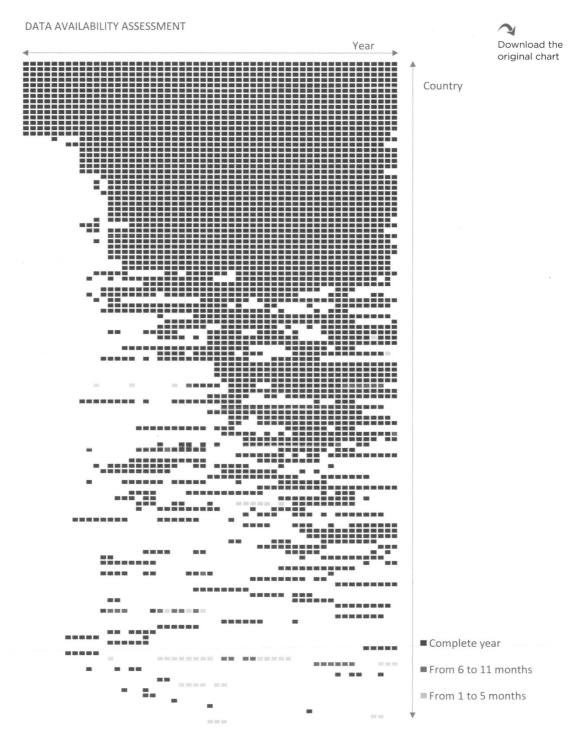

Figure 6.8 Visualization for meta-analysis: assessing data availability.

Assessing Data Quality

When we start analyzing the data, a new surprise awaits us: The data quality is lower than expected. Here are a few examples and how I dealt with them:

- **Inconsistent data between Eurostat and the national statistical offices.** For example, there are 12,789 births in unknown months in Italy in 2003, according to Eurostat. Istat, the Italian statistics office, confirmed this by email, but the data on their own website contains no births in unknown months. I used the data from Istat.

- **Missing months.** Most of the time, I used linear interpolation to fill in missing data.[5] I didn't apply the same rationale in all cases. Rather, I tried to come up with the least bad solution in each case.

- **Missing years in the U.S. data.** I found provisional data in the Centers for Disease Control (CDC) website in PDF files. I used Tabula software for conversion, and it worked fairly well.

- **Wrongly reported data for New Zealand.** Until 1990, the data for December are highly suspicious. I tried to correct for it, but, judging by the chart, I don't think I succeeded.

I'll spare you the details, but this example is getting more realistic than I expected. Perhaps a bit too realistic and too much of a cautionary tale of the many unforeseen issues impacting project costs and deadlines. **After all the cleansing and filtering processes, only 36 countries remain.**

Adjusting the Data

Our goal is to evaluate whether the proportion of live births in each month changed over time, so we're not using absolute values but rather percentages. By default, each month accounts for 8.33 percent of all births (100 percent divided by 12), so we need to compare the actual proportion to this reference value. The problem is that there are four reference values, one for each possible month length (28, 29, 30, and 31 days), which makes analysis pretty confusing. We can simplify it by defining a standard month length and adjust the data accordingly, and that's what I've done.

---

5 Linear interpolation allows you to estimate missing values based on neighboring values.

Exploring the Data

Since we've got a nice, long time series, it's hard to fight the urge to draw a line chart. After all, that's what line charts are for, right? **Figure 6.9** displays the line chart we get when plotting the entire time series for Sweden. There's clearly a cyclic pattern, and something is changing, since the cycle is different between the 1960s and the last decade. I think we need to dig a little deeper.

PROPORTION OF MONTHLY BIRTHS IN SWEDEN

Download the
original chart

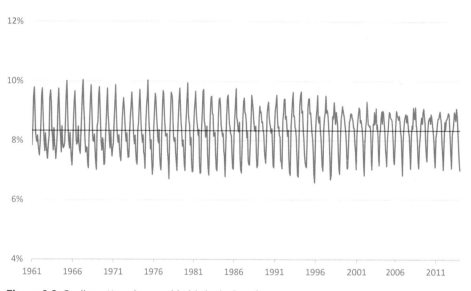

Figure 6.9 Cyclic pattern in monthly births in Sweden.

Let's try something else. In **Figure 6.10**, each line encodes a year. Now it's clear that there are many more live births in spring than in the colder months. It's also obvious that the weight of each month changes from year to year. Unfortunately, we can't say that this is a random variation or a trend. There are so many years that trying to find something by color-coding them would be futile.

PROPORTION OF MONTHLY BIRTHS IN SWEDEN

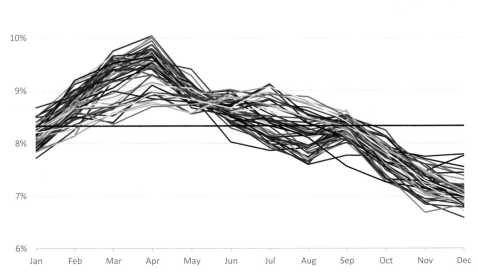

Figure 6.10 The proportion of each month in the number of live births.

These are interesting insights that can help us better understand the data, but this is not exactly what we're looking for because we aren't paying attention to the problem. We are applying an autopilot solution that says we should use a line chart to display a time series. That's not completely wrong, but **we keep comparing a month with the adjacent months, while our actual goal is to check whether the proportion of births in each month changes over time and if that change is meaningful**. We already know they do, but this approach is not telling us how.

Embracing Seasonality

The first chart did reveal the cyclic pattern. A cyclic pattern in monthly data usually means that the data fluctuate seasonally. What we really need to do isn't to compare January to February, but rather to compare all the months of January over the years. This is what the original problem asks us to do, and the seasonality we found adds another reason to do it.

Figure 6.11 shows a fragment of the complete chart presented in Figure 6.12 for Sweden. I decided to copy the idea of the horizon chart and fold the *y* axis, displaying negative values up, but in red.

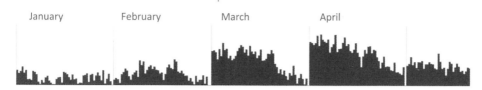

Figure 6.11 A declining pattern in Sweden.

As you can see, January is mostly composed of little red bars, meaning that the proportion of births in this month is a bit lower than the reference line (8.33%). February, on the other hand, is mostly blue and the bars are higher, which means that in many years there are more births in February than the reference.

March is even stronger, but now we can see something very interesting: At some point, March's weight starts trending down. This is even clearer in April. Is this an isolated case? Maybe we should check the entire chart in **Figure 6.12**. I kept all the available data for the selected countries. Therefore, the period spans from 1961 to 2014, even though we don't have data for the entire range in all countries.

I'll leave it to you to study the chart, as I think it deserves a few minutes of your attention. Here are a few highlights:

- **Seasonality is real.** There are more births in spring and summer than in fall and winter, although in the Mediterranean countries the season starts and ends later.

- **Geography matters.** Neighboring countries display a similar behavior: Nordic countries; Mediterranean countries; Germany, Switzerland, and Austria; France, the Netherlands, and Belgium.

- **Things are changing.** There is a clear reduction of births between October and January, but in March more babies are born again. However, the Nordic countries are having more babies in the summer months. In other countries, September is becoming a popular month to have them, and even the winter months no longer seem so negative.

Figure 6.12 The full picture: monthly proportions of live births in 36 countries.

PROPORTION OF LIVE BIRTHS IN EACH MONTH: VARIATION TO THE REFERENCE VALUE (8.33%)
From 1961 to 2014

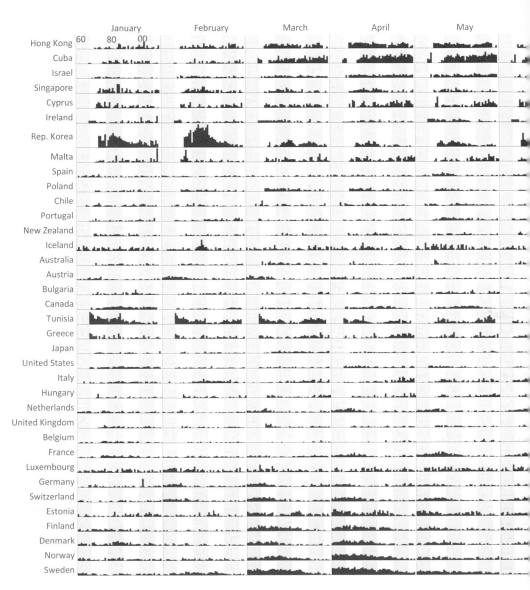

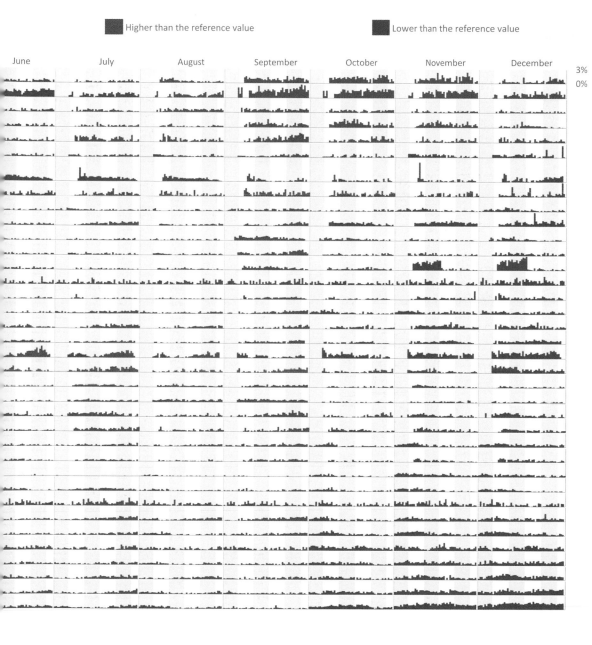

This is the right chart format to answer our question. Its overall design shows that the problem was correctly understood, and it provides a precise and detailed answer. Whether we need this much detail is something that we can determine afterwards, but a lot of detail puts you in data exploration mode. You may want to stay there for a while, trying to understand whatever captures your attention.

The chart also reinforces some doubts about data quality. There are several outliers that are hard to justify, and others, such as the data for November and December in New Zealand, are hard to understand. And as I had been unable to determine why there are so many live births in January and February in the Republic of Korea, I had to enlarge the chart and change the scale (it remains comparable with the other charts, though).

Download the
original chart

LIVE BIRTHS IN THE EUROPEAN UNION ARE MOVING FROM SPRING TO SUMMER

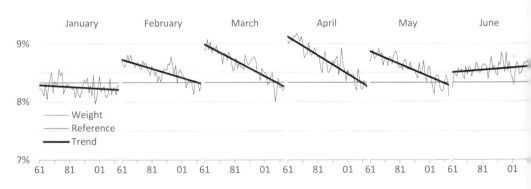

Figure 6.13 Answering the question: What are the changes in the proportion of live births in the European Union?

Communicating Our Findings

It wouldn't be easy to choose a different format as compact as the one in **Figure 6.10** to amalgamate all the data. The chart does create a rich display, full of detail, and encourages the reader to spend some time studying it.

However, if I were going to share it, I might need to make some changes. And, more important, our questions remain unanswered: Is the proportion of births changing globally? If so, in what direction? After observing the chart, we can safely say they are indeed changing. But are changes in one country reinforcing or canceling out the changes in other countries?

The chart in **Figure 6.13** summarizes the data at a higher level, answering our question for Europe (the group of countries for which we have more data). The design makes it simple to read, and the metric is just the proportions of live births, instead of a more complex one, such as the variation to a reference value.

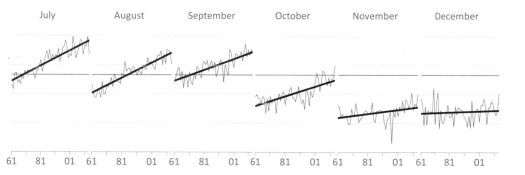

The reference line makes it clear which months are above and below, and there is an interesting conversation between them and the trend lines. Now we can answer the question: We can confirm that the spring months are trending down in favor of the summer months, while the winter months remain at the same level. We can use the same format to drill down, comparing the profiles we found, such as comparing the Nordic countries to the Mediterranean countries.

Takeaways

- Structuring your data visualization process will make it more efficient and will yield higher returns. However, this doesn't mean that you should always follow a predefined path.

- Sometimes, the data themselves will force you to consider further analysis, but looking at known data from a different perspective can reveal unsuspected insights.

- The visual information-seeking mantra and focus plus context can help you find a starting point and your overall approach to the data.

- Translate the problem you're trying to solve into a few questions.

- The best questions deal with order, composition, distribution, evolution, relationships, profiling, and exceptions in the data.

- These questions must be very specific and clear. Find tips on how to write questions in a market research handbook.

- Come up with questions that allow the audience to understand the broader context, while using other questions to add detail.

- Get the data to answer these questions and be prepared to go back and let your curiosity work to formulate a few more questions.

- When selecting data sources, make sure the data meet your multiple needs (Can you trust the data? Are concepts and methodologies aligned with your project?).

- Make sure your charts are answering the real questions, not apparently similar ones.

- *Simplify to clarify.* You'll need simplification as much as your audience will.

7

HOW TO CHOOSE A CHART

We've already met many of the actors of our visual theater. Now it's time to introduce them more formally.

In Chapter 1, we defined "chart type" as a set of standardized transformations applied to the data points in the "proto-chart." We have complete freedom in the way we use the data points. Line segments connect points to make a line chart; rectangles connect points to the axis to make a bar chart. Whatever the result of these changes, there is a difference between *seeing* the chart and *interpreting* it. The audience may not always be able (or have the interest) to decode a new chart type and may prefer a familiar one.

We also saw in Chapter 1 that there can be significant differences in the effectiveness of two charts. The effectiveness of a chart type is relative and determined by its suitability to the specific situation: the task, the message, the audience's profile, the medium, and the context.

Even if we consider every single chart within the Excel chart library as a unique chart type (which we shouldn't), that only scratches the surface of the myriad chart types available today.[1] If you're forced to choose from a vast number of options without a clue as to how to group or filter them, this leads to paralysis. Barry Schwartz shows this in his book *The Paradox of Choice*.[2]

The best way to avoid a choice such as this is to have a clear understanding of your goals and how to achieve them using data visualization. If your inner wizard is not yet ready, you might try an application wizard, although it will never understand the specifics that make your project different from every other project.

A third option (the one we'll be discussing in this chapter) is to classify the charts into categories. Consider this as only a rough starting point, though, because even subtle design options can make a chart jump from one category to another. For example, when you add a variation band to a line chart, it probably means that you're less interested in a trend than in spotting outliers, effectively moving the line chart to a different category. There's no unambiguous relationship between charts and tasks, and more generally, a particular chart type does not have a direct relationship with any single task.

Look again at the Excel charts library (**Figure 7.1**). Each category is broken down into some subtypes, but unfortunately the multiplicity of choices is more illusory than real. There are actually fewer chart types here than you may think at first. You might notice that the obnoxious cones and pyramids available in previous versions of Excel are nowhere to be found. It's not that Microsoft came to its senses and removed them; it just demoted them to column options. If you look closely, you'll notice that Microsoft could have applied the same reasoning to several of the other chart subtypes.

---

1   If you want to know how much a myriad is, Robert L. Harris's *Information Graphics: A Comprehensive Illustrated Reference*, New York: Oxford University Press, 2000, contains more than 850 entries and nearly 4000 illustrations, according to Amazon. Even if it misses a few of the new chart types, it's still a great starting point.

2   Schwartz, Barry. *The Paradox of Choice*. New York: Harper Perennial, 2005.

EXCEL 2016 CHART LIBRARY

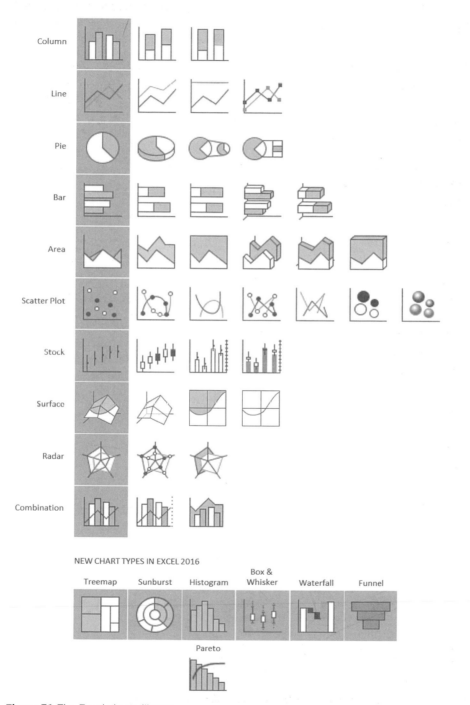

Figure 7.1 The Excel charts library.

In a book intended for spreadsheet users, it's tempting to accept this classification as based on visual characteristics. You can't deny that it is an objective classification, just like grouping people by the color of their eyes. But the question is, how useful are these classifications? Can you infer computer skills from someone's eye color? Can you infer a chart's adequacy for a task based only on visual characteristics?

Also, if you go beyond the basics, you'll soon find yourself making what Excel calls "combo charts," which might include bars, areas, and lines (see "Combination" in Figure 7.1). If most of your charts are combination charts, what's the point of having this classification in the first place?

No matter how objective its criteria seem to be, any classification will start to crack at some point. If we use more subjective criteria, such as task type, the first thing we have to accept is that each of the main chart types can belong to more than one category. For example, a connected scatter plot can be grouped either with scatter plots (both display relationships) or line charts (both display patterns of change over time).

Even though chart classifications are not as arbitrary as constellations, they're not neutral. They induce us to think on their own terms. A classification like the one in Excel, which emphasizes visual characteristics, leads us to a more decorative approach to data visualization. On the other hand, **when we use a classification based on task adequacy, it's easier to forget about useless visual effects and focus on the options that make the chart more effective.**

While the connection between chart effectiveness and task type is clear, you can't forget that there are other criteria influencing your choice. In this chapter, we'll devote some attention to two criteria: the profile of the audience and the form of distribution.

Task-Based Chart Classification

I don't think we'll start speaking of "proportion charts" instead of "pie charts" or "relationship charts" instead of "scatter plots" any time soon, but finding a better balance between form-based naming and function-based naming would be an undeniable improvement. We could start by making sure that the task type and chart type always appear together in the same sentence—the former justifying the latter.

Figure 7.2 (on the following page) proposes a task-centered classification. The key to grouping tasks is to consider that a task makes a question operational to some extent. So it makes sense that we share the same categories discussed in the previous chapter: order, composition, distribution, trend, relationship, profiling, and alerts/exceptions. These categories can be further grouped into point comparison tasks and data reduction tasks as major categories, and data-driven annotations as a supporting category.

The first row displays the most commonly used chart in each category. From the second row on, charts were selected based on their potential to answer the question. As noted above, a chart may appear in more than one category.

People often explore and come up with new chart types. I did so myself when I created the "bamboo chart" (Figure 3.8). Trying to make this list exhaustive by listing most chart types by category would be impossible, so the charts are included as a representative sample of concepts in each category. There is a practical limit to the examples given: the ability to make the chart in Excel. If you can't make it, or the cost does not justify it, the chart is not included. The following chapters are structured around this group of chart types.

This last category deserves further explanation. Check the red circles below. They represent the days I ate chocolate in March.

● ●

In this case, we're visualizing *on/off* states, but if I shouldn't eat chocolate, the *on* state can be regarded as an exception. We should call this visualization an "outlier detection chart." As such, it doesn't fit into the major categories of point comparison or data reduction tasks. At the same time, we can see outlier detection as a special case of annotation, driven by some kind of underlying data. When you add these data-driven annotations to a chart, they can take the shape of dots, variation bands, or contextual bands (such as when you have a gray band marking a recession period).

Let's call these data-driven annotations a supporting category, cutting across the other categories but also using their own graphical devices.

A CLASSIFICATION OF CHART TYPES

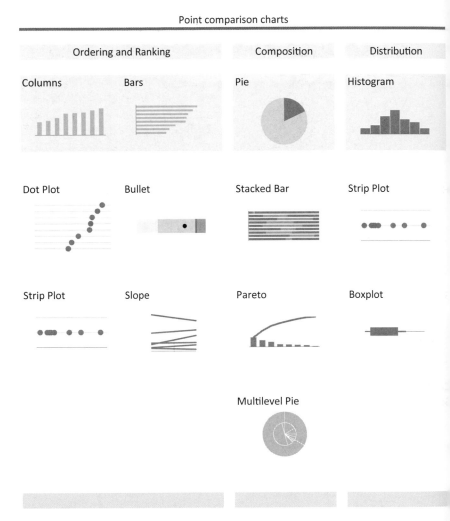

Figure 7.2 A new task-based classification of chart types.

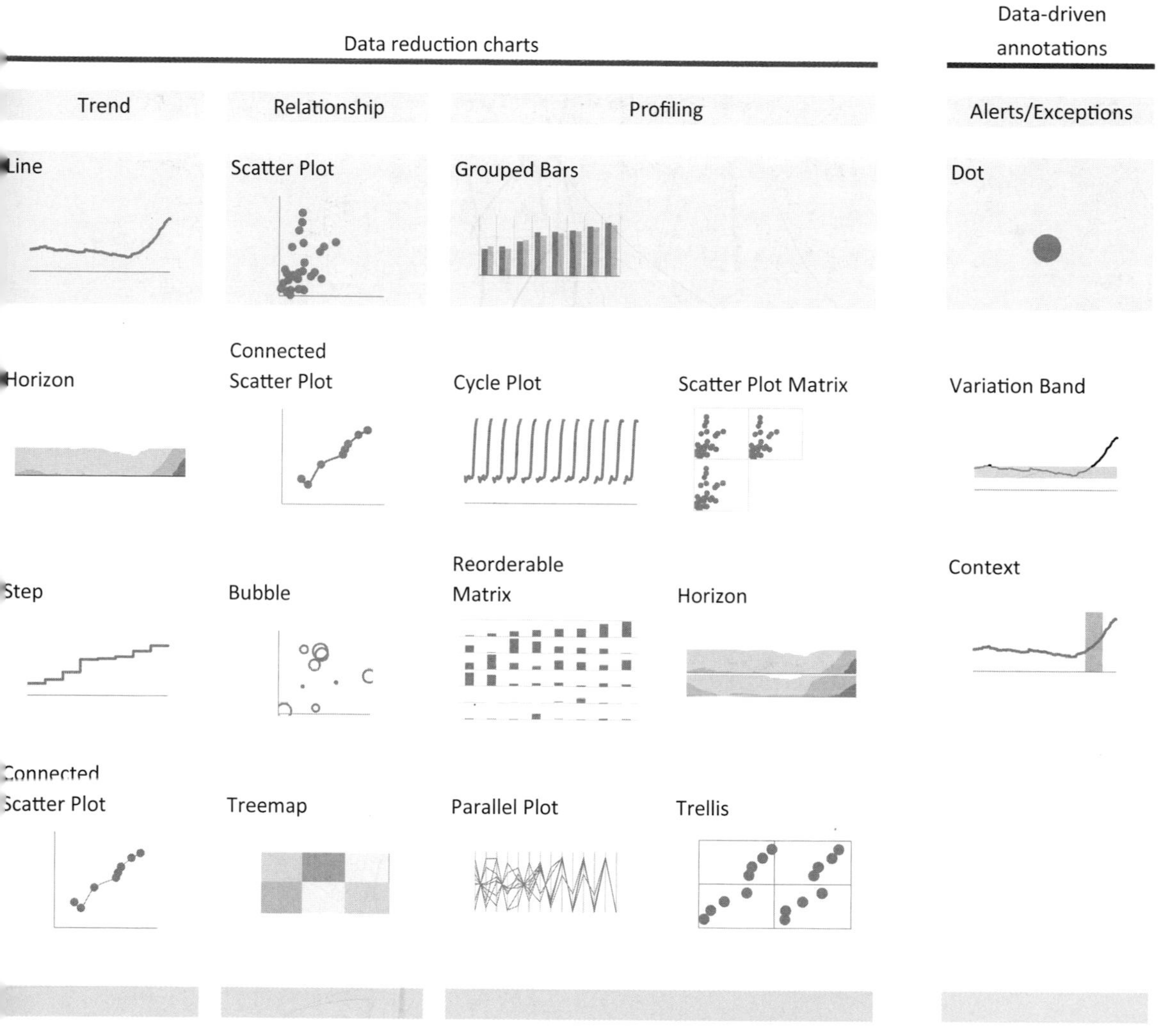

Data reduction charts			Data-driven annotations

Trend	Relationship	Profiling	Alerts/Exceptions

Line

Scatter Plot

Grouped Bars

Dot

Horizon

Connected Scatter Plot

Cycle Plot

Scatter Plot Matrix

Variation Band

Step

Bubble

Reorderable Matrix

Horizon

Context

Connected Scatter Plot

Treemap

Parallel Plot

Trellis

Audience Profile

I once had the bad idea of sharing a draft of a dashboard that included a very colorful bubble chart. But colors had no functional justification in this dashboard and created serious overlapping issues. I removed the color fill in the final version, to some users' bitter disappointment. It was like taking lollipops away from children while explaining how bad they are for their teeth.

I also had someone trying to convince me of the superior accuracy of a pseudo-3D pie chart (I kid you not!). It's tempting to attribute this to a bad case of illiteracy, but I think that's an overly simplistic explanation for an organization that's accustomed to a consistent flow of data visualization production and consumption. In both of these examples, we must also factor in emotions, impression management, and even classifications that emphasize aesthetics over effectiveness.

Go to the web page

The great graphics team at the *New York Times* is not afraid to experiment with new ways of communicating visually. This is at odds with their scatter plot avoidance of just a few years ago for fear that their readers would be unable to make sense of them.

This example of the *New York Times* is also relevant from the point of view of information asymmetry, as discussed in Chapter 3. It is acceptable to assume that charts for consumption within an organization can deliver a more complex message because the audience shares a common knowledge base. With the media, however, information asymmetry is harder to deal with. The message needs to take into account a more complex context that includes factors beyond information, such as graphic literacy, consumption circumstances, interest, and attention.

As a creator of information products, your customers want you to deliver results that meet their expectations. The easiest path, with the greatest probability of success, is to do exactly that, even if that means poorer visualizations and lower return on investment. Trying to go beyond customer expectations means that you will probably have to fight for your ideas and will have a hard time explaining why they're better for the organization. This applies to basic things, like removing pseudo-3D effects to improve readability and effectiveness, but also to charts that force the audience to change the way it thinks and reasons about the data.

Go to the web page

In **Figure 7.3,** the line charts at the top represent unemployment rate and job vacancy rate independently. You don't have to be an expert to sense that there must be some type of connection between these two rates. When you plot them one against the other, as is done in the bottom chart, you get the so called Beveridge

curve.[3] You can infer more about the state of the economy by reading this chart
than by comparing the two line charts.

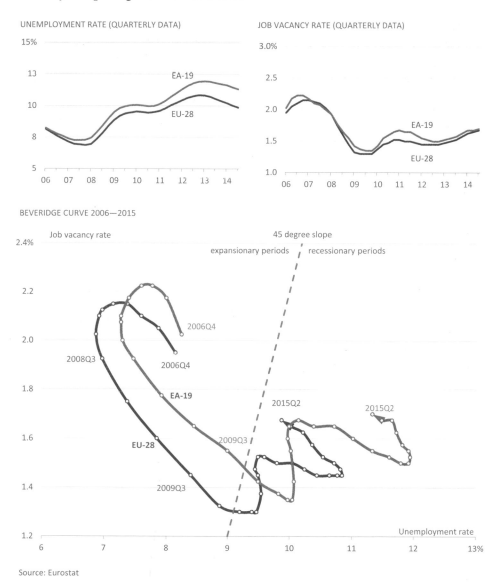

UNEMPLOYMENT RATE (QUARTERLY DATA)

JOB VACANCY RATE (QUARTERLY DATA)

BEVERIDGE CURVE 2006—2015

Source: Eurostat

Figure 7.3 The Beveridge curve versus two independent charts. Observing relationships can
shed new light on old line patterns.

3 This chart was redrawn from a chart published by Eurostat. If you want to know more about the
Beveridge curve, the web page offers a basic explanation.

While you should fight established routines if you think you can improve them, you must have the humility to recognize that people within the organization know the organization and the data it needs better than you. So this requires effort on both sides and often goes from the technical level to management.

For example, a manager assumes that the sales force will not understand a dashboard and that this will create some friction in the short term, so an information product with a more familiar design is the better choice. You, in turn, will try to show management the main advantages of using a dashboard and find ways to minimize friction. You might do this, for example, by annotating profusely and making sure that you provide answers to all their needs.

Here's a concrete example. A basic visualization rule is that a chart is not a table. When you label every single data point, all you get is a bad chart and a bad table. That's why only a few data points should be labeled, such as the highest, the lowest, the first, the most recent, and the one at which something happened. For many cases, this is the right thing to do. Also, because extensive labeling requires more space, that would require enlarging the chart. Some tasks, however, require access to precise values. Sales incentives, for example, are based on precise metrics, not on the answer we get from our impressions of a chart. We must find a solution that satisfies both the added value that visualization brings to data analysis and the precise result that turns into actual incentives.

The bullet chart (**Figure 7.4**) is a better alternative to speedometers. (We'll discuss bullet charts more in the next chapter.) One of its advantages is that we can stack them, using very little space, where we can both visualize the data and get the values from a table-like structure, satisfying both needs.

Figure 7.4 The bullet chart, where we can pair the chart with the values.

Sharing Visualizations

The distance between the charts displayed on a screen and the audience is usually greater than we realize. That path is filled with technical barriers and incompatibilities, the political management of information, and the profile of the audience. Hence, it's useful to assume that the audience will never see your graphical representations the same way that you see them on your screen, and this should be factored in from the beginning of your project.

Consider an interactive visualization, for example. It seems to be a wise choice for any audience. But is it? Take a top manager. Perhaps she has no time to explore the data and delegates this task to middle managers, who should provide her with only a static synthesis of essential findings.

Middle managers, in turn, believe that interactivity distracts sales teams or makes them analyze the data on sales performance in ways that are impossible to reconcile, destroying a shared knowledge base. So, rather than an interactive visualization, perhaps a standard PDF report will ensure that everyone is on the same page regarding the way the organization analyzes the data. In this example organization, interactive visualization may be relevant only to a small fraction of the total personnel.

Screens and Projectors

If I had to choose an object to symbolize Murphy's law ("what can go wrong will go wrong"), I would choose a projector. It will mess up sizes and aspect ratios, wash out your carefully selected color scheme, or evilly replace things. We will never be fully prepared for a temperamental projector; we can only minimize its impact.

Your computer screen probably has a different aspect ratio and higher resolution than a projector. If you don't consider these differences and instead focus only on your visualization, the projector will make you pay at show time, cropping your images or making fonts too small to read from afar. Make sure that, from time to time, you switch your screen resolution to the projector's resolution. Also, you'll probably want to increase distances between color hues and add saturation (**Figure 7.5**).

Go to the web page

Not LCD-friendly palette

LCD-friendly palette

Figure 7.5 You may need to switch to an LCD-friendly palette (palettes from ColorBrewer).

Above all, always test your visualizations on a projector and screen before using them in your presentation. (By the way, this also applies to dashboards and other visualizations that are meant to be shared and used on other computers.)

Smartphones and Vertical Displays

⊜
Go to the
web page

According to Hannah Fairfield, senior graphics editor at *The New York Times*, more than half of the newspaper's website traffic comes from smartphones, which forced them to rethink the way they structure their stories. Unlike print or large desktop screens, where a large amount of data can be presented simultaneously for user exploration, small screens mean that space must be used wisely, beginning by editing out any unnecessary features. Layering and sequencing provide means for moving from one screen to the next, like reading one paragraph after another. Transitions must be smooth and the connections must be obvious.

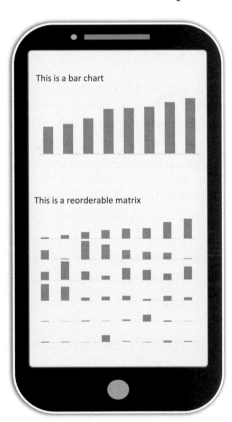

In data visualization, the vertical display is great. Not because we're going to switch the typical aspect ratio of bar charts or line charts, but because the width in a vertical display is sufficient to display them (**Figure 7.6**), leaving the lower half of the screen for text or for a second chart. For a horizontal display, we would enlarge the chart to fit the screen.

Figure 7.6 A vertical screen allows for more than one chart.

PDF Files

We discussed in Chapter 4 the senselessness of using PDF files to share tables and raw data, but if you want to share a static visualization almost exactly as you designed it, a PDF file is a great option. A PDF is much better than, for example, a raster image like PNG or JPEG formats. You can create large pages that readers will be able to zoom in and zoom out, or you can go the smartphone way and create multiple small pages.

Excel Files

In a closed and standardized environment, sharing your visualization in Excel not only can add interaction but also can give users access to the raw data. Things will get a bit rougher if you factor in multiple Office versions, localization issues, or security settings (regarding mail attachments or allowing for running macros), but sharing in Excel is a serious option.

Sharing Online

If you compare the Insert menu of Excel online and Excel 2016 (**Figure 7.7**), you'll see that a severe adjustment to your visualization may be needed if it uses several of the features not present in Excel Online.

Figure 7.7 Comparing Excel 2016 with Excel online.

Sharing full-featured interactive visualizations online that were made in Excel would be the best of many worlds, but it's still a bit frustrating (and expensive, if you use a Microsoft infrastructure, including SQL Server and SharePoint). There are a few nice spreadsheet controls for .NET applications that you can use, but they don't fully replicate Excel functionalities, so make sure they meet your needs.

As your literacy and experience grows, you'll become more impatient when using Excel as your data visualization tool. Interactive online visualizations such as Tableau Public or Power BI may bring about those impatient moments, and you may decide that you need to replace Excel with a specialized data visualization tool.

Go to the web page

Takeaways

- The way a chart looks matters, not as the starting point, but as the result of a process—the process of answering a question or completing a task. That's why a task-based classification of chart type is preferable to other types that are based only on their visual characteristics.

- When you subordinate your chart choice to the task type, you become more aware of the task itself and how you can fulfill it effectively. Keeping your goal in mind makes it much less likely that you'll add useless decoration and visual junk.

- Other criteria should also be taken into account, such as the expected audience literacy. In some contexts, you may need to choose a more familiar chart, while in other cases using extensive annotations can be enough to introduce a less familiar chart.

- Another criterion for selecting a chart is how it will be shared. Interactivity, file formats, and the hardware involved may require changes to the design that can range from details (such as font size) to large structural changes (such as using animation instead of multiple charts).

8

A SENSE OF ORDER

This chapter is mostly about comparing data points. Some of the tasks you can do when comparing data points are ordering, sorting, and ranking. Comparisons are found everywhere in data visualization, so much so that Edward Tufte says that "compared with what?" is "the deep, fundamental question in statistical analysis."[1] In a more or less explicit way, you'll find comparisons at the heart of every category in our chart classification. If you aren't comparing data points, you're comparing trends or profiles.

So, in this chapter we'll be comparing things but in a very strict sense: We're working at the data point level, with points that are ordered, sorted, or ranked by a relevant key. They're not compared to the total (otherwise, we would be talking about composition) and we're not turning them into shapes by perceptual reduction and generalization.

---

1 Tufte, Edward. *Visual Explanations*, Cheshire, CT: Graphics Press. 1997.

First, however, we must ensure that comparisons are possible. Let me show you three examples where comparisons are not possible or relevant (**Figure 8.1**).

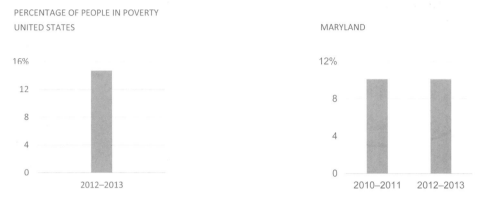

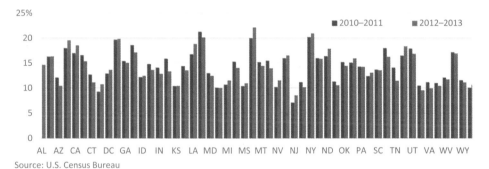

Source: U.S. Census Bureau

Figure 8.1 These three images make us unable to compare the data: absent in one case, irrelevant in another, and impossible in the third.

We might format a chart so badly that we can read nothing from it or, even worse, what we read is the opposite of what the data actually says. That's not the case for the top left image in the figure. It's clean, everything is there for a reason, and it can't possibly mislead you. Now, it looks like a chart, it reads like a chart, it's made like a chart, but it's actually a duck[2] because it violates the most fundamental principle: There is no data visualization with a single data point. Data visualization is like the tango, and the more data points, the merrier.

---

2 This is a word play with a Tuftean background: "When a graphic is taken over by decorative forms or computer debris…then that graphic may be called a *duck* in honor of the duck-form store, 'Big Duck.'" Edward Tufte. *The Visual Display of Quantitative Information and Envisioning Information*, Second Edition, Cheshire, CT: Graphics Press. 2001.

Formally, it's acceptable to consider the top right image in Figure 8.1 as a proper chart. After all, it's well formatted, and it contains enough data points to make comparisons possible. But the thing is, what's the point? If there is no variation, there is no reason to make a chart.

The image at the bottom of Figure 8.1 is an example of data dumped into a chart without any visible criteria. There is indeed a lot of variation, but the way the chart is formatted turns interpretation into a mission impossible.

Of course we can come up with scenarios, rhetorical ("See? In spite of all the propaganda, it didn't move an inch") or forced by the nature of the data (missing data), where these charts might be used, but as a rule, a chart is relevant only when it displays multiple data points, when it allows for their comparison, and when variation is interpretable.

The most popular chart in ordering data points is the bar chart. It's also the most familiar example of a chart taking advantage of "position along a common scale," the most accurate of basic perceptual tasks according to the Cleveland study that we discussed in Chapter 2.

A chart that combines familiarity and accuracy combines two qualities that make a good chart, so shouldn't we use the bar chart even more often? Let Amanda Cox from the *New York Times* answer that: "There's a strand of the data viz world that argues that everything could be a bar chart. That's possibly true but also possibly a world without joy."

Go to the web page

She's exaggerating, of course. No one will ever argue that data visualization can be reduced to boring bar charts only. What she means (I think) is that the emotional dimension and creativity can't be removed from data visualization. You can see it as a trade-off, whereby you sacrifice some effectiveness and expect more engagement in return. This is a central equation in infographic design. In an ideal world, the joy of aesthetics and the joy of understanding (our Eureka moments) would go hand-in-hand, but we often need to accept a less-than-perfect compromise.

The Bar Chart

A bar chart encodes the values of a discrete variable into the height of columns or the length of bars.[3] In **Figure 8.2**, the variable "expenditure" contains 14 categories. The vertical axis (y) represents expenditure amounts in a predefined unit of measurement (in this case, U.S. dollars). Usually, the vertical axis ranges between zero and a round value slightly above the maximum data point value. From this chart, it's easy to conclude that Housing is the highest expenditure, almost double that of the second highest, Transportation.

Download the
original chart

ANNUAL MEAN EXPENDITURE

Consumer Expenditure Survey, 3rd quarter 2013 through 2nd quarter 2014

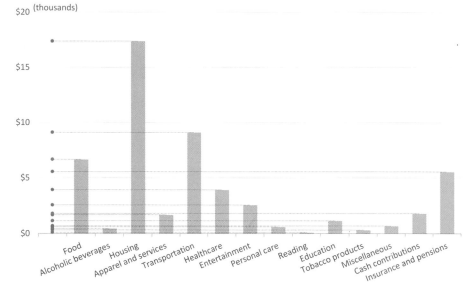

Source: Bureau of Labor Statistics

Figure 8.2 A bar chart and how it originates from the proto-chart.

---

3   To make things simpler, from now on let's identify them as vertical bars and horizontal bars.

Vertical and Horizontal Bars

As we saw in Chapter 1, and represented here again in Figure 8.2, the data points for a vertical bar chart are placed along the vertical axis and then offset at equally spaced distances along the horizontal axis to allow for better discriminability and easy labeling.

I'm sure you noticed the awkward position of the labels along the horizontal axis. Rotating them makes it harder to read them and takes a lot of room. If you don't rotate them at all, they'll overlap. Sometimes you can solve this problem by splitting the labels into two or more lines, but that wouldn't help in this case. Instead of rotating the labels, a better idea is to rotate the bars, creating a horizontal bar chart (**Figure 8.3**).

ANNUAL MEAN EXPENDITURE
Consumer Expenditure Survey, 3rd quarter 2013 through 2nd quarter 2014

Download the original chart

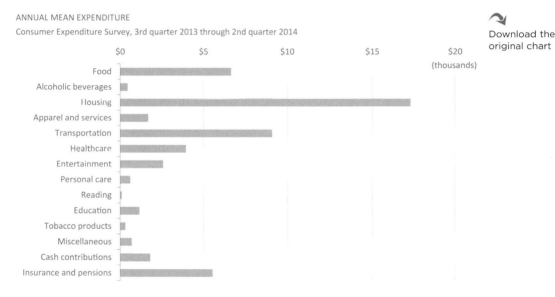

Source: Bureau of Labor Statistics

Figure 8.3 Rotating the bars when there is no room for labels.

It's often said that the difference between horizontal and vertical bar charts is the room available for labeling each data point. It's not quite that simple, however, because there are no two identical chart types. If there is a time dimension, for example, it's better to keep the bars vertical, so that time flows as usual from left to right. We have more flexibility if we're using nominal variables without an explicit order. Fortunately, charts that use nominal variables are usually the ones where longer labels are more common. Also, if you're creating multiple bar charts, try to be consistent and avoid randomly switching between vertical and horizontal bars. If you must make the change, be sure your audience understands why.

Color Coding

I'm trying not to be too dogmatic, but if I had to choose the single most useless formatting option in Excel, I would probably choose "Vary colors by point." I have never found a good reason to use this option. Sure, you should identify every series in a bar chart by a unique color. That's one of the uses of color. But randomly assigning a color to each bar adds empty meaning and confuses the audience.

That said, you *can* and *should* use multiple colors in a single series if (and only if) doing so enriches the chart. You do that by assigning meaning to each color you use. **Figure 8.4** shows the differences between these encoding options. The chart on the left is the typical, one-color bar chart. I wanted to call the audience's attention to a specific data point, so I made a slight change that forces the audience to compare Florida to all the other states. The middle chart is more interesting. It adds a kind of geographic dimension, color-coding each state by the U.S. Census Bureau regions.[4] Now we know that there is a geographical pattern to poverty, because most of the poorer states are in the South. This is a good reason to add a map to our analysis.

The last chart uses the Excel option "Vary colors by point." You'll find that Excel loops in a sequence of 12 colors. Does this provide any useful insights? I don't think so!

Ordering

Ordering values alphabetically makes it easy to locate a single value in a table. We also order people by name when we want to emphasize that no one is more important (tough luck if your name is Zuckerberg...hmm, or maybe not). Used like this, the alphabet allows us to generate a good enough random order.

Unlike with tables, however, it's easy to see why data visualization abhors alphabetical order: It destroys patterns and makes it very hard to compare data points. It's like a new version of Excel's "Vary color by point."

---

4 In specialized data visualization applications, instead of a categorical variable, like region, we could use a continuous one, like population density, but in Excel that is almost impossible and would require far too much work.

PERCENTAGE OF PEOPLE IN POVERTY BY STATE, 2012–2013

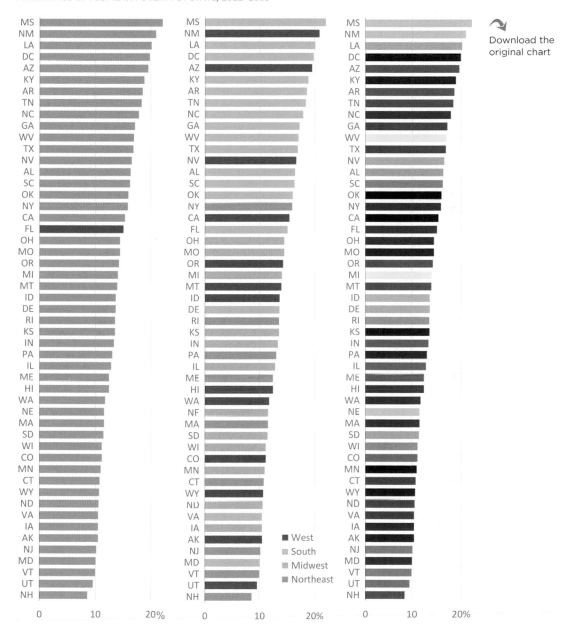

Download the original chart

Source: U.S. Census Bureau

Figure 8.4 Three ways of using color in bar charts.

Figure 8.5 displays the population density for each U.S. census division, using three ordering criteria. Even though there are only nine data points, three of the top four regions are so close that, in the left chart, you have to spend some cognitive resources trying to figure out which one comes second, third, and fourth. Your job becomes much simpler if you sort the data points by population density, as the chart on the right does. Now your precious cognitive resources can be applied to more relevant tasks.

POPULATION DENSITY BY DIVISION

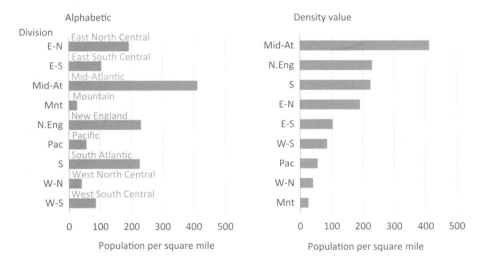

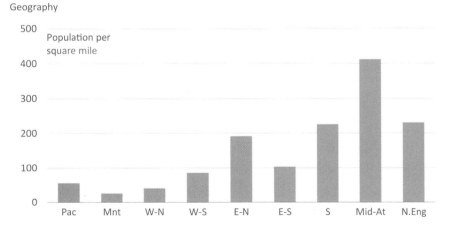

Source: U.S. Census Bureau

Figure 8.5 Sorting keys.

In the bottom chart, you have to think of the U.S. as a horizontal axis where the census divisions are approximately ordered geographically from west to east. We can easily conclude that the East is much more densely populated than the West (although excluding Alaska would make population density in the Pacific division much higher).

Especially when there is more than one series, there is never a predefined good way to order the data points. Each key may reveal unexpected insights, so it's better to test with several keys. Again, ordering alphabetically is usually counterproductive, so don't order alphabetically unless there seems to be a mysterious relationship between category names and the data, or your goal is to force your audience to focus on individual data points.

Chart Size

Charts are often larger than they need to be for the message that they convey. A textured, pseudo-3D bar chart could take as much space as four carefully designed charts, or even more, if we're prepared to lose some detail. For creating a graphical landscape, each chart should be as small and compact as possible, within the limits of viewing comfort, the audience, the context, and the type and level of detail to be displayed.

Due to its high level of accuracy, the bar chart allows for a significant level of compression without losing the essence of its message. In **Figure 8.6**, the chart displays the percentage change of GDP for 38 countries or regions. Edward Tufte proposed these "word-size" charts and called them "sparklines."[5]

As this example shows, the crisis that started in 2008 affected all countries on the list (with the red vertical stripe marking negative growth), so if that was your core message, these sparklines could fit the bill. But the chart also shows one of the major weaknesses of sparklines: the difficult management of vertical scales. The version on the left uses a common range for all the countries, which almost turns the bars into a sequence of dashes but allows for a better comparison between countries. The one on the right uses country-specific scales, which improves resolution, but you will no longer be able to compare countries.

---

5 Tufte, Edward, *ibid*. The original design uses lines rather than bars.

Download the
original chart

GROSS DOMESTIC PRODUCT AT MARKET PRICES
Percentage change over previous period, 2000–2013

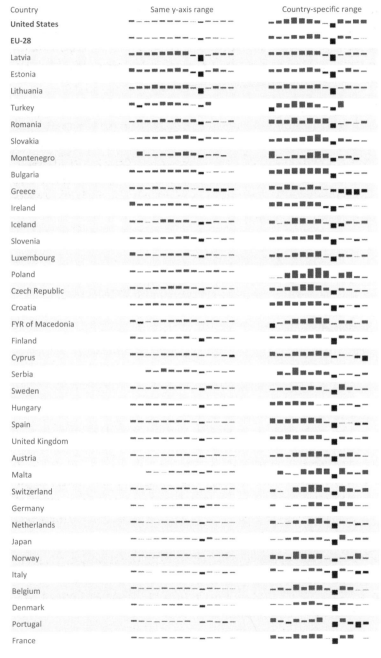

Source: Eurostat

Figure 8.6 Sparklines pack a lot of data into a small space.

This example shows that you can make very small charts and still retain much of the message. It doesn't mean you have to go that far, however. A trick you can use is to create a regular-sized chart and then resize it to make it smaller. If it starts looking cluttered, change the font size or remove something that will make the chart look uncluttered again. Repeat the process until you can no longer remove or change anything without influencing the message beyond an acceptable level.

Breaks in the Scale

The chart at the left in **Figure 8.7** leads us to conclude that we spend much more money on Transportation than on Food. The right chart confirms that we spend more on the former than on the latter, but the gap is much less pronounced than the first chart leads us to believe. The data are the same in both charts, so the error must come from somewhere else.

WE SPEND MUCH MORE ON TRANSPORTATION THAN ON FOOD. OR MAYBE NOT?
Consumer Expenditure Survey, 3rd quarter 2013 through 2nd quarter 2014

Download the
original chart

Source: Bureau of Labor Statistics

Figure 8.7 Breaks in the scale can lead us astray.

The scale in the left chart doesn't start at zero. Since, in a bar chart, we compare bar heights, their variation in this chart is not proportional to the variation in the data. As we know, cognitive tasks should complement, but not correct, perceptual tasks. Failure to do so, as in this case, is one of the most common techniques of manipulating the message in a chart.

You break the scale when you remove a section from it. In the example, the scale was broken at the bottom, thus not starting with zero. But you can remove a section anywhere in the scale. Fortunately, in Excel you can do this only at the bottom (but there are tricks to simulate other breaks).

By default, you should avoid breaks in scale because they invalidate reading and comparing distances from the axis to the data points. In chart types where we don't visually connect the axis to the data point, as in line charts, this issue is less relevant, but that's not the case with bar charts.

In some cases, the scale is broken out of malice, but let's forget about those. We break the scale to improve resolution—that is, to see in more detail the differences between very similar data points. Take gross domestic product (GDP), for example. We don't usually see charts with absolute values of GDP, because only in extreme circumstances are there impressive variations. A 2 percent change could go almost unnoticed, and that's normal, but these small changes have tremendous effects in the economy. That's why we use variation instead of absolute volumes.

Changing Metrics to Avoid Breaks in the Scale

Unfortunately, setting the scale at zero is the best recipe for creating dull charts, in both senses of the word: boring and with little variation. The solution is not to break the scale, but rather to find a similar message that can be communicated using alternative metrics.

Take the absolute value of GDP in Ireland in **Figure 8.8**. Although it displays a consistent growth for over a decade, only a soul of rare sensibility will be impressed by the small increases from one year to the next. They are important but hard to quantify, and what does a few million more or a few million less mean?

Figure 8.9 tells a different and richer story. It represents the year-to-year variation in the same period. What we only sensed in the previous version becomes very clear. And, to make the chart even more explicit, a reference (variation in the European Union) and two annotations (the shading in the euro period and the reversal of the color for negative growth) were added.

This change in perspective helps us better understand the behavior of GDP over the years, using a bar chart but without having to manipulate the scale.

IRELAND: GROSS DOMESTIC PRODUCT AT MARKET PRICES

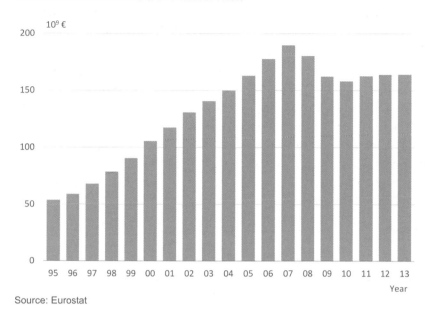

Source: Eurostat

Figure 8.8 Absolute value of GDP in volume in Ireland.

IRELAND: GROSS DOMESTIC PRODUCT AT MARKET PRICES
Change over previous period, based on 2005=100 and the euro

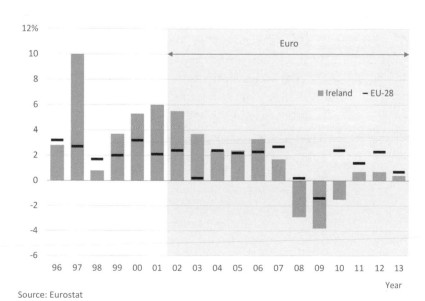

Source: Eurostat

Figure 8.9 Changing to relative growth makes the chart more interesting.

Evolution and Change

The concept of evolution suggests some degree of stability in consecutive periods that creates recognizable patterns when using a line chart. Change, in turn, is more unstable, and a pattern is harder to detect. Keep this in mind when choosing between bar charts and line charts. When the ups and downs are so pronounced that no pattern or trend is detectable, use a bar chart. If there is a glimpse of a pattern, a line chart may be a better choice.

A Special Bar Chart: The Population Pyramid

Traditional population pyramids contain numerous confusing features. As an example, in the left chart of **Figure 8.10**, each gender is placed on one side of the axis. First, this prevents an accurate comparison between genders. It also shows that using a bar chart itself is less than useful because it makes it difficult to add more series. And finally, since each gender is on opposite sides of the axis, color coding for each gender as used here holds no value.

POPULATION AGE STRUCTURE IN THE U.S.: 1960 VS. 2010 VS. 2100   FOLDED POPULATION PYRAMID

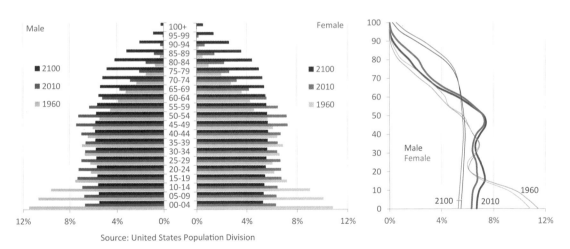

Source: United States Population Division

Figure 8.10 Using bars and lines to make population pyramids.

Download the
original chart

In Figure 8.10, let's now compare the traditional pyramid bar chart to a new chart, on the right, that replaces the bars with lines. The bar chart feels so busy that it's almost impossible to extract any meaningful knowledge from it. The line version respects the need to identify the population profile, with the added benefit of allowing for a better comparison between genders, because the axis is now folded. As you can see, in 2010 there are more males in the lower age groups, and only in the population aged 50 and older are there more females (this would be difficult to see in the bar chart version). It's also easy to compare the profiles in each year. All of this while taking up much less space.

In **Figure 8.11**, we take this line chart concept to an extreme level, summarizing in a single chart the age structure of the population in the Maldives islands between 1985 and 2050 (projected), or 66 series for each gender. Notice how the darker tones, corresponding to the first years of the time series, draw a typical pyramid. Notice also how over time the population gets old, revealing more weight at the top of the pyramid and less at the bottom.

AGE STRUCTURE IN THE MALDIVES

Source: U.S. Census Bureau

Figure 8.11 Aesthetics and effectiveness don't have to be mutually exclusive.

I believe the chart looks beautiful while keeping a good level of effectiveness, but my actual goal was to show that an aesthetically pleasing Excel chart is not an oxymoron. There are more effective ways of conveying this population change (such as an animation or a series of small pyramids for every 10 years, for example), but this is the kind of balance between aesthetics and effectiveness you should experiment with.

Well, it might be a good idea to take a break now. If possible, get a lemon sorbet to cleanse your palate, and close your eyes for a few seconds. Then you'll be ready to appreciate some softer stimuli.

Dot Plots

After a few pages of circumspect bar charts, a few dots hanging on wires (**Figure 8.12**) may not look like much, but actually they're an excellent alternative to bars for two major reasons: clutter and break in the scale.

Try to imagine Figure 8.4 with dots instead of bars. I can assure you it would look much less cluttered. Visual clutter is one of the most serious issues with bar charts. Using a bar to represent a simple data point is clearly overkill that results in no room for more data. At times, this may make us overlook less obvious things. The population pyramids offer a glaring example of this.

But dot plots are not only about reducing clutter and avoiding overstimulation. Because we don't compare heights, dot plots actually allow us to break the scale to improve resolution, and that's a big plus over bar charts.

Notice in Figure 8.12 that Washington, D.C., is a strong outlier when it comes to population density. One of the solutions to keeping chart resolution at a reasonable level is to remove outliers and explain why you've done so in the form of an inset. In this case, the inset shows that the range between the top and the bottom values is much smaller than between the top value (New Jersey) and the outlier (Washington, D.C.). Using the inset allows us to have a good resolution in the chart and at the same time be aware of the outlier, the much higher population density in Washington, D.C.

Go to the web page

If you want to have fun and use a bar chart without the bars, try adding a tail to the dots (using error bars). The resulting chart was named by Andy Cotgreave the "lollipop chart." I did that for Maryland in Figure 8.12, just as an example. Note, however, that you can't break the scale with lollipop charts, since the lollipop stick is just a thin bar (see also the lollipop in Figure 5.17).

POPULATION DENSITY PER STATE, 2010

Download the
original chart

Source: U.S. Census Bureau

Figure 8.12 Dots, lollipops, and how to deal with outliers.

Slope Charts

The chart in **Figure 8.13** shows that people in the bottom 20 percent and the top 20 percent quintiles of income before taxes display significant differences in the weight of some expenditure items—namely Housing, Food, and Insurance and Pensions.

WEIGHT OF MAJOR EXPENDITURE ITEMS BY LEVEL OF INCOME

Consumer Expenditure Survey, 3rd quarter 2013 through 2nd quarter 2014

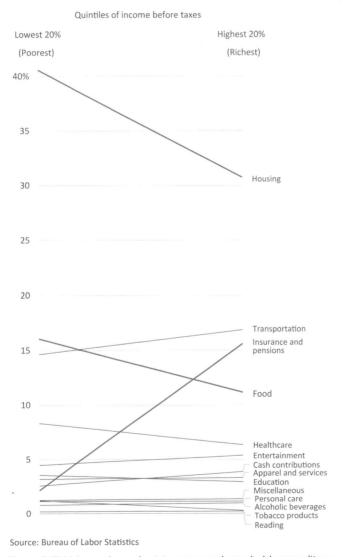

Source: Bureau of Labor Statistics

Figure 8.13 Using a slope chart to compare household expenditure.

Had we used a bar chart, we would face again the problem of how to order the data, an even more serious problem now because we have two series to choose from instead of one. But since the best way to solve a problem is to prevent it, we can use this slope chart and stop worrying about it.

The slope chart is already familiar to us: We saw it in the first chapter as an alternative to pie charts, Figure 1.17, and now we use it again as an alternative to bar charts. In Figure 1.17, we were comparing two dates, while here we're comparing two categories, or more specifically, lowest to highest quintiles. This shows that a slope chart is not just a short line chart, and that the lines shouldn't be seen as indicating a trend. The slope chart's purpose is to represent variation between two states, which you can define by two dates but also by any other pair of categories. Traditionally, there is the notion that we shouldn't draw lines between categories, because there are no intermediate states between them (for example, a chart displaying data for male and female would read "the more male...," which wouldn't make sense). This rule is now more flexible, and you can use lines to show differences, not only in change over time, but in many more contexts.

Strip Plots

The strip plot (or one-dimensional scatter plot) has been with us since the beginning of this book; this may lead you to suspect some form of favoritism, which is not far from reality. Strip plots are the basis of all one-dimensional charts, including bar charts and dot plots. They differ from bar charts and dot plots because points are not offset along the opposite axis.

The strip plot in **Figure 8.14** is the one-dimensional version of the first chart in this chapter, on average annual expenditure.

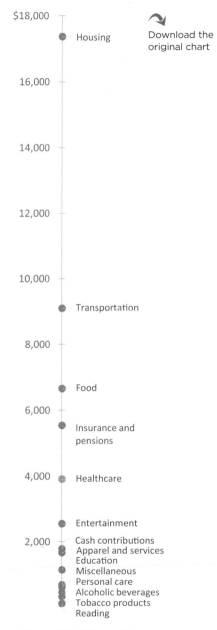

ANNUAL MEAN EXPENDITURE
Consumer Expenditure Survey,
3rd quarter 2013 through 2nd quarter 2014

Download the original chart

Figure 8.14 Strip plot: the most compact chart type ever?

Strip plots are naturally ordered, so that's something that we don't have to worry about. They also take a lot less room than the equivalent bar chart, although labeling is not so easy. I believe strip plots will become more popular once we get rid of this need to identify every single data point (interaction can provide identification on-demand, allowing us to focus on more interesting data points or clusters).

Speedometers

Driving a car may seem like a great metaphor for managing an organization, but you risk a nasty accident if you take the metaphor too far. And you're taking it too far if you're using speedometers and other ill-suited charts in an executive dashboard. As you can see from a simple Google search for "executive dashboard," things can really go overboard (**Figure 8.15**).

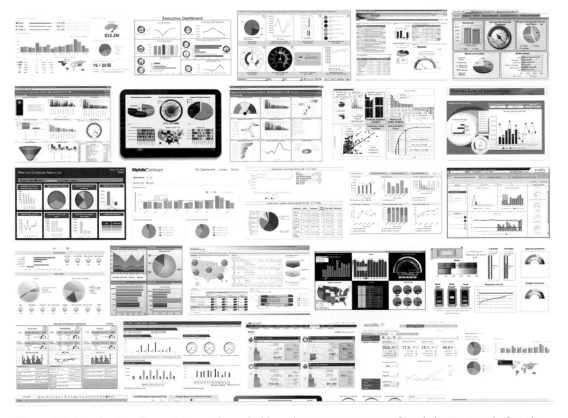

Figure 8.15 You don't really want to use these dashboards to run a company. *Google image search. Google and the Google logo are registered trademarks of Google, Inc. Used with permission.*

A car dashboard shows you all you need to know about the car *now*, in the simplest possible way, so that you don't have to take your eyes off the road for more than a split second. Focus on driving and forget the data. Sooner or later a red light will tell you that you need to refuel.

Data at non-alert levels are more relevant for a manager than for a driver. This is truer when you factor in a time dimension: Your current speed is not explained by the past, whereas it is important to check how your market share changed over time. When using the car dashboard metaphor, designers often neglect this time dimension, probably because the corresponding object in the car dashboard is missing.

Download the original chart

Speedometers usually have a much glossier look than the simple one in **Figure 8.16**, but they share the same nature: a needle encoding a data value and a red–yellow–green scale to help read it. This makes them champions of low data density.

Figure 8.16 An Excel speedometer made of a donut chart.

Bullet Charts

If you need a visual representation of a key performance indicator (KPI), how do you design it so that it communicates effectively and reduces the amount of required real estate? Stephen Few suggested something he called the "bullet chart," which is basically a strip plot where we plot actual values and target values, while reference values are represented as shades of gray and are embedded in the axis.

Go to the web page

The bullet chart in **Figure 8.17** is the result of my own interpretation and translation of Few's specifications to Excel. In several examples, Few combines the bullet chart with an alert, so it seems appropriate to make those a single object.

Download the original chart

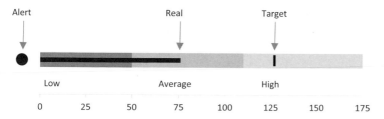

Figure 8.17 A bullet chart is a compact chart for displaying KPIs.

If one can get beyond shiny things, it's easy to see why bullet charts are much better than speedometers: They are much more compact while displaying two data points instead of one (a 100 percent improvement!). Also, when it makes sense to compare KPIs you can stack bullet charts, making comparisons much easier than the equivalent speedometer design (**Figure 8.18**).

Download the
original chart

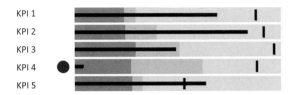

Figure 8.18 Stacked bullet charts.

Bullet charts and speedometers do share the issue of indicator polarity, whereby in some cases more is better (such as GDP growth) and in other cases more is worse (such as unemployment rate). When comparing multiple indicators, they should share the same polarity. If that's not possible, there must be visual clues to make the audience aware of the inversion.

Alerts

It may seem strange to include a point in a chart classification. In fact, the point is not a chart, but its role is crucial for visual monitoring tasks, and we can argue that the point represents a comparison to a normal state.

Look again at Figure 8.18. It displays five bullet charts, but only one is asking for closer attention because an immediate action may be required. An alert is not a summary. There are always values within an acceptable fluctuation range that shouldn't be associated with them.

Figure 8.19 shows some types of alerts available in Excel as conditional formatting. Often, the yellow alarms correspond to "all cases that are not green or red," which makes no sense. Alert design should ensure that they trigger salience in pre-attentive processing, which is lost if we color code all data points.

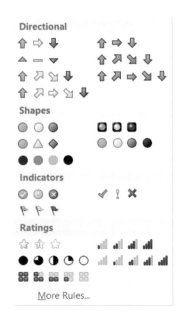

Figure 8.19 You can use conditional formatting to display alerts in Excel.

Keep in mind that people managers usually agree in making alerts more exceptional, but at the same time suggest that positive (green) alerts should also be in place to counter the negative impact of red alerts. Compromise, if you need to, but don't forget that alerts are *rare*, by definition.

Takeaways

- ■ When comparing data points, most charts force you to choose an ordering key. Always choose a key that is aligned with your task. Since alphabetical order is virtually random, you should never use it.

- ■ Bar charts are perceptually very accurate. Take advantage of this and try making them much smaller than usual.

- ■ Don't break the scale in bar charts. If you have high absolute values that don't change much, switch metrics and display the relative change.

- ■ Slope charts, strip plots, and dot plots are less sensitive to the chosen ordering key or to breaks in the scale, making them the right choice when these issues arise.

- ■ Use bullet charts when you want to show one or more KPIs, especially if you want to display multiple thresholds (such as target, below, and above).

- ■ Use alerts sparingly and only when the data requires them. Don't use yellow alerts or other colors to signal intermediate states.

9

PARTS OF A WHOLE: COMPOSITION CHARTS

As all parents know, no two slices of cake are exactly the same. In the eyes of children, their piece is always smaller than the others' pieces, which triggers the inevitable cry of "It's not fair!" Evaluating the actual size of the slice is one of our first failed experiments in our assessment of proportions, something that will never change. Just like *our irresistible fascination with all things circular.*[1]

---

1   Few, Stephen. "Our Irresistible Fascination with All Things Circular." *Visual Business Intelligence Newsletter*. El Dorado Hills, CA: Perceptual Edge. 2010.

There is another reason that explains our everlasting love for proportions. Some charts, such as scatter plots, are very abstract, while others resemble real objects with which we interact on a daily basis, thus requiring a minimal learning curve. We tend to favor the latter. Few people know what a sectogram is, but they are familiar with its objectification in the form of a pizza, a cheese wheel (such as the French Camembert), or pseudo-3D pies. A sectogram is just a pie chart with a boring name.

When thinking about composition, the goal is to understand how the whole is constituted, and how much each segment contributes to the whole. Let's define *composition* as a generic term referring to any whole, expressed in absolute or relative terms, while *proportion* is a subset that refers to charts in which the total is expressed in relative quantities and the slices add up to 100 percent. The most common chart for representing composition is the stacked bar chart, while circular charts like the pie chart are the most popular for representing proportions (**Figure 9.1**). The pie chart is also the most popular chart in general, if we measure popularity by the number of results in a Google search.

CONSUMER EXPENDITURE IN THE U.S. PER MAJOR ITEM GROUPS

Download the
original chart

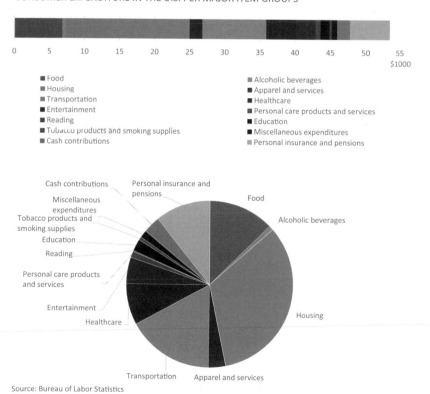

Source: Bureau of Labor Statistics

Figure 9.1 Displaying the composition of consumer expenditure in a stacked bar chart and in a pie chart.

Composition charts (especially pie charts) are controversial like no other—loved by many (the charts are fun and our customers really love them!) and despised both by others and by experts (they are wrong on so many levels!). As we discussed earlier, reducing the usage of pie charts and other composition charts to a minimum is indeed a kind of rite of passage in data visualization. **That's why a chapter on composition charts in a data visualization book is essentially an exercise in damage control.**

What Is Composition?

The "whole," expressed in absolute or relative terms, is central to any composition chart. No matter what, the whole must be displayed in each and every composition chart. Again, *no matter what*. And there is no mystery or complex notion of *meaningful* whole: it is the exhaustive and exclusive (meaning no overlapping parts) sum of all its parts.

Let me show you how damaging hiding the whole can be. In the stacked bar chart on the left of **Figure 9.2**, it appears that around 90 percent of the exports of manufactured industrial products are medium-to-high tech, which is great... until you actually read the labels in the vertical axis and realize that the chart is deceiving you: It's truncated at the top and at the bottom, which is something a responsible chart maker should never do, for reality is much less bright after fixing the scale and showing the whole. In the chart on the right of Figure 9.2, instead of 90 percent, medium-to-high technology accounts for a little more than 60 percent of the exports in this country.

Composition or Comparison?

Let's approach composition from a ridiculously strict (albeit true) perspective. If a composition chart represents parts of a whole, then *the whole* is the reference to which each value must be compared. For example, a pie chart can tell me that my market share is, say, 25 percent. I can then check my competitor's market share, but *I can't compare both* (I told you this is ridiculously strict). A composition chart must be read in sequence, as illustrated in **Figure 9.3**. The moment I start comparing both market shares, I move away from a composition task to a comparison task, without even realizing it.

EXPORTS OF INDUSTRIAL PRODUCTS BY TECHNOLOGICAL INTENSITY

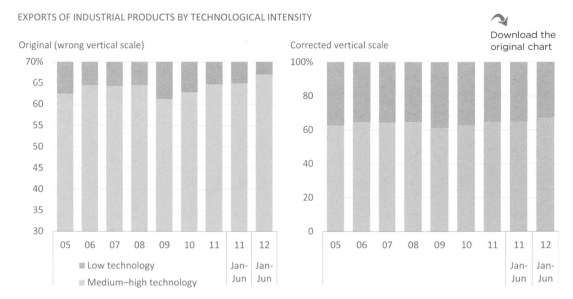

Source: Portuguese State Budget 2013

Figure 9.2 Correcting the vertical scale after a seriously bad error.

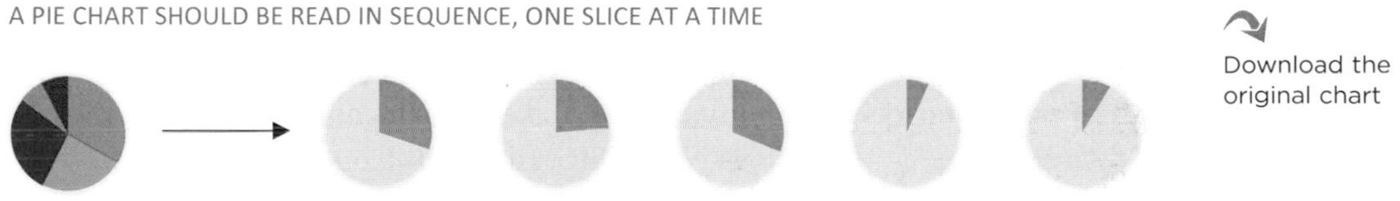

A PIE CHART SHOULD BE READ IN SEQUENCE, ONE SLICE AT A TIME

Figure 9.3 Reading a pie chart in sequence, comparing each slice to the whole.

Let's add just one more argument in this extreme approach to composition charts. Unless a slice falls into what Simkin and Hastie[2] call "anchor points" (easy-to-spot, perceptually salient angles, such as 0°, 90°, or 180°) (**Figure 9.4**), you'll always get a less-than-optimal perception of the actual slice size, even more so if the slice doesn't *begin* at one of those well-defined angles. So, only in very specific and simple cases can composition charts actually be useful and relatively accurate.

Remember how hard it was to determine which of two non-aligned bars was higher in the section on Weber's law in Chapter 2? That was a theoretical example, but later in this chapter you'll see how the use of composition charts can hide useful insights that become obvious when you realize you're *comparing* things and switch to a more effective chart type for that task.

2 Simkin, David and Reid Hastie. "An Information-Processing Analysis of Graph Perception." *Journal of the American Statistical Association*. 82:454–465, 1987.

ANGLES TO PERCENTAGES IN A PIE CHART

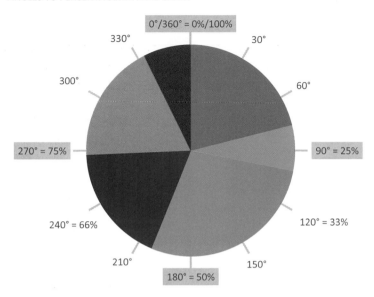

Figure 9.4 Angle degrees and their percentages in a pie chart, where you can identify anchor points.

Chart selection ultimately boils down to two things: what the task is really about, and the trade-offs you're willing to accept.

Composition is a comparison with a framework (the whole). Rationally, however, you almost never need the framework. You may argue that people like to see it, and you would be right. The problem is that there is a price to pay in effectiveness and the accurate assessment of the data points. You must decide whether you're willing to pay that price to get your audience's attention.

Go to the
web page

In his scathing article "Save the Pies for Dessert,"[3] Stephen Few does concede that pies are better than other charts when you want to compare grouped values, although he believes there is no significant real-world usage to make this a relevant feature. As an example, Figure 9.1 clearly shows that Food and Housing account for almost 50 percent of total expenses, something that is much harder to see using bar charts (in a bar chart you'll have to read the axis first and perform mental calculations). See the section on donut charts later in this chapter for a more complex example.

---

3 Few, Stephen. "Save the Pies for Dessert." *Visual Business Intelligence Newsletter*. El Dorado Hills, CA: Perceptual Edge. 2007.

Pie Charts

A pie chart is a circular chart in which each value is encoded by a proportional slice that can be read using its area, angle, or arc (**Figure 9.5**). As seen in Chapter 1, we can take the pie chart as a variation of a stacked bar chart. The pie chart is one of the charts furthest away from the proto-chart, measured by its number of transformations. In addition to this, the pie chart is often subjected to decorative transformations to make it more similar to an actual physical object (**Figure 9.6**).

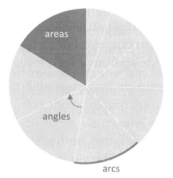

Download the original charts

Figure 9.5 You can use arcs, areas, or angles to read a pie chart.

Figure 9.6 One of the dangers of using pie charts is the temptation to make it look like a real-world object.

Critique

Pies are an easy target. Edward Tufte says that they shouldn't be used, because they lack a real axis, before adding that a "worse design than a pie chart is several of them."[4] Stephen Few doesn't use pies and advises his readers against using them,[5] suggesting that they should be left to dessert.[6] Few's criticisms are mostly related to the difficulty of comparing slices and the objectification through pseudo-3D effects and glossy textures.

---

4 Tufte, Edward. *The Visual Display of Quantitative Information*, 2001. Cheshire, CT: Graphics Press, Second Edition.

5 Few, Stephen. *Show Me the Numbers: Designing Tables and Graphs to Enlighten.* Burlingame, CA: Analytics Press, Second Edition. 2012.

6 Few, Stephen. "Save the Pies for Dessert." *Visual Business Intelligence Newsletter.* El Dorado Hills, CA: Perceptual Edge. 2007.

My position is closer to Ian Spence's,[7] who stresses that criticism comes from people who ask too much of the "humble pie." The pie chart is just an "attractive device for the display of a small number of proportions." Perhaps this is the ultimate criticism: not taking the pie chart seriously, seeing it as nothing more than a design device to add some fun, the Comic Sans of data visualization. In theory, I do not exclude them, because I believe that in certain circumstances they are useful, but in practice I always find a better alternative.

We can view the pie chart as a sign of low graphical literacy. When Albert Einstein said that "everything should be made as simple as possible, but not simpler," he could hardly find a better example than pie charts to demonstrate oversimplification. When an organization uses too many pie charts, either it doesn't take data visualization seriously or it downplays the complexity of the issues it has to tackle.

Damage Control

The pie chart at the left in **Figure 9.7** is an example of using a we-are-trying-to-fool-you asterisk in data visualization, and is based on a real-world example of a city budget. If you sum the slices, they will not add up to the total value displayed. The mystery of the missing slice is solved after reading the note. The result is as misleading as the stacked bar chart from Figure 9.2: You can't say you have a budget of 301 million euros and then make a pie chart showing only the interesting expenses.

Download the
original chart

CITY BUDGET PROPOSAL

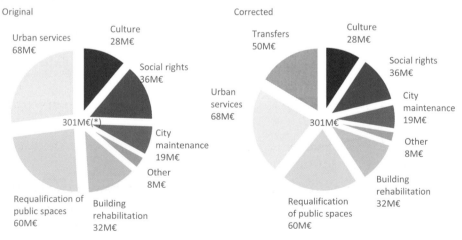

(*) Including 50M€ in financial transfers

Figure 9.7 Does correcting a pie chart even make a difference?

7   Spence, Ian. 2005. "No Humble Pie: The Origins and Usage of a Statistical Chart." *Journal of Educational and Behavioral Statistics.* 30-4: 353–368, 2005.

The right pie replicates the left one but adds the missing slice. All other slices are now smaller to accommodate for the new one. Strangely, this doesn't seem to matter; it's too much work to check all the slices, one by one, and compare sizes in both pies. The fact that adding such a significant slice is met with such perceptual indifference speaks volumes about how insensitive to variation we are when using a pie chart.

If your organization has developed a bad pie chart addiction, the first step is to help it recognize that it has a problem, because that's the moment inertia is broken and interesting things start to happen. Meanwhile, you'll need to implement a damage control policy. You can start with this checklist and then add your own items:

- For any composition chart, the whole must be obvious and meaningful. If some slices are missing and others don't seem to belong to the concept, the audience may suspect a strong tendency for cherry-picking values.

- Does it make sense to sum the categories? Don't use a pie chart to represent time series.

- Can the metric be summed? Pie charts can't represent averages or growth rates.

- Are percentages in the data consistent with the proportion in the chart? Verify that they add up to 100 percent. Rounding justifies 100.1 percent or 99.9 percent and can be tolerated. Everything else is wrong.

- I don't know how one would include negative proportions in a pie chart, but even if you find a way, don't do it.

- Make sure you group values visually (using similar colors) when they have something in common.

- Sort the values in descending order within each group.

- Do not use special effects or pseudo-3D or exploded slices. Use color contrast for emphasis.

- Do not use a legend. A pie chart allows for direct labeling. If the labels overlap, perhaps you are displaying too many slices.

You should be aware that there are no direct alternatives for representing proportions, because the most effective alternatives actually represent something else. The question is whether we want to observe proportions or to compare values that happen to be expressed in percentages.

The Fan Chart

I was playing with this idea of making reading pie charts more accurate, such that they would provide the ability to compare to the whole and to compare slices, while retaining their "pie-ness." I came up with what I call the "fan chart." I must tell you upfront that I still tag these charts as "fun" and "pie." In other words, they lie at the bottom of the usefulness scale. But these chart types show that we can play with Excel and try to find a way to solve a specific issue.

In **Figure 9.8**, pie charts display the age structure by broad age groups for the U.S. and Brazil. Then, below each pie chart, I added a fan chart. (You'll see in the next figure why I called them "fan charts"). In a fan chart, all slices start at zero degrees (vertical) and they are not stacked. Notice how the U.S. and Brazil have almost exactly the same proportion of adult population, at around two thirds? The big difference is in the proportion of children (much more in Brazil) and elderly (much more in the U.S.). It's much easier to compare the proportions of children and elderly in the U.S. using the fan chart, isn't it?

In **Figure 9.9**, each chart represents the proportion of an age group for all countries in each continent. The charts reveal very different demographic profiles (compare Europe with Africa, for example), while a sub-continental analysis for Asia is needed. It would be useful to add interactivity to explore the data, or at least adjust the length of each

Download the
original chart

COMPARING AGE STRUCTURES: UNITED STATES VS. BRAZIL IN 2010
By Broad Age Groups

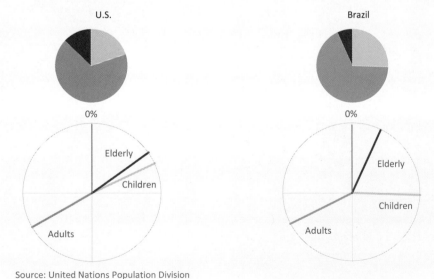

Source: United Nations Population Division

Figure 9.8 Using a fan chart to compare age structures in the U.S. and Brazil.

line to the absolute value of the population, allowing the differentiation of China from a small island in the Pacific. This chart allows this, thereby introducing a second metric, which is not common in proportion charts.

Every new chart type should be met by a healthy amount of both enthusiasm and skepticism. Perhaps a new chart offers a solution to a visualization problem you were previously unable to solve, or perhaps it forces you to look at the data from a different perspective. Or a new chart type may provide an answer to a question that no one asked. If the new question is asked, does the new chart answer the question more effectively than other chart types? Above all, does the chart respect the data?

AGE STRUCTURE BY COUNTRY, CONTINENT, AND BROAD AGE GROUP, IN 2010

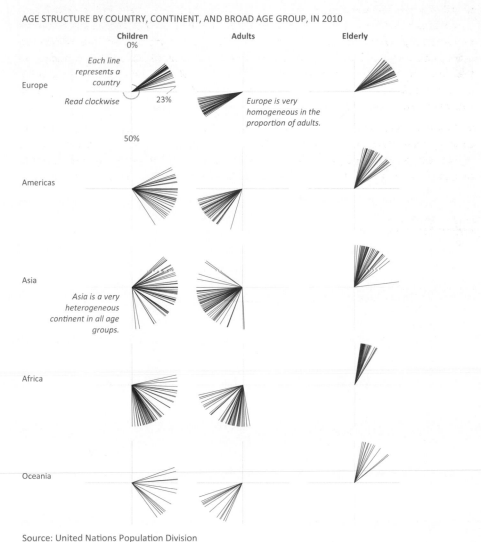

Download the
original chart

Source: United Nations Population Division

Figure 9.9 Using fan charts to compare age structure per country.

Donut Charts

While the pie chart attracts strong criticism, the donut chart is almost ignored. Why? Because it's seen as a minor chart, and every bad thing you say about pie charts can be applied to donut charts, and then some: The absence of a visible center makes it even more difficult to compare slices.

Donuts appear to have the advantage over pie charts of allowing for the comparison of multiple series, one in each ring, which makes them the circular version of stacked bar charts. In fact, though, there is little value in this, for it only helps to compare the first and last values of each series, just like the stacked bar chart.

Figure 9.10 shows how a donut is typically used for comparing two or more independent series, one in each ring. Let me ask you this: Do people spend more time in leisure and sports activities (which really means watching TV, for the most part) when they spend fewer hours working? The correct answer is "yes," but you have to spend some (too much) time comparing the segments in each ring to come up with the answer. The same happens with most of the other categories.

Download the
original chart

WHEN EMPLOYED FULL TIME, PART TIME, AND NOT EMPLOYED

Own household children, youngest under 6. Average for the combined years 2009–13

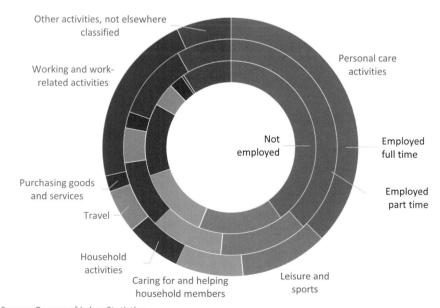

Source: Bureau of Labor Statistics

Figure 9.10 Typical donut usage: comparing three independent rings.

The slope chart in **Figure 9.11** makes everything more obvious. The time spent working is just another segment in each ring in a donut chart, while its salience in this slope chart defines how we read pretty much everything else.

WHEN EMPLOYED FULL TIME, PART TIME, AND NOT EMPLOYED

Own household children, youngest under 6

Average for the combined years 2009–13

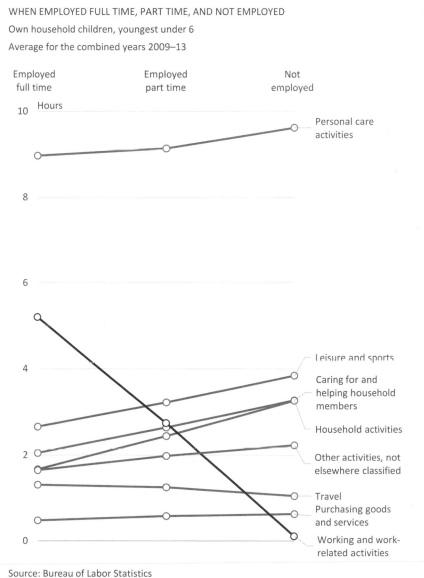

Source: Bureau of Labor Statistics

Figure 9.11 Slope chart to the rescue (again)!

Donuts as Multi-Level Pies

Although its close relationship to the pie chart isn't the best calling card for donut charts, they're not totally useless. They're great at improving upon the only thing pie charts are good at: aggregating slices. It goes without saying that you must get rid of the hole first, turning the donut into a multi-level pie chart.

The donut chart in **Figure 9.12** shows the expenditure breakdown in the U.S. using a three-level hierarchical structure. You can see both how each major item contributes to the whole and how each sub-item contributes to the parent item. To take advantage of a chart like this, you need to add interaction to identify each item or sub-item on demand, since you can't possibly label every single one (in Excel, you can identify segments when hovering the cursor over each item).

This example shows that, while a donut chart shouldn't be used to compare independent series, it can help when there is a hierarchical relationship between them.

This raises again the issue of the editorial dimension when making charts. It's often advised (rightfully) to minimize the number of slices in a proportion chart to

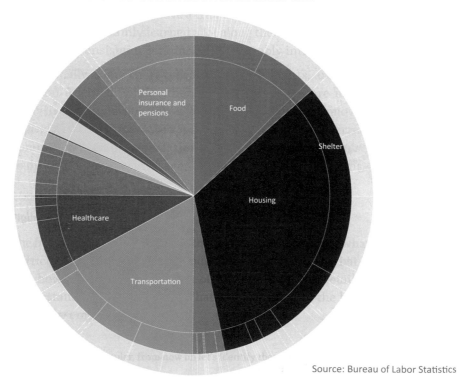

Download the
original chart

STRUCTURE OF HOUSEHOLD EXPENDITURE IN THE U.S. IN 2012–2014

Source: Bureau of Labor Statistics

Figure 9.12 A multi-level pie chart made with a combination of pie charts and donut charts.

from two to six. This chart contains 76 categories—far, far beyond that acceptable range. But because it's structured in a way that allows us to switch between levels, we can safely move from a simplistic definition about absolute limits to a loose interpretation that takes into account the way the data is organized and displayed.

Actual Hierarchical Charts: Sunburst Charts and Treemaps

Beginning in Excel 2016, you can actually make multi-level charts without having to resort to tricks and combination charts. **Figures 9.13** and **9.14** show the same household expenditure data using the new sunburst chart and the treemap.

STRUCTURE OF HOUSEHOLD EXPENDITURE IN THE U.S. IN 2012–201⸱

Figure 9.13
A multi-level pie chart, a.k.a. the sunburst chart.

Download the original chart

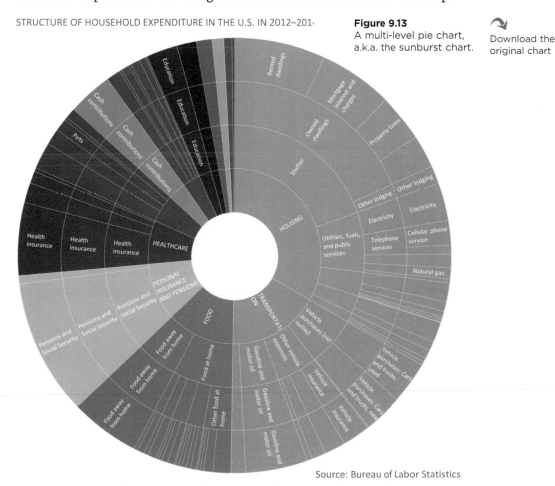

Source: Bureau of Labor Statistics

Download the
original chart

STRUCTURE OF HOUSEHOLD EXPENDITURE IN THE U.S. IN 2012–2014

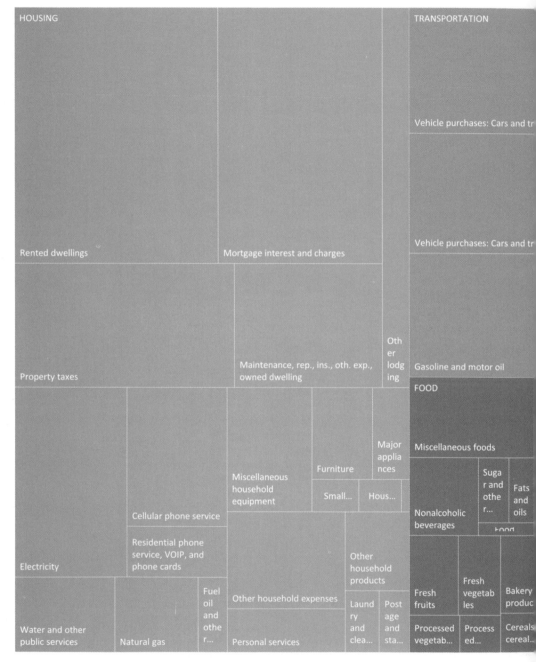

Source: Bureau of Labor Statistics

Figure 9.14 The basic implementation of treemaps in Excel 2016.

Vehicle insurance

Vehicle. rent., leas., licen., oth. charges

Vehicle maintenance and repairs

Vehicle finance charges

Public transportation

PERSONAL INSURANCE AND PENSIONS

Pensions and Social Security

Life and other personal insurance

HEALTHCARE

Health insurance

Drugs: Prescription and nonprescription

Medical services

Medical supplies

ENTERTAINMENT

Entertainment: fees and admissions

Pets

Toys,...

Audio and visual equipment and services

Entertainment: other supplies, equip., & services

CASH CONTRIBUTIONS

APPAREL AND SERVICES

Apparel, Women, 16 and over

Apparel, Men, 16 and over

Apparel, Girls, 2...

Apparel...

Other apparel products and services

Footwear

Appar...

EDUCATION

Education

k

h

d

a...

E...

s

ilk

am

Food away from home

Cash contributions

MISCELLANEOUS EXPENDITURES

Miscellaneous expenditures

PERSONAL CARE PRODUCTS AND SERVICES

Personal care products and services

ALCOHOLIC BEVERAGES

Alcoholic beverages

TOBACCO PRODUCTS AND SMOKING SUPPLIES

RE AD IN G

These are nice additions to the Excel chart library, especially the treemap. Unlike in other Excel charts, the way you order the data doesn't really matter, because each level is algorithmically sorted. You do need to be careful how you structure your data table; Excel must know exactly which labels correspond to which values so that there are no aggregate values. **Figure 9.15** shows the table structure for the item Food. You can use the same structure for both chart types.

TABLE STRUCTURE FOR MULTI-LEVEL CHARTS

Level 1	Level 2	Level 3	Level 4	USD
Food	Food at home	Cereals and bakery products	Cereals and cereal products	176
			Bakery products	343
		Meats, poultry, fish, and eggs	Beef	232
			Pork	177
			Other meats	123
			Poultry	172
			Fish and seafood	129
			Eggs	58
		Dairy products	Fresh milk and cream	147
			Other dairy products	276
		Fruits and vegetables	Fresh fruits	274
			Fresh vegetables	240
			Processed fruits	109
			Processed vegetables	133
		Other food at home	Sugar and other sweets	139
			Fats and oils	115
			Miscellaneous foods	702
			Nonalcoholic beverages	375
			Food prep. by consumer unit, out-of-town trips	51
	Food away from home	Food away from home	Food away from home	2787

Figure 9.15 The table structure for hierarchical charts in Excel 2016.

Probably because they're new implementations, the sunburst chart and treemap don't feel like real Excel charts right now (early in 2016). The level of control we usually have over the details is nowhere near what we can find in the other charts. The treemap is actually very basic and is nothing more than a rectangular version of the sunburst chart. For example, a treemap usually encodes two variables: one for rectangle size and one for rectangle fill color. A popular encoding combination is volume and growth, where growth is encoded by a color ramp. This is an important feature that is missing in the treemap's initial implementation, in Excel 2016. And being able to remove the hole in the sunburst chart would be a nice improvement, too!

Stacked Bar Chart

The stacked bar chart in **Figure 9.16** belongs to a report by the European Commission. This chart has many issues, including the inverted order of proficiency level, the intrusive comment in the middle of the chart, the color palette, and missing data. In addition to these problems, this chart demonstrates how difficult it is to read and compare intermediate bars in a stacked bar chart—not only in this chart but in all composition charts with more than two categories.

Go to the web page

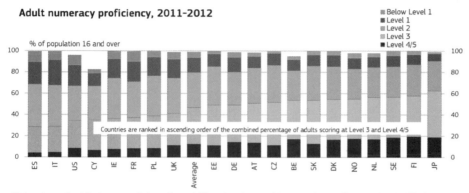

Figure 9.16 Multiple problems in a stacked bar chart.

This example makes it even more obvious that in most cases we are not interested in comparing a data point to the whole but rather in comparing multiple data points with each other. So the right chart for this data table is the one that allows for better comparisons between proficiency levels and also within each level, like the one in **Figure 9.17**.

This panel chart,[8] in addition to not requiring color coding for level identification, shows variations that can be detected only if the series are aligned. Using color, as we have done previously to highlight the countries of Eastern Europe, we can see that they generally have higher values in levels 2 and 3 and lower levels in 4/5.

8　We'll discuss panel chart and similar chart types in Chapter 13.

NUMERACY PROFICIENCY AMONG ADULTS

Percentage of 16–65 year-olds scoring at each proficiency level in numeracy

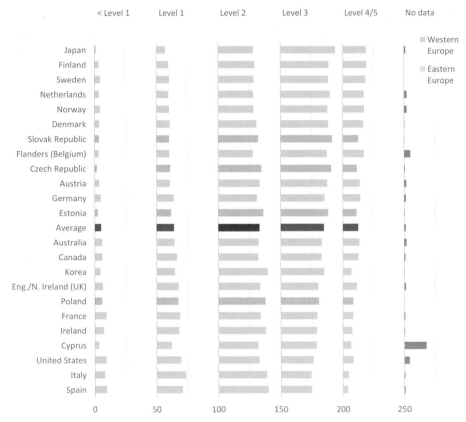

Source: OECD Skills Outlook 2013

Figure 9.17 The same baseline makes intermediate levels easier to compare.

Pareto Chart

Since in most cases a composition task is in reality a comparison task, and representing the whole is irrelevant, the bar chart is often the suggested alternative to proportion charts. But one issue remains to be solved: how to show the cumulative values. The Pareto chart can reconcile this need with the need to compare categories effectively.

The Pareto principle, from which the Pareto chart gets its name, postulates that for many events, 80 percent of the effects are the result of 20 percent of the causes (the 80/20 rule). The Pareto chart lets you compare the relative weight of each category as well as their cumulative effect, showing the individual values of each category in vertical bars arranged in descending order, while a line displays the cumulative value.

The bars in the top chart in **Figure 9.18** (on the following page) would give us a very clear idea of the difference in population size between the major EU countries and the rest. However, the cumulative line makes it even more obvious: There are 28 countries in the EU, but more than half of the population is concentrated in only four countries (Germany, France, the UK, and Italy), and nine countries compose 80 percent of the population.

The version of the Pareto chart at the top displays two unsynchronized axes: the left axis for individual absolute values and the right axis for cumulative percentages. Using two axes should ordinarily be avoided, but in the case of the Pareto chart, the reading of the variables is clearly independent and there is no risk of the reader drawing conclusions based on their relationships. Still, it's useful to make sure that the reader uses the correct axis to read each series. You can do this using the same color encoding.

The chart at the bottom uses two synchronized axes. They represent exactly the same quantities at each grid line, although one represents absolute values and the other represents relative values. The problem with this approach is that it degrades resolution: The clear split between countries in the top chart is missing in this. When you have many categories, you can end up with a flat chart where you can't discriminate each one, so testing both options is a good idea.

Some authors in quality control suggest that the way Excel users design Pareto charts is not entirely correct: In the first bar, the line should run from the bottom left corner to the top right corner, and not in the center of the bar. I'd like to know more about this and other apparently debatable rules, but as an exercise, I followed them in the bottom version. I used a scatter plot, because it's easier to implement the chart with this than figuring out how to do it with a bar/line combination chart.

Go to the
web page

POPULATION IN THE EUROPEAN UNION BY COUNTRY IN 2012

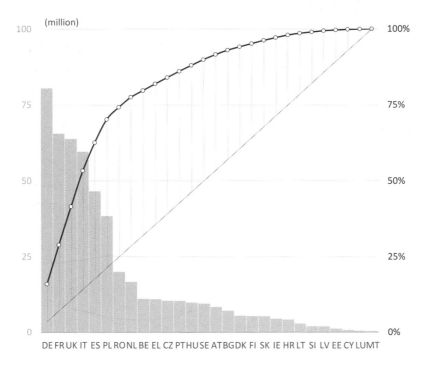

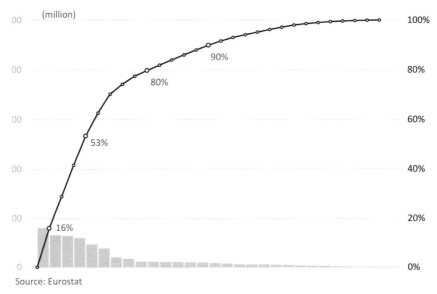

Source: Eurostat

Figure 9.18 Using a Pareto chart as an alternative to proportion charts.

Takeaways

- The distinctive characteristic of composition or proportion charts is the representation of the whole, defined by the cumulative values of all categories. The most common examples of composition charts are stacked bar charts, pie charts, and donut charts.

- Composition should be seen as a minor task in data visualization. From an extreme point of view, we can argue that all we can do when using composition is compare a single data point to the whole.

- In almost all cases, especially when dealing with relative values, composition analysis is in reality a comparison analysis, where the whole is of little importance.

- Intermediate categories are difficult to compare using pie charts or stacked bar charts.

- Although there are scenarios in which a pie chart is simple and familiar enough to give the audience a general idea of the values and their relative proportions, the frequent use of pie charts should be taken as a symptom of low numeracy and graphicacy within the organization.

- Overall, the best alternative to pie charts is the Pareto chart, which allows for a more effective comparison of individual data points and also gives a sense of the whole through the display of cumulative values.

10

SCATTERED DATA

Henry Ford once remarked that "Half of my advertising budget is wasted, but I don't know which half." Similarly, we could say that half of our data are noise, but we don't know which half. There is always *signal* (useful information) and *noise* (irrelevant variation) in a data set. Not only can we not always tell which is which, but signal and noise also change from task to task and from user to user.

In our pursuit of simplification and the good form, it would be ideal if we could reduce an entire data distribution to a single indicator like the mean, with an acceptable level of information loss. We *can* find such variables, but they'll lack relevant variation and they'll ultimately be useless.

However, we may be luckier than Henry Ford. All distributions have a shape (or form), and once we know that shape we can start trimming the noise while keeping the shape intact, for the most part.

A traditional way of learning the properties of a distribution is through the extensive use of descriptive statistics, but if you think you can always trust statistics to help you discover a distribution's shape, think again. Let me show you what I mean with a famous example that the data visualization community loves.

The four data sets used to create the charts in **Figure 10.1** are identical. Or at least that's what you would have concluded had I concealed the charts from you and shared only some of the most common statistical measures of each data set, such as mean, variance, correlation, and linear regression. These measures are identical for all four charts. And yet a simple glance at the charts is enough to confirm that the values in each data set are far from identical.

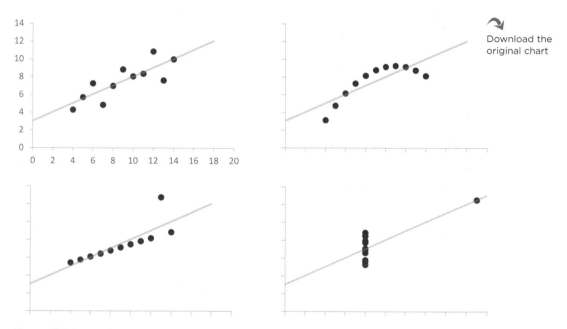

Download the original chart

Figure 10.1 Anscombe's quartet illustrates the need for a complementary relationship between statistical measures and data visualization.

These four scatter plots are called the Anscombe's quartet, from its author's name, the British statistician Francis Anscombe. He wanted to show (successfully) that data sets with identical statistical properties may correspond to very different distributions.

Anscombe's quartet demonstrates one of the reasons why we need to visualize the data: not to replace, or even minimize, the role of traditional statistical methods but to be aware of their complementary relationship, where both perspectives are important and where only the nature of the task allows us to decide the best combination.

This complementary relationship takes many forms. When you have all points of a distribution plotted on a chart, you get a very detailed picture—much more detailed than anything you can get through statistical measures, naturally. But there are two issues with this. First, you may get lost in all the detail and become unable to "see the big picture," with all the noise canceling out the signal. Second, you'll want a quantitative value that you can use as a reference, such as "a sales increase of 10 percent" rather than "move this point from here to there."

Visualizing a data set also helps us choose the best statistical measure. Take, for example, the bottom right chart in Anscombe's quartet. There is no variation in x, except for a strong outlier. If you had to choose between the mean and the median, the latter would better describe the distribution, because it's not influenced by the outlier.

This chapter explores the intertwined nature of data visualization and statistics. We will not go beyond basic descriptive statistics, but that should be enough to understand the reasons why visualization and statistics need each other. Often people evolve from a purely visual perspective to a more balanced approach because statistics provide a solid framework for improving their visualizations. The inverse is also true: Many statisticians (including Francis Anscombe, William Cleveland, and John Tukey) realize the need of data visualization for better statistical analysis.

I must confess that I remember well when I was unable to understand one of the examples presented later in this chapter—the box-and-whisker plot. I thought I needed to put a couple of hours aside to decipher it. Then one day I saw it superimposed on the data points and it took me less than a minute to realize how simple the chart is, and that there was nothing complex to decipher. The box-and-whisker plot is just a visual list of cut-off points. Sometimes, the right image is all you need to understand something that immediately becomes simple and obvious.

The Data

I will risk asserting that if you visualize data on the distribution of housing, auto sales, or medical appointments at the U.S. state level, you'll get very similar charts or maps. No divining talent is required to foresee this, for these, and many more variables, are strongly correlated to population. These charts and maps basically display population distribution. A more interesting approach is to measure how much the variable actually diverges from that distribution.

All data comes with its own baggage of surrounding knowledge, opinions, and misconceptions, which simply can't be avoided. But I wanted to use a data set that could minimize this baggage. Since I was free to choose whatever data I wanted for this book, the 2012 U.S. Census of Agriculture seemed a good choice (**Figure 10.2**, on the following page). Of course, this means that you'll learn more about the distribution of goats or bee colonies than you'd expected. When I chose this data set, I assumed that the correlation with population distribution would be weak and perhaps even negative. I added humans as one of the species, so we can analyze that too.

When data have a spatial dimension, we're naturally curious about any spatial patterns. In fact, you should always check for those patterns, but if they prove uninteresting, don't bother keeping the maps. Maps aren't easy to make in an out-of-the-box Excel installation—although it became easier with Excel 2016. As a bonus, I'll include a section on maps (made in Excel) for the data we're using. But until then we'll work with unidentified data points.

POPULATION PER SPECIES IN THE U.S. IN 2012

(000)

State	Cattle and calves	Beef cows (*)	Milk cows (*)	Hogs and pigs	Sheep and lambs	All goats	Colonies of bees	Broilers	Turkeys	Horses and Ponies	Human Population
Alabama	1,236.5	722.8	9.1	142.6	21.1	52.7	11.6	172,955.4	7.4	63.7	4,822.0
Alaska	10.7	3.4	1.1	1.0	0.8	0.6	0.5	1.9	3.0	1.6	731.4
Arizona	911.3	197.9	193.6	169.6	180.6	71.7	58.5	8.5	2.5	92.4	6,553.3
Arkansas	1,615.8	813.3	9.0	109.3	18.8	41.6	23.3	170,380.4	8,821.8	61.1	2,949.1
California	5,370.5	583.6	1,815.7	111.9	668.5	140.0	945.6	42,268.5	4,532.3	142.6	38,041.4
Colorado	2,630.1	683.3	130.7	727.3	401.4	34.8	34.8	19.6	3.8	110.4	5,187.6
Connecticut	48.3	8.1	17.7	4.7	6.1	4.4	5.6	79.6	9.4	17.4	3,590.3
Delaware	18.2	3.8	4.5	5.9	1.0	2.0	0.8	43,206.5	0.8	6.2	917.1
Florida	1,675.3	982.8	123.2	14.9	18.2	52.1	206.7	11,031.7	5.6	121.0	19,317.6
Georgia	1,033.7	469.9	79.5	153.7	21.8	71.7	64.2	243,463.9	2.7	69.9	9,919.9
Hawaii	134.0	73.2	1.5	11.4	21.9	13.0	8.6	3.4	0.1	5.1	1,392.3
Idaho	2,397.5	485.0	578.8	45.1	231.1	18.1	103.6	9.6	6.7	61.4	1,595.7
Illinois	1,127.6	344.0	98.8	4,630.8	54.7	31.5	10.0	115.9	739.7	62.7	12,875.3
Indiana	821.3	182.6	174.1	3,747.4	52.2	38.6	13.0	6,238.6	5,084.8	97.4	6,537.3
Iowa	3,893.7	885.6	204.8	20,455.7	165.8	56.2	30.0	1,949.0	4,383.2	62.2	3,074.2
Kansas	5,922.2	1,270.5	131.7	1,886.2	62.5	42.3	10.7	17.9	131.2	74.9	2,885.9
Kentucky	2,270.9	985.1	71.8	313.4	54.6	64.1	12.7	51,189.7	34.6	141.8	4,380.4
Louisiana	789.0	434.3	16.1	6.8	9.8	18.8	34.9	25,061.5	1.4	59.8	4,601.9
Maine	86.3	10.5	32.1	8.9	11.9	6.4	14.5	47.3	5.6	12.0	1,329.2
Maryland	194.5	39.2	50.9	19.9	19.3	10.7	7.9	64,192.4	77.4	28.7	5,884.6
Massachusetts	35.7	6.2	12.5	11.2	12.5	8.6	4.7	18.1	12.1	20.3	6,646.1
Michigan	1,130.5	108.1	376.3	1,099.5	86.5	27.1	79.0	1,125.6	2,190.5	88.0	9,883.4
Minnesota	2,412.7	357.8	463.3	7,606.8	126.5	33.7	101.4	7,765.2	19,450.0	66.4	5,379.1
Mississippi	921.5	495.4	14.5	401.9	13.0	24.5	36.1	134,479.9	1.5	58.7	2,984.9
Missouri	3,703.1	1,683.7	93.0	2,774.6	92.0	103.7	14.6	46,880.7	7,572.5	117.3	6,022.0
Montana	2,633.7	1,439.7	13.9	174.0	236.6	10.3	119.0	89.9	20.2	97.9	1,005.1
Nebraska	6,385.7	1,730.1	54.6	2,992.6	71.8	25.8	44.9	909.0	195.6	64.3	1,855.5
Nevada	420.3	220.2	29.5	2.7	91.9	21.4	10.2	3.8	1.3	22.5	2,758.9
New Hampshire	33.4	4.1	13.5	3.3	8.1	4.9	2.9	28.9	2.6	9.1	1,320.7
New Jersey	31.4	9.5	7.2	7.9	14.9	8.3	13.3	19.9	13.7	27.7	8,864.6
New Mexico	1,354.2	461.6	318.9	1.3	89.7	31.0	15.1	3.9	6.4	50.7	2,085.5
New York	1,419.4	86.0	610.7	74.7	86.3	36.4	70.6	591.6	143.5	90.2	19,570.3
North Carolina	829.7	348.2	46.0	8,901.4	29.2	66.4	24.2	148,251.5	17,191.3	66.9	9,752.1
North Dakota	1,809.6	881.7	17.9	133.7	64.6	4.7	370.5	24.7	419.3	45.3	699.6
Ohio	1,242.3	277.9	267.9	2,058.5	112.0	51.6	21.4	12,194.0	2,096.4	114.1	11,544.2
Oklahoma	4,246.0	1,677.9	45.9	2,304.7	53.7	89.1	21.0	38,430.0	102.1	158.9	3,814.8
Oregon	1,297.9	504.3	125.8	12.7	214.6	33.2	82.2	3,294.8	4.8	70.4	3,899.4
Pennsylvania	1,626.4	148.2	532.3	1,135.0	96.6	50.2	32.0	29,248.1	2,956.0	119.9	12,763.5
Rhode Island	4.7	1.4	1.2	1.8	1.8	0.9	0.7	13.4	6.3	2.4	1,050.3
South Carolina	297.3	166.7	16.0	224.1	12.7	38.7	10.1	44,296.2	6,999.6	52.4	4,723.7
South Dakota	3,893.3	1,610.6	91.8	1,191.2	257.7	16.5	210.4	57.6	2,449.8	68.9	833.4
Tennessee	1,856.3	874.6	48.0	147.8	43.8	91.7	14.2	30,400.7	4.0	96.5	6,456.2
Texas	11,159.7	4,329.3	434.9	800.9	623.0	878.9	136.8	107,351.7	1,747.5	395.8	26,059.2
Utah	776.8	369.7	90.4	731.7	287.9	14.7	26.1	5.6	2,894.9	59.0	2,855.3
Vermont	274.3	11.5	134.1	3.9	18.8	10.6	8.6	48.5	3.8	11.7	626.0
Virginia	1,631.9	657.3	94.1	239.9	85.0	50.8	14.3	38,386.3	5,160.8	86.8	8,185.9
Washington	1,162.8	211.9	267.0	19.9	44.9	27.1	96.7	7,511.1	5.3	64.6	6,897.0
West Virginia	414.9	191.4	10.1	5.9	31.6	18.8	9.3	14,781.3	1,817.3	26.5	1,855.4
Wisconsin	3,494.1	248.3	1,270.1	311.7	80.1	61.1	49.7	7,818.7	3,468.5	103.5	5,726.4
Wyoming	1,307.7	664.3	6.2	85.4	354.8	9.2	45.0	4.9	0.9	72.5	576.4
Total	89,994.6	28,956.6	9,252.3	66,026.8	5,364.8	2,621.5	3,282.6	1,506,276.8	100,792.2	3,621.3	313,281.7

Note: Beef cows are cattle raise for meat production and milk cows are cattle raised for milk production. These two columns are subsets the first column, cattle and calves.

Sources: USDA Census of Agriculture and U.S. Census Bureau

Figure 10.2 The data set for this chapter: livestock and human population.

Download the original table

Distribution

"Distribution" refers to how the values of a variable are placed along an axis, keeping the proportional distances taken from the values in the table. In descriptive statistics, there are two complementary ways to study a distribution: searching for what is common (the measures of central tendency) and searching for what is different along with how much different it is (measures of dispersion).

Plotting the individual points of a variable along an axis results in the creation of a strip plot that mimics the characteristics of the proto-chart. We have to add titles and labeling, but changes are otherwise minor and result from the need to ensure that all points are visible, even when they overlap.

Showing Everything: Transparencies and Jittering

Making all points visible ensures maximum accuracy (unless the presence of an outlier jeopardizes the chart's resolution). Showing all the points is useful, but it can also prove to be excessively noisy, not allowing the reader to generalize the results.

When there are many similar or identical data points, they'll overlap, and the chart reader may not be able to evaluate how much the data points are concentrated. A single dot can hide many others. A strong concentration combined with a wide range makes this even more serious. That's why a single outlier can ruin an otherwise acceptable resolution.

When you still get overlapping data points after changing marker size and type, chart size, or scale range, you have a few options you can resort to (**Figure 10.3**). Choosing a dark tone for the marker and setting a high percentage of transparency can help create a sense of density. Or you can go all the way and simply remove the fill color and use a simple shape, like a ring.

NUMBER OF HORSES AND PONIES BY STATE

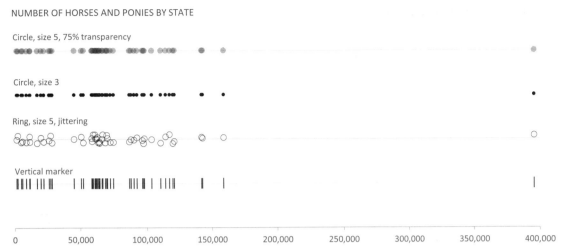

Source: USDA Census of Agriculture, 2012

Figure 10.3 How to minimize visual overlapping.

If everything else fails, adding a very small amount of random variation to separate the dots ("jittering") can minimize overlapping without influencing the way you read the data. When you use jittering, it's always advisable to add a note explaining it.

Quantifying Impressions

One of the first things we'll notice in the distribution of horses and ponies is the strong outlier at about 400,000, which is far above all other states. The remaining states seem to be loosely grouped in three clusters. We can guess that the mean should fall in the middle one, so it should be around the 70,000 mark.

It would be useful to validate and quantify our impressions: Where exactly is the center of the distribution? How much variation should we consider "normal"? Can we quantify the limits above or below which a point should be considered an outlier? **Figure 10.4** can tell us more about this. Let's remove the outlier for a moment so that we can use the chart at a higher resolution.

Take a look at the position of the two triangles, representing the median and the mean. The median is clearly to the left of the mean and near the darker area.

NUMBER OF HORSES AND PONIES BY STATE

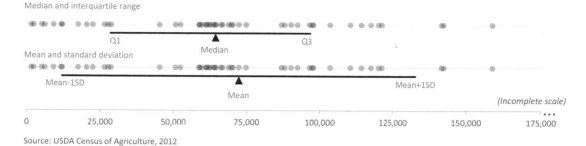

Source: USDA Census of Agriculture, 2012

Figure 10.4 Comparing central points and deviations.

Mean and Standard Deviation

The mean is useful when variation is small and when the values are distributed more or less symmetrically to the left and to the right. A quick look shows that this is not the case here: Even without counting the outlier, the three values to the right skew the distribution and impact on the mean. For this reason, the mean seems somewhat inflated and is not the best measure to represent the center point of this distribution. The horizontal dark red line marks the standard deviation (the amount of dispersion) from the mean, and is also clearly influenced by the values above 130,000.

The Median and the Interquartile Range

Another measure, the median, is the middle point of an ordered list of data points. For example, in (1,2,3,4,5), the median is 3. Because the median takes into account the *position* of the data points more than it does the actual values, it's unaffected by outliers. If instead of (1,2,3,4,5) you have (1,2,3,4,500), you still get the same median. That's why the median is lower than the mean in the example of horses and ponies. When a distribution is symmetrical, mean and median have the same value.

As you can see, the median is not a calculation that takes into account the whole data, but rather just a cut-off point that splits the distribution in two. You can use this logic and split the distribution in other places. A common split is in three places, to get four sections, or *quartiles*, where each quartile contains a percentage of the data points in the ordered list: Q1 contains the bottom 25 percent, Q2 contains 50 percent and Q3 contains 75 percent. It follows that 50 percent of the data points fall between Q1 and Q3. This is called the *interquartile range* and it's represented in the top chart of Figure 10.4 by the red line. Unlike the mean, where the range of the standard deviation is equal to the left and to the right, the median does not have to be at the center of the interquartile range. The fact that the median is not at the center reveals the distribution skewness.

Outliers

In **Figure 10.5**, I temporarily set the value of the outlier to zero. If you compare this chart to the previous one, you'll see that the impact on the median and the quartiles is negligible (it changes a bit because the value was moved to the bottom half of the list), while the mean becomes much closer to the median and the standard deviation is greatly reduced.

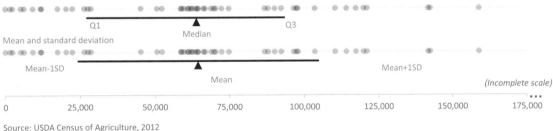

NUMBER OF HORSES AND PONIES BY STATE

Source: USDA Census of Agriculture, 2012

Figure 10.5 The impact of outliers on the mean and standard deviation.

In the analysis of distributions, the treatment of outliers has been gaining increasing interest. An outlier may correspond to an error (for example, when on a scale from 1 to 5, a value of 6 is entered). Outliers are a common feature of certain distributions (Washington, D.C., for example, will appear as a clear outlier in a list of states by population density) or something that needs further investigation. Imagine, for example, that sales in a sales territory are much better than expected. It's useful to understand why this is happening and if it can be replicated elsewhere. Whatever the case, **an outlier is almost always interesting and should not be overlooked.**

It seems easy to identify an outlier when we see it, but it's helpful to define the acceptable thresholds, because in many cases what qualifies as an outlier is not as obvious as it is in this case.

There is no single methodology to define an outlier and how it should be calculated. **Figure 10.6** displays a red tick line, corresponding to the interquartile range (top) and the standard deviation from the mean (bottom). Think of the thinner, light red line as marking a transition zone beyond which we should consider any point an outlier. The range of this transition zone is calculated:

- For the **median**, by multiplying the interquartile range by 1.5 and adding this product to Q3 and subtracting it from Q1.

- For the **mean**, by adding or subtracting two standard deviations.

If there are no outliers, these limits are capped at the minimum and maximum values. Both methods agree that there is a single outlier in this distribution.

NUMBER OF HORSES AND PONIES BY STATE

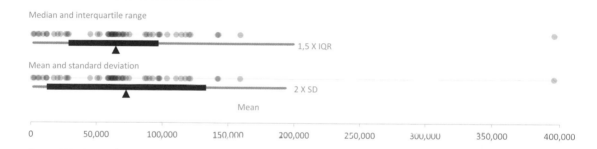

Source: USDA Census of Agriculture, 2012

Figure 10.6 Two methods of calculating outliers.

Download the original chart

Box-and-Whisker Plots

The strip plot gives us an accurate picture of the distribution of points along the axis. However, it's easy to feel that there is nothing concrete that we can hold on to. We need something that summarizes those values and at the same time provides anchor points that help us read the distribution. That's the reason we've been adding metrics that help us understand the structure in a more quantified manner.

Now that we have a pretty good idea of the distribution, perhaps we're getting overzealous by displaying all the data points. Aren't we risking not seeing the overall picture, with all those distractor points? Perhaps we should simplify and emphasize only the key points, and find a way to compare all the series in the table. Wouldn't that be a better allocation of our resources?

It certainly would be, and the best way to do it is through the box-and-whisker plot. We don't really have much to do, because the chart is already present in Figure 10.6: If you consider the top distribution, the "box" is the thick red line (the interquartile range) and the "whiskers" are the light red lines extending from there, defining the thresholds beyond which only the outliers remain.

One of my clients was somewhat uncomfortable with a suggestion to use the median instead of the mean (the presence of strong outliers justified it). He wasn't sure whether users were aware of the difference between the two metrics. If we're at this level of numeric literacy, the box-and-whisker plot may not appear to be the best graphical representation, because of its abstraction and its use of less familiar statistical concepts like quartiles. However, this chart deserves some investment because, in most instances, it satisfactorily describes the distribution with an acceptable loss of detail.

The box-and-whisker plot may not give a perfectly correct image of the distribution where there are two very populated areas around the median creating a bipolar distribution, which is not visible on the chart. However, we can compensate for this weakness of the box-and-whisker plot by keeping the data points visible, by varying the width of the box depending on the density of points, or by some other creative solution.

Z-Scores

It would be nice to compare distributions, but a glance at the table from Figure 10.2 will make us think twice: We can't compare 1.6 billion broiler chickens with a few million horses.

To make comparisons possible, we need to transform the data. One of the common ways of achieving this is by calculating the *z-scores*, whereby each variable is transformed so that its mean is set to zero and its standard deviation is set to one. All data points in each distribution become positive or negative, depending on whether they fall above or below the mean.

After calculating the z-scores, we can compare the distributions (**Figure 10.7**). It's clear that all have strong outliers. There are several variability profiles. For example, variability in goats is much lower than in the number of horses and ponies.

DISTRIBUTION OF EACH SPECIES PER STATE

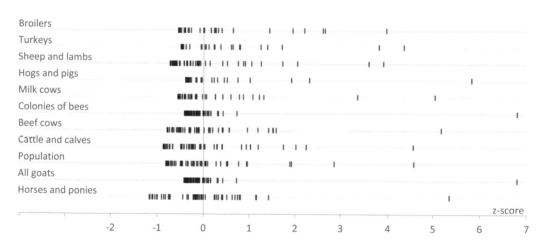

Source: USDA Census of Agriculture, 2012

Figure 10.7 Using z-scores to compare distributions.

Download the
original chart

Figure 10.8 allows us to compare the distributions using multiple box-and-whisker plots.[1] We can see that they're ordered by the median value, and many other details are now clearer. In the bottom two distributions, goats have a much lower variability than horses and ponies, but its outlier is much stronger. In several distributions, deciding whether a data point is an outlier is not as simple as in the example of horses and ponies, but the box-and-whisker plot sets a criterion we can follow.

Note that I opted to keep all the data points, although usually a box-and-whisker plot displays the outliers only.

Download the
original chart

DISTRIBUTION OF EACH SPECIES PER STATE

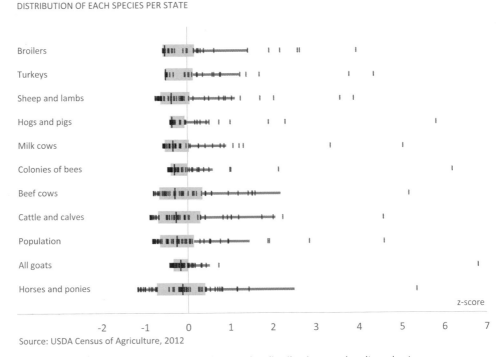

Source: USDA Census of Agriculture, 2012

Figure 10.8 Adding box-and-whisker plots to the distributions makes it easier to compare them.

---

1   Microsoft implemented box-and-whisker plots in Excel 2016. Like the other new charts, they're not as flexible as the existing charts in the library. For example, in the current version, there is no option for making horizontal box-and-whisker plots. Those in Figure 10.8 were made from a scatter plot, which is a very time-consuming process.

The Pareto Chart Revisited

Outliers and variability suggest another way of reading distributions, which is by analyzing their cumulative values. So, let's return to the Pareto chart. In a Pareto chart, the line of cumulative values always lies within the shaded top triangle (**Figure 10.9**), wherein the diagonal line represents the minimum concentration, and a single data point at the topmost left corner would correspond to the highest concentration (all horses in a single state).

You'll certainly wonder whether the distribution of horses and ponies is similar to other species. The answer is no, as we see in Figure 10.9, where you can compare their distribution to hogs and pigs. It's clear that although you can find many horses almost everywhere, hogs and pigs are much more concentrated. A single state holds more than 30 percent of the population.

CUMULATIVE INVENTORY PER STATE

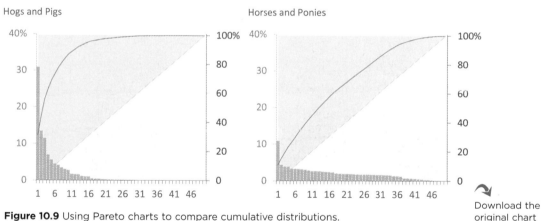

Figure 10.9 Using Pareto charts to compare cumulative distributions.

Download the original chart

In **Figure 10.10,** you'll find a Pareto chart for each of the animal species in our livestock analysis (and also for humans). I shaded part of the top left triangle to show how cumulative values vary for all these distributions. For each state, I recorded the maximum and minimum values. I also added reference lines in the 50 percent and 80 percent cumulative values. For example, turkeys follow the Pareto principle: 80 percent of the population can be found in 20 percent of the states, while you need 56 percent of the states to get 80 percent of horses and ponies.

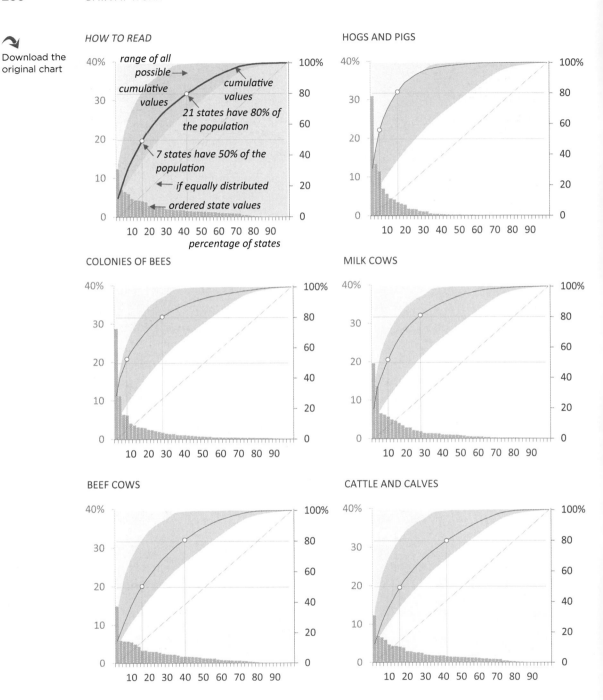

Figure 10.10 Pareto charts of all animal species in our livestock analysis.

TURKEYS

BROILERS

SHEEP AND LAMBS

ALL GOATS

POPULATION

HORSES AND PONIES

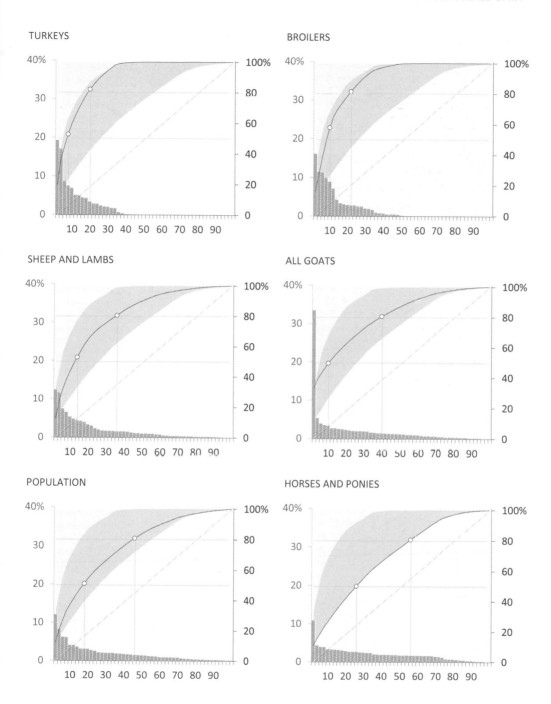

Excel Maps

It's a pity that, for far too long, basic thematic mapping was absent from an out-of-the-box Excel installation. To circumvent that before Excel 2016, I kept playing with the available options, such as:

- Using shapes (a state is a shape) and coloring them through programming.

- Using very small cells to draw low-resolution regions, with conditional formatting and without programming. The resulting maps look somewhat rustic, but good enough for most basic tasks.

- When mapping Walmart stores (recall Figure 5.20), I used a scatter plot to display counties and stores.

Excel 2016 now comes with 3D Maps. The name is alarming, but you can make a Region map and ignore the other options. I used 3D Maps to map our livestock data in **Figure 10.11**. I split the distributions into five bins, using percentiles 20, 40, 60, and 80.

Figure 10.11 Mapping livestock and human populations.

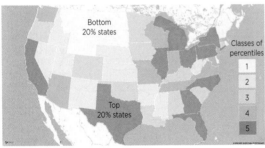

Legend

Beef Cows

Cattle and Calves

Turkeys

Hogs

Bee Colonies

Sheep

Goats

Horses and Ponies

Human Population

Milk Cows

Broiler Chickens

Don't forget that sometimes we pay too much attention to the spatial dimension just because we can make a map, even if it doesn't reveal significant patterns, and we overlook other dimensions and relationships that can be revealed by a simpler, non-spatial display.

Histograms

Each of the counties in the U.S. is shown in **Figures 10.12** and **10.13**. There are so many points that vertical jittering was applied to facilitate seeing the density of points. In Figure 10.12[2] the technique worked well and allows for an acceptable breakdown of data points. In Figure 10.13, on the contrary, the distribution is so skewed that the only remedy to improve discrimination would be to use a log scale.

POVERTY PERCENT IN ALL AGES BY U.S. COUNTY IN 2010

Source: U.S. Census Bureau

Figure 10.12 Distribution of U.S. counties by percent poverty.

POPULATION BY U.S. COUNTY, 2012 ESTIMATES

Source: U.S. Census Bureau

Figure 10.13 Distribution of U.S. counties by population.

2 Note that we are taking into account the number of counties only, regardless of their population. In a more thorough analysis, you should weight them.

We saw how useful the box-and-whisker plot is at synthesizing a distribution through a set of measures such as the median and the interquartile range. But what if we want to know how many cases there are in an interval? For example, how many counties fall within the 15 percent to 20 percent poverty range? That's something you can't really answer with a box-and-whisker plot.

The histogram answers questions like that, however. Unlike in the box-and-whisker plot, we need to define bins (classes or intervals) and count how many cases fall inside each bin. The problem is that there is no simple way of defining those bins and their cut-off points, which opens the door to malicious manipulations. But let's assume good faith. Figures 10.12 and 10.13 show that we need different approaches to get a good portrait of each of these distributions.

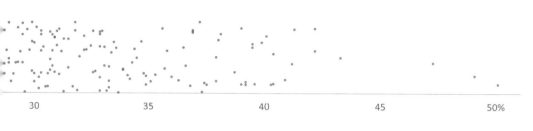

Bin Number and Width

When defining the number of classes (bins) in a histogram, you must find the right balance between resolution and the task. On the one hand, the number of bins should be as small as possible without loss of relevant details. On the other hand, the task may impose a specific goal that forces a predefined bin number or bin width. Take the preceding example: If you want to know how many counties fall within the 15 percent to 20 percent poverty range, you'll have to use a 5-point bin width, but you'll want to check if and how this influences the overall shape.

There is no simple way to determine the appropriate number of bins, because this number depends on the range of the data, the number of points (n), and the actual profile of the distribution. You can find suggestions ranging from general impressions, such as "5 to 20," to more formulaic alternatives. You can approach the problem from two perspectives:

- **The number of observations (n).** With the Rice rule ($2n^{1/3}$), we would get around 30 bins for 3143 counties.

- **Bin width.** Freedman–Diaconis's rule: $2(IQR(x)/n^{1/3})$, where IQR is the interquartile range. The result for the population data can be rounded to a bin width of 7,500. The use of IQR means that the result will not be influenced by outliers.

Whatever the methodology used, it should not avoid a qualitative assessment of the appropriate number of bins. Freedman–Diaconis's formula seems to be a good compromise between a fully empirical decision and overly complex formulas for something that does not prevent an arbitrary decision.

The distribution of counties by percent poverty draws a reasonably symmetric bell-shaped curve with a few not-too-pronounced outliers. We can easily justify any number of bins or any bin width, and we'd have to try hard to mess up the curve. As you can see, all bin widths in **Figure 10.14** do an acceptable job of showing the shape of the distribution. For the top histogram, I calculated the number of bins and rounded the width to 2. The bottom left and bottom right histograms use 5-point and 1-point bin widths, respectively. The 2-point bin width will not tell you how many counties there are in the 15 percent to 20 percent poverty range, but if you find the 5-point width acceptable, you should use that histogram.

NUMBER OF COUNTIES BY POVERTY PERCENT
2-point bin width

Download the
original chart

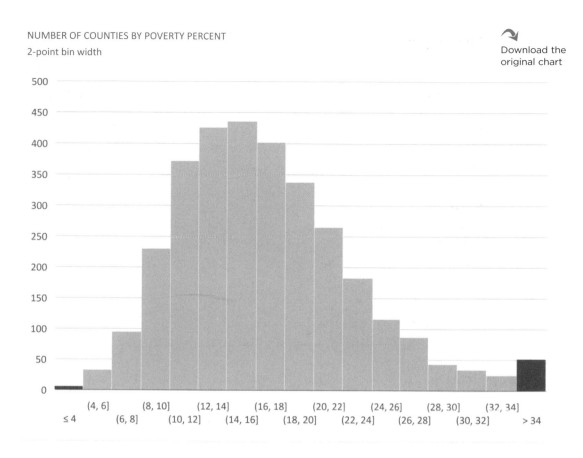

5-point bin width

1-point bin width

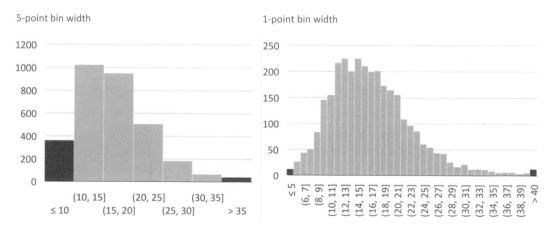

Figure 10.14 Testing with different bin widths.

The population histogram is much harder to set up (**Figure 10.15**). Since we're using same-width bins, we'll always end up with a strong overflow bin (the last bin on the right). I decided that the overflow bin should not include more than 10 percent of all counties, so the cut-off point will be counties with more than 210,000 inhabitants. If you set the bin width at 7,500, you'll get 29 bins, close to Rice's formula.

NUMBER OF U.S. COUNTIES BY POPULATION IN 2012

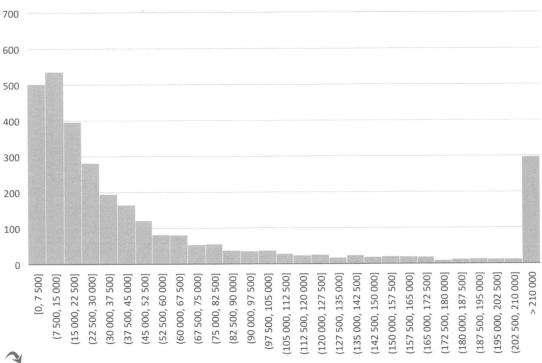

Download the
original chart

Figure 10.15 A distribution that requires more editorial judgment.

Now, do you think that a county with 2,500 inhabitants is similar to another with 7,501? Or is a county with 200,000 inhabitants not much different than another with one million? If you believe they have significantly different qualities, you may need to tweak the bin width, number of bins, and overflow bin until you find a suitable result. Make sure that your message is consistent with your design and that both are consistent with the overall shape of the data.

Histograms and Bar Charts

It's important to clarify the difference between histograms and bar charts, as they are very similar visually. A bar chart represents categorical values with an arbitrary order. To show that there is no continuity between values, the bars should be represented with a gap between them.

The histogram, in turn, refers to sections in a quantitative axis, wherein a bin's upper limit coincides with the next bin's lower limit. In histograms, bars are not separated by spaces. In **Figure 10.16**, the chart on the left is a histogram, where class limits are clearly defined. In the bar chart on the right, I defined seven categorical classes, and I can even rank them, something that I can't do with a histogram.

One of the new charts in Excel 2016 is the histogram, and I used it to make the histograms in this section. Again, this is still a bare-bones implementation that doesn't allow for the level of control we're accustomed to with other charts. Hopefully, we'll be given more control over Excel histograms in the future.

NUMBER OF COUNTIES BY POVERTY PERCENT

Download the original chart

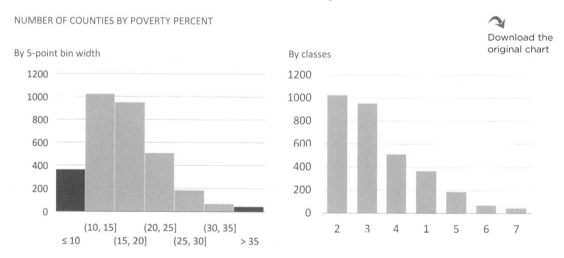

Figure 10.16 The difference between histograms and bar charts.

Cumulative Frequency Distribution

Adding a bit of jittering to a strip plot helps reduce overlapping points, but it might not be a bad idea to also make the vertical axis a bit more informative. How about displaying a cumulative value, like the Pareto chart does?

CUMULATIVE FREQUENCY DISTRIBUTION OF COUNTIES BY NUMBER OF INHABITANTS

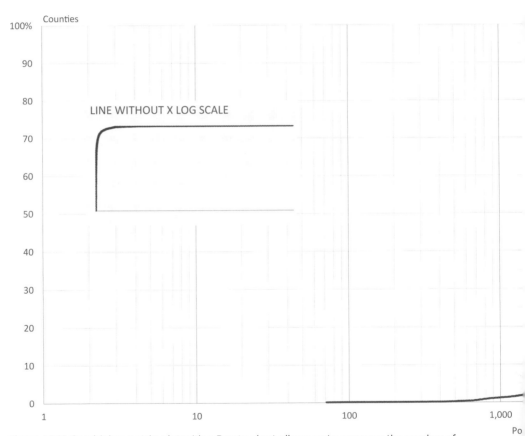

Figure 10.17 Combining a strip plot with a Pareto chart allows us to compare the number of counties for each cumulative percentage.

Figure 10.17 shows what happens when we order the counties in ascending order of population, set the vertical axis to display the cumulative frequency, and set the horizontal axis to display county size. Since we have a very wide range, the horizontal axis must be set to log scale.[3] I added an inset to show what the line would look like in a linear scale as opposed to the log scale.

A log scale with secondary gridlines allows for a more precise reading. With a linear scale, it would be impossible to determine the number of counties for each cumulative percentage.

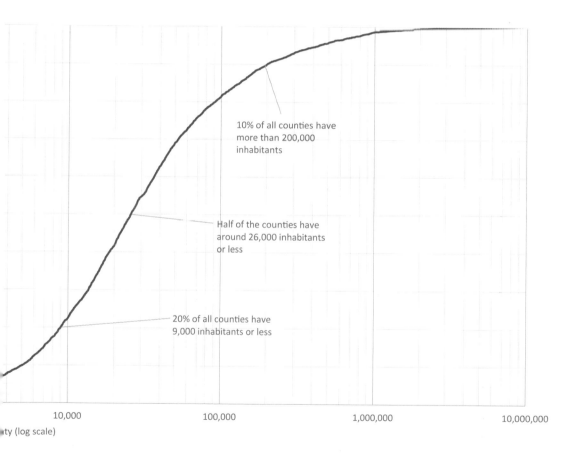

10,000   100,000   1,000,000   10,000,000

ity (log scale)

---

3   Log scales are discussed in Chapter 14.

Takeaways

- Statistics and data visualization should be seen as complementary methods, where one reinforces the other and both have advantages.

- When plotting data points, always minimize point overlapping by choosing transparencies, rings, alternative marker sizes, or all three. Or, if necessary, add a small amount of random variation.

- A distribution is often too noisy to yield meaningful insights without additional help, in which case you can use statistical methods to find key anchor points.

- Often, noise is not necessarily bad. You may choose to mute it but keep it in the chart.

- Have a plan for dealing with outliers, because they are interesting.

- Box-and-whisker plots are great charts for comparing distributions.

- Use Pareto charts to display the cumulative frequency of distributions to learn more about cumulative effects.

- Unlike bar charts, histograms show continuity between adjacent values and therefore have no gaps between their vertical bars.

- When using histograms, test several bin widths and numbers of bins to find the best combination for the task.

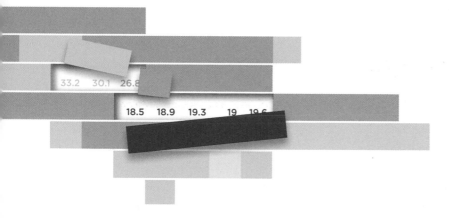

11

CHANGE OVER TIME

Tobler's first law of geography ("Everything is related to everything else, but near things are more related than distant things") could be applied to both space and time. For many variables, variation from one time period to the next tends to follow a reasonably smooth path. Any abrupt changes draw our attention and must be investigated.

It's perfectly acceptable to focus our attention on describing the now, but in most cases a larger time frame helps us understand where we are, why we are here, and where we should expect to go. But the importance of time also depends on the complexity of our economic or social systems (more, and more vocal, social minorities make societies more complex). Today, many variables vary more sharply than they did 50 years ago. For example, high-frequency trading is an extreme example within the extreme example of stock volatility. Also, the past is not uniform: There are almost invisible long-term patterns and cycles with unwanted consequences (such as population aging and the credit cycle), and there are short-term patterns (like unemployment rate) that we are more aware of because they affect our daily lives more immediately.

Focus on the Flow: The Line Chart

Most rivers flow relatively smoothly. Their general flow tends toward a point, even if, at the local level, it appears to keep twisting and turning and changing course unexpectedly (**Figure 11.1**).

Since at least the time of ancient Greek philosophers, the river has been the preferred metaphor for describing the flow of time. It's natural, therefore, that a metaphorical river, a line, is the primary representation of time in data visualization. We do use other charts to represent time, and we do use line charts to display non-temporal data, but the combination of time series and the line chart is especially useful. It respects the direction of time (from left to right) and focuses on the flow (rather than on individual data points) that will be read as meaningful trends and patterns.

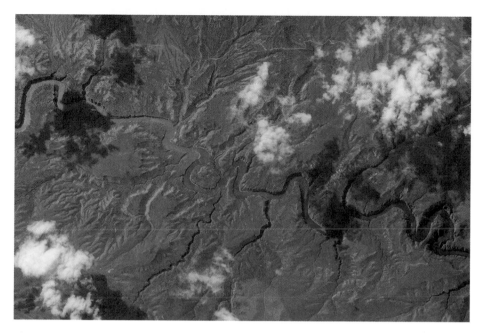

Figure 11.1 The Bighorn River. Source: NASA/ISS

The line chart is one of the best and most flexible types of charts for displaying change over time. It isn't perfect, though. Some nuances may escape it, and at times it may also suggest nonexistent relationships, so we'll discuss alternative formats as well.

The line chart at the top in **Figure 11.2** shows a clear and stable evolution in the volume of nights spent in tourist accommodations by residents in Spain. The evolution of non-residents is more complex: an upward trend that increases and turns into exponential growth, followed by a plateau during the first decade of this century, and then a return to growth over the last years.

Although we focus on the flow when reading line charts, if there are significant changes it's a good idea to make data points in the line more prominent (using labeled markers, in this case) to help quantify local variations.

The bottom bar chart uses the same data but suggests a different approach. Instead of patterns and trends, it favors pair-wise analysis (annual and between the two series).

AFTER PLATEAUING, TOURISM IN SPAIN IS ON THE RISE AGAIN
Nights spent at tourist accommodation establishments

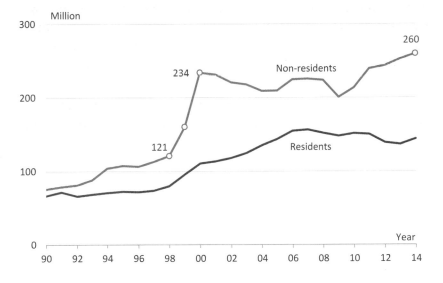

THE GAP BETWEEN RESIDENTS AND NON-RESIDENTS IS RISING AGAIN
Nights spent at tourist accommodation establishments

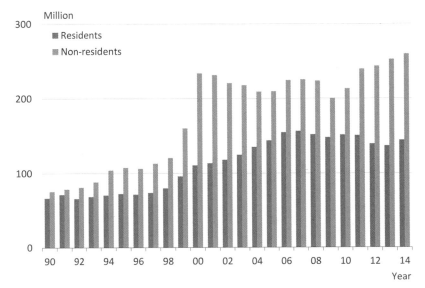

Source: Eurostat
Note: Nights spent in hotels; holiday and other short-stay accommodation; campgrounds,
recreational vehicle parks, and trailer parks

Figure 11.2 Using the same data, line charts and bar charts yield different messages.

When reading a line chart, we need to realize that we can discuss patterns and trends in each series, but we must be careful when drawing any conclusions about the *relationship* between two variables. As an example of exploring the relationship between variables, a quick chart made using William Playfair's 18th-century data (**Figure 11.3**) reveals a huge depression in the first half of the time series when using the *ratio* of exports to imports rather than absolute values. These two charts complement each other—one revealing details that are missing in the other.

Ratios have the additional advantage of making the message clearer: In 2000 and 2001, non-residents spent two nights in tourist accommodations for each night spent by residents (**Figure 11.4**).

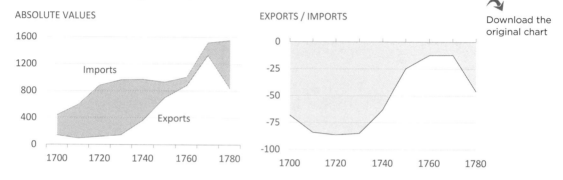

Figure 11.3 Using complementary charts to reveal more insights.

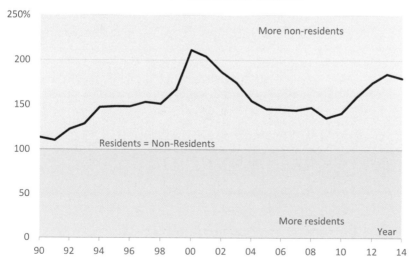

Figure 11.4 Ratio between non-residents and residents in nights spent at tourist accommodations.

Using ratios is a simple and familiar way of getting some sense of the relationship between two variables. Variables that are often seen together, such as imports versus exports, budget versus actual, or female versus male, gain meaning when presented both with absolute values and with ratios.

Scales and Aspect Ratios

When you're dealing with scales, line charts are more complex than bar charts. We compare heights in bar charts, and the only way to do so is to keep the scale intact (starting at zero, with no breaks). No matter what you do, if you don't break the scale you'll always be able to compare two bars correctly and calculate their absolute or relative difference.

There isn't a general rule to apply regarding what a line chart should look like, or what the "right" slope should be. When you change a chart's aspect ratio you change the slope. You can also manipulate it by changing the scale. This means that we can break the scale and take advantage of it to improve resolution by defining a scale range around the maximum and minimum data points. A good reference to start with is to set the average slope to around 45°. (This "banking to 45°" was first proposed by William Cleveland.[1])

The slope of the line is a design issue and to a lesser extent a functional issue. One slope can make a pattern easier to spot than another slope, so you should test aspect ratios and scales that push the slope below or above 45°.

Whatever angle you choose, a slope is always meaningless on its own because there are no reference points (except for the horizontal reference line that marks an upward or a downward trend). It acquires meaning only when compared to other slopes.

The top charts in **Figure 11.5** illustrate a discussion held a few years ago on the federal tax rate for the 1 percent richest Americans. The chart on the top left shows a sharp decline, while in the chart on the top right, the authors, arguing that the scale should include all potential tax rate levels, show that it had essentially stabilized. (This rationale would flatten out every chart under the sun, by the way.)

We can say that the chart on the top left is better because it allows us to see change in more detail. But we can't infer from it that the tax rate for the super-rich is nose-diving, nor we can say after reading the chart at the top right that the tax rate is flat.

---

1   Cleveland, William S., Marylyn E. McGill, and Robert McGill. "The Shape Parameter of a Two-Variable Graph." *Journal of the American Statistical Association*. Vol. 83: 289–300, 1988.

THE TOP 1% IS PAYING LESS AND LESS TAX
Average federal tax rate for top 1% households

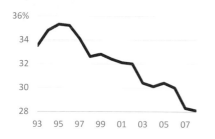

TAXES PAID BY THE TOP 1% REMAIN UNCHANGED
Average federal tax rate for top 1% households

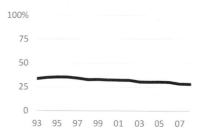

Download the
original chart

THE TOP 20% IS PAYING LESS AND LESS TAX, BUT THE TOP 1% BENEFITS THE MOST
Average federal tax rate for top 20% households

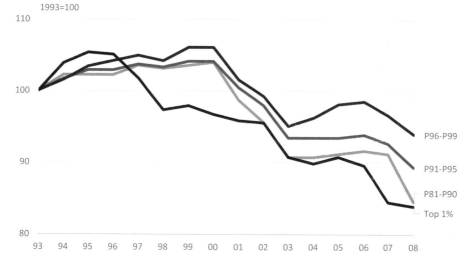

Source: Tax Policy Center

Figure 11.5 Applying different scales in line charts.

The only real solution is to add references so that the slope in this series can be compared to other similar series and thus gain meaning.

The bottom chart may have an answer. First, we need to display not the top 1 percent of households but all four groups within the top 20 percent. Next, we want to know, not how much federal tax each group actually pays, but how much it has changed since 1993 (because the original discussion was focused on how much it changed).

Now, when we display the data we can almost say that, the less rich a household is, the less tax it's paying (when comparing to 1993). This works perfectly for the bottom three groups, but not for the top 1 percent, which is enjoying a higher cut in its tax rate than all the others (and it started earlier). You still can't judge the meaning of a slope, but you can say for certain one of the groups has been treated favorably when compared to other groups.

When you have more than one series you have more flexibility to change aspect ratios or the scale on the vertical axis, and you should take advantage of it to improve resolution or make patterns clearer. When you have a single series, consider using a bar chart instead of a line chart if you have only a few data points and if you can get good resolution without breaking the scale. Above all, make sure your audience doesn't jump to conclusions based on a single slope.

Focus on the Relationships: Connected Scatter Plots

We can view a line chart as a special form of scatter plot, in which the relationship is established between the variable value in the vertical axis and the corresponding time period in the horizontal axis. Variables in a line chart vary independently, which means that when we have two or more variables, we can't infer much about their relationships, even if they appear to vary in the same direction. When we establish a relationship between the variables in a scatter plot, we lose the temporal dimension and are left with only a snapshot of the moment.

This need not be so. There are cases where a similar evolution hides deep changes in the relationship, and in other cases we detect changes but are unaware of how significant they are.

Figure 11.6 shows a rendition of a chart published by *Time* magazine (international edition, November 4, 2013). The use of two axes and the broken scale on the left mean that the author wanted to highlight a relationship between the evolution of the two variables. As we'll see in Chapter 14, however, the secondary axis should not be used in these circumstances.

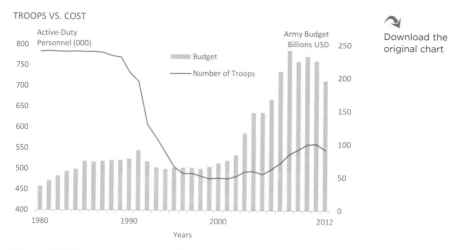

TROOPS VS. COST

Download the original chart

Figure 11.6 There is a better way of comparing these variables.

If we do want to know what kind of relationship is established between two variables over time, we have to plot one against the other. Each data point marks the values in both variables for a given year (or other time period), and by connecting the data points we can see how the relationship evolved over time.

Figure 11.7 shows what happens when you apply this connected scatter plot to the data from Figure 11.6. It becomes obvious that there are four phases in the relationship between troops and army budget:

■ Ronald Reagan keeps increasing the budget without changing the number of troops. Russia (then the USSR) was unable to cope with this and the Cold War finally ends.

■ With the end of the Cold War, the U.S. begins a decade-long period of troop reduction, even during other wars (such as the Gulf War, in 1991).

■ The next decade begins with the 9/11 attacks, the Afghanistan War, and the Iraq War (2003). This forces a significant increase in the army budget, but only a marginal increase in the number of troops.

■ After the 2008 financial crisis, there is a downward trend in the budget and no change in personnel.

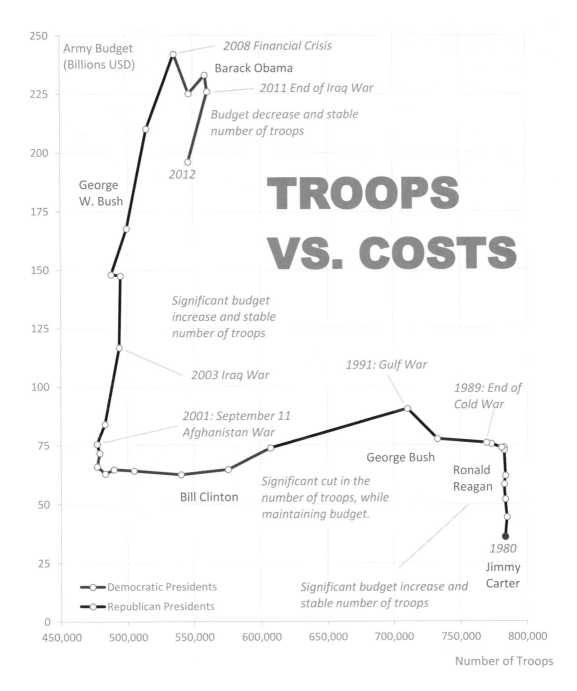

Army Budget
(Billions USD)

2008 Financial Crisis

Barack Obama

2011 End of Iraq War

*Budget decrease and stable
number of troops*

2012

George
W. Bush

TROOPS
VS. COSTS

*Significant budget
increase and stable
number of troops*

2003 Iraq War

1991: Gulf War

*1989: End of
Cold War*

*2001: September 11
Afghanistan War*

George Bush

Ronald
Reagan

Bill Clinton

*Significant cut in the
number of troops, while
maintaining budget.*

1980

Jimmy
Carter

—O—Democratic Presidents
—O—Republican Presidents

*Significant budget increase and
stable number of troops*

Number of Troops

Figure 11.7 A connected scatter plot reveals interesting relationships.

Download the
original chart

This chart clearly shows how during the turn of each decade significant changes took place in the relationship between the number of troops and the army budget. Probably due to the nature of new challenges and technological advances, a repeat of the inflated number of troops during the Cold War now seems unlikely.

Because we should, whenever possible, try to understand relationships between variables and not only describe each one of them in isolation, scatter plots are the most powerful charts available to us. The connected scatter plot is not easy to read at first, but I strongly encourage you to become familiar with it—at least during the exploratory stage—to check for relevant shapes in the relationships. Whenever you feel the need to use a dual-axis chart with two independent variables, you should try the connected scatter plot first.

Go to the
web page

Sudden Changes:
The Step Chart

In most circumstances, it's reasonable to assume that the evolution from one state to another is a continuous and smooth process: If a product sells 100 units in a month and 110 in the following month, it's likely that the sale of additional units has spread over the entire month. Based on the evolution of sales by the middle of the month, it may be possible to estimate the final sales.

In other cases, a change is abrupt and has no intermediate steps. The ranking of a football team has no decimal values. In certain product categories, prices can be left unchanged for several months or even years. A standard line chart is not the ideal method for displaying these changes that lack intermediate states, because the line chart represents a slope instead of a vertical line.

Since 1998, several postal services throughout Europe underwent restructuring and privatization, following an EU regulation. In some cases, you need only look at the price index for these services to guess when the company was privatized. The chart in **Figure 11.8** shows that the index for postal services hardly changed over the years, with only minor corrections in January each year, if any. After they were privatized, frequent price hikes became the new normal. This is a step chart, and the orange series captures the nature of the price index in postal services much better than a standard line chart.

Download the
original chart

POSTAL SERVICES: PRICE HIKES AFTER PRIVATIZATION IN PORTUGAL

Harmonized Indices of Consumer Prices: Postal Services vs. All-Items

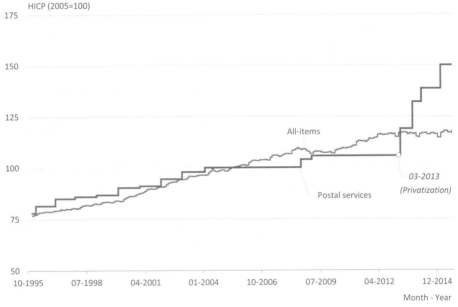

Source: Eurostat

Figure 11.8 Use step charts to display sudden changes.

If you look closely, you'll see that the all-items index (the gray line) also evolves in steps. However, the use of a step chart in this case clearly misses the point, because only on rare occasions is the index left unchanged from one month to the next.

The step chart is between a line chart and a bar chart. It still displays a trend like a line chart halfway, and because of the vertical lines, it forces you to pay more attention to variation between data points, like a bar chart. You could take this as the best of both worlds, but Figure 11.8 proves that you have to have the right data and the right variation to make a useful step chart.

Seasonality: The Cycle Plot

A simple representation of the flow of time is the most obvious way to display change, but it can be inadequate in certain circumstances. In the U.S., for example, you would want to compare turkey sales in November with turkey sales from November of the previous year, rather than from October. Or if you are a sandwich restaurant owner, you might want to compare attendance between 12:00 PM and 1:00 PM each day of the week.

Tourism is a good example of seasonality. **Figure 11.9** (on the following page) shows how strong the tourism cycle is in Italy. We can see that nights spent by non-residents plateaued at about 50 million and that nights spent by residents are consistently increasing.

We can't really say much more when the data is presented this way. When there is a clear cyclic pattern in the data, we have to gather and analyze all the data for each moment of the cycle to find the underlying structure. See what happens when we compare the data for each of the twelve months (**Figure 11.10** on the following page). The cycle is still there, but now we get a lot of details:

- The large increase in nights spent by residents in July and August over the last years.

- The months when residents spend more nights than non-residents.

- The traditional huge gap between residents and non-residents in August.

- The drop in non-resident nights in recent years.

- The sudden drop in nights spent in 2002. (I couldn't find a good reason for this, but I don't want to assume without further investigation that this is a data error.)

NIGHTS SPENT AT TOURIST ACCOMMODATION ESTABLISHMENTS IN ITALY

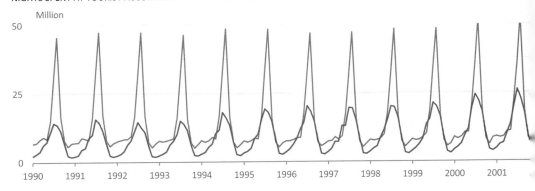

Source: Eurostat

Note: Nights spent in hotels; holiday and other short-stay accommodation; campgrounds, recreational vehicle parks, and trailer parks.

Figure 11.9 After confirming the cyclic pattern with a peak in summertime, there isn't much to see here.

NIGHTS SPENT AT TOURIST ACCOMMODATION ESTABLISHMENTS IN ITALY 1990–2015

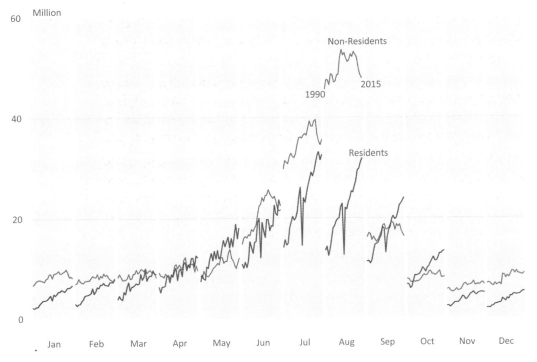

Source: Eurostat

Figure 11.10 With cycle plots, you can see both the overall cycle and the variation in each moment of the cycle.

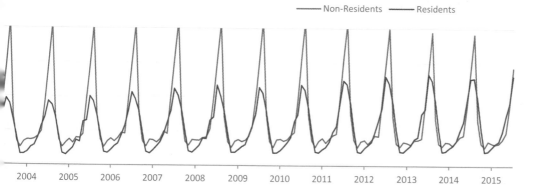

Sparklines

Sparklines is a term coined by Edward Tufte to designate "intense, simple, word-sized graphics"—that is, graphics that could be integrated into the text flow to show, for example, how the results evolved ▮▮▮▮▮▮▮ ▮ ▮▮ ▮▮▮ ▮▮ ▮▮ for the Spanish soccer team Real Sociedad during the 2014–2015 season (red: losses; black: wins; spaces: ties).

As the name implies, sparklines began as very small line charts, but bar or area charts are also used successfully as sparklines. The most notable feature of a sparkline is its extremely reduced size. Its compactness is obtained at the expense of removing all support elements and through miniaturizing data-encoding objects.

Beyond Tufte's books, I couldn't find many examples of sparklines integrated into the text, as suggested by Tufte, but several vendors, including Microsoft, have added sparklines to their products. Now it's very common to find sparklines, especially when available space is scarce, as in dashboards. You'll also find that they've become popular on the sports page (**Figure 11.11**).

2014–2015 SPANISH SOCCER SEASON
Outcome in each week

FC Barcelona	
Real Madrid CF	
Atlético Madrid	
Valencia CF	
Sevilla FC	
Villarreal CF	
Athletic Club	
RC Celta de Vigo	
Málaga CF	
RCD Espanyol	
Real Sociedad	
Rayo Vallecano	
Elche CF	
Levante UD	
Granada CF	
RC Deportivo	
Getafe CF	
SD Eibar	
UD Almería	
Córdoba CF	

Week 1   Week 38

Key   **Black**: victory
        Red: defeat
        Space: tie

Source: La Liga

Figure 11.11 You can see the outcomes of all
games in a season. Ties in soccer are common,
so there should be a symbol for that (a dot or
an underscore character, perhaps) to make sure
the number of ties is correctly counted.

Download the
original chart

Using sparklines is not as simple as it might
seem. You must ensure that variation is as clear
as possible. Figure 11.11 represents a best-case
scenario: Only three possible states (positive,
neutral, or negative) mean that you don't have to
worry about the level of detail or how to choose
the right scale, while color helps separate positive and negative values.

Sparklines are an interesting concept, but there
are a few issues associated with their extreme
miniaturization, among which is the removal
of the vertical axes and the consequent absence
of quantitative references.

Figure 11.12 represents the monthly unemployment rate at the U.S. state level. The first group
of two columns displays the actual rate, while
the second group displays the ratio between
the state rate and the national rate, where red
means "above national rate" and blue means
"below national rate." Within each group, the
sparklines in the first column are comparable
because they share a common scale, while in
the second column of each group you can't
compare states because each sparkline has an
independent scale, allowing for a better resolution. Both of these options are legitimate,
but it's likely that your audience will tend to
compare sparklines. You should make it clear
which option is currently applied and, if possible, let the audience choose between them.
Compare this display with the horizon chart in
Chapter 13, which uses the same data.

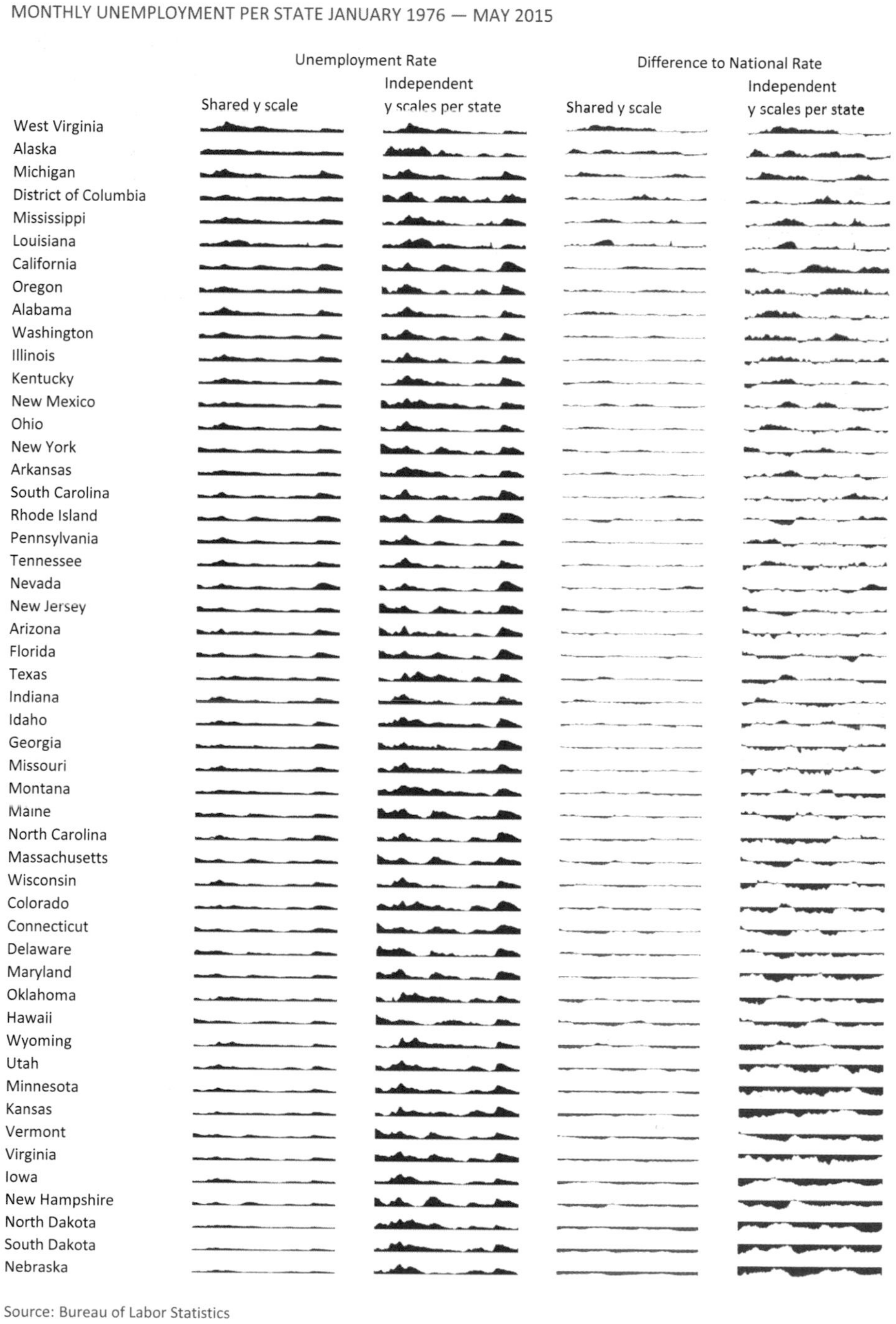

MONTHLY UNEMPLOYMENT PER STATE JANUARY 1976 — MAY 2015

	Unemployment Rate		Difference to National Rate	
	Shared y scale	Independent y scales per state	Shared y scale	Independent y scales per state

West Virginia
Alaska
Michigan
District of Columbia
Mississippi
Louisiana
California
Oregon
Alabama
Washington
Illinois
Kentucky
New Mexico
Ohio
New York
Arkansas
South Carolina
Rhode Island
Pennsylvania
Tennessee
Nevada
New Jersey
Arizona
Florida
Texas
Indiana
Idaho
Georgia
Missouri
Montana
Maine
North Carolina
Massachusetts
Wisconsin
Colorado
Connecticut
Delaware
Maryland
Oklahoma
Hawaii
Wyoming
Utah
Minnesota
Kansas
Vermont
Virginia
Iowa
New Hampshire
North Dakota
South Dakota
Nebraska

Source: Bureau of Labor Statistics

Figure 11.12 Sparklines are difficult to manage when you have a continuous vertical scale.

Tufte suggested some ways to minimize this problem of multiple individual scales versus a single shared scale, particularly by indicating the values of certain relevant points (first, last, major, minor), but also by overlapping a fluctuation band of typical values in order to emphasize the points outside this band.

Stephen Few sought to address the problem of scales[2] and then proposed the concept of bandlines,[3] in which the background color encodes quartiles in an attempt to find a middle ground between the individual scales and a shared scale.

Animation

Watch the video

Go to the web page

Earlier I mentioned Hans Rosling's first TED conference, "The best stats you've ever seen." If you haven't done so already, watch it now. Rosling's conference is a great example of skilled communication with data and of using animation the right way. He uses a tool named Trendalyzer, and you can find an interactive online version and play with some datasets at Gapminder's site.

What is "animation"? If you're a PowerPoint user, you know that Animations is one of the top menu options. You use it to make objects pulse, teeter, spin, grow, shrink, swivel, bounce, flow in, fly out, or fade—or simply appear, if you aren't an imaginative person. Apple's Keynote animations are even cooler, and include fireworks and flames.

But animation in data visualization is not exactly that. In data visualization, animation happens when a bar gets shorter, a point changes position, or a line slope is smoothed over time. These changes result from changes in the underlying data, usually when a new period in a time series is selected.

If you stop a movie, you can see what's happening in the still image—for example, a donkey talking to a heavy green creature with funnel ears. But why are they talking and what will happen next? You don't know, because only a sequence of frames will tell you that.

2 Few, Stephen. "Best Practices for Scaling Sparklines in Dashboards." *Visual Business Intelligence Newsletter*. El Dorado Hills, CA: Perceptual Edge. 2012.

3 Few, Stephen. "Introducing Bandlines: Sparklines Enriched with Information about Magnitude and Distribution." *Visual Business Intelligence Newsletter*. El Dorado Hills, CA: Perceptual Edge. 2013.

The same is true for animation in data visualization. If you stop Hans Rosling's talk while he's displaying data for a given year, you won't be able to detect any patterns beyond those currently visible in the image. But after watching the entire sequence, you'll see a global movement of countries in a particular direction, even if that movement is less than linear in individual cases.

Just as you need a map to discover spatial patterns, you need a sequence to discover time patterns. Animation not only helps you detect patterns, but it's also a *cool* way of presenting change over time. If you can add great verbal communication skills, you'll deliver a memorable presentation.

But there is a catch. Animation doesn't show you a pattern; *you* use the sequence to build a pattern in your brain, and working memory plays an active role in this. The small storage space and volatility of our working memory mean that animation can't be used in data visualization when the data display multiple and complex patterns over time. In Rosling's talk, you see that countries simply moved from the bottom right corner of his chart to the top left corner. No other patterns emerge. If you want to show an animation, you must ensure that there is a single pattern, that the pattern is easy to detect, and that it flows as smoothly as possible.

If, instead of a presentation with a fixed sequence, your audience is given an interactive tool to play with, things can be a bit more interesting. The tool doesn't need to be as sophisticated as Trendalyzer, but it should at least allow for basic interaction, with pause, forward, and back/rewind buttons.

If, for whatever reason, it's not possible to use animation, using several small charts (also known as "small multiples") is a great alternative. **Figure 11.13** contains 31 small population pyramids that show how the age structure of the U.S. population changed since 1950 and how its evolution is projected until 2100. The pattern is clear, so it's a good candidate for animation, but with a multitude of small images you can study the changes in more detail. Having today's age structure fixed in each background in a lighter color shade acts as a reference and helps us better evaluate both past and future changes.

UNITED STATES POPULATION PYRAMIDS FOR ESTIMATES AND PROJECTIONS 1950–2100

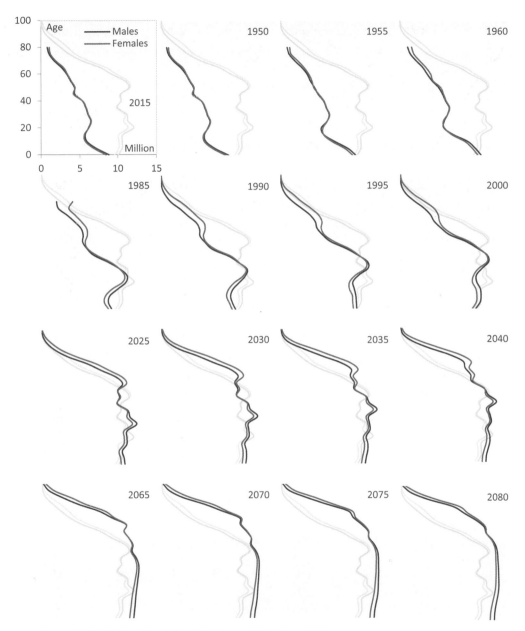

Source: United Nations Population Estimates and Projections 2015

Figure 11.13 Using a multitude of small images like the individual frames of an animation. Reflecting the trend in population aging, the top class (85+ years old) is detailed and replaced by a new top class (100+ years old) after 1985.

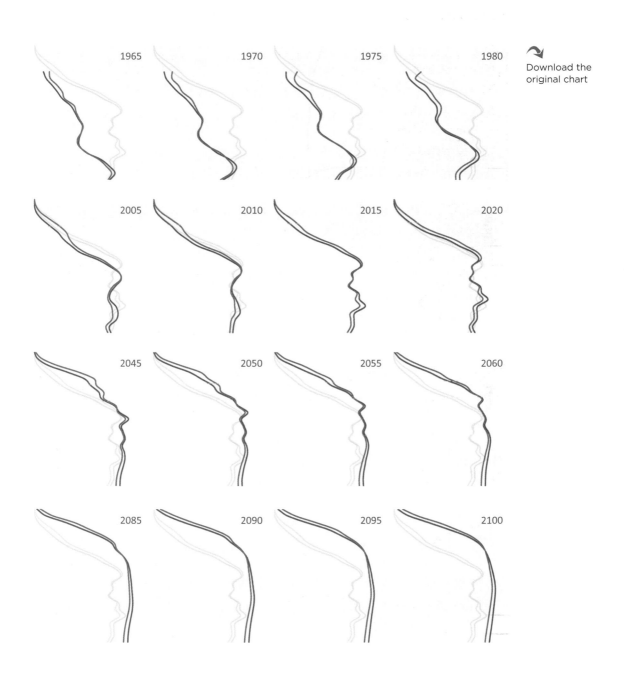

Takeaways

- Time is one of the fundamental dimensions in data analysis, and it should be represented whenever possible.

- The line chart is the default chart for visualizing a time series, because the line emphasizes the flow (and thus the trend). Use a bar chart if you want to compare data points instead.

- Markers are not required in a line chart, but you should use them for substantial turning points, outliers, or other significant cases.

- Don't assume that because two series seem to vary in a similar fashion, there is a direct relationship between them. Better yet, show both.

- Instead of showing a pair of variables (men/women, imports/exports), show the ratio between them. Better yet, show both.

- To better observe how the relationship between two variables evolves over time, you need a connected scatter plot.

- When a variable displays a strong cyclic pattern, many of the details are hidden by the cycle. Slice it up and show how each moment of the cycle changed over time (how January changed, how February changed, and so on).

- Because in a line chart you compare slopes and not heights, you can break the vertical scale, within reason.

- Try changing the chart's scale and aspect ratio so that you get an average slope of 45°. Then check if that's the right format to show the patterns.

- Avoid single-series line charts. Add some type of reference, such as the expected variation, or a second series (for example, by comparing one series to a higher-level series, such as a state to the national average), or even consider using a bar chart.

- For some variables, change is abrupt rather than gradual. A step chart offers a more accurate picture of this sudden change.

- Animation works best when there's a single and simple pattern. When you can't use animation or when you want the audience to calmly go through the details, you can display the same sequence using small multiples.

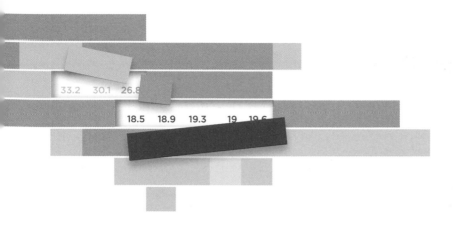

12

RELATIONSHIPS

As we've seen, to explain the world is to look for relationships among the facts we observe. While you'd think it would then be easy to take the next step, to answer the "why," most of the time it isn't so easy.

Since discovering relationships is an essential step to knowledge-building, it's only natural to think that data visualization would have the right tools for revealing the why in these relationships. But in fact, that's only half true at best. When we see two series in a line chart varying in the same direction, it's tempting to conclude that there's a direct correlation between them. However, as we learned in the preceding chapter, this may not be true (even if the author has tried to prove it by adjusting scales in the vertical axes).

We can only infer the existence and nature of a covariation between two variables when we plot them one against the other and measure the results. But the fact that two variables show a similar variation does not necessarily mean that there is a causal relationship—that one causes the other.

A popular chart on social media showed a strong linear relationship between chocolate consumption by country and the number of Nobel laureates (**Figure 12.1**).[1] This is not a license to eat chocolate. A country's wealth, among other contributing factors, allows for a higher consumption of chocolate and also an increased investment in science. It's not some miraculous property of flavonols found in chocolate.

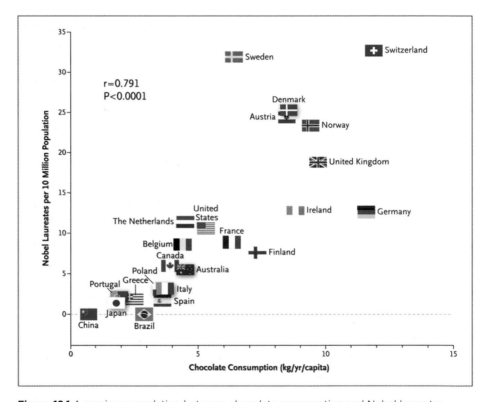

Figure 12.1 A spurious correlation between chocolate consumption and Nobel laureates.

---

1   Franz H. Messerli, M.D. "Chocolate Consumption, Cognitive Function, and Nobel Laureates." *New England Journal of Medicine*. 367:1562–1564, 2012. This paper should be read as a parody.

The analysis of covariation between two variables is important and has several implications. If one thing changes when something else changes, it's natural to assume that one causes the other. Many arguments implicitly make that assumption, from political discourse to debates around the water cooler. In a true causal relationship, there is indeed a strong correlation between the variables. That must be analyzed to ensure that we get the causality right (for what is the cause and what is the effect is not always clear).

Understanding Relationships

Relationships are complicated. Sometimes an action triggers the expected reaction, sometimes it triggers the opposite reaction, and sometimes it's met with indifference. We're interested in knowing what the reaction for a given action will be, or at least we would like to minimize the range of possible outcomes.

Figure 12.2 summarizes what we should be looking for when analyzing relationships:

- **Direction.** *Positive,* or direct, relationships mean that variation in both variables has the same sign: When one increases, the other also increases; when one decreases, the other also decreases. A perfect positive relationship, or correlation, has a value of 1. *Negative,* or inverse, relationships have opposite signs: When one increases, the other decreases. A perfect negative correlation has a value of -1. If there is no correlation, its value is zero.

- **Strength.** If there is a very narrow range of outcomes, the variables have a *strong* relationship (approaching either 1 or -1). If that response widens, the relationship becomes *weak* and the correlation tends toward zero. When the range is so wide that the response seems nothing more than a random value, there is no relationship and the correlation is zero. The meaning of a strong relationship is different for different people: A physicist will look for values above 0.9, while a value of 0.6 could be more than enough in psychology studies.

- **Shape.** In its simplest and most common model, relationships are *linear:* A variation in a variable triggers a proportional variation in another variable. But the nature of the relationship may change, like when it turns into an *inverted-u* shape.[2]

---

2   The Laffer curve is an example of a u-shaped relationship. It models the relationship between the level of taxation and revenue. The more taxes, the more revenue, but after a certain level the relationship becomes negative and a tax hike actually induces lower revenue.

■ **Visualization.** Some characteristics are hard to spot without visualizing the relationship in a scatter plot. They can be useful at finding *clusters* of data points, showing gaps, and identifying *sub-populations*. As shown by the Anscombe quartet (recall Figure 10.1), *outliers* influence several statistical metrics, so quickly spotting them may prove invaluable for selecting the right metric or the right analysis. For example, when you analyze the relationship between income and another variable, a weak relationship might improve if you split the data by gender—something that will probably be obvious once you display the data.

Curve Fitting

If the ideal result of reading a scatter plot is to understand the true nature of the relationship, this may prove an elusive goal. You can easily get lost in a forest of data points that prevents you from seeing the overall pattern.

In Figure 12.2, take a look at the third scatter plot under Nonlinear Shapes. Now imagine applying a force so powerful that it compresses the data points until a line is all that remains. This is the line that best describes, or *best fits*, the data. The closer the original data points are to this line, the better the fit. The values R^2 are called *coefficient of determination* and tell us how much of the variation of *y* is described by *x*, and vary between 0 and 1, or between zero percent and 100 percent. We can easily see that the red curve fits the data much better than the blue one, and the higher R^2 value confirms it.

There are many ways to improve curve fitting, but at some point the curve becomes so specific to the data you're working with that you can't generalize the model (for use with other data), so be careful of *overfitting*. To improve your model, you should also plot and interpret the residuals—that is, the difference between the observed value and the value estimated by the curve (check the second scatter plot under Strength in Figure 12.2).

This is the moment when general data visualization becomes visual statistics. I won't continue this path in this book, but I strongly encourage you to learn more about how using both visualization and statistical methods can dramatically improve your data analysis.

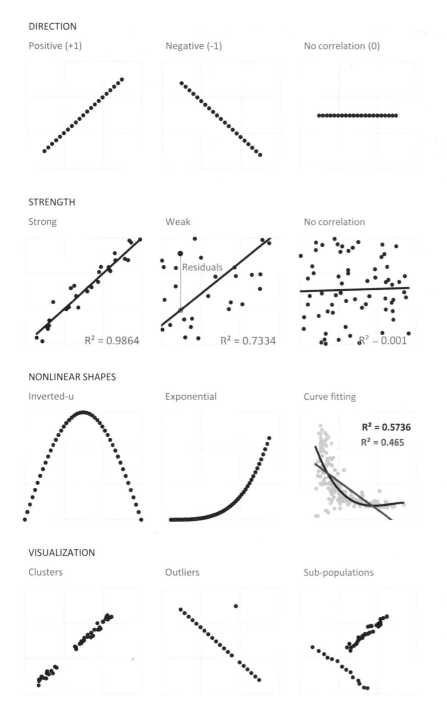

Figure 12.2 You can get a good sense of a relationship if you know about its direction, strength, and shape. Visualizing it will make you aware of less obvious features.

The Scatter Plot

Some chart types suffer a significant number of changes from the proto-chart, turning them into some recognizable physical object with which the audience has some sort of familiarity. The pie chart is the most obvious example. Charts displaying relationships are not immune to design excesses, but they are more resilient than other chart types. The scatter plot is at the opposite pole to the pie chart, suffering a minimal transformation and having a level of abstraction that is difficult to overcome. This makes it hard to add pseudo-3D effects (the third dimension in a scatter plot almost always carries some meaning).

Let us return to the data on livestock that we examined in Chapter 10. I'm sure the data will continue to suggest new questions. We analyzed livestock data within each species, but it's also legitimate to ask whether there is any relationship between species. For example, can the high concentration of pigs and poultry lead us to conclude that the two species are concentrated in the same regions? To answer, we must analyze the correlation between pairs of species.

The scatter plot is the chart that best displays covariation between two variables, so it's the most suitable type for verifying the degree of association between them.

Consider a case with a positive association between horses and goats. With a correlation of 0.86, as shown in **Figure 12.3,** we can conclude that in each region it will be common to find both species with a proportional variation between them.

GOATS VS. HORSES

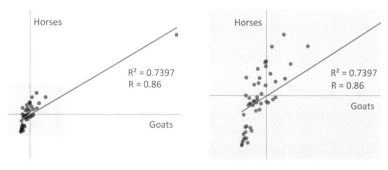

Figure 12.3 A scatter plot displaying the relationship between horses and goats (we're using z-scores, and each dot represents a state). The chart on the left displays all states. Because the outlier reduces resolution, the version on the right zooms into the gray area.

Comparing the maps in Chapter 10 confirms the similarity. Also, in this case, R^2 is around 74 percent, which means that the remaining 26 percent will be determined by other factors. If after inspecting the scatter plot, you feel that a correlation of 0.86 looks too high, you're right: If we exclude the outlier, the correlation coefficient drops to 0.77. So make sure you *always* check for the impact of outliers.

If there seems to be a positive association between certain species, the reverse does not seem to occur with intensity. The minimum association is only –0.08 between broiler chickens and beef cows.[3] A more negative value would indicate that larger poultry populations would be associated with smaller beef cow populations, and the other way around. In the case of these two species, only 4 percent of the variation is described by the variation of the other variable.

Showing all the possible relationships between pairs of variables in a matrix helps form an overall picture of these relationships, as is visible in **Figure 12.4**. Note that there are several instances in which the regression line is near horizontal, which shows the lack of correlation between them.

This graphic color table allows us to draw some conclusions about the data through just two conditional formatting rules in Excel, one for each triangle. The limits of the ramps were set to the theoretical limits and not to the values found in the table. The middle point was set to zero in the case of correlation coefficients and to 0.5 for the coefficient of determination. This allows us to realize immediately that the positive associations are much stronger than the negative associations (lower triangle), and the coefficient of determination is low in almost all cases (upper triangle).

---

3 Bear in mind that, according to the U.S. Department of Agriculture, beef cows are cattle raised for meat production and dairy cows are raised for milk production. These two are subsets of the category "Cattle and calves." This should be taken into account when reading the charts in this chapter.

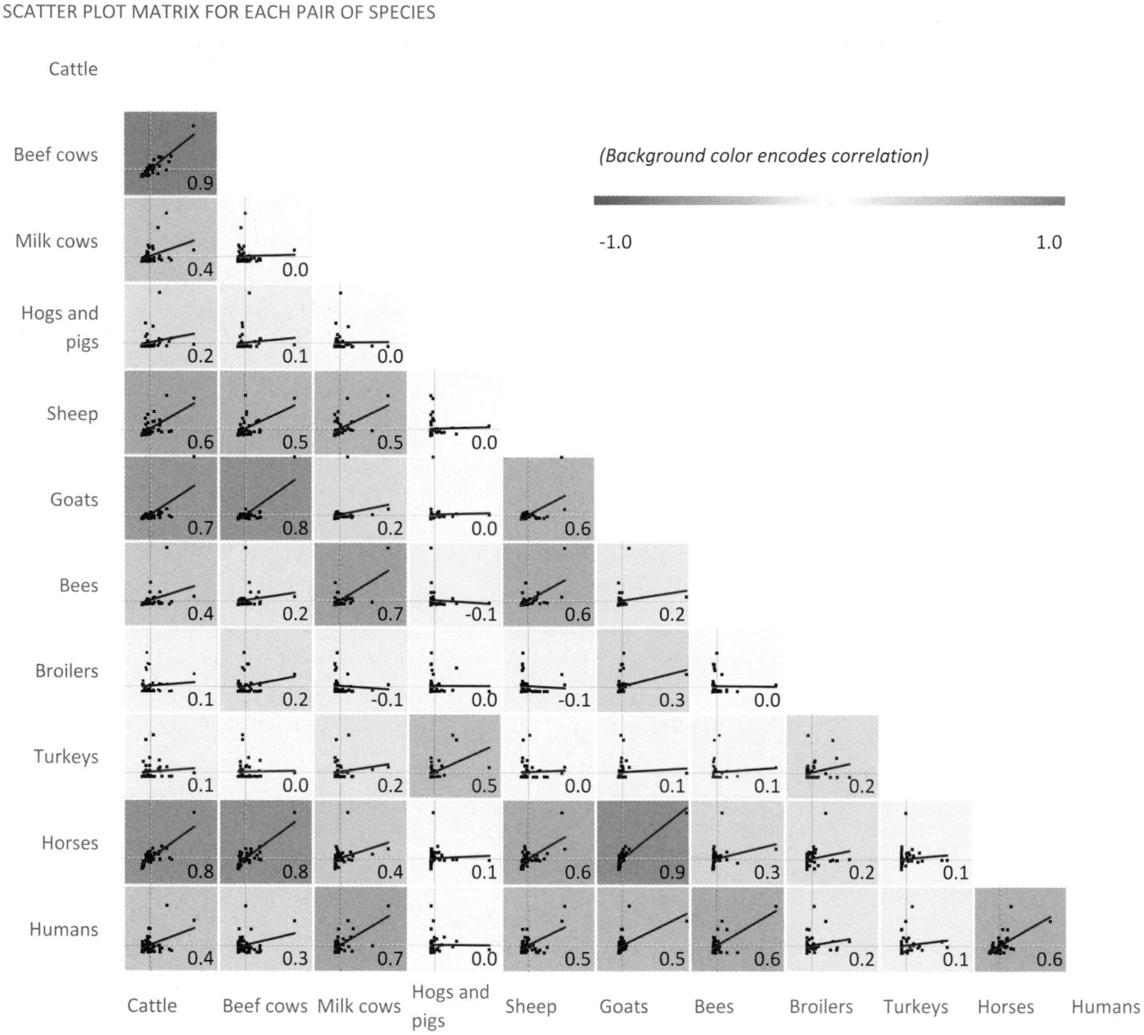

SCATTER PLOT MATRIX FOR EACH PAIR OF SPECIES

Figure 12.4 This scatter plot matrix allows the reader to study each pair of variables and compare scatter plots.

Download the
original table

The table in **Figure 12.5** summarizes the relationship between the variables, with the correlation coefficient in the lower triangle and the coefficient of determination in the upper triangle.

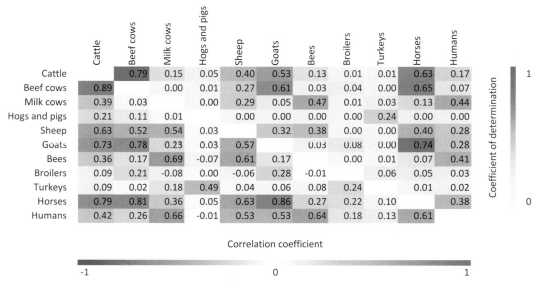

	Cattle	Beef cows	Milk cows	Hogs and pigs	Sheep	Goats	Bees	Broilers	Turkeys	Horses	Humans
Cattle		0.79	0.15	0.05	0.40	0.53	0.13	0.01	0.01	0.63	0.17
Beef cows	0.89		0.00	0.01	0.27	0.61	0.03	0.04	0.00	0.65	0.07
Milk cows	0.39	0.03		0.00	0.29	0.05	0.47	0.01	0.03	0.13	0.44
Hogs and pigs	0.21	0.11	0.01		0.00	0.00	0.00	0.00	0.24	0.00	0.00
Sheep	0.63	0.52	0.54	0.03		0.32	0.38	0.00	0.00	0.40	0.28
Goats	0.73	0.78	0.23	0.03	0.57		0.03	0.08	0.00	0.74	0.28
Bees	0.36	0.17	0.69	-0.07	0.61	0.17		0.00	0.01	0.07	0.41
Broilers	0.09	0.21	-0.08	0.00	-0.06	0.28	-0.01		0.06	0.05	0.03
Turkeys	0.09	0.02	0.18	0.49	0.04	0.06	0.08	0.24		0.01	0.02
Horses	0.79	0.81	0.36	0.05	0.63	0.86	0.27	0.22	0.10		0.38
Humans	0.42	0.26	0.66	-0.01	0.53	0.53	0.64	0.18	0.13	0.61	

Coefficient of determination 1 ... 0

Correlation coefficient

-1   0   1

Figure 12.5 This graphic table summarizes the correlation coefficient and the coefficient of determination for each pair of species.

Download the original table

Scatter Plot Design

Your goal when designing a scatter plot is to make the relationship between two variables as clear as possible, including the overall level of association but also revealing clusters and outliers. This is easier said than done. The data and a few bad design choices can make reading a scatter plot too complex or misleading.

Figure 12.6 shows the structure of a basic scatter plot. If you're plotting one variable against the other, in a perfect relationship all data points would lie along the 45° diagonal. This is the line that splits the plot area into a top and a bottom triangle. In some cases, this is the reference line, and your goal is to check the distances between the line and the data points (for example, earnings by gender in Figure 5.5).

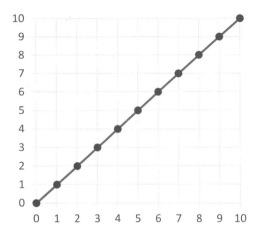

Figure 12.6
Modeling a basic
scatter plot.

Scatter plots are naturally square, because this makes the 45° diagonal more obvi-ous, and identical distances between data points maintain their relationship both horizontally and vertically. You need to scale both axes accordingly.

Figure 12.7 shows that if we follow these rules by the book, we'll get a very low-resolution chart (top chart). However, if we trim the empty areas, we get better resolution without distorting the proportions (bottom chart). Since we're not using bars or other similar objects, we can break the scale.

Download the
original chart

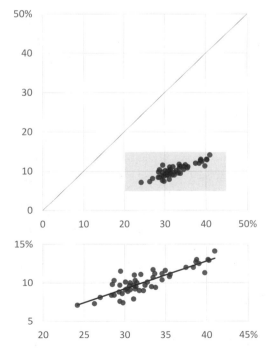

Figure 12.7
Trimming a scatter plot
to improve resolution.

Having the same scale in both axes and, if needed, trimming the scale to show only the useful area is the ideal case. If you think one of the axes could have better resolution, you should add clues to make sure the reader adapts to this change in proportions. In the chart on the right of **Figure 12.8**, we improved resolution of the y axis cutting it by half (1:2), kept the 45° reference line, and added the line of best fit.

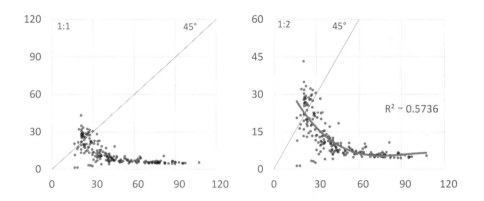

Download the original chart

Figure 12.8 Improving resolution in one axis and adding reading clues.

Clusters and Groupings

Often as interesting as the relationship between two variables is the way data points cluster together. When visualizing data on European countries, we come to expect some groupings: Western Europe versus Eastern Europe, Baltic countries, Nordic countries, Mediterranean countries. Sometimes, these groupings are obvious due to the Gestalt law of proximity. In other cases, you'll have to explore and add more variables that make these groupings emerge.

Likewise, in the U.S., in many variables we expect to find states in the West and South regions (as defined by the U.S. Census Bureau) in opposite poles. When plotting hypertension versus diabetes, for example (**Figure 12.9**), it's clear that not only is there a strong relationship between the two but also that when adding a categorical variable (Region), a spatial pattern seems to be uncovered. Furthermore, within the South region is a cluster clearly separate from the main cloud. How does this translate into a spatial pattern and spatial continuity? The map in **Figure 12.10** shows that, with the exception of Texas, all South Central states belong to this cluster, which also includes two states of the South Atlantic division: South Carolina and West Virginia.

When creating a scatter plot, it's easy to overlook details in the distribution of each variable. To make sure this doesn't happen, add marginal distributions along each axis. Figure 12.9 exemplifies this.

HYPERTENSION VS. DIABETES AT STATE LEVEL IN 2015

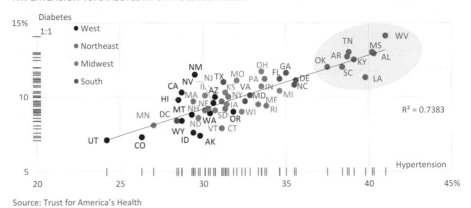

Source: Trust for America's Health

Figure 12.9 Adding a categorical variable (Region) helps the reading of the scatter plot.

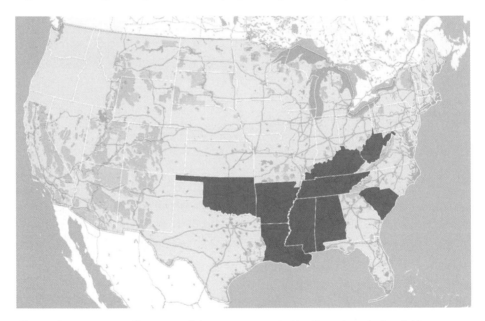

Figure 12.10 A map confirms a spatial pattern suggested by the categorical variable.

Multiple Series and Subsets

You're not restricted to a single line of best fit for each scatter plot. You can define a meaningful group and analyze it, while not forgetting that you can't generalize insights from the group to the whole population. A "meaningful group" also means that you can't go cherry-picking the data points that validate your message. In **Figure 12.11**, each region gets its own line of best fit, and it's easy to see that the South (blue dots) follows the line of best fit much closer than the West (the red dots), which is much more diverse. Overall, the relationship is much stronger in the South than in any other region, although we should question whether we have enough data points in each region to draw meaningful conclusions.

You can also analyze multiple variables, such as in **Figure 12.12**, where it is clear that inactivity and hypertension have a similarly strong relationship with diabetes, and that obesity has a much weaker relationship.

HYPERTENSION VS. DIABETES AT STATE LEVEL IN 2015

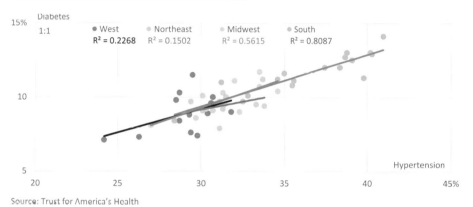

Source: Trust for America's Health

Download the original chart

Figure 12.11 The relationship between hypertension and diabetes is not uniform in all regions.

DIABETES VS. INACTIVITY, OBESITY, AND HYPERTENSION

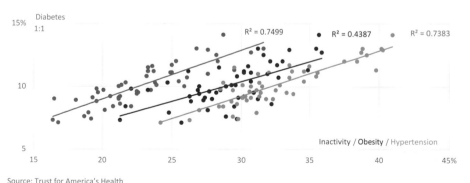

Source: Trust for America's Health

Download the original chart

Figure 12.12 The relationship between diabetes and inactivity, obesity, and hypertension.

Profiles

Remember the bamboo chart from Chapter 3, Figure 3.9? It starts from an overall value (national average) and shows how sub-groups diverge from that value. The goal is similar in **Figure 12.13**: From the overall share of imports and exports in Germany and the Netherlands, we can check how each country performs for each product group.

Download the
original chart

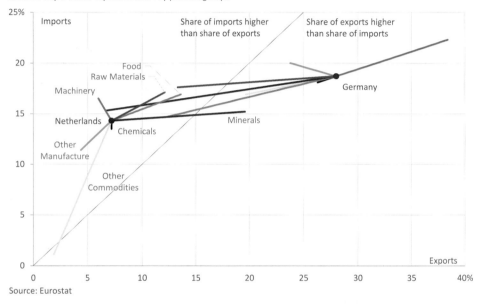

GERMANY AND THE NETHERLANDS: TRADE WITH THE REST OF THE WORLD (EXTRA EU)

Share of imports and exports in 2014 by product groups

Source: Eurostat

Figure 12.13 A connected scatter plot displays differences to the overall share. Color palette based on one from ColorBrewer2.org.

The chart shows that Germany's share of trade outside the EU is clearly to the right of the 45° reference line, which means that it exports much more than it imports. This is influenced by sales of Machinery, with a share of exports of 38 percent. Compare this with Minerals, where exports are half of imports. The Netherlands has a different profile. The overall position is to the left of the 45° line, but Minerals has a much higher share of exports than imports.

This technique of displaying country profiles can be seen (in a more complex, interactive, and aesthetically pleasing display) in the Better Life Index (**Figure 12.14**) from the Organization for Economic Cooperation and Development (OECD). Each flower represents a country, its height represents the index, and each petal's height encodes the score for each item in the index. Users can emphasize or deemphasize item relevancy by changing each petal's width.

Go to the
web page

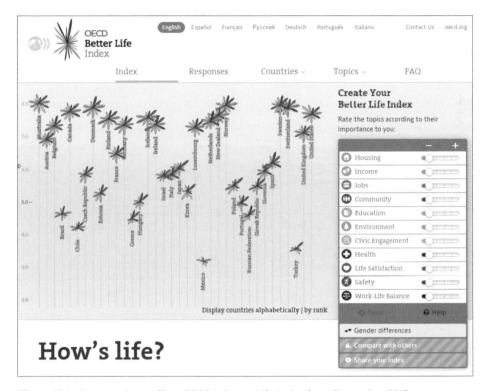

Figure 12.14 Scatter plot profiles: OECD's Better Life Index from December 2015.

Bubble Charts

Think of the bubble chart as a scatter plot in which the size of the dots (bubbles) encodes a quantitative variable. In addition, because the area is larger, it's possible to use color to add a fourth quantitative or qualitative variable.

We discussed Stevens' power law in Chapter 2. It tells us that we underestimate larger areas and overestimate smaller areas. When applied to bubble charts, this means that we can't accurately compare the areas of the bubbles. But the bubble chart has a strange feature: It combines this low-precision retinal variable (area) with perceptually precise retinal variables (x and y positions).

Don't dismiss bubble charts because we can't accurately read and compare bubbles. Instead, think of a bubble chart as a scatter plot to which you added interesting, but not critical, data. We must accept (but be aware of) some level of inaccuracy when comparing bubbles if we can benefit from the additional insights. Otherwise, we should consider other visualization options.

The bubble chart in **Figure 12.15** is a redraw of Figure 12.9, where bubble sizes encode total population. For improved accuracy, the point that happens to match the bubble center was maintained. You can read the chart like you'd read a scatter plot, but now you also know, for example, that three of the larger states are relatively close together.

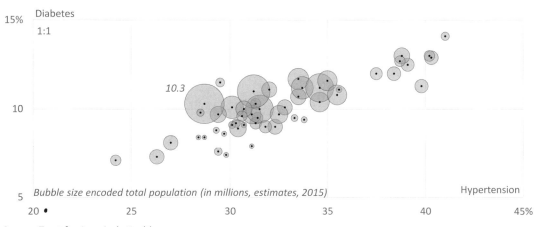

HYPERTENSION VS. DIABETES AT STATE LEVEL IN 2015

Source: Trust for America's Health

Figure 12.15 Bubble size shouldn't be used to encode critical data.

If you watched Hans Rosling's talks (as described in Chapters 2 and 11), **Figure 12.16** will look familiar. This Gapminder chart plots two development indicators (life expectancy and gross domestic product *per capita*) and uses bubble size to encode population and bubble color to encode region. In this chart, we don't really care about how big China and India are. The major insights are the strong correlation between gross domestic product and life expectancy and the distribution of the countries along this line, with African countries at the bottom left and European countries at the top right. It's nice to have population, but basically it only contributes to making the chart prettier.

Check the section Size by Population in the legend. It's hard to believe that the 1000 million bubble is ten times larger than the 100 million bubble, confirming Stevens' law and our inaccurate assessment of areas.

Because each data point uses a larger area, the bubble chart allows for fewer points than a scatter plot, and the probability of overlapping data points is also much higher. In Gapminder's chart, it's clear that the designer worked hard to ensure that only smaller bubbles could overlap larger ones, so that all remained visible. In Figure 12.15, I used a high percentage of transparency to make sure all bubbles are visible.

Go to the
web page

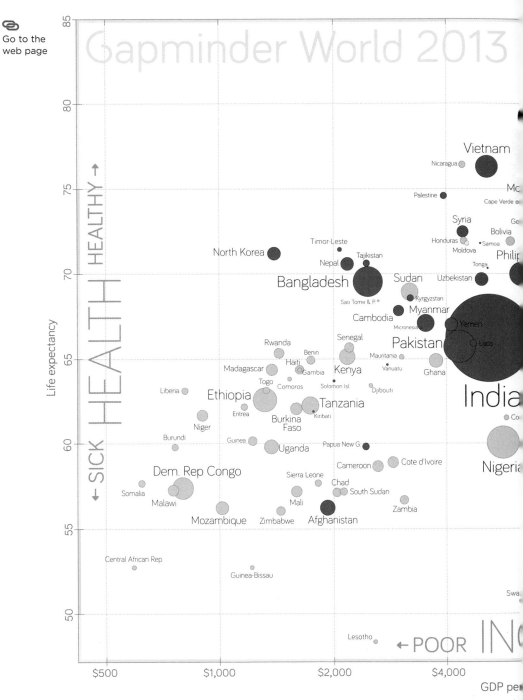

Figure 12.16 In this Gapminder chart, bubble size encodes country population and
color represents region.

Japan

Italy

Iceland

Switzerland

Israel

Cyprus

Australia

Sweden

Norway

Singapore

Qatar

Malta

France

Canada

Luxembourg

Spain

Austria

Netherlands

Kuwait

South Korea

UK

Germany

Greece

N.Zeal.

Ireland

USA

Portugal

Finland

Denmark

Slovenia

Belgium

Maldives

Costa Rica

Lebanon

Cuba

Bahrain

Iran

Chile

Brunei

Jordan

Croatia

Czech Rep.

Tunisia

Serbia

Panama

Uruguay

Peru

Argentina

Turkey

Poland

Estonia

Algeria

Libya

Slovak Rep.

Saudi Arabia

Colombia

Monten.

Romania

Hungary

United Arab Emirates

Barb.

Venezuela

Latvia

Thailand

Mexico

Lithuania

Malaysia

Oman

Bulgaria

Seychelles

Brazil

Mauritius

Bahamas

St.Vincent & G.

Azerbaijan

Trinidad &
Tobago

Grenada

nican R.

Iraq

Egypt

Suriname

Belarus

Russia

donesia

Turkmenistan

Kazakhstan

Botswana

olia

nibia

South
Africa

Gabon

Equatorial
Guinea

HEALTH & INCOME
OF NATIONS
IN 2013

This graph compares Life Expectancy
& GDP per capita for all 182 nations
with more than 100 000 inhabitants,
recognized by the UN.

COLOR BY REGION

SIZE BY POPULATION

0
1
10

100

1 000
million

www.gapminder.org/world

version 8

ME RICH →

$16,000 $32,000 $64,000 $128,000

rnational $

scale to show doubling of incomes as same distance on all levels. — LIFE EXPECTANCY: IHME 2014. Available from http://vizhub.healthda-
vorld. LICENSE: Creative Commons Attribution License 3.0, which means please share! "Based on a free chart from www.gapminder.org".

Note that a bubble chart always contains at least three meaningful variables (*x*, *y*, and bubble size) and should not be confused with what I like to call a *helium chart*, as schematically represented in **Figure 12.17**. We can assume that, for all relevant purposes, the helium chart lacks the variables *x* and *y* because they are not linked to the data table.

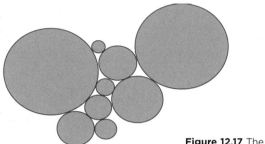

Figure 12.17 The helium chart.

The helium chart is often an interactive chart in which you can toss the bubbles around. This is fun but rarely useful or insightful. Because the only relevant variable is bubble size, a helium chart is really just another bar chart, but without the level of accurate reading we can expect from a bar chart.

Takeaways

- Relationship charts provide the highest level of data integration, showing the true shape of the variation when two variables are plotted one against the other.

- Your goal should always be to reduce the noise until the basic structure of the relationship becomes apparent. Play with Excel's options for the line of best fit, but don't over-fit.

- Complement what you see with statistical metrics such as the correlation coefficient.

- Characterize the variables' relationship in terms of direction, shape, and strength.

- Never forget that correlation doesn't imply causation. Even when we are aware of doing so, it's easy to describe the data with an implicit cause and effect relationship.

- When you use the same units of measurement for both axes in a scatter plot, also apply the same range and make the chart square. Then zoom in and select the relevant section, maintaining the correct proportions.

- Use reference lines such as the 45° line as annotations for a more precise reading.

- When using bubble charts, emphasize position and use bubble size for a less relevant variable.

- Don't use helium charts, whose only relevant variable (prone to inaccurate reading) is size.

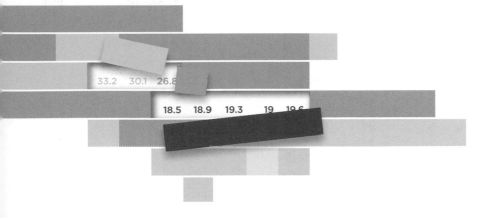

13

PROFILING

To introduce the topic of this chapter, let me first show you a visual display that will help you realize the significance of profiling: a chart with a lot of data points that could benefit from a structure to process a large amount of data. The graphical table in **Figure 13.1** represents the estimated percentage of people in each single-year age group (0 to 100 years old and more) in each of the 3,141 U.S. counties. Row height encodes population size for that county. Counties were sorted by median age. Higher proportions are encoded in red, while lower proportions are encoded in gray.

Counties by median age
and population size

Single-year age groups

Lower
percentage

Higher
percentage

**More red to the right
= higher median age**

Figure 13.1 Percentage of population at each single-year age group at the county level in the U.S. Data from the 2010 census. Source: U.S. Census Bureau (American FactFinder).

Download the
original chart

Go to the
web page

This visualization contains *hundreds of thousands* of data points. If I used Italian *comuni*, instead of U.S. counties, I would end up with a table with more than *half a million* data points. So visualizing a large number of data points in Excel is *possible*, and even *useful* for revealing patterns that might otherwise remain hidden. This is not Big Data,[1] but it is clearly bigger than the data sets used less than 250 years ago, when most charts used today were invented.

The point with this display is that, although *more* data is not necessarily *better* data, low-data-density Excel charts are often the norm, because low-density charts are also easier to make and read. At this level, it's useful to constantly ask "What data can I add?" "How will additional data improve the analysis?" and "How can I design the chart for more data?"

Perhaps in a few years' time, immersive technologies will turn current chart types into the silent movies of data visualization. While we wait for the future to arrive (or until a new marketing fad replaces Big Data), it's worth thinking of ways to add more data and extend the lifespan of the chart types we have today. If you think about it, many of the ideas discussed in the book will have that side effect.

One way of adding more detail to a chart is by creating **profiles**. Profiling is the representation of entities by creating an array of similar charts in which there are two readings: a reading of each individual profile and a comparison reading with other profiles. The integration and interdependence of these charts should lead us to consider them as a whole—as a single chart rather than as separate charts. We've already seen an example of a profiling chart: the scatter plot matrix in Figure 12.4. We'll explore other types of profiling charts over the next pages.

---

1   Remember that Big Data is, in a humorous but not too accurate definition, "Anything that won't fit in Excel."

The Need to Solve

We are now facing an interesting conundrum. On the one hand, the average number of data points per chart has to grow, because the data and their relationships are more complex, and higher graphical literacy means more sophisticated visualizations of larger data sets.[2] On the other hand, the audience may not appreciate having to deal with a visualization that goes beyond their attention span.

If we simply add more data to the charts found in the Excel library, we'll end up with undetectable patterns within spaghetti line charts or a chaotic forest of bar charts. We must impose a structure that minimizes cognitive load so that the audience can effortlessly process a larger volume of data. Profiling is one of the solutions.

Over time, various forms of profiling have been proposed with different designations: scatter plot matrices, panel charts, reorderable matrices, and small multiples. There are different nuances among these concepts, but they're all rooted in the same essential principle of juxtaposing multiple entities and making comparisons based on the same criteria.

One of the features of profiling charts is that individual chart position is not arbitrary; it must be deduced from the data whenever possible. This is particularly explicit in the reorderable matrix, in which either the points are ordered along a quantitative axis or the juxtaposition criteria obey some rules, as discussed below.

Panel Charts

The National Snow and Ice Data Center (NSIDC) is a U.S. organization dedicated to the study of the cryosphere, the frozen regions of our planet. One of its activities is to monitor the sea ice in the Arctic and the Antarctic regions. In one of their web pages, you can play with the interactive chart shown in **Figure 13.2**, visualising the extent of sea ice through the years since 1979. What insights can we get from this chart? Basically, that there is more ice in the winter than in the summer, and there are variations from year to year. That's relatively little insight for such a noble task.

Go to the web page

---

2 Having to deal with a data set just an order of magnitude larger could make Excel users aware of the need for better visualization and data management skills.

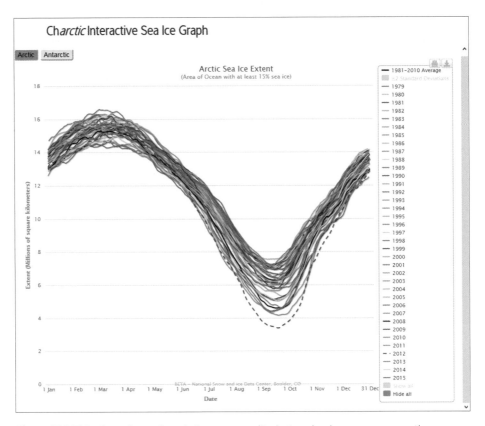

Figure 13.2 This chart shows the obvious seasonality but uselessly compares months.

When used with all the data, this is the typical spaghetti chart that tells us nothing, apart from the obvious seasonality. The problem, as you've already guessed, lies in the useless comparisons between months, when the right way to analyze the data is to profile each month over time in a cycle plot, just like we did in Chapter 6 with the monthly live births. The charts in **Figure 13.3** also show seasonality, but they go far beyond that: They reveal a serious decrease in sea ice extent in the Arctic over time. They also show that variation in each month is higher in the Antarctic but variation is increasing in summer months in the Arctic.

SEA ICE EXTENT 1978–2015

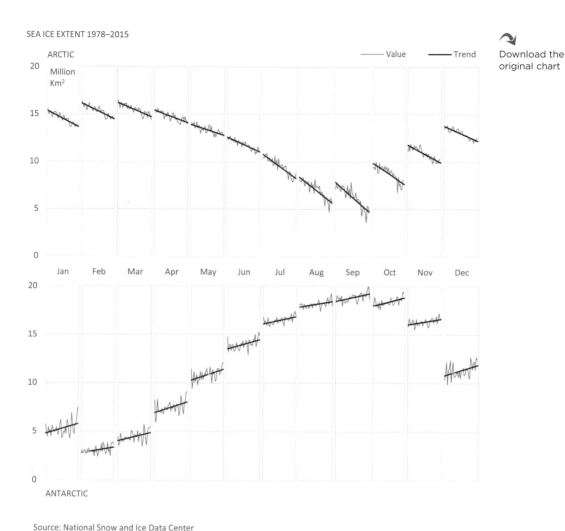

Source: National Snow and Ice Data Center

Figure 13.3 More relevant insights are revealed with a cycle plot.

Seasonality is just one of many factors that impede traditional line charts from providing insights effectively. In this case, as in others, profiling is the solution to visually organize and get insights from larger tables. Profiling shows the data, not in a single chart but in juxtaposed *panels* (profiles). This creates individual representations that can be studied case by case, as well as profiles comparable as a whole. Even if you focus on the month profile, you can still observe the seasonal data evolution.

Bar Charts with Multiple Series

The grouped bar chart in **Figure 13.4** displays the profile of several household types regarding expenditures. I don't want you to compare individual expenditure categories across multiple household types, so I added vertical gridlines to raise perceptual barriers between them. The implicit suggestion is that you should make comparisons inside each household type or compare between household expenditure profiles. If you want to emphasize expenditure categories, you may want to switch the data table and group by category rather than by household type. The chart is not very effective, though. There are too many categories, and except for Housing, profiles seem very similar. **Profiling assumes that there are sufficient differences between profiles to justify visualizing them.**

AVERAGE U.S. HOUSEHOLD EXPENDITURE

Per type of household and expenditure category, in 2014

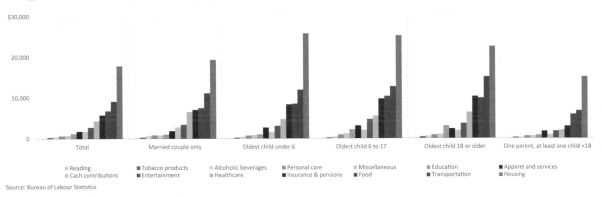

Source: Bureau of Labour Statistics

Download the
original chart

Figure 13.4 A poorly grouped bar chart.

The new version, in **Figure 13.5**, addresses these issues, starting by aggregating expenditure categories into broader groups that make sense to the author and, hopefully, to the audience. Then, reference points make it easy to compare the item with the overall expenditure structure. Now the gaps are much more obvious.

AVERAGE U.S. HOUSEHOLD EXPENDITURE

Per type of household and expenditure category, in 2014

Download the
original chart

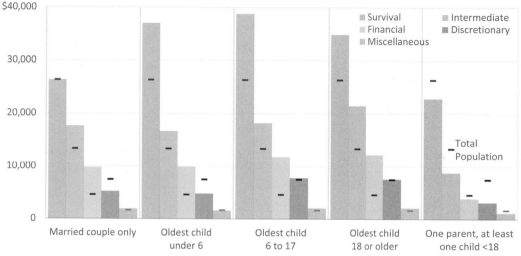

Source: Bureau of Labor Statistics

Figure 13.5 An improved grouped bar chart.

Horizon Chart

Only a fraction of the top chart real estate in **Figure 13.6** is actually used to display data. Perhaps we could do something about this, because the more compact your display is, the more data you can add. For example, since a variable can have positive and negative values, but not at the same time, there's always wasted space in the other side of the axis. We could "fold" it, assuming that the vertical axis represents an absolute scale, and use color to encode sign (red = above, blue = below). The middle chart in Figure 13.6 shows the result. We just have to switch gears and read the variable as having two states. This isn't too difficult, and nothing is lost from the previous version.

STANDARD AREA CHART

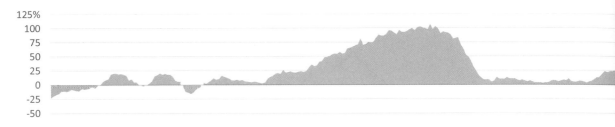

FOLDING VERTICAL AXIS AND USING COLOR TO ENCODE POSITIVE AND NEGATIVE VALUES

FOLDING VERTICAL AXIS FOR THE SECOND TIME

Download the
original chart

Figure 13.6 From a regular area chart to a horizon chart.

What if we take this a step further and create a diverging color scale to signal levels of variation, as we did in the middle chart of Figure 13.6? Then, nothing prevents us from collapsing the axis so that only the top class for each data point remains visible. We can use color to deduce into which class the point falls. The result is the bottom chart of Figure 13.6. Jeffrey Heer *et al.* named this design the "horizon chart" and defined its specifications.[3]

I won't tell you that no perceptual precision is lost. It is. That's inevitable when you use color to encode quantitative data. Folding the axis is also a strange concept that takes some time to get used to.

3   Heer, Jeffrey, Nicholas Kong, and Maneesh Agrawala. "Sizing the Horizon: The Effects of Chart Size and Layering on the Graphical Perception of Time Series Visualizations." *ACM Human Factors in Computing Systems* (CHI). pp. 1303–1312, 2009.

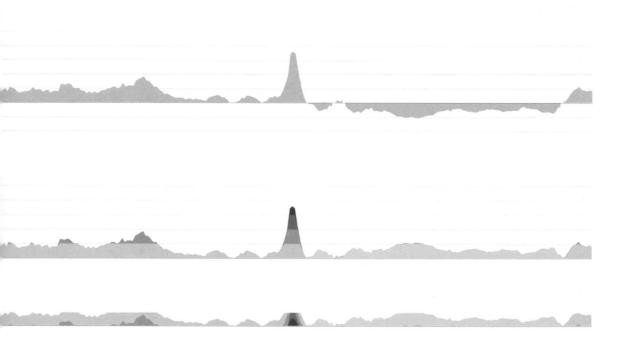

This looks like too much work for its dubious return, but I don't think the authors of the horizon chart wanted to go this far just to end up with a long stripe of colored bands. Where the horizon chart really shines is when you treat it as a profiling chart. In **Figure 13.7**, you get 52 profiles of unemployment by state for a whopping 473 months. Much happened in nearly 40 years, and you can discover it here. Regardless of the national unemployment rate, some states will consistently be above it.

If you wanted to display the same data using regular area charts, you would get a chart seven times taller and spread over multiple screens or pages. Its compactness is what makes the horizon chart so great: You get a lot of detail, but at the same time you can zoom out and get the overall picture.

MONTHLY UNEMPLOYMENT PER STATE JANUARY 1976 – MAY 2015: DIFFERENCE TO NATIONAL RATE

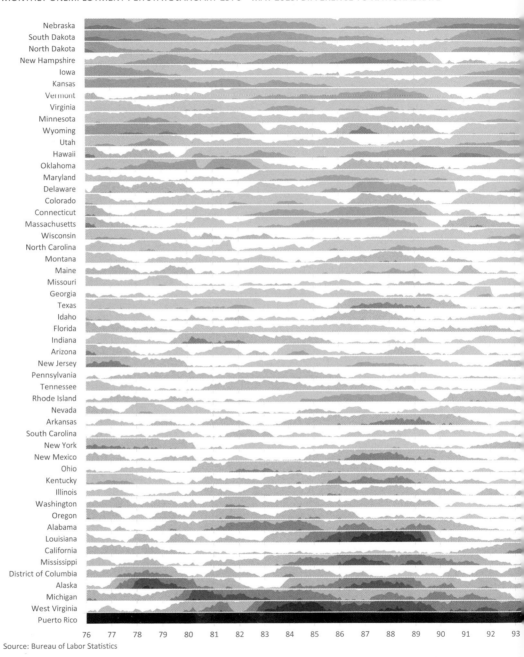

Source: Bureau of Labor Statistics

Figure 13.7 Except for the scatter plot, the horizon chart is probably the most data-dense chart type.

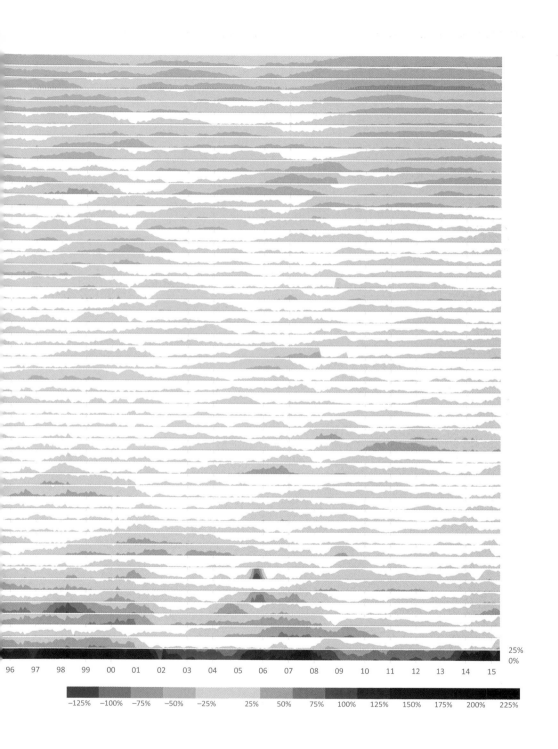

Reorderable Matrix

In the top display in **Figure 13.8**, a set of entities (places) identified by letters is associated with a set of characteristics. It's not easy to draw any conclusions from the display, as neither features nor entities are sorted to help create a recognizable pattern. In the second version, on the bottom, we have ordered both lines and columns, and have discovered that certain characteristics are associated with certain types of entities. From these associations, we can identify three levels of human settlements. A simple table sorting allowed us to find patterns that would otherwise remain hidden. The existence of one or more diagonals is a typical result of a reorderable matrix.

UNORDERED DATA

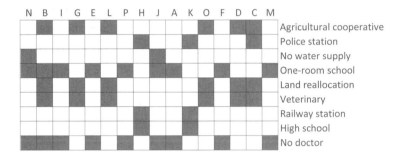

ORDERED DATA

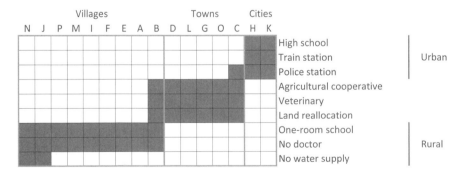

Figure 13.8 Bertin's reorderable matrix using dummy data.

This is an example of Jacques Bertin's reorderable matrix, purposely simple and designed by himself. With real data, patterns may be less clear, be less easy to spot, or have multiple solutions.[4]

Inspired by the reorderable matrix, the chart in **Figure 13.9** shows the U.S. retailer Walmart's store growth between 1962 and 2006. States were ranked by opening date and number of stores, and colored according to their U.S. Census region. Combining the sort and color reveals several interesting details, including the gradual Walmart entry into every state of the South and Midwest, intense store openings throughout the 1980s, and sudden expansion into the Northeast and West since 1990, making it a truly national chain. Unlike the preceding matrix example, in this case only the states can be sorted because the horizontal axis is a time series.

The reorderable matrix demonstrates the importance of finding the right sorting key for data. As we've seen, this is valid for any type of graphical representation. In simple charts, there is a proper sort key. With profiling charts, there is no single key to the diagonals. We might need to manually adjust each of the rows and columns to obtain the appropriate grouping.

---

4 In the 1960s, reordering matrices was done manually with cards, but now you can play with an interactive version online.

Go to the
web page

GROWTH OF WALMART 1962–2006
Stores open per year and state

Figure 13.9 The reorderable matrix applied to Walmart store opening data.

Small Multiples

Edward Tufte coined the expression "small multiples." Like other profiling charts, a small multiples chart consists of a grid layout where entities share the same display rules. Any chart can be used in a matrix of small multiples, although using pie charts is guaranteed to yield great loathing from Tufte.

One of the most interesting uses of small multiples is as an alternative to animation. In this case, each multiple functions as a frame of a movie, allowing us to study each frame and make pair-wise comparisons.

In **Figure 13.10**, a U.S. map is used to again show Walmart store openings. Ordering is obvious, since it's a time series. Each year represents existing stores and those that have opened that same year. The gray dots in the background represent the location of each county of the United States.

The reorderable matrix and small multiples complement each other nicely. Notice on the small multiples map how the store network has spread like a virus from a central point, while it's easier to observe entrance and coverage profiles in each state in the reorderable matrix.

Using exactly the same data, we're able to prove what has been emphasized throughout this book—namely, that there are many ways to extract knowledge from a table, and we must search for them using a multitude of visualization types.

Download the
original chart

GROWTH OF WALMART: 1962–2006

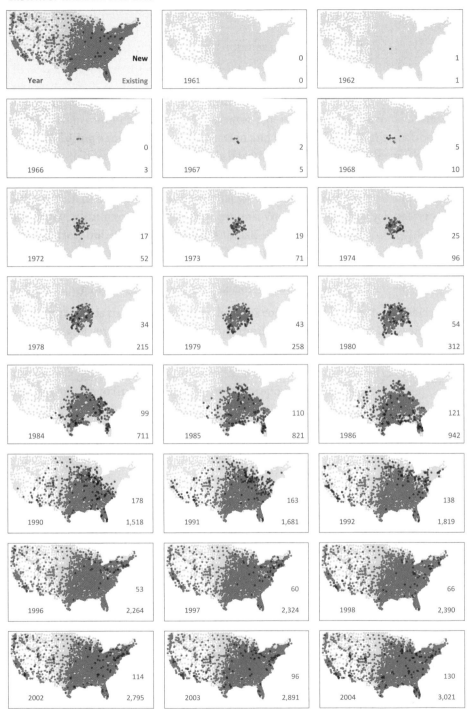

Figure 13.10 Using small multiples to display Walmart store openings.

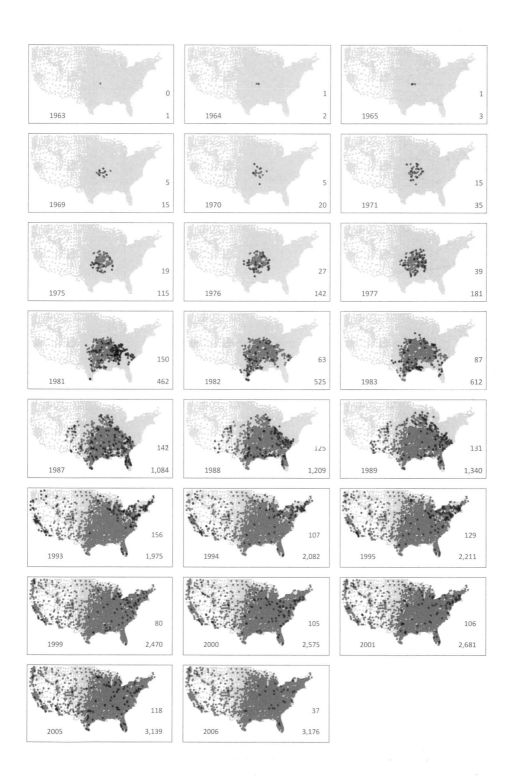

Profiling in Excel

In Excel, you can select a data range and drop it into a chart object, and it will be added as a new series. It would be great if you could drop a categorical data range and automatically split the chart into small multiples. But you can't.

When working on profiling charts, first build an initial chart that will serve as a model. Do your best to ensure that this will be your final design. Ensure that the scales cover the maximum and minimum values of the entire table, and set them to manual mode so that they don't change when you change categories. When you have your final version, save it as a template and use it to make the remaining charts in the set.

With a data visualization tool other than Excel, creating profiling charts is as easy as dragging a variable to the appropriate field. When there are many variables with potential for segmentation, this is an invaluable aid. This is one of the features whose absence in Excel exasperates me the most.[5]

Note that the maps presented in Figure 13.10 to exemplify small multiples are made of scatter plots where each point coordinate is a geographical coordinate. The high number of points allows us to recognize the overall shape as the United States.

Since the position's variables do not encode values beyond the geographical locations of the point, an alternative is to create multiple series, each color-coded. For these Excel maps, three series were used: counties in gray, existing stores in orange, and new stores in blue.

---

5 The good news is that this has been addressed by Microsoft in Power BI. You may want to try it if you have a recurrent need.

Takeaways

▪ The more data points you add to a chart, the higher the risk of hiding patterns. When you split a chart into multiple profiles, you get a more structured display that is easier to read and interpret.

▪ In a profile chart, all profiles share the same design, especially the aspect ratio and the scales, to make them comparable.

▪ In general, reading each profile should be as easy as reading the full-size original chart type, but when you perform pair-wise comparisons it's harder to spot smaller differences. Adding reference points simplifies this task.

▪ Sort the profiles such that you're able to see the overall pattern.

▪ Often you can use small multiples instead of animation. Check the pros and cons of each option for each specific visualization.

▪ Profiling means that you split the data set into as many profiles as the number of categories in the profiler variable (year, state, month, etc.). Explore the data by testing multiple profiler variables, if the tool you're using allows you to do so without too much effort.

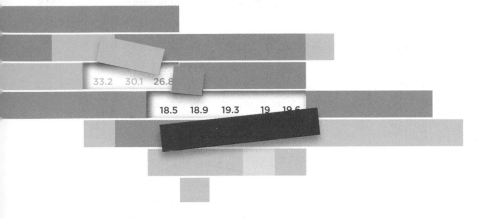

14

DESIGNING FOR EFFECTIVENESS

It's easy to agree on what "effectiveness" means, but finding a consensus on how to measure it is much harder. Effectiveness doesn't exist on its own; there is "effectiveness to whom" (where who defines the parameters) and "effectiveness regarding what" (the task).

In data visualization, the word "effectiveness" is thrown around a lot, so let's try to understand its scope. First, imagine yourself in the role of:

- **A scientist**, sharing with fellow scientists the results of your team's latest experiment on vaccine safety.

- **A policy maker**, trying to change the behavior of reluctant mothers regarding vaccine safety.

- **An artist**, creating a beautiful piece of data art that raises awareness of the issue of unvaccinated children.

Now imagine that you need to create effective visualizations for each. In this scenario, you'll reuse some of the data in all three roles, but everything else is different: information asymmetry, tasks, goals, and audience attention span. You simply can't use the same visuals and send the same message. You realize this and design three different visuals accordingly. You are certain that each one will tackle the task very *effectively.*

But wait. Suppose something goes terribly wrong in this perfect scenario. Your daily agenda somehow got completely mixed up and you deliver the wrong presentation in each meeting: You tried to change the behavior of your audience at the art gallery, who were there to see art, not an infographic about how safe vaccines are; you shared your piece of art with your team, who instead wanted to see hard statistics and complex charts; and you discussed the results of your experiment with the reluctant mothers, who had no idea what those scatter plots and regression analysis were all about. In this case, your visuals were actually so *ineffective* that you ended up inciting an angry mob. Your perfectly crafted messages were the right ones for the originally intended audience, but the moment they were mixed up and you delivered the wrong presentation in each meeting, all their effectiveness was lost.

To prevent this kind of disaster, always double-check that you're presenting the right visuals to the right audience.

The point is, effectiveness in data visualization is task-dependent and design-dependent (not to mention data-dependent). You have to create a visualization that addresses the issue, and you must design it in a way that generates a meaningful communication for your select audience. Some people will tell you that "insights" is the metric you should use to evaluate its effectiveness. Others will insist that "engagement" is the right metric, and you achieve that by prettifying your visualizations. This leads to aesthetics.

The role and importance of aesthetics define one of the major lines separating data visualization practitioners. On one hand, we have a huge group of anonymous practitioners who use common software tools such as Excel and PowerPoint in their daily data-related tasks within organizations. On the other hand, infographics created by graphic designers have a growing presence in the media. Also, organizations have found in infographics a way to increase the audience for their websites. Neither of these two groups is uniform, but the distinction between them is clear.

Since graphic designers' visualizations are more visible and more aesthetically appealing, it's natural that they serve as a model to common organizational practitioners. This aesthetic appeal is leveraged by software application vendors who promise artistic accomplishment through the use of their canned effects.

When graphic literacy in the organization is low, these are seductive arguments, especially because alternative models to suit the organization's needs are non-existent, unknown to them, or labeled "boring."

Many journalists and infographics designers fight against stylistic excesses that result in an inability to understand the visualizations' content. Alberto Cairo, a journalist and lead author writing about data visualization for the media, says in his book *The Functional Art* that "[G]raphics, charts, and maps aren't just tools to be seen, but to be read and scrutinized. The first goal of an infographic is not to be beautiful just for the sake of eye appeal, but, above all, to be understandable first, and beautiful after that; or to be beautiful thanks to its exquisite functionality."[1] Cairo does not minimize the importance of aesthetics, but he subordinates aesthetics to the functional reading and understanding of graphical representations, even in infographics, an area in which consumers expect greater creative freedom.

Data visualization in organizations follows a specific model (business visualization), and the adoption of inappropriate models negatively impacts the value we can extract from the data. Adhering to basic visualization principles discussed throughout this book not only helps you create more effective graphical representations, but also builds a safety net in the organization that helps avoid aesthetic calamities such as the pie charts presented in the first chapter.

There are no charts without aesthetics, however. Aesthetics create an emotional response that translates into rejection, indifference, or continued attention. Our aim is to always capture attention and interest in learning more, because this is the only way to help the audience acquire knowledge.

1   Cairo, Alberto. *The Functional Art: An introduction to information graphics and visualization.* Berkeley, CA: New Riders. 2013.

The Aesthetic Dimension

Many of the charts in **Figure 14.1** are real, by which I mean they're charts that someone has used in their analysis and communication. In most of them, we do not intuit any particular artistic talent of its author, not even some basic graphic design skills, but rather just the use of the flashiest options available in the application.

When artistic talent is scarce, common sense would suggest adopting a more conservative and neutral attitude. Judging from the number of 3D effects, bright colors, and exploded pie slices, we might be tempted to conclude the opposite. At least the authors are aware of the importance of the aesthetic dimension.

Figure 14.1 Google search results for "charts and graphs." *Google and the Google logo are registered trademarks of Google Inc. Used with permission.*

Bad designs result from a lack of skills, customer and peer pressure, and a unique aesthetic sense supported by canned effects available in software applications. The consequences are visible on the search results page. But artistic talent is not a necessary condition for making good charts. If your daily tasks are analyzing your organization's data, design skills are not a requirement.

It is no coincidence that we only began data visualization in Chapter 5 of this book, after having discussed perception, context, and data preparation. While aesthetics are discussed in this chapter, this structure aims to highlight the functional component of visualization and reduce the pressure for allegedly needed artistic talent or, even worse, the unrestrained use of special effects.

A Wrong Model

If, instead of "charts and graphs," we search for "data visualization," we get results dominated by graphic design, as exemplified by **Figure 14.2**. Many of the images are unique and attention-grabbing, and some are pure poetry.

Comparing both search results shows the immense distance between the canned effects of "memorable" charts and the true talent of many designers. But I'm not trying to demonstrate the aesthetic deprivation of the former search results. We have a more important goal, which is to evaluate whether the data visualization model of the latter is relevant to us. Here are some evaluation criteria:

- **Can they be made in an organizational environment?** Being unique objects, these visualizations do not fit the production processes that are expected of a sales or marketing department; they are best suited for the creative process of a design studio or a media outlet.

- **Are they effective?** They are no doubt beautiful and effective in drawing the attention of the audience, but many of them pose serious reading problems, either for point comparison or for pattern detection.

- **Are they consistent and recognizable?** Any chart type requires a learning period, but a production environment is not compatible with a continuous visual innovation that requires constant relearning of the process.

- **Are they adapted to office tools?** These visualizations are produced using specific programming languages and applications such as Adobe Illustrator—tools that are not generally available to typical office users.

- **Are they aligned with office users' skills?** These visualizations emphasize graphic design skills and artistic talent, which in general are not expected or required for data analysis positions in an organization.

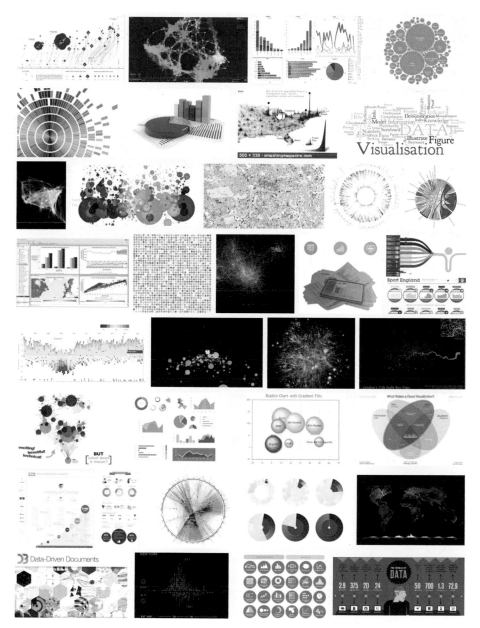

Figure 14.2 Google search results for "data visualization." *Google and the Google logo are registered trademarks of Google Inc. Used with permission.*

The Design Continuum

It's not hard to conclude from the answers to the questions above that data visualization as practiced by graphic designers isn't compatible with the day-to-day needs of organizations. Although appealing, it can't serve as a role model for business visualization. But design is inevitable from the moment when points are mapped. How can we integrate design more explicitly in the organizational routine? To understand it, we must recognize that the nature of design changes along a continuum whose characteristics are represented in **Figure 14.3.**

- **Encoding.** In the first phase, the design task is to encode the data using a set of transformations that create a recognizable chart, with which we've likely had prior experience and which we know how to read and interpret. This is the passage of the proto-chart to the chart, as discussed in Chapter 1.

- **Function.** The functional stage takes into account the situation (task type, audience profile, and other context variables) and represents the most rational way to optimize the message, by taking advantage of the rules of perception, for example.

- **Makeup.** At this stage in the continuum, the criterion is no longer effectiveness at all costs but the creation of an emotional reaction that arouses attention and promotes the interest of the audience for the message you want to convey.

- **Decoration.** Excessive makeup, distortions, or the introduction of elements irrelevant to chart reading bring about this stage. The display becomes narcissistic and more concerned with its own aesthetic effect than with effective communication.

Talented graphic designers stay within the makeup stage, creating visualizations that tend to be both informative *and* engaging, while decoration is mostly found in pseudo-3D Excel charts and many bad infographics. Decoration is the wrong goal, but its relationship with aesthetics can trigger a transformation and become art. In data art, the data are merely the starting point for the development of an artistic expression with the goal of offering an emotional experience.

THE DESIGN CONTINUUM

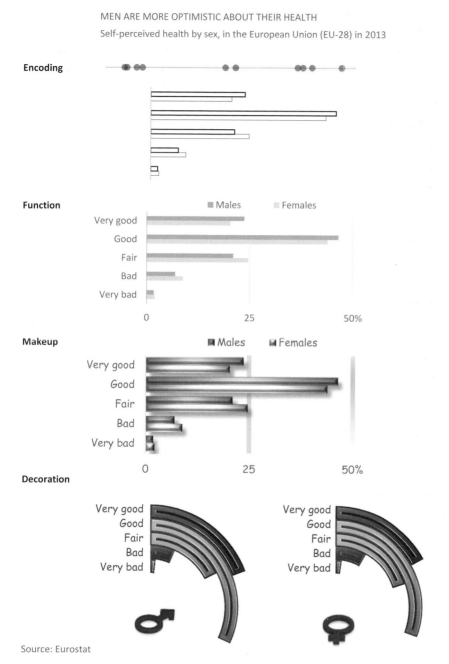

MEN ARE MORE OPTIMISTIC ABOUT THEIR HEALTH

Self-perceived health by sex, in the European Union (EU-28) in 2013

Source: Eurostat

Figure 14.3 Design changes its nature along a continuum.

Tools Are Not Neutral: Defaults

Have you heard the fable about the scorpion and the frog? The scorpion asks the frog to help it cross the river. When the frog refuses for fear it will be stung, the scorpion reasons it would never sting the frog because both would then die. The scorpion eventually persuades the frog but then stings the frog in the middle of the river crossing, dooming them both. Before dying, the frog asks why the scorpion stung him, to which the scorpion responds, "It is in my nature."

Every tool also has "its nature:" its default settings, its purpose, and the way the vendor understands the needs to be addressed. Different tools lead to different results for the same task. Edward Tufte wrote a famous essay[2] in which he says that PowerPoint favors a type of linear presentation and an unpleasant sales pitch: "PowerPoint presentations often look like a high school drama: very loud, very slow, very simple." This can trigger an interesting discussion. The vendor likes to claim that misuse or poor use is not the application's fault but instead is the fault of the tool user. This, however, hides a lot of the truth.

Then we have the additional issue regarding application defaults; they're a balm for users, because they save time, avoid the anxiety of multiple choices, and give the illusion of skills that do not exist. Moreover, it's easy to believe that the vendor has chosen the best options.

Excel proves that this is far from reality.

We can't deny that the defaults have improved since the ugly Excel 2003. The purple bar on gray background is gone, as is the silly legend used for a single series. But much remains to be done. All of Excel's predefined designs cater to the user's sense of aesthetics, and not a single one suggests a more *functional* approach to the design. Here are just a few examples of bad defaults for bar charts:

- Bar charts can have far too many grid lines, because the algorithm is more interested in finding round numbers. Setting the default limit to three in order to split the plot area into four sections would be an improvement.

- The default gap width between bars is set to an obscure 219 percent. Setting it at 100 percent would be more sensible.

- Once variation falls below a predefined threshold (around 20 percent), Excel will break the vertical scale. This can't be the default behavior for bar charts.

---

2   Tufte, Edward. *The Cognitive Style of PowerPoint: Pitching Out Corrupts Within*. Cheshire, CT: Graphics Press, Second edition, 2006.

If you want to follow Stephen Few's or Edward Tufte's data visualization recommendations while using a tool like Excel, you will constantly fight against the majority of chart types and their default settings.

Reason and Emotion

How experts define data visualization is almost as personal as their fingerprints. Most definitions can be easily placed in a section of the design continuum, which best discriminates the many varying perspectives.

The design continuum is not just about aesthetics. The continuum also reflects the relative weights of reason and emotion on a graphical representation. The conflict between reason and emotion is one of the constants of the human condition, and it doesn't seem likely that scientific and technological advances will ever substantially change the relationship between them. It seems much simpler to capture attention through emotion—because it's more immediate—than to capture attention through reason—which requires greater investment.

Data visualization does not escape this confrontation. Graphic illiteracy leads to a preference for simple charts with few data points that recreate physical objects, to which are added very obvious stylistic "wow" effects. Increased literacy does not eliminate emotional components but leads to subtler preferences that seek to integrate emotion into visualization.

A.I.D.A.

A.I.D.A. is an old marketing acronym that models expected behaviors toward an advertising message. The initial objective is of course to attract potential consumer's **Attention**, because this is the necessary step to evoke **Interest**, which may become the **Desire** for the product, which leads to a purchase **Action**.

These four steps are important, and message effectiveness is measured by the final result, the sales volume, but nothing is possible without the first **A**—the foot in the door that establishes a communication channel. The larger the number of messages to which we are subjected, the more advertisers seek some form of differentiation that makes their message stand out.

Now, because most of the time you're not actually selling a product or service when you share a chart with an audience, let's adapt the model:

- ■ **Attention.** A visualization stands out on a page and attracts our attention.

- ■ **Interest.** A quick scan and evaluation of visual objects, and perhaps reading titles, helps us decide whether this is interesting.

- ■ **Desire.** We now want (desire) to read the visualization in full and capture whatever message it communicates.

- ■ **Action.** As managers, we can actually take action based on what the data tell us. As magazine readers, we might take the action of ceasing to purchase certain products or simply becoming *aware* of a social issue.

In business visualization, the resources available for representing data are sparse. There are only a handful of chart types (although they have multiple variations). For many infographics authors, making a bar chart is almost a sacrilege, because that represents an immediate transformation of Attention into Boredom. For others, the key focus is on the data only. Edward Tufte, for example, says that "if the statistics are boring, you chose the wrong numbers."

We find levels of reason and emotion on four elements of a chart: in the data themselves, in the visual variable that encodes them, in the title, and in the background.

Compare the charts in **Figure 14.4** and **Figure 14.5**. It's the same chart type displaying the same data, but a world of emotions separates them.

Both charts represent the annual evolution since 1960 of live births in Portugal, one of the countries in the world with the lowest fertility rates. In the first version, only in the data do we find some emotion, due to the significant reduction in live births. This first version seeks to be correct, neutral, and descriptive, or in one word, rational. The designer believes that the reader will know how to incorporate the chart into his or her overall knowledge on the subject. It's a chart formatted to complement an accompanying text that one is already reading. Few readers will be attracted to the text after seeing the chart. It is common to find this kind of chart in a report or in an official statistics agency publication.

LIVE BIRTHS IN PORTUGAL 1960–2014

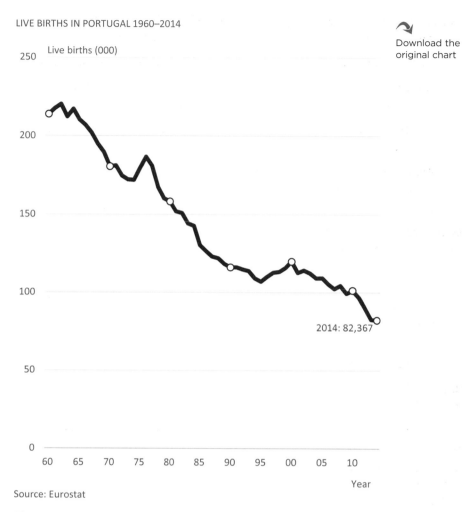

Download the
original chart

Source: Eurostat

Figure 14.4 Displaying live births from a rational perspective.

IS THIS COUNTRY FOR THE ELDERLY?

Never before have so few babies been born in Portugal. This is a demographic time-bomb set to destroy health systems and social security. Is it too late to avoid?

Figure 14.5 Displaying live births with an emotional touch.

Live births (000)

250

200

150

100

50

0

2014: 82,367

60 65 70 75 80 85 90 95 00 05 10

Year

Source: Eurostat

The second version is much different. This chart does not include any additional quantitative information to make us better understand what's happening, and yet it draws our attention and evokes our interest. If this were the initial pages of an article in a magazine, it's likely that it would have incited us to read it to learn more. This is because we feel that it's talking about a real drama, not just showing a few statistics. Let's see how this is done:

- **Data.** Like the skyrocketing unemployment rate in Greece, the sharply plummeting trend is so "in-your-face" that it tells the whole story.

- **Line.** The chart line is the only color element, so it attracts attention. The use of red gives us a clue that it is not good news (a blue line would soften the message).

- **Title.** The title is not descriptive; it makes a comment that is complemented by the text below. Formulating a question, it suggests that the reader will find the answer in the article.

- **Background.** The dark background, with an empty playground picture, bridges the gap between data and reality.

I added a few questionable details to enhance the dramatic effect, as the subtle continuity between the series and the object in the background image makes it look like the line is tending toward zero. The much larger size of the image also gives this chart an emphasis that the previous version does not.

These details don't alter the message in the data, but you must be aware of the dangers you face when entering this emotional dimension. You'll typically know when you've gone too far, but one example is to avoid depicting people in the picture, as they evoke too much undefined emotion.

Does Reason Follow Emotion?

With the clear, simple, and immediate message in the chart from Figure 14.5, we set the emotional tone. From a rational perspective, it would make sense to add more data, such as comparing Portugal to the European Union. But should we do this in this chart? The chart tells us that there is a significant drop in live births in Portugal, and the text tells us that this will have dramatic consequences. This is the scenario that we have set up. From here on, we'll build our story with more data and cleaner charts.

The chart in **Figure 14.6** shows that Portugal is diverging quite a lot from the European Union, with continuous drops in live births throughout the twenty-first century. This means that the scenario is very serious, both in absolute terms and in comparison with the EU.

Download the original chart

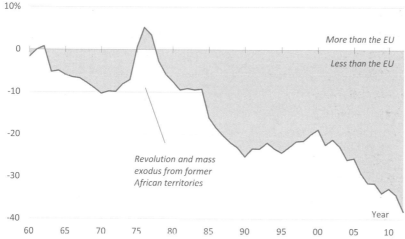

Source: Eurostat

Figure 14.6 Taking advantage of the previous emotional framework.

The chart in **Figure 14.7** would also be a good candidate for an emotional approach. It shows us that, because the fertility rate is below 2.1 children per woman (the minimum needed to replace generations), there is a scarcity of more than one million children since 1990, an average of over 50,000 per year. This is a very high number for a country the size of North Carolina.

Because the chart in Figure 14.5 has established the central idea and set the emotional framework, none of the remaining fertility rate charts need to have that same dramatic effect. The other charts enrich the story in a subordinated manner and without conflict with the central chart, like our planetary system orbiting the sun.

Download the
original chart

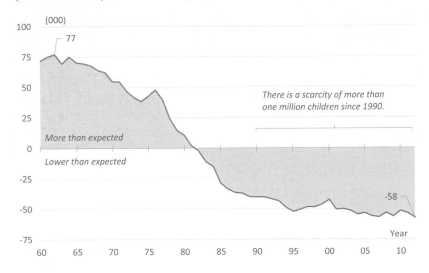

DIFFERENCE BETWEEN TOTAL LIVE BIRTHS AND EXPECTED TOTAL
Expected total: If fertility rate = 2.1 live births per woman

Source: Eurostat

Figure 14.7 No added emotion is necessary.

Emotion and Effectiveness

Some studies show that an aesthetic evaluation of an object affects the perception of its functionality, so neglecting this dimension and any other form of emotion when reading a chart proves to be a mistake. The question is therefore whether we should continue to evaluate the effectiveness of a chart strictly by functional criteria, or if instead emotional components should be taken into account and exploited to attract the audience's interest.

There is no universal answer. One reason for this is that the interpretation of functional criteria and emotional components differ between the time of analysis and the time of communication (we don't make 3D pie charts for personal consumption).

The second reason relates to the asymmetry between the information producer and the consumer. The larger the asymmetry, the more likely it is that the producer will prefer an emotional representation, as in the case of infographics in media. In business organizations, however, information sharing starts from a more balanced position and common interests that minimize the need to attract attention.

It's also most likely that people will remember an unusual and emotional graphical representation when compared to another one they have seen a million times before. Although this is a goal sought by infographics, memorable and emotionally appealing charts are generally not necessary or relevant in a business organization, even though they may be used at times when the organization as a whole must be made more aware of something or when personnel need specific motivation.

Note that there is a decline in communication effectiveness associated with a monotonous constant repetition of the same graphical model, whether it's that of pure rationality or the emotional memory. One introduces boredom; the other produces desensitization and requires increasing doses of emotion to maintain the same level of audience response.

Occam's Razor

If the aesthetics suggested by the "data visualization" search results presented earlier in this chapter are not suitable for everyday data visualization in an organizational environment, what's the alternative?

In the fourteenth century, the Franciscan monk William of Occam (or William of Ockham) formulated a principle that came to be known as Occam's razor, which states that "plurality is not to be assumed without necessity." That is, we should always prefer simple hypotheses or explanations over the more complex, as the introduction of complexity must result from necessity. Invoking parsimony and simplicity to explain reality is a common theme of many philosophers, artists, and scientists over the centuries, from Aristotle's writings to the more prosaic KISS (*Keep it simple, stupid*).

It's important to note that parsimony and simplicity are not absolute principles. We should not take them to the extreme and risk losing useful elements for understanding. This is implied in Occam's razor and is explicit in the famous Einstein quote: "We should make things simple, but not simpler." Also, you shouldn't assume that "simplifying" equates to "removing things": You do have to eliminate the irrelevant, but that's the starting point that should be followed by minimizing the accessory, fixing the necessary, and adding the useful. This metaphorical razor proves valuable when it comes to Excel and visualizations in organizations, because much of the formatting work of an Excel chart consists of deleting useless objects and fixing a lot of details.

Let's now observe Occam's razor in action, as applied to a chart in which we have added only a clip-art image using the default settings of Excel 2003.

The charts in **Figure 14.8** represent the evolution of annual per capita availability of meat from various sources, in the United States, over a century. We're interested in the evolution of beef and chicken availability in particular. (In case you're wondering: According to my research, no single factor explains the abrupt reversal of the trend in beef consumption after 1976. Health concerns are often cited, but an article in *California Agriculture* suggests that a widening gap between beef and chicken price indexes, coupled with lower consumer purchasing power, played a major role in this shift.)

Go to the
web page

Figure 14.8 shows the original chart along with the modified chart after applying Occam's razor. The line chart is the right chart for representing the data. Let's discover how functional design options render the chart most effective and most appealing.

- **Eliminate the irrelevant.** Initially, our intervention is *subtractive*, removing excess and bringing out the nature of the data. To cite another familiar phrase, now is the time for "less is more." Although the sharp decline in beef consumption makes the cow happy, this does not justify keeping the image of the smiling cow on the chart. The gray background, the borders, the legend, the markers... all that must go, because they add no value whatsoever.

- **Minimize accessory objects.** In the second phase, we can do a better job with the axis. Removing the decimal places on the vertical axis, the four-digit years, and the excessive number of grid lines are examples of minimizing accessory objects.

- **Correct the necessary.** In the third phase, we make corrections in the representation of the data itself, aligning it with the message. Some of the series are residual, and pork availability remains more or less flat over the years. The more interesting analysis seems to be comparing beef to chicken. We'll emphasize these two series, identify pork, and mute the others.

- **Add the useful.** In the last phase, we add useful elements such as the maximum value in beef and a visual annotation highlighting a period of price increase that triggered the reversal in the trend.

These four phases show that removing clutter is indeed a necessary first step, but this will not magically unveil hidden gems. It will only prepare the chart for the real work.

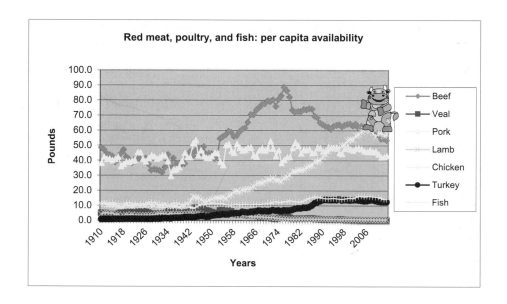

DECLINING SINCE THE LATE 1970S, BEEF CONSUMPTION WAS RECENTLY SURPASSED BY CHICKEN MEAT
Meat availability per capita in the U.S.

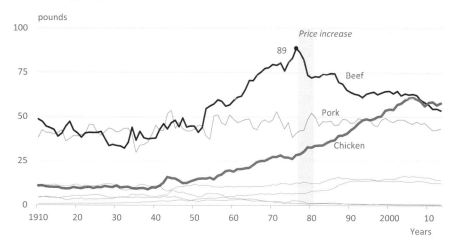

Source: U.S. Department of Agriculture

Figure 14.8 Applying Occam's razor to make a chart more effective and elegant.

Before considering the task completed, make sure that this chart is aligned both with your message and with the overall communication. Don't forget to check logistical issues, since the chart is now much lighter than the original (for example, will it look OK when projected?).

All of these changes result in a cleaner chart that is much more focused on the message we want to convey. While it is hard to forget the smiling cow from the first version, the second version looks more professional in the true sense of the word. All changes have a rationale, keeping the chart functional and resulting in more elegant and proper aesthetics in the organizational context.

Except for a few annotations we could add, there isn't much we can do to make this chart significantly more functional. However, do we want to add an emotional tone? Perhaps we should start with a less insipid title. If we want to go even further and start changing the visual objects, things suddenly get a lot more slippery, and *you will always lose functionality*. If you don't go overboard and the emotional dimension nicely complements or illustrates your message, you'll get more attention and, hopefully, more interest. So this is a potential tradeoff when you're willing to lose some functionality, without significantly impacting the message, in order to gain more attention and interest from the audience.

Designing Chart Components

Let's go over some of the chart components and see how Occam's razor and our generic design perspective apply.

Keep in mind that just as important as making good decisions with the chart's formatting options is ensuring that they're consistent throughout the presentation or report. When you create a chart, you also create rules, which the audience internalizes. If for no apparent reason you modify the rules, that will generate a disorienting effect in the audience and a need to relearn what was once considered acquired.

Inconsistency is not always bad, however; if it's planned and it takes advantage of salience, it may reinforce a message that otherwise would go unnoticed. Inconsistencies take multiple forms and multiple levels, so I cannot be exhaustive, but they occur:

- **At the detail level,** when the same entity is coded with different colors in two charts, or when using multiple fonts, or when several similar charts that should be compared have different scales.

- **At the intermediate level,** regarding the selected type of chart. If you've chosen a chart type to answer a certain question, don't change the chart type if you have the same questions later, as when doing the same analysis for various products, regional levels, or socioeconomic groups.

- **At the top level** of the process and in the overall representation structure. If the chosen option is a global analysis followed by filtered data focused on one aspect, don't confuse the audience with similar analyses but different structures.

Pseudo-3D

It's impossible not to love impossible objects, like the Penrose triangle (**Figure 14.9**) and at the same time feel uncomfortable staring at them. It's funny how if you fixate on any point in the triangle it looks absolutely believable, but not the triangle as a whole. When art takes advantage of this, like in M.C. Escher's lithographs, where a waterfall feeds on itself or stairs become endless loops, it looks so easy to make unique and memorable illustrations!

Go to the web page

It would be really nice to have something like this in data visualization. Something to add to a visual display to make it unique, worthy of attention, and, as vendors like to proclaim, professional and memorable. (I've already told you "professional and memorable" is a pet peeve of mine.) Whatever it is, this *je ne sais quoi* must have an instantaneous effect and be quick and easy to add, regardless of the author's design skills. It must transform an abstract chart into a concrete image that resembles a day-to-day physical experience.

Figure 14.9 The Penrose triangle.

Well, there is something that exists, but would it be considered good news or not? This thing is called the *pseudo-3D effect*. In most software applications, it's available as an option and it comes with what we might call an "Escher bonus," or in other words, the inability to make sense of the position of objects in space. The Escher bonus is visible in **Figure 14.10**. The charts on the left have a default 3D rotation, so they look bad without any other modifications. If you didn't know that the value of the first data point was 424, it could be anything, depending on the 3D rotation.

Download the
original chart

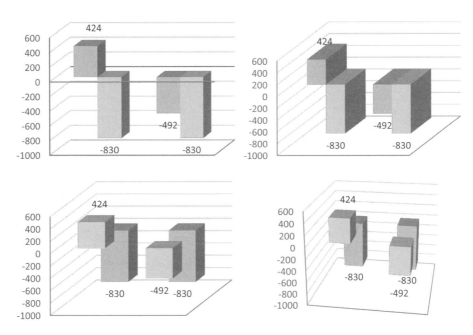

Figure 14.10 You can't accurately compare bars and get the correct values from a 3D chart.

These four charts show how useless grid lines are in a 3D chart. You can't count on them to get a reliable reading. Your only option is to compare column heights. After all, there are no scale breaks, so that should be OK, right? Well, not so fast. I wouldn't trust the bottom right chart if I were you. You would need to check whether the proportions are correct, and you'll have to be aware that your perception is compensating for distances. Because you can never be sure about the position of objects in space, any 3D chart fully deserves the Escher Career Achievement Award. And that is one award you don't want as a chart maker.

The top left chart in Figure 14.10 was redrawn from a real chart in a supposedly serious document: a government budget report. When we see the pseudo-3D effect applied to charts at this level, it makes us realize the long road ahead to achieving acceptable graphical literacy. The forest of colorful pipes in **Figure 14.11** is effective for a four-year-old child. Now that we know that we can't trust grid lines, what values are really being represented?

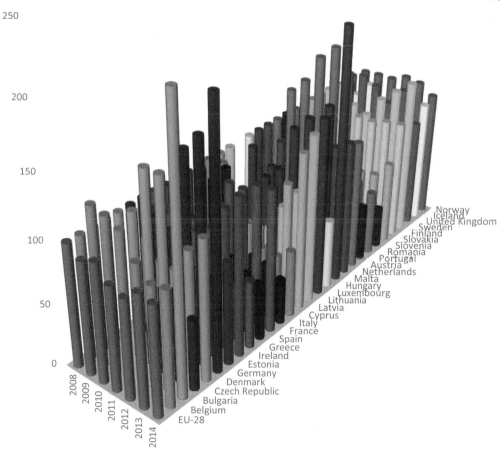

RESIDENCE PERMITS IN THE EUROPEAN UNION, PER COUNTRY

2008=100

Download the
original chart

Source: Eurostat

Figure 14.11 A chart or a child's toy blocks?

Let's examine the arguments against the use of pseudo-3D effects in data visualization. The use of pseudo-3D effects:

- **Distorts the relationship between objects.** The distances between objects and their relative magnitude are poorly evaluated. In a pie chart, nearby segments seem larger than those farther away; in a bar chart, it's hard to see which side of the bar serves as a reference and comparison with the grid lines, which are of no use.

- **Creates an erroneous communication concept.** Some studies conclude that those individuals who make charts with pseudo-3D effects do so not for personal consumption but only at the time of communication, believing that this will have a positive impact on the audience's attention and memory. As we have seen earlier, surprising the audience with a design is something that makes sense in the media but does not fit the production process of business organizations, where hundreds of charts are made every day.

- **Extinguishes the surprise effect.** Special canned effects, such as those available in software applications, have a very short lifespan. Once the surprise element fades away after their initial use, boredom soon follows.

- **Produces over-stimulation.** As can happen with color, 3D generates an over-stimulating effect that leads to eyestrain.

- **Hides data points.** As in the previous chart, when points are represented in the apparent third dimension, it's natural that the most distant points are hidden by closer points.

- **Takes up too much space.** The introduction of pseudo-3D effects forces an increment on the average space occupied by each point, which demands an increase in chart size or a reduction of the amount of data represented. Either option proves to be a mismanagement of the available space.

- **Is immature.** Most adults acquired the ability of abstract thinking required to read a chart at around the age of 12. Representing data with blocks and disc slices is really regressing to an earlier age and would only make sense if it were accompanied by a clown nose.

Textures

If the whole point of adding pseudo-3D effects is to create "physical objects," then coloring the area within a slice or a bar using a flat color defeats that purpose. In 3D, the area of a slice or a bar becomes a surface that needs to be filled with a glossy texture. Texture makes things real, and the more real the objects look, the better.

In **Figure 14.12**, only the small pie chart represents proportions correctly, but it's easier to overlook it when pies in pseudo-3D look so real that you feel like touching them. (Note that in this case I added the dubious flourish of reflections and shadows to make them even more real, while purposefully making the shadow position incompatible with the position of the light, which is a typical error.)

Textures are not an exclusive attribute of pseudo-3D charts, but it makes sense to use them when an author intends to give a physical quality to the chart. Because data visualization deals with abstract concepts and images, translating them into some physical shape is certainly a noble endeavor; however, we should call this something else, perhaps some form of data art that has to be measured by artistic criteria rather than by its compliance with the objectives of data visualization.

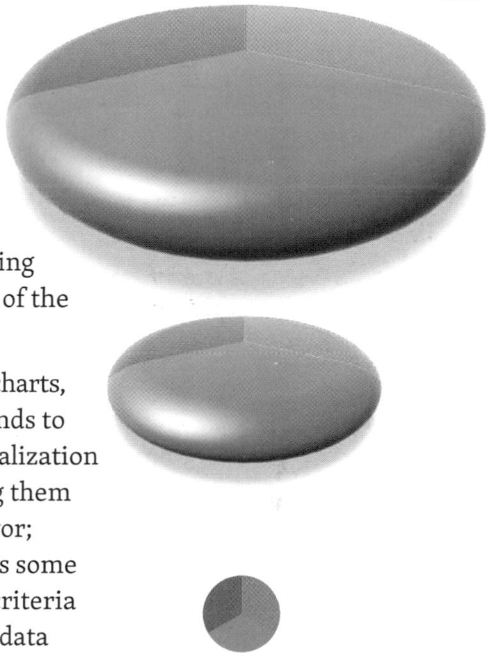

Figure 14.12 Pies made to be touched.

How about the sizing issue when using texture? Chelsea fans have good reasons to be unhappy with their team in the 2015–16 English Premier League soccer season ▪▪▪▪▪▪▪▪▪▪▪▪▪▪ ▪▪▪, especially when compared to its performance of the previous season ▪▪▪▪ ▪▪▪ ▪▪▪ ▪▪▪▪ ▪▪▪ ▪▪ ▪▪ ▪▪▪▪ ▪ ▪▪ . Now tell me: How much larger would these two charts need to be if I wanted to add textures? If, instead of flat colors like blue and red, you use a texture with a range of colors for each category (like the green slice in Figure 14.12), you'll need many more pixels for the texture to communicate the physicality of the object. The objects must have a minimum dimension that allows the texture to be perceived and decoded, which means that the chart will necessarily be larger than a version without texture. The alternative is to reduce the number of data points displayed, if possible.

Textures also incur a serious productivity problem. While I was able to make the pie chart in the bottom of Figure 14.12 in just a few seconds, the others took me much more time, because I kept playing with lighting and materials and angles and rotations and everything else that Excel puts at our disposal for adding useless formatting.

Titles

A chart has two basic groups of objects. The first group includes all the data-encoding objects: lines, bars, areas. Everything else is in a supporting role to help identify the data and to help in reading the chart or defining its limits. Let's start with the title. At first you'll build on the title, adding more and more detail so that it serves to help you define your information. Later, you'll trim it to be comprehensive but extremely concise.

The most common way of titling a chart is to describe its contents—for example, "Age Structure of the German Population in 2050." This tells us all about the variables involved but nothing about its insights.

A descriptive title is appropriate, but consider demoting the descriptive portion to a subtitle, using as the main title the chart's message: "Germany in 2050: A Shrinking and Aging Population [as we can see from the chart]." The phrase "as we can see from the chart" helps to write the conclusion, although it should not actually appear in the title, naturally.

Now take another step and make it a more complex story: "In 2050, Germany will have a shrinking and aging population. This is due in part to the increase in life expectancy but above all the drastic decrease of birth rate, where an average of [value] children needed to replace generations will not be born, despite the immigrants whose share of the birth rate is increasing."

Writing sentences like this helps us organize the information and lets the story flow and make sense. This text is perfectly suited to describe a made-up model of the German demographic evolution. Now break it into several pieces that will be used in the chart titles. You can do it literally using ellipses (...drastic decrease of birth rate...) or by making some adjustments:

- A shrinking and aging population *(population pyramid)*
- Life expectancy will keep increasing *(line chart)*
- Number of live births keeps trending down *(line chart)*
- Number of live births will continue to be below generation replacement *(bar chart displaying ratio of actual live births versus target live births)*
- Live births will remain high among immigrants and will account for a larger share of total live births *(line chart displaying live births by mother's country of birth)*

Regarding formatting, I rarely use the title object in an Excel chart. Most of the time I write titles in a cell above the chart, which usually allows for better control. I also tend to accept the suggestions of several style guides and align titles to the left, which enhances readability when compared to centered titles.

Go to the
web page

Fonts

There aren't many opportunities for playing with extravagant fonts in business visualization. However, I still have fond memories of the time I used a "gore" font in a slide, looking perfect in all that gory black and red. Wouldn't it be nice to use a gore font in a chart once in a while? Or perhaps a childish font, like Comic Sans? Well, the problem is that fonts help set the tone, and usually, a terror scene or a playground is not the best tone for regular quarterly business reviews.

In most charts, use a font that looks clean, neutral, and readable. Most standard sans serif fonts are OK, but you may not like a font at a given size, small or large.

For this book's charts, I had to choose a standard Windows font, and it had to look good at a size of 8 points. After testing several fonts, I had to accept that Calibri was the best, given these constraints.

Annotations

Plotting unemployment rates (**Figure 14.13**) only shows us a sudden reversal of trend in 2008, but they tell us nothing about the possible causes. Add a few written or visual annotations such as the date of the Lehman Brothers bankruptcy and the subsequent sovereign debt crisis that led to the two Greek bailouts. They can help us contextualize the data, giving the audience additional elements for interpreting the chart.

We saw how playing with salience allows us to create layers of data relevance in a chart. Now imagine a thin transparent film over your chart, where you can freely add comments, notes, or contextual data. This "annotation layer" (as the *New York Times* graphics team calls it) can really help your audience read your chart. Annotate a chart as much as you need, but any notes should be useful and accurate and should not compete for attention; they should be a discreet but helpful whisper.

MONTHLY UNEMPLOYMENT RATE BY AGE GROUP AND SEX

European Union and other countries

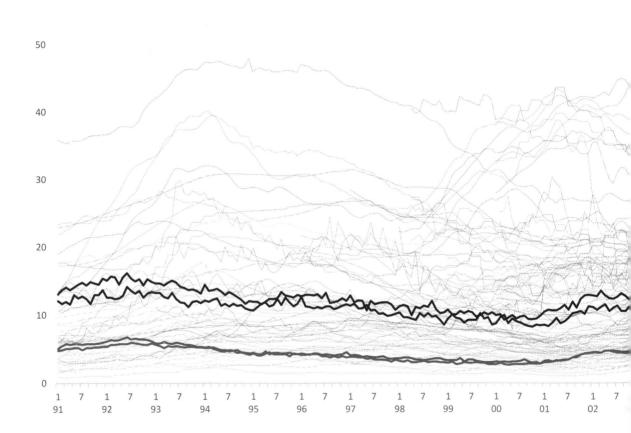

Source: Eurostat

Figure 14.13 Using dozens of series to create a sense of density.

Download the
original chart

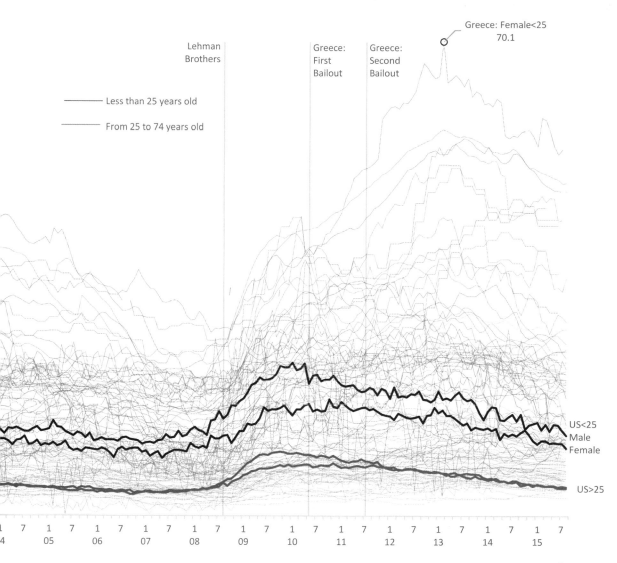

Lehman
Brothers

Greece:
First
Bailout

Greece:
Second
Bailout

Greece: Female<25
70.1

————— Less than 25 years old

————— From 25 to 74 years old

US<25
Male
Female

US>25

7   1   7   1   7   1   7   1   7   1   7   1   7   1   7   1   7   1   7   1   7
4   05   06   07   08   09   10   11   12   13   14   15

Month/Year

Grid Lines

Grid lines range from an excess of unjustifiable prominence to their complete removal, which they do not deserve.

I removed grid lines from Figure 14.13. Can you point to exactly where the 50% grid line would be on the *left* axis? That's easy: You can expect it to be aligned with the middle of the "50" label. But will it be as easy to point to the same grid line on the vertical axis on the *right*? Actually, that would be a bit trickier, and I wouldn't be surprised to find an error margin of up to 0.1 inches, up or down.

We saw in Chapter 2 that Weber's law justifies grid lines and reference lines, because they facilitate the comparison among points, especially if the points are far apart. Bear in mind that the Gestalt law of figure/background tells us that they should only support the reading of the chart; they are not leading actors.

Grid lines should be present most of the time on the vertical axis, and also along the horizontal axis when using scatter plots or similar charts. Their number cannot be defined at the outset, as that depends on the data itself, the scales, the chart size, and the chart's aspect ratio. When you have a profile chart, where multiple entities share the same scale, you will probably need more grid lines to accommodate all the differences.

That said, we saw that we often split a distribution into four quartiles. We can borrow that reference and use three grid lines, dividing the scale into four sections, which will be a reasonable number for a typical chart. See this applied in **Figure 14.14**. Note that additional lighter, minor horizontal grid lines were also applied, but as you can see they're not needed. And just imagine how busy the chart would look if they were at the same level as the major grid lines.

NUMBER OF LIVE BIRTHS PER 1000 WOMEN IN EACH AGE GROUP

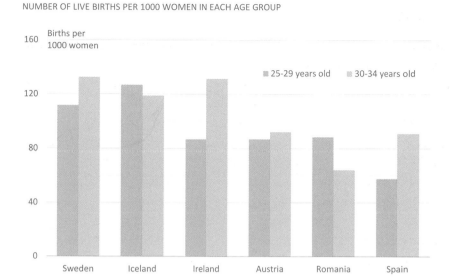

Source: Eurostat

Figure 14.14 Grid lines must help reading the chart without interfering.

Clip Art

Clip art is sometimes used to add a touch of humor to a chart. Don't do this. If the chart was designed to be fun, great, but adding a canned joke just "because" is a very bad idea, as we have seen in bad examples at the beginning of this book.

That said, any text that could be replaced by an image may be replaced. For example, using known symbols to replace legends is a good idea. Corporate logos, country flags, and club emblems are some of the possible candidates. A symbol renders reading more universal, but do not assume that because you can identify these symbols, all your audience will be able to do the same.

Download the
original chart

The Secondary Axis

A chart with a secondary axis might seem to acquire an aura of seriousness and ability to harmonize the patterns in the data that no chart with one mere axis can achieve. Note the gravitas and seriousness of the chart in **Figure 14.15** and the seemingly great harmony among the three series.

INTEREST RATES (NEW LOANS)

Figure 14.15 A dual-axis chart is always misleading.

Hmm, well, not really. I'm afraid a dual-axis chart with different scales is nothing more than a sophisticated form of misleading. You could elect it as one of the deadly sins of data visualization.

Two *independent* scales mean that there is no relationship between them, so the limits and range of each scale depend only on the author's discretion. However, the natural tendency of the author is to assign a series to each axis in a way that *suggests* similar patterns or a non-existent relationship (or unproven by the chart).

For some bizarre reason, economists seem to love dual-axis charts, judging by the numerous examples in financial reports. In Figure 14.15 I'm replicating one of those examples. The series Consumption is arbitrarily associated with the secondary axis, and the range was adjusted to coincide as much as possible with the series Business.

If we do use a dual-axis chart, our first priority must be to ensure that the reader immediately sees which series is assigned to which axis. This must be done visually, not in text. In this example, the association between Consumption and the secondary axis is made only after reading the legend. Add the break in scales of both axes and you're left with a chart that is nothing more than a repository of malpractices.

Now compare the chart with the one in **Figure 14.16,** and you'll be surprised to see that interest rates for Consumption loans are far above the rest.

INTEREST RATES (NEW LOANS)

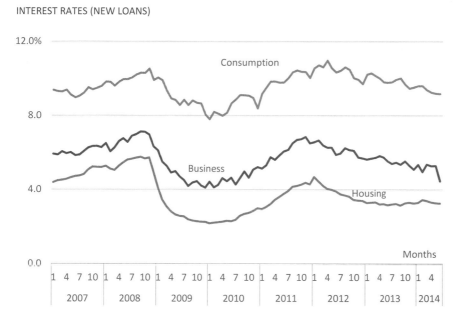

Figure 14.16 Removing the secondary axis offers an accurate comparison of all series.

Be very clear about this point: Even if there is a perfect match between two series, even if this match is reinforced by a perfect correlation, and even if everything makes sense, there is never a good reason to use a dual-axis chart when there is a risk that the reader will compare series in both axes.

If we want to observe how similar or how correlated two variables are, there are correct forms for doing so. In most cases, the existence of two axes means that the author believes there is a relationship between variables. For time series, it's easy to verify this using a connected scatter plot. Manipulating the scales until they "look good" is not one of the best practices—not by a long shot. In such a flexible field as data visualization, this particular rule stands almost as dogma.

Let's look at the exceptions. There aren't any that I'm aware of *when comparing variables*. However, redundancy, equivalence, and perspective can justify the use of a secondary axis:

- **Redundancy.** You have the same scale in both axes. It makes sense, in large charts, to help minimize saccadic movements and provide an equal reference on the far side.

- **Equivalence.** The scales are different but equivalent and, obviously, are synchronized. Euros and U.S. dollars, or Celsius and Fahrenheit are examples of equivalent scales.

- **Perspective.** You want to see a series from two perspectives and it doesn't make sense to compare them. The Pareto chart (from Chapter 9) is the most common example.

Legends

Think of legends as necessary evils. They're evil because they disrupt the chart reading flow but are necessary for identifying the series when no better alternative is available.

As we've seen, legends force continuous back and forth (saccadic) eye movement and color-matching tasks and should be avoided whenever possible through the use of the direct labeling of the series. This is an easy rule to apply to static line and pie charts, but may compromise readability in dynamic charts where labels risk overlapping when the data change. In cases where there is such risk or formats in which the direct identification is difficult, set up the legend as close as possible to the data. Do not be afraid to put the legend within the data area. Just ensure, though, that it does not interfere with reading.

When encoding the series with colors, check whether you can tell them apart in the legend and whether it's easy to match the key and the series. Because the color area in the legend is very small, it needs more color separation than when we compare large areas.

The legend border is at the top of the list of useless object formatting options available in Excel. Not surprisingly, until recently it was enabled by default. It might be possible to justify its use in some obscure scenario that, so far, I have not found. If you have an older version of Excel, it also presents a legend when there is only one series. Delete it as soon as you see it.

Backgrounds

Remember the heavily saturated yellow background of the bad example chart you had to endure at the beginning of this book, and how it contributed to its over-stimulation? What about the chart with the photo of an empty playground, a few pages back?

These two examples show that the background influences the way we read the chart, so it should be carefully evaluated. Of all the elements of a chart, the background should be less prominent (it's called "background" for a reason). As a rule, it should have the same color as the surrounding area, although many exceptions may be considered.

In his 2004 book *Show Me the Numbers*, Stephen Few says that a background that is not neutral undermines data integrity, and any image useful to supplement the data should be used in proximity to the chart but not as background. That's your safest bet, but if you want to define an emotional framework as was done in the live births example, you may get more attention using a background image.

Note that defining an emotional framework and manipulating your audience's feelings are not the same thing. The empty playground image in Figure 14.5 sets the stage, but our eyes are naturally drawn to the red line. It doesn't compete with data for the audience's attention and interfere with data perception as a color image would (don't use color images as backgrounds). From there, it's difficult to establish other criteria for selecting the right image. The image must translate the message without excessive emotional manipulation. It should only be a foot in the door that leads people to want to know more.

Ordering the Data

We know that a chart lets us compare points, but an effective comparison depends on choosing the right ordering key. Some keys, like time, seem so obvious that we don't think much about them (although we *should* think about them, as we saw in the monthly births project in Chapter 6). When there's a categorical scale, as in most bar charts, it's more difficult to determine the ordering key. Alphanumeric ordering is almost random, which makes it useless in graphical representations. We have to look for the right ordering key among the data.

In **Figure 14.17**, you'll need some time to find Colorado (CO), because none of the charts are using an alphanumeric key. But because that's a state we're interested in, I have emphasized it for you. (You're welcome.)

A CENTURY OF POPULATION CHANGE: SHARE OF POPULATION IN EACH STATE AND CHANGE IN RANK

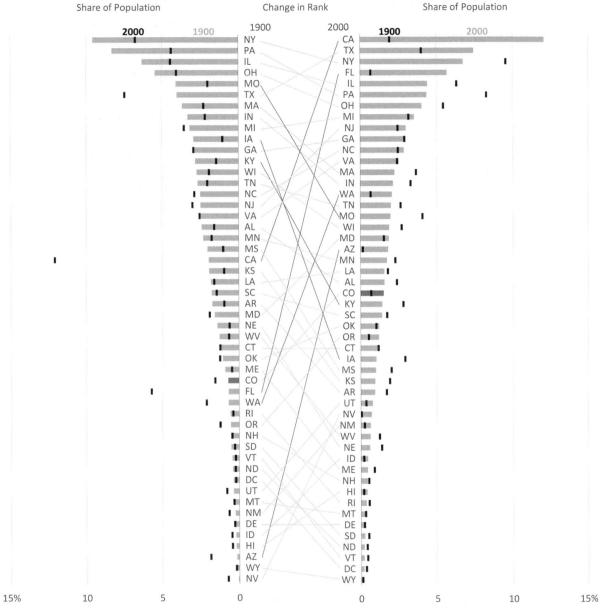

Source: U.S. Census Bureau

Figure 14.17 Different ordering keys result in different insights.

Download the
original chart

This is a very common situation: comparing two years for a bunch of categories. There is no right ordering key, because it depends on the task. If you want to emphasize the current status, you'll use one key, and if you want to emphasize the starting point, you'll use another key. The chart actually shows you both keys (current and starting point), while displaying the change to the other key. This makes it easy to spot that strong outlier on the left (California). The slope chart in the middle helps to make sense of the changes.

Making a decision on the ordering key is not always this easy. Take household expenditure. If you look carefully at the categories, you'll see that they're not ordered arbitrarily. In **Figure 14.18**, the pie chart makes it clear that the most basic items (Food, Housing, and Apparel) account for half of household expenditure (the right half of the pie). This is an interesting insight. The bar chart looks unordered and doesn't seem very useful.

STRUCTURE OF HOUSEHOLD EXPENDITURE IN 2012–2014

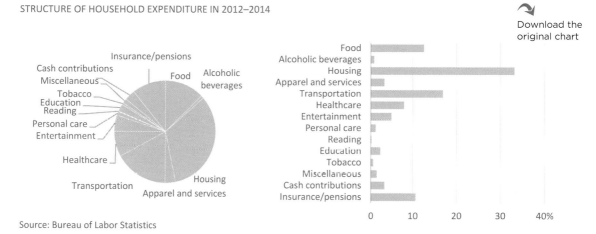

Download the
original chart

Source: Bureau of Labor Statistics

Figure 14.18 Keeping the implicit order key.

In **Figure 14.19,** the insights change a bit, as does the role of each chart. Any implied order in the categories was ignored in this alternative representation, and ordering is based only on the value of each category. Now, the bar chart is very effective for comparing the categories, while the pie chart shows that Housing and Transportation account for half of the expenditure.

A third version (**Figure 14.20**) lies somewhat between the two previous ones: This version groups categories, orders the groups first, and then categorizes within each group.

STRUCTURE OF HOUSEHOLD EXPENDITURE IN 2012–2014

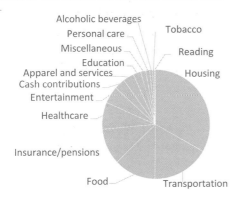

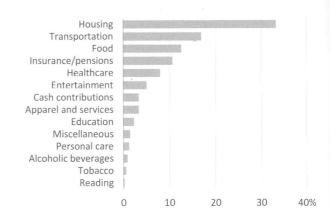

Source: Bureau of Labor Statistics

Figure 14.19 Using the data values to order categories.

Download the
original chart

STRUCTURE OF HOUSEHOLD EXPENDITURE IN 2012–2014

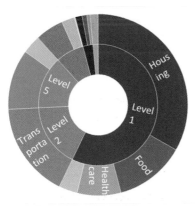

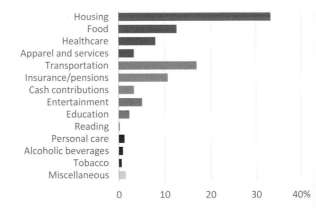

Source: Bureau of Labor Statistics

Figure 14.20 Grouping and ordering the data.

Download the
original chart

This classification of expenditure, as well as other classifications (occupations, economic activities) shows how an apparently nominal variable may have an implicit order that we should be aware of, and that we must decide whether we want to respect. In other cases, although there is an implicit ordering, it may not be obvious to a layperson, so it's useful to understand the rationale applied.

Any chart that uses a categorical axis requires making more or less arbitrary additional decisions regarding ordering. If possible, use chart types for which these decisions need not be made. The default ordering is by values (**Figure 14.21**). Use the nominal axis for special purposes, such as when you do want to change ordering, as was done in the example in Figure 14.18.

STRUCTURE OF HOUSEHOLD EXPENDITURE IN 2012–2014

Figure 14.21 The default ordering key.

Download the original chart

Number of Series

The maximum number of series in an Excel chart is set to 255. Of course, no one is going to represent 255 series, as this is a theoretical limit. Or is it?

In our classification of chart types, we defined two major groups: point comparison charts and data reduction charts. When thinking about the number of series or categories in a chart, the same rationale applies. When you want each series to remain unique and identifiable (in the legend), then six is a reasonable maximum reference value. When the series is diluted and what matters is the overall pattern created by numerous series, then you can have hundreds or even thousands.

When three is the maximum number of objects stored in working memory and six is the number of colors we can discriminate comfortably[3] (the number of "accents" in an Excel color theme), it's justifiable to limit the number of series to a value between these two references. Take this with a grain of salt, however, because the number of series must be evaluated for each specific case.

---

3 Ware, Colin. *Information Visualization: Perception for Design.* Waltham, MA: Morgan Kaufmann, Third edition, 2012.

The chart type, the variability, or overlapping and crossing points may or may not support the upper (more series) or lower (fewer series) thresholds. As we've seen since the beginning, more important than the number of series is creating a display that helps us make sense of the data, understand the distances between points, and observe patterns and detect extreme values.

Let's look at some ways to reduce and manage the number of series and the number of points per series.

Chart Type

As we know, a point requires less space than a line, and a line requires less space than a bar. Hence the type of encoding we use is important for maximizing the number of series while maintaining the chart's readability.

Remember when we compared pie charts to a slope chart in Chapter 1? With a little irony, we could say that both chart types could handle more data: The slope chart would be able to maintain its readability level, while for pie charts it would be somewhat irrelevant to add more slices because they had already reached their level of absolute ineffectiveness.

Also, in the case of population pyramids, two series for each gender are sufficient to hamper reading the bar chart, while using lines supports a larger number of series.

Grouping

The level of detail should be appropriate to the task. Sometimes, over-aggregating hides (innocently or maliciously) the most relevant information. On the contrary, abundant details will attract attention to spurious variations, hiding the tree under the excess of leaves.

In our example, data on household consumption expenditure has 14 categories, making them candidates for some level of aggregation. The proposed grouping in Figure 14.20 to 5+1 (five plus a miscellaneous group) is displayed in the inner ring, while the outer ring details each of the groups. Regardless of the selected chart type, this is a useful solution: It aggregates and emphasizes categories at a higher grouping, while allowing us to explore the details.

Residual Category

In **Figure 14.22**, we decided that a hierarchical structure is not relevant to the analysis, and observing
the main items is all that matters. Hence we have
ordered them by value, creating a residual group of
around 14 percent.

These criteria are naturally adapted to the task, and
one must ensure that the definition of a residual category does not hide important details. We don't have
to aggregate the residual categories by consolidating
them into a single value; a visual aggregation (by
color) is enough, as in Figure 14.22, where residual
categories remain separate (but in Excel, placing the
cursor over them would identify them).

MAJOR ITEMS IN THE STRUCTURE OF
HOUSEHOLD EXPENDITURE IN 2012–2014

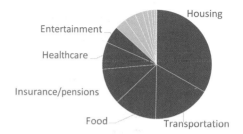

Figure 14.22 Visual residual categories.

Context

We saw, in Figure 14.13, the evolution of the unemployment rate in several countries,
grouped by gender and age group (youth and adults). This segmentation has generated 128 series, still far from Excel's limit but incompatible with the traditional
data visualization philosophy, wherein each series has to be clearly identified.

Our first goal in this type of representation is to observe the overall patterns
generated by a wide range of series. In this case, the chart draws attention to the
sudden growth in unemployment after 2008 and the fact that unemployment is
consistently higher among young people than among adults. The chart shows the
typical values of a set of data series given by their proximity and a denser zone,
as well as cases in which the values are significantly different than this pattern.

These are important elements that you can see in a static version of the chart, but
you can only learn more about the phenomenon represented here through some
sort of interaction. You could switch between the differentiation by gender and
age, for example, or emphasize the four series of a particular country. Imagine
that this picture illustrates what happens in the Excel file: You click a line and all
four series for the selected country are emphasized.

"But isn't this a spaghetti chart?" you might ask. Well, it surely looks like spaghetti.
But a "proper" spaghetti chart occurs when you actually want to identify each
series and you are unable to do so, or you're unable to clearly see a pattern or trend.

In other words, you have failed to capture the individual characteristics of each series. In this case, however, we're providing a context to one or a small number of series, which we can clearly see, and through interaction with the Excel file, we can choose whatever series calls our attention.

Small Multiples

Figure 14.23 is split into four small multiples, each representing one of the four groups of variables. We can immediately see the difference between youth unemployment and adult unemployment. We also see a denser pattern for men and a more dispersed pattern among women in both age groups, without having to observe this behavior through interaction. The interaction could be programmed so that, for example, by placing the cursor over a series in a chart, that country would also be highlighted in the remaining charts.

MONTHLY UNEMPLOYMENT RATE BY AGE GROUP AND SEX

European Union and other countries

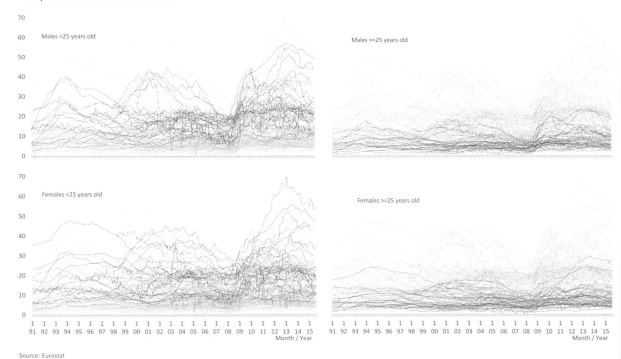

Source: Eurostat

Download the
original chart

Figure 14.23 Splitting the unemployment rates into four small multiples allows us to see the behavior of each group.

Interaction is another way of managing a number of sets greater than would be usefully represented in a single chart.

Lying and Deceiving with Charts

If you allow me to update the famous quote attributed to Disraeli, there are four kinds of lies: lies, damned lies, statistics, *and visualization*. This puts data visualization at a higher level of wickedness and persuasiveness.

If someone wants to twist the facts beyond what is legitimate, they will do so, regardless of the means chosen. Blind trust in our eyes (pun intended) makes us more vulnerable to visual lies.

Charts are always an interpretation of data, in the same way that a photo is an interpretation of reality, no matter how objective it may seem. This should be not only recognized but encouraged (the editorial dimension we have talked about throughout this book) within an ethical framework that seeks to identify its own subjectivity and minimize its influence on choices. There can be no contradiction between "what I want to say" and "what the data say." This difference is often difficult to detect, especially when the subject's message is fully determined by his beliefs, ideological position, and activism.

The examples we'll see below do not exhaust the diversity and subtlety of visual lies; they only purport to identify some of the most pathological cases. If you want a more systematic and exhaustive list, Gerald Everett Jones's *How to Lie with Charts* is the obvious reference. Alberto Cairo's *The Truthful Art* also deals with truth and lies in visualization, but Cairo takes a subtler approach. He wants to help readers recognize the truth and make it stronger (by combining visualizations with statistical methods, for example).

As a follower (and also as a member) of social network communities interested in data visualization, I frequently stumble upon links to the daily changing "worst chart ever" (many people in social networks are addicted to their daily dose of outrage). In most cases, the "worst chart ever" is just a chart in which the designer exaggerated his willingness to do things differently, combined with a profound numerical illiteracy. All these charts lie, but in most of them there is more ignorance than malice. The more extreme the actor's voice, the greater his likelihood for manipulation.

Data, Perception, and Cognition

The first requirement for a chart not to lie is, naturally, that the data don't lie either. As we have seen, the hidden agenda of those who produce and disseminate data, the way they want to frame their reality, and how metrics, concepts, and parameters are defined may make the degree of data's truth vary. Having verified these conditions, we can only check whether choices in the graphical representation truthfully reflect the data.

One of the most transverse and insidious forms of a lie is the conflict between the perceptual and cognitive dimensions of a chart. As we know, what we see in the chart can't be corrected by the legend or other objects.

Exaggerating Differences

The quantitative scale in a chart should start at zero by default. This rule conflicts with the need to observe in more detail (with better resolution) the differences between points. Any solution that breaks the scale has to be studied to ensure that the message's essence is not biased. Some charts are more sensitive to the absence of the origin: Bar charts and area charts do not tolerate it, as the scale must represent all values, beginning with zero.

In **Figure 14.24**, the small difference between the two values is magnified to an absurd level because the minimum value was set to 49. This example seems to exceed the limit of common sense, but the proportions are identical to a chart that was featured on Venezuelan TV showing the results of presidential elections.

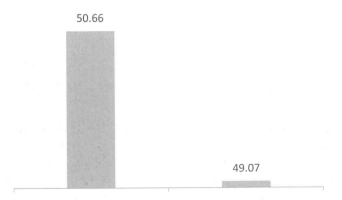

Figure 14.24 Manipulating the vertical axis to exaggerate differences.

Distorting Time Series

In a time series, the intervals between periods should remain constant. If that's not possible, the scale should reflect this fact, varying the distances *proportionally* along the axis. The left chart in **Figure 14.25** shows that if you have time intervals of one, five, and ten years and you don't take that into account, you'll generate an exponential curve. If you respect proportions, you'll get a linear projection. This is a case of numeric illiteracy that influences how the chart is rendered. I often see this in newspapers. To correct this problem in Excel, set the horizontal axis as a date.

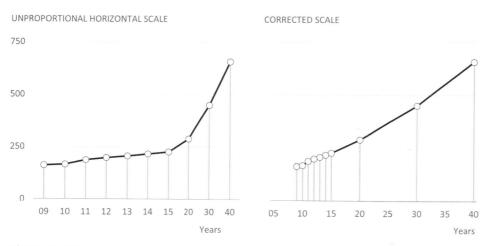

Download the original chart

Figure 14.25 Time periods must be spaced proportionally.

Aspect Ratio

The charts in Figure 14.25 respect the original chart aspect ratio, which is almost 1: 1, or in other words, almost square. This accentuates the curve slope, which, along with the error in scale, accentuates the difference regarding the reliability of the data.

There is no rule defining the relationship between the width and height of a chart. In general, charts should be rectangular, except for the scatter plot, which should be square. In this book, the aspect ratio of the plot area is usually around 1.6: 1. William Cleveland suggests a line chart's aspect ratio depends on its slope, which should be adjusted to a value of around 45° (the slope of the corrected version in the preceding example).

The best rule is to maintain consistency, justify any inconsistencies, and, in line charts, apply the rule to include two or more series so that the slope is analyzed in relation to the various series, not in absolute terms.

Omitting Points

In **Figure 14.26**, compare the darker gray bar with the remaining gray bars, ignoring the white ones. Now, repeat the analysis including all bars. I don't think you'll come up with the same conclusions, because the context of the dark gray bar was altered. If the set of all bars form a coherent group, cherry-picking only a few that support an argument is obviously a lie.

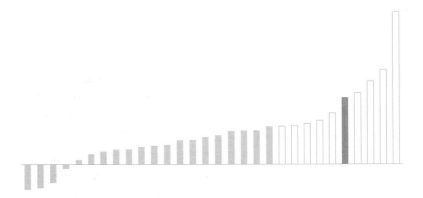

Figure 14.26 Cherry-picking data to make a point.

Mistaking Variation for Evolution

The difference in values between two dates is just a variation; it's not possible to draw any conclusions about the evolution in the data because there aren't enough data points.

When we choose two points only, we have more freedom to select the variables that we want to represent, as we're not conditioned by their long-term evolution. This is probably one of the reasons why variation charts are common in annual reports.

The chart in **Figure 14.27**, inspired by a bank's annual report, uses only two time periods in addition to the capital sin of transforming a real variation of –15.1% into a graphical variation of –49% by eliminating the origin without warning.

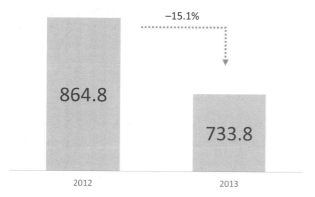

Figure 14.27 Mistaking variation for evolution *and* playing with the vertical axis.

Double Axes

The use of dual-axis charts is a subtle form of graphical lie through which, as we have seen, a spurious relationship is established between variables. Considering that the author of a dual-axis chart tries to harmonize the representation, it's natural to break some rules: The vertical scale is one of the first victims.

In the rare cases where two axes are acceptable, as in the Pareto chart, it's essential that the audience make an immediate visual association between the series and the corresponding axis and not through a mere reference in the legend.

Pseudo 3D

The pie chart in **Figure 14.28** shows how, in addition to all other problems, the pseudo-3D effect distorts chart reading. The labeled segments both have the same value, but the one "closer" to the observer is perceived to be larger (and it *is* graphically larger). In a bar chart, as we saw earlier in this chapter, the second kind of chart most affected by this malformation, the parallax effect renders bar comparison impossible and, in some cases, hides a substantial number of bars that are "behind" the higher bars.

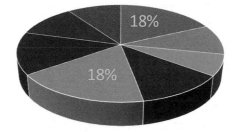

Figure 14.28 3D changes the way we perceive nearer points.

Context

Most graphic lies are stupid or ignorant, and can be easily spotted by a trained eye. On rare occasions, ideological debate becomes interesting, and if it includes aspects of data visualization, all the better. Let me give you an example.

Figure 14.29 shows the steep decline of the infant mortality rate in Spain and in Portugal. In the 1970s, both countries underwent regime changes, from dictatorships to democracies. Now, let me ask you this: Judging from the chart, do you think these regime changes had a disruptive impact in infant mortality? I presume you'll say "yes" for Spain and "no" for Portugal. If you were a Portuguese conservative, you would like this idea that the left-wing revolution didn't do much to improve infant mortality, while in Spain conservatives would say democracy actually harmed infant mortality.

Download the
original chart

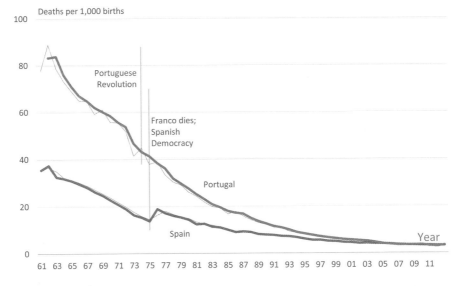

Figure 14.29 Absolute comparison can hide significant developments.

We must understand that these countries were not exactly North Koreas of the time. Hard trends in Europe also occurred in the Iberian Peninsula, even if more tenuously. The 1960s and the 1970s were years of strong decline in infant mortality rates, especially where they remained high.

So it makes sense to check whether the infant mortality rate in a country was declining at a speed above or below the regional average (say, the future eurozone EZ-17). As you can see in **Figure 14.30**, Spain always remained a little below the average, except for a period of about eight years before dictator Franco's death, when mortality decreased a lot (between 1965 and 1973), and returning to the EU average after that. So apparently democracy was bad for the infant mortality rate in Spain. One day I'll need to understand the reasons for this.

Download the
original chart

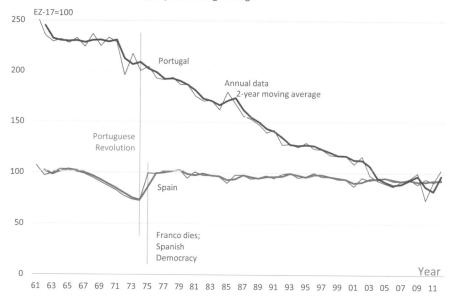

Source: Eurostat

Figure 14.30 Comparing to a reference can bring more interesting insights.

In Portugal, the dictatorship kept the infant mortality rate at much more than double that of the EU during the 1960s. And suddenly, three years before the revolution in 1974, they changed public healthcare and infant mortality started a long and consistent downward trend.

You can have both the absolute and the relative interpretations. Politicians often choose one of the two, depending on which one better fits their agenda. Just like many variables follow the regional distribution of population, a majority of phenomena are influenced by hard trends, and you should identify them and factor them in.

When Everything Goes

Data visualization also has to endure its share of outright lies (and liars). From a biased "infographic" that reflects only the author's agenda to a bar that goes up instead of down (you need only search Internet images for "Fox News charts" to find them), you should be prepared for everything.

At the top of **Figure 14.31** you can find a helpful template for preposterous lies. It basically contains two arrows free from any constraints of scale. Then you add a fake time series to make it look like a real chart. One of the arrows demonstrates that your adversary is not doing what it should be doing. The second arrow shows that the bad things it was already doing are now skyrocketing. At the bottom of Figure 14.31 is a real-world example of applying this template.

Interestingly, when caught with such lies, the typical author's response is, "Well, you could read the numbers; they were there," which is basically the same argument used to defend pie charts. This is outright poor business practice.

TEMPLATE FOR PREPOSTEROUS LIES

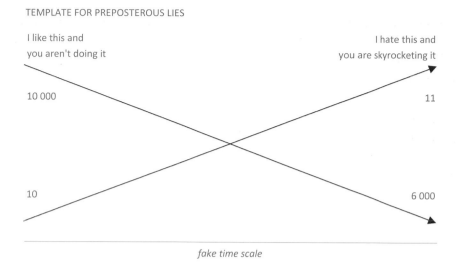

I like this and
you aren't doing it

I hate this and
you are skyrocketing it

10 000

11

10

6 000

fake time scale

Go to the
web page

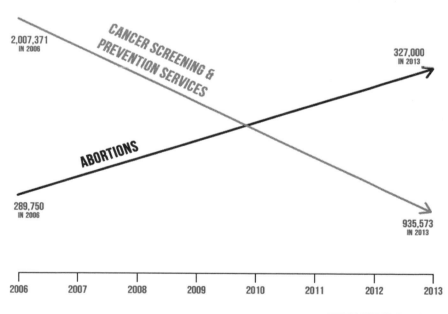

PLANNED PARENTHOOD FEDERATION OF AMERICA:
ABORTIONS UP — LIFE-SAVING PROCEDURES DOWN

CANCER SCREENING &
PREVENTION SERVICES

2,007,371
IN 2006

327,000
IN 2013

ABORTIONS

289,750
IN 2006

935,573
IN 2013

2006 2007 2008 2009 2010 2011 2012 2013

SOURCE: AMERICANS UNITED FOR LIFE

Figure 14.31 Two arrows that pretend to be a chart and an actual application of the template by Americans United for Life. The chart was taken from their website.

Takeaways

- Design is always present in data visualization, but its nature changes from functional to decorative.

- While it remains at a functional level, design depends more on data management skills than on graphic design skills.

- Apply Occam's razor to remove all that is irrelevant in a chart, minimize the accessories, adjust what is needed, and add what is missing.

- Provide an emotional hook if you think your audience needs one. A title that frames the question, a background image with a real or symbolic link to the reality the chart is portraying, and the promise of an answer can keep the audience interested. Then, since you already provided the emotional framework, your following charts can be more functional and complex.

- Pseudo-3D effects, textures, and dual-axis charts have no place in business visualization.

- Annotate your charts in meaningful ways.

- Finish the sentence, "As you see in the chart..." and use your response to write chart titles.

- Use the titles to write one or more sentences. This will make it easier to find the right sequence for presenting your charts.

- There are many ways to lie with charts. Do your best to avoid them, while retaining your editorial discretion.

33.2   30.1   26.8

18.5   18.9   19.3   19   19.6

15

COLOR: BEYOND AESTHETICS

Avoid catastrophe. According to Edward Tufte, this is "the first principle" when using color in data visualization.[1] Given the complexity contained in this warning, avoiding catastrophe is not an easy task to achieve.

Color is a complicated physiological phenomenon associated with symbolic, aesthetic, and emotional qualities. Each of these qualities is enough by itself to wreak havoc in data visualizations if not treated with care. Together, they make disaster almost inevitable and justify Tufte's principle.

---

1   Tufte, Edward. *Envisioning Information*. Cheshire, CT: Graphics Press, 1990.

In an organizational environment, the talent of applying subtle color harmonies isn't one of the most valued skills, as proven by the frequent use of primary colors splashed onto spreadsheets. Other factors that affect color in business visualization include corporate branding guidelines and the differences between what you see on a computer monitor and what you see on a projector screen.

It's natural to assume that a color disaster will take the shape of an aesthetic aberration. But in fact (and this will be a relief to some readers and heresy to others), **the aesthetic quality of color has little relevance in business visualization**. Let this sink in for a moment. It is the key that opens the door to a functional approach to color, in which certain aspects are handled in a rational way to achieve the goals of the graphical representation:

- The first and most important functional quality of color is its **suitability to the task**. For example, color selection differs depending on whether you want to encode either a categorical variable or a variable with a continuous range of values.

- The second functional quality of color is **stimuli intensity**. Pure primary colors and pastel colors have different intensity levels, which allow us to establish various levels of chart reading and evaluate the stimulus intensity of each object on the chart.

- The final functional quality of color is, in a broad sense, its **symbolism**. As we saw in the vegetable availability chart in Figure 3.3, for example, switching expected colors creates a cognitive dissonance that is difficult to overcome.

These are the functional qualities of color that we should focus on. If we succeed, the result will be an effective chart. We are also likely to avoid an aesthetic disaster, even if the result may not be worthy of an art gallery.

The aesthetic quality of color is more subjective and difficult to functionalize, but we can even improve color aesthetics if we follow the classical rules of color harmony. As you'll see later in this chapter, these rules correspond to positions on the color wheel, facilitating their selection while also allowing the expression of personal sensibilities.

But before all this, let's analyze the physical components of color and the ways in which we try to quantify it.

Quantifying Color

Like sound, color does not have an absolute value. Both result from the way our senses *respond* to certain wavelengths, and the way our senses respond to color depends on surrounding colors, lighting, and the physical composition of our photoreceptor cells in the retina, among other factors. We can confirm the relative and subjective value of color in **Figure 15.1**, which represents one of the most basic optical illusions dealing with color. Compare the blue tone in each square. The blue square on the right appears darker, but believe it or not, the blue tone is exactly the same in both squares.

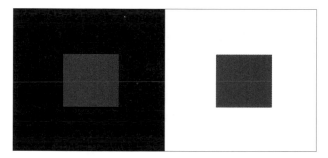

Figure 15.1 Which one is darker? Are you sure?

The way people *verbalize* color is also different. This is evident when comparing men's and women's color preferences. Women often appear to be more sensitive to small color variations, while men are easily satisfied by broader color categories.

We categorize color when we say that the rainbow has seven colors (red, orange, yellow, green, blue, indigo, and violet), but where are the cut-off points, and how can we guarantee that the color spectrum is covered in a reasonably comprehensive way and that there are no overlapping categories? In fact, one can't do it without a more objective classification. Hence, a quantitative approach is necessary so that, for example, a computer can tell a mobile phone what "Prussian blue" is and how to represent it.

The RGB Model

We saw in Chapter 2 that photoreceptor cells are sensitive to wavelengths corresponding to colors near red (R), green (G), and blue (B), from which the remaining colors are obtained. Your computer uses a similar color-coding model, where each color (channel) has a value between 0 and 255. The total number of colors is the result of multiplying the three channels: 256 x 256 x 256 = 16.8 million combinations, approximately.

The image in **Figure 15.2** shows the Colors dialog box in Excel where you can choose a custom color, with the RGB model selected. Note the values for Red, Green, and Blue below. In this model, the RGB code (0,0,0) is the minimum value of each channel and consequently the absence of color, so it's the code for *black*. On the other extreme, the RGB code (255,255,255) corresponds to the maximum value of the three channels, and it's the code for *white*. When the three colors have the same value, we obtain a shade of *gray*. Several of the most common colors are combinations of the values 0, 128, and 255. *Red* has the RGB code (255,0,0), *green* has the RGB code (0,255,0), and *blue* has the RGB code (0,0,255). The "classic" green is much darker than the one in the electromagnetic spectrum and is closer to the RGB code (0,128,0).

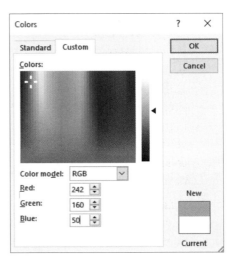

Figure 15.2 Choosing colors using the RGB model in Excel.

The HSL Model

Taking into account the examples above, we might be led to believe that the RGB model is intuitive and we can easily realize which color corresponds to a certain code or which code we need to obtain a particular color. But with the exception of the maximum, minimum, and the middle values, it isn't easy to determine which color corresponds to a certain code combination or how to vary a color tone.

The HSL model is more intuitive. Unlike RGB, it doesn't refer to color combinations. Instead, it uses three dimensions of color: hue (H), saturation (S), and luminance (L):

■ **Hue** corresponds to the colors we observe in the electromagnetic spectrum, ranging from zero (red) to 255 (violet), and runs along the horizontal axis in the Custom tab of the Colors dialog box in Excel (**Figure 15.3**).

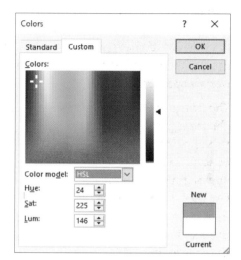

■ **Saturation** is the second dimension, the measurement of color purity. The more saturated, the purer the color. When we reduce saturation, every hue eventually fades into a uniform shade of gray. Saturation runs along the vertical axis of the Custom tab of the Colors dialog box. As you can see, no matter which hue you select, you always get gray when you minimize saturation.

Figure 15.3 Choosing colors using the HSL model in Excel.

■ **Luminance** is the intensity of light. Regardless of whether hue is highly saturated, color varies according to the intensity of incident light. The more intense the light is, the lighter the hue becomes; the less intense the light, the darker the hue. If you minimize the luminance, there is no light, and no matter what hue and saturation values you choose, you'll always get black. Pure color corresponds to the intermediate point in the range (128 in Excel, 50% in other systems). A light gray tone, for example, has low saturation and high luminance and does not depend on the chosen hue. In Excel, you change luminance using the vertical strip to the right of the Custom tab of the Colors dialog box.

To understand the difference between color and hue, think about brown: Most people will agree that brown is a color, but a brown hue doesn't actually exist; the color is the result of combining orange hues with saturation and luminance.

A simple exercise shows how much more intuitive the HSL model is. In Excel's Colors dialog box, select the Custom tab and, with the RGB color model selected, enter the values 162, 90, 18, a brown tone. Move the slider for luminance as if you were creating a color ramp for a chart. You'll notice that the values change in all RGB channels. Now re-enter the same codes, choose the HSL model and change the luminance strip again. Notice that only the luminance value is modified. Combining values for three switches is harder than changing a single one. That's why applying a continuous variation in luminance, a characteristic of most color ramps, is simpler in HSL than in RGB.

The table in **Figure 15.4** displays some colors and allows us to compare values for the RGB and HSL models. The first seven hues are pure: saturation remains at 255 and luminance at 128. Note that brown and orange have the same hue (21), but brown has lower saturation and lower luminance. (Other definitions of brown will have slightly different codes.)

SAMPLE COLORS AND THEIR VALUES IN THE RGB AND HSL MODELS

Color		RGB			HSL		
		Red	Green	Blue	Hue	Saturation	Luminance
Red		255	0	0	0	255	128
Orange		255	127	0	21	255	128
Chartreuse		127	255	0	64	255	128
Lime		0	255	0	85	255	128
Cyan		0	255	255	127	255	128
Blue		0	0	255	170	255	128
Magenta		255	0	255	213	255	128
Brown		162	90	18	21	205	90
White		255	255	255	170	0	255
Black		0	0	0	170	0	0
Gray		128	128	128	170	0	128

Figure 15.4 Comparing RGB and HSL values for selected colors.

Stimuli Intensity

Etiquette tells us that WE SHOULD NOT WRITE WITH ALL CAPITAL LETTERS, because that's equivalent to shouting, which is not very polite. If we want to emphasize something, we should use **bold** or *italics* instead. This modulation of the writing tone is useful for distinguishing between various parts of speech.

In data visualization, color is one of the instruments that we have to play this role. Pure colors produce intense, vibrant, and often aggressive stimuli, and are the chromatic equivalent of shouting, while pastel shades are soft and ease conflict, even if your choice of hues is not harmonious.

The impact of the intensity of chromatic stimuli differs, depending on the size of the color patch. The colors of the squares on the left in **Figure 15.5** generate stimuli that are too intense and aggressive. Their use in a bar chart would be classified as a catastrophe. While maintaining the same intensity, the impact of the thinner lines is lower due to the reduced area they occupy. The thicker lines increase the conflict again.

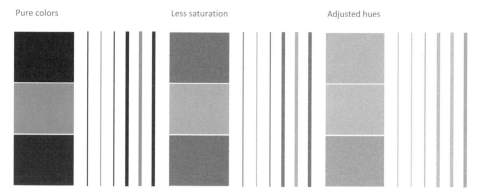

Figure 15.5 The impact of stimuli intensity depends on the size of the color patch.

The second group uses the same hues of the first one, with added luminance and less saturation. Although the results are still not an example of harmony, and while these transformations have generated an intensity imbalance, this version is less troublesome than the first one.

To those less sensitive to color harmony, there is a useful corollary to this adjustment: **A reduction in stimuli intensity increases the tolerance for errors in the selection of a color palette.** This means that, even if the basic hues are not harmonious, managing luminance and saturation reduces the intensity of the stimulus and the result becomes less unpleasant.

I made slight changes to the hues in the third group, adjusting them to fit one of the rules of color harmony that we'll mention later in this chapter. With the HSL model selected, I adjusted saturation and luminance to balance the intensity between the three colors. The result is clearly better than in the other two groups. The categories remain very distinct, are not overstimulating, and offer a more pleasant combination.

We increase or reduce the intensity of the stimuli depending not only on the type of chart but also on the technology involved, because there are substantial differences in how various tools process colors. Your chart will have some color differences among monitors, when printed, or when projected on a screen. There are some ways to minimize these differences, such as increasing saturation and hue separation when planning to use an LCD projector, but it is advisable to always check the result in advance.

The Functional Tasks of Color

The colors of both sets of squares in **Figure 15.6** are ordered (first by luminance and then by hue). While this statement is evident for the set on the left, it's less obvious for the set on the right. Although the hues are distributed along the electromagnetic spectrum, we cannot associate them to continuous values. Instead, we associate only categories: Blue is simply different from red, and both blue and red are different from yellow, which is neither higher nor lower than green. Hence, the statement that both sets of squares are ordered is open to doubt. Except when they are very close, hues represent unordered categories.

Ordered by luminance   Ordered by hue

Figure 15.6 Unlike changes in luminance and saturation, ordering hues by wavelength doesn't translate into a perception of order.

Unlike hues, other color dimensions are related to the perception of intensity levels ordered along a quantitative scale, as shown in the first set of squares.

This distinction between different hues and variations in intensity fits the classification of qualitative and quantitative variables, in which the quantitative variables are continuous by nature, while qualitative variables can be categorical (having no implied order) or ordinal (having some sort of order).

In short, the encoding of categorical variables is associated with the selection of hues, while encoding continuous variables is associated with luminance and, to a lower extent, saturation (it's better to consider saturation a dimension that helps with fine-tuning hues).

Another factor must be considered here, which is *how we interpret the data* and how our interpretation is reflected in the message that we try to communicate through a graphical representation. From the intersection between "how to encode" and "how to interpret" result six major functional tasks of color in data visualization:

- Categorize
- Group
- Emphasize
- Sequence
- Diverge
- Alert

Let's detail each one of these.

Categorize

The first (and most common) functional task of color in data visualization is to categorize the data. Each series or category acquires its own identity, which is expressed in the chart legend. When other criteria are not taken into account, series identification takes place primarily by selecting hues. Hues should be perceptually distinct and the perceptual weight of each series must not differ significantly, unless we have justification for it. In **Figure 15.7**, the criterion for choosing hues far apart for the two series is the qualitative difference (gender), without any ordering.

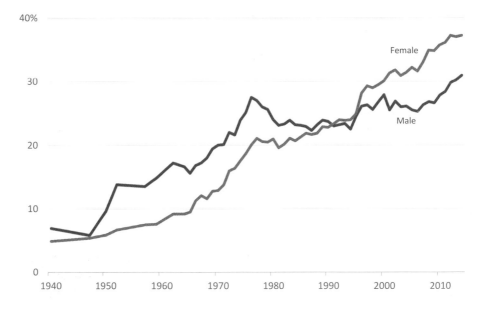

AFTER MORE THAN 30 YEARS, ARE MEN PLAYING CATCH-UP IN EDUCATION?
People aged 25 years and over who have completed college

Source: U.S. Census Bureau

Figure 15.7 Using opposite hues to encode gender.

None of the functional tasks of color should be left to software application default settings. However, because of the sequence of default colors, categorizing will probably suffer less than other tasks by letting the application color-code the series, provided the default color palette is well chosen. Still, this will only be valid for a small number of series. The higher the number, the more author intervention in color management will be needed.

The legend in **Figure 15.8** was generated by Excel. There seems to be a purpose of encoding countries based on cool and warm colors. If it made sense to color-code 32 series in a chart, this encoding would be quite useful. However, a closer inspection shows no obvious criteria, beyond the rotation of colors available in the palette.

Figure 15.8 An apparently interesting color coding is in fact meaningless.

Anyone without significant vision impairments can differentiate at least a few hundred thousand colors under optimum viewing conditions. It is difficult, however, to perform a color-matching task when you have 32 series in a chart. It's therefore natural to ask ourselves what is the practical limit on the number of colors. *A palette of never more than 12* (including white, black, and gray) is a defensible answer, but the best one is to *use as few as possible,* because having to make an effort to discriminate colors is contrary to the spirit of visualization.

Depending on your perspective, other values may pop up.

The colors of the rainbow are universal and easily discriminated, so seven is a good number to start with. This is the number suggested by Stephen Few, or more precisely, a palette with 7 + 1 colors where gray is the additional color code.[2]

In many circumstances, even using seven colors is excessive. A large data variation can hide patterns or hinder comparisons. When we use legends, it's necessary to take into account the reduced capacity of short-term memory, which also contributes to reducing the real maximum limit. But there is a trick to maximize the number of colors we can use, and that is by grouping them.

2   Few, Stephen. "Practical Rules for Using Color in Charts." Perceptual Edge. Visual Business Intelligence Newsletter. February 2008.

Group

A chart results from the interaction of many factors. That's why looking at categorization and assuming that all categories are distinct and independent is insufficient. For several reasons (for example, data variation and the limits of the working memory), we can argue (as we did in the preceding chapter) that the maximum number of series should be set between three and six, where six series should sound a warning to the strong probability that we are making an ineffective chart.

However, the greater the number of categories, the greater the possibility and usefulness of grouping them. Take household expenditure items such as food, beverages, communications, and transportation. Instead of four distinct hues, we could create one group of food and beverages and a second group of communications and transportation. We don't have to actually sum them; we can visually group them using two hues and then vary the other dimensions of color. The pie charts in **Figure 15.9** are an example, which we saw earlier in Figure 2.22 in the discussion of the Gestalt laws.

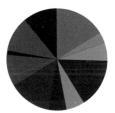

Figure 15.9 Grouping categories by hue.

It's easy to select four different base hues and four equally different variations for each base hue, so that without much effort we can use 16 color codes on a chart, far surpassing the limit of 12 hues that seemed to exist and that has already guaranteed some chart reading difficulty.

This shows how important it is not to take these rules as absolute and literal references, but only as indicators that need to be adapted to specific circumstances. It also proves that rules can be bent when we actually think about the data.

Let's return to the issue of identifying 32 countries. In **Figure 15.10**, identifying each country by color would be catastrophic. Having to increase the chart's size to accommodate the legend would be unwieldy, but also expecting the reader to perform color matching for all 32 countries seems overly optimistic. The chosen option facilitates the identification of countries by group and suggests a geographical/political reading based on the use of only two color codes (for Western Europe and Eastern Europe, and gray for the EU-28).

Although identification is a functional task of color, this example shows that individual identification is not always necessary at the actual level of the entities, which can free color to offer another level of reading. We've been reusing this idea since the beginning of this book.

IN MOST COUNTRIES, WOMEN ENJOY A LONGER AND HEALTHIER LIFE THAN MEN
Large gap in life expectancy at birth in Eastern Europe

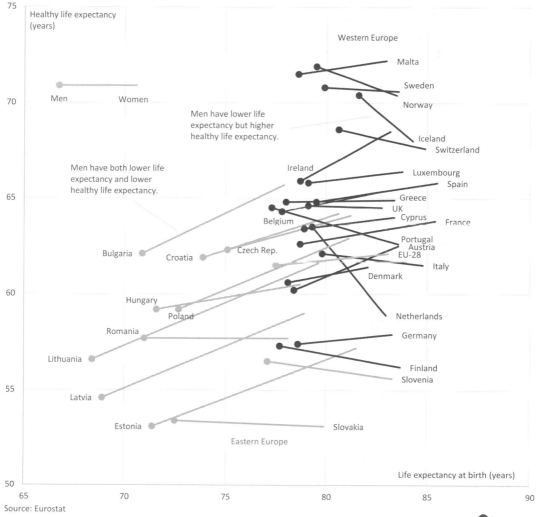

Figure 15.10 Using color as a grouping strategy.

Download the
original chart

Emphasize

As a general principle, we should avoid any unwanted perceptual imbalance, in which some entities receive more attention only because of the characteristics of their chosen color.

The operative word in the previous paragraph is "unwanted." When we make a chart, it's natural that our knowledge and editorial decisions lead us to suggest an interpretation of the data, or of formatting the chart for ease of reading based on the audience profile.

When emphasizing an element in the chart, we give it more perceptual weight than others, through a degree of contrast and salience. We might provide more saturation over less saturation, less luminance over more luminance, or an opposite hue to a set of similar hues.

In addition to directing focus through manipulating object colors, we can also do so by adding context variables, such as adding background shading during periods of recession in a time series.

We applied the functional task of color in many of the charts in this book. In **Figure 15.11,** we use it to emphasize a subset of countries—namely, those where the gap for healthy life expectancy between men and women is more than three years.

We're dealing with an editorial decision that could be different, depending on the context and the message. More than any other functional task, emphasis is based on an evaluation of data relevance and on how it could be read. This kind of prerogative must therefore be exercised with full awareness of its implications.

The chart from Figure 14.5 in the previous chapter, displaying the evolution of live births, reaches an extreme level of emphasis by using a single red line that evolves on a gray background.

Sequence

Unlike previous tasks, a sequence through a color ramp assumes the orderly display of points or series.

Although used more often to represent intensities in thematic maps (such as population densities or changes in terrain features), color ramps are useful for facilitating the perception of the order or continuity, when it exists.

COUNTRIES WHERE THE GAP IN HEALTHY LIFE EXPECTANCY
BETWEEN MEN AND WOMEN IS MORE THAN THREE YEARS
Healthy life expectancy by sex and country, in 2012

Download the
original chart

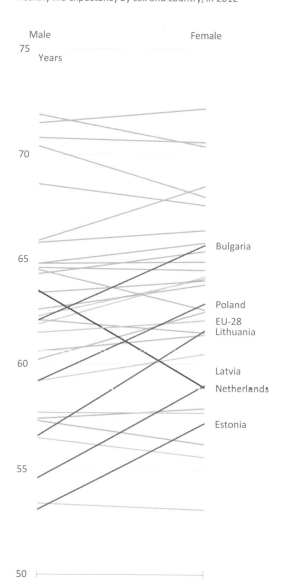

Source: Eurostat

Figure 15.11 Using color to emphasize healthy life
expectancy gaps.

The chart in **Figure 15.12** displays the percentage of expenses on food by income levels in each quintile, in Spain (Q1 corresponds to the bottom 20 percent of families by income, while Q5 represents the top 20 percent of families).

LESS IN FOOD, MORE IN HOUSING: CHANGES IN EXPENDITURE IN SPAIN

Proportion of household expenditure per category and income quintile

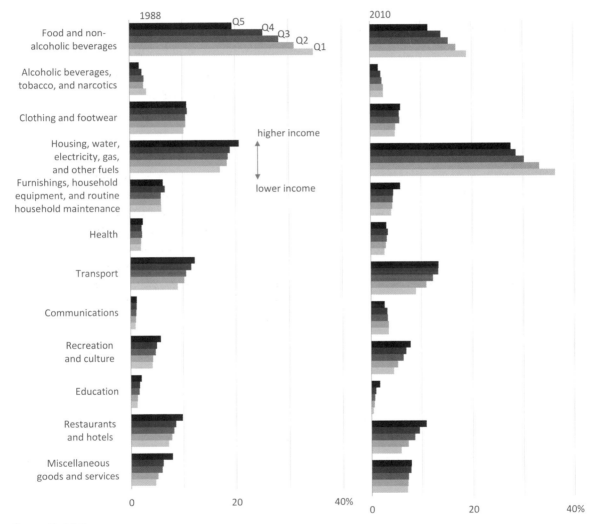

Source: Eurostat

Figure 15.12 Changes in household expenditure in Spain.

Download the
original chart

The bars in **Figure 15.13** are a fragment of the chart in Figure 15.12 where I used multiple hues instead of a single hue with multiple luminance levels. Apart from an excessive use of color, the left chart induces a discrete reasoning of comparing category to category. The chart on the right, on the other hand, induces some continuity and a reasoning of association and correlation. It's easier to see here an example of Engel's law (*with increasing income, the food share in total expenses decreases*) than in the version on the left.

LESS IN FOOD, MORE IN HOUSING: CHANGES IN EXPENDITURE IN SPAIN

Proportion of household expenditure per category and income quintile

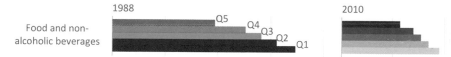

Figure 15.13 Hues favor discrete reasoning.

The HSL model facilitates the creation of color ramps. Just choose the hue, set the minimum and maximum luminance, and divide this range in equal parts, as in the example of **Figure 15.14**, where a new level of luminance was applied at intervals of 32. From a cursory glance, this seems like a very useful color ramp. But if you look more closely, you'll notice some unpleasant inconsistencies—for example, the distance between the 96 and the 128 seems greater than between other pairs. This occurs both in color and in shades of gray, where variations in lighter shades seem greater than variations in darker shades.

Figure 15.14 A color ramp with equal intervals.

In some more sophisticated color models, this lack of linearity in color perception is adjusted, but it does not happen in any of the models available in Excel, HSL, and RGB.

There is no simple way to create a color ramp whose distances are perceptually similar. If the ramps available in your Excel color theme are not suitable, try to create a new one by varying the luminance as done above. Starting from regular intervals, increase the distance in low luminance and reduce it in high luminance until the steps look right. At the end of the chapter, you will find references to sources of color palettes that include the ability to create these color codes so you don't actually have to do it yourself.

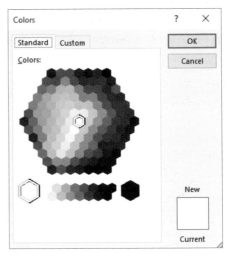

The ramp in Figure 15.14 was created with the default Excel Colors dialog box (**Figure 15.15**), starting from the exterior colors and moving toward the center.

Figure 15.15 Excel dialog box for choosing standard colors.

Diverge

The diverging scales represent the intensity of a deviation from a central point or reference point. It's important to underline the word "intensity," because it gives us the key to the design of divergent scales, which must use two contrasting hues, not a multitude of hues (rainbow scale).

When it comes to diverging scales (**Figure 15.16**), just choose (in the Excel Colors dialog box) the center line that clearly distinguishes two diverging scales. It's likely that you'll have to manually adjust the luminance or saturation of some colors.

Figure 15.16 Two versions of a diverging scale: continuous and categorical.

Unlike their use in cartography, diverging scales are rarely used when making traditional charts. They could be used more often to represent the results of scales in questionnaires, such as the Likert scale.[3]

---

3   Robbins, Naomi B. and Richard M. Heiberger. "Design of Diverging Stacked Bar Charts for Likert Scales and Other Applications." *Journal of Statistical Software.* Volume 57, Issue 5. 2014.

To create a diverging color scale in **Figure 15.17**, items below the middle category are displayed to the left of the axis and items above the middle category are displayed to the right. The middle category was split, half to the left and half to the right. As suggested in the Robbins *et al.* article, this category is not visually split by the axis line.

FREQUENCY OF BEING HAPPY IN THE LAST 4 WEEKS

Population over 16 years old in 2013

Download the
original chart

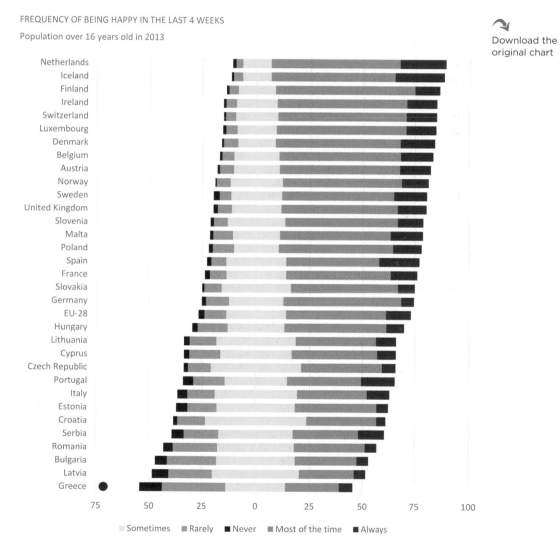

Source: Eurostat

Figure 15.17 Diverging color palette applied to a Likert scale.

A much more common use of color scales is in graphical tables, where you can apply conditional formatting. In **Figure 15.18**, I defined 10 color codes using the diverging scale presented in Figure 15.15. This is granular enough, and you have better control over the color scale than using a true color ramp.

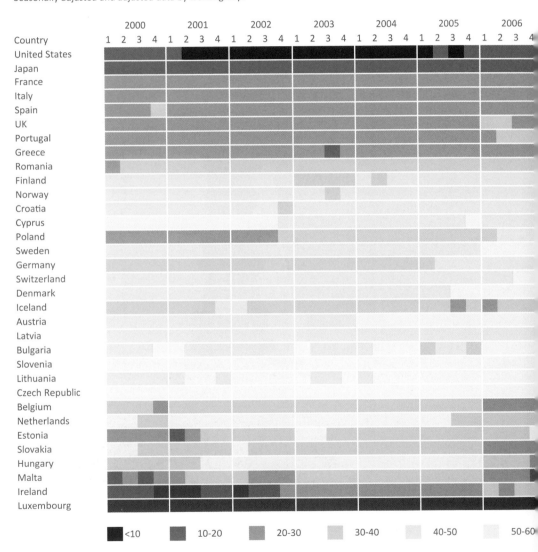

Download the original chart

EXPORTS OF GOODS AND SERVICES PERCENTAGE OF GDP
Seasonally adjusted and adjusted data by working days

Source: Eurostat

Figure 15.18 Using a diverging color ramp to make a graphical table in Excel.

Year - Quarter

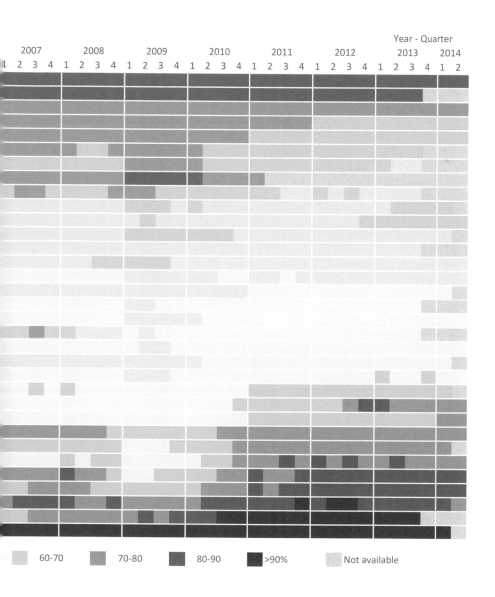

Alert

In Figure 15.17, you'll notice a small red circle in front of Greece. This is to alert you that Greece is the only truly unhappy country, because negative responses outnumber positive responses.

We already saw other examples of alerts in previous chapters. Depending on how you size and format an alert, you will want to use a high-intensity chromatic stimulus, along with a conventional meaning (such as the use of red to signal danger), to make sure the alert is not overlooked.

Color Symbolism

We know the color of our organization, of the sports team we cheer for, and of the flag of the country where we were born. We know that the sky is blue, the land is brown, and the snow is white. We know that love is red, hope is green, and envy is yellow. The boy is blue and the girl is pink. In Christianity, the color purple is associated with the Passion of Christ. In Hinduism, saffron is the color of fire and is the most sacred color.

The audience expects us to honor the symbolic use of color, from the colors shared with the whole community down to the colors specific to a group.[4] Using conventional color symbolism simplifies communication, recognizes group values, and does not generate unpleasant and somehow annoying situations, such as using pink for boys and blue for girls.

Unsuitable color choices are not always obvious. Do you remember the red line showing the evolution in the number of births (Figure 14.5)? As the color associated with danger, it's natural for red to be chosen when something goes wrong. But it's also part of the basic rules of political communication not to give bad news wearing a red tie. For internal presentations within organizations, colors tend to be chosen in order to minimize the impact of negative product sales and to maximize the impact of their growth.

---

4 Tip: If you want to use the colors of your organization, request their RGB codes instead of trying to guess them.

Color symbolism should be seen not only as a cultural construct but also as a representation of the physical world, although the relationship to the physical world can be more flexible, depending on the situation. But we should avoid certain associations: Meat is not green, water is not red, human skin is not purple (most of the time).

The Role of Gray

An excessive use of adjectives is considered a bad sign in literature, and it's easy to see why: The author has not been able to engage the reader through subtler writing and, to compensate, smacks you with prepackaged emotions. In data visualization, color resembles the adjectives in literature, and like adjectives, color should be used sparingly.

Believe it or not, a colorless chart is a great starting point. Yes, the notion of a monochrome chart will be strange to those born in the world of PowerPoint and color printers, and may induce painful memories for those who suffered through presentations with transparencies and other artifacts of the computer Stone Age. But removing color is a common experiment in the creative process of a graphic designer. Testing monochrome versions allows the designer to focus on other qualities, such as the shapes, sizes, and position of objects. It is commonly said that if a monochrome version works, a color version will also work.

As we've seen, a chart supports a very limited number of colors. Using shades of gray helps us identify this limit. If you can no longer differentiate between shades of gray, it's likely that you have reached the limit and you'll have to use an alternate form of representation.

We can always count on pie charts as a source of bad examples. In this case, a pie chart can illustrate the unnecessary use of color. **Figure 15.19** shows only a few results of an image search for "pie charts" and demonstrates how difficult it is to imagine a pie chart without several rainbow colors.

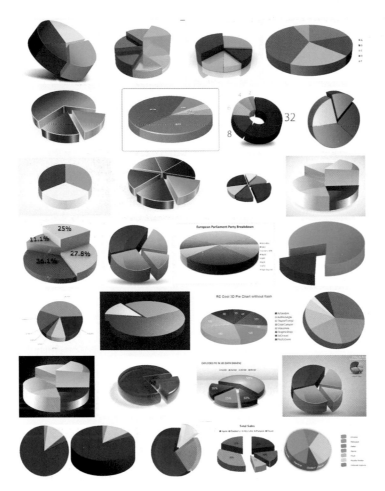

Figure 15.19 Colorful pies in search results. *Google and the Google logo are registered trademarks of Google Inc. Used with permission.*

However, the grayscale example in **Figure 15.20** shows that color is unnecessary for identifying segments or for emphasizing a particular segment. The grayscale pie chart exhibits an understated but effective elegance (if one can say that about pie charts), which makes it even more obvious that there are too many colors in the version on the left.

An emotional reaction to color is inevitable, which influences the assessment of other aspects of the chart. The way we look at the grayscale pie chart on the right is more neutral and rational. Also, printing grayscale images is much less costly than color printing and ensures that variations are noticeable even by those with color blindness.

MAIN REASONS FOR PART-TIME EMPLOYMENT BY SEX

From 15 to 64 years old, in the European Union (EU-28), in 2014

Download the
original chart

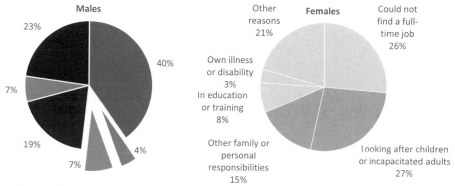

- ■ Could not find a full-time job
- ■ Looking after children or incapacitated adults
- ■ Other family or personal responsibilities
- ■ In education or training
- ■ Own illness or disability
- ■ Other reasons

Source: Eurostat

Figure 15.20 Because slices don't overlap and can't be misidentified somehow, color-coding them is purely discretionary.

Of course, the world is not black and white, and I don't intend to persuade you to use only shades of gray in all your charts, but experimenting with grays will help you create a focused foundation for using color stimuli that better fit the message you want to convey.

The latest versions of Excel include a palette of gray tones, so you will be able to experiment with formatting your charts this way.

Color Staging

While it would be excessive to say that a good chart is a colorless chart, we might more reasonably say that *a good chart is a staged-color chart.*

Contrary to what an Internet image search may lead us to believe, a chart is not a pocket rainbow. And it's useless to compare rainbow-colored charts to the idealized effectiveness and rationality of grayscale charts. The answer lies in the middle: Reasonable color management in a chart depends on the functional balance of color, its intensity, and its absence.

There are two groups of objects in a chart: objects that encode the data (bars, lines, dots, areas) and objects that support and identify them (axes, grid lines, text, legend, background). Think of the former as the actors and the latter as the stage.

In addition to its strict role of helping to identify data encoded objects, the stage has an emotional quality that you can explore (the empty playground in Figure 14.5, for example). However, we should not make use of this emotional dimension without clear justification, and we must use it within reason. With or without justification, the stage must always be forced to retreat into the background through variations in shades of gray, thereby giving prevalence to the representation of data (the actors).

Applying priorities as defined in Chapter 6, but keeping this theatrical analogy, it's also up to us, as directors of this play, to establish a subtler distinction among the actors—between leading, supporting, and extra roles. The extra roles are important as context but are not essential to the play. The extras often don't have names and can be encoded with gray. Two good extras candidates are the categories "Other" and "Do not know/No answer" used in market surveys.

Other cases depend on the message we want to convey. For example, in the chart in **Figure 15.21**, mozzarella, cheddar, and other American cheeses are highlighted as the main actors. Remaining merely as context, all other cheeses are included to add context. In an interactive chart, we could define a fixed set of cheeses according to other criteria and highlight some others only when hovering the mouse over the line.

In another example (**Figure 15.22**), we wanted to emphasize that personal and family responsibilities are the key reasons that most distinguish men and women working at part-time jobs.

Except for the examples of bad chart choices, all charts in this book seek to apply functional color management, including the application of gray, creating reading levels that all charts should provide.

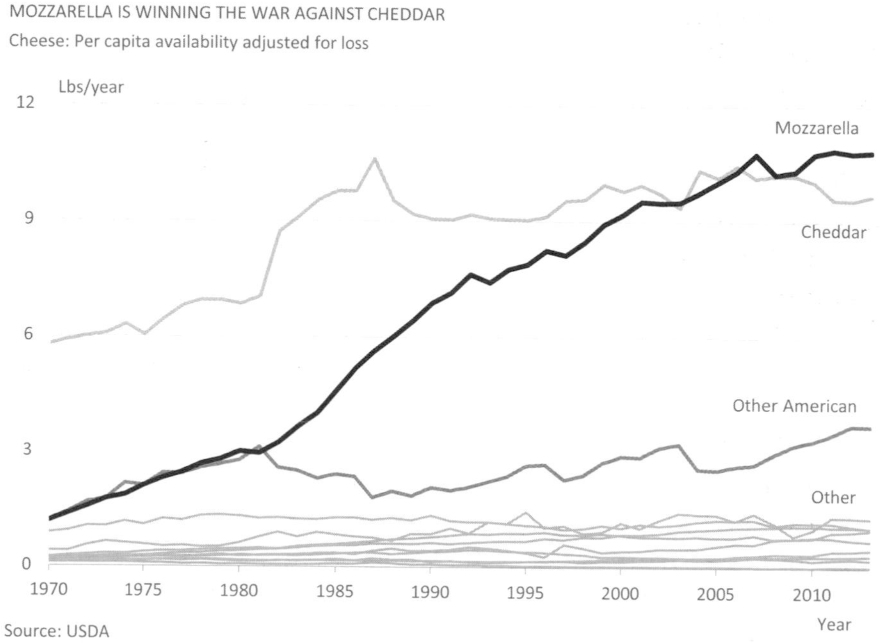

MOZZARELLA IS WINNING THE WAR AGAINST CHEDDAR
Cheese: Per capita availability adjusted for loss
Lbs/year
12
9
6
3
0
Mozzarella
Cheddar
Other American
Other
1970
1975
1980
1985
1990
1995
2000
2005
2010
Year
Source: USDA

Download the original chart

Figure 15.21 The leading actors (Mozzarella), the supporting actors (Cheddar and Other American cheeses), and the extras (the gray lines).

MAIN REASONS FOR PART-TIME EMPLOYMENT BY SEX
From 15 to 64 years old, in the European Union (EU-28), in 2014
Males
Females
45%
30
15
0
Looking after children or incapacitated adults, 27.1
Could not find a full-time job, 26.3
Other reasons, 20.6
Other family or personal responsibilities, 15.1
In education or training, 7.5
Own illness or disability, 3.4
Source: Eurostat

Download the original chart

Figure 15.22 Emphasizing family reasons for part-time employment.

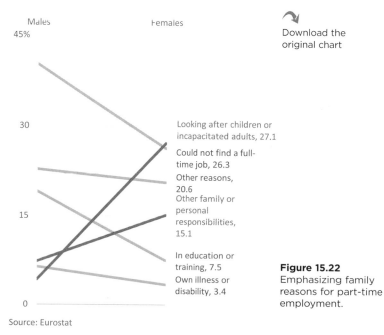

Color Harmony

From a functional point of view, colors *per se* don't really matter, and if you can avoid strong symbolic meanings, it doesn't matter if you pick them randomly. Data visualization deals with discriminating among visual stimuli, defining their relationships, and establishing the intensity of these stimuli. The colors you pick just need to meet these requirements. Realizing this helps us overcome our fears of aesthetic catastrophe.

If you use color according to the principles we've discussed so far, it's difficult to believe that any catastrophe will happen. But it is equally unlikely that your chart will be remembered for your rare talent for selecting and combining colors.

Is it possible to seek a comfortable balance somewhere between unappealing trash and something worthy of an art gallery? Can we make a chart more attractive even without the right artistic skills?

The answer is a clear "yes, but...." I do believe that color harmony is not tamable by rules and algorithms, nor is it possible to gift aesthetic sensibility to those who do not have it or do not cultivate it. But learning about the rules of color harmony can have a surprising effect on the way we think about the message we want to convey and how our visualization brings it to life.

General Principles

Color harmony depends a lot on culture and individual subjectivity, so take these rules as suggestions and allow for potential variations according to the specific real-world situation.

It's easier to choose colors if we find a good starting point, and there are several ways to do this:

- **Symbolism.** We've seen that if the audience associates colors with the data, we should at least ask ourselves whether there is any reason not to use those colors. For example, is it appropriate to differentiate data by gender in using blue and pink? Is it appropriate to use the colors of our organization?

- **Message tone.** Is the message we want to convey positive or negative? If the former, we could use blue or green, while for the latter you may want to use red, and so on.

- **Standard palette.** Before exploring the 16 million colors that your computer offers, try a palette other than the software's default color palette. Excel 2016 has 23 palettes and room for creating many more.

The Classical Rules

If it's true that color combinations are a result of the author's very personal choices, it's also true that some color choices create conflict, while others suggest similarities. If you map colors to a circle or a *wheel*, these chromatic relationships become apparent.

What's really interesting is that there is an almost perfect overlap between chromatic relationships and data relationships: If you want to emphasize a certain kind of relationship, there is a matching rule of color harmony for that. For example, if you want to oppose two series, you'll choose complementary colors, one from each side of the color wheel. You don't even have to think about specific colors or hues. At this point, only positions in the color wheel matter.

The color wheel is like a flat map that helps you familiarize yourself with the lay of the color space. But it's a flat map because it doesn't take into account the other two dimensions of color, luminance and saturation. To manage chromatic stimuli, these dimensions will have to be factored in. Also, the color wheel provides a structure, but you must adjust it to your needs.

The color wheels in **Figure 15.23** contain 12 hues and are formed by concentric rings, where the outer ring represents maximum saturation (255) and the standard luminance (128). The inner rings represent decreasing luminance levels in the first wheel and decreasing saturation levels in the second wheel.

COLOR WHEEL WITH LEVELS OF LUMINANCE

For a Saturation value of 255

Download the original chart

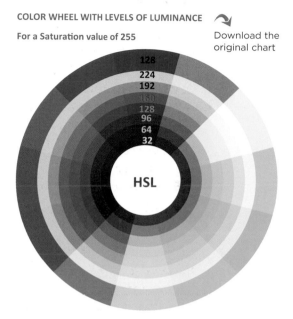

COLOR WHEEL WITH LEVELS OF SATURATION

For a Luminance value of 128

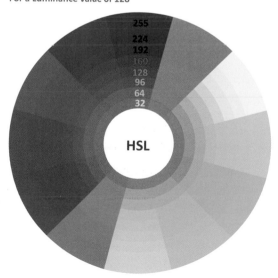

Figure 15.23 Color wheels with varying luminance and saturation.

A close look at the outer ring shows that the pure hue can result either in an un-necessary overstimulation or in an unjustified imbalance due to the difference in brightness. This must be compensated for, using the other dimensions of color.

The examples that follow illustrate the classical rules of color harmony. Each example shown includes a color wheel that defines the rule and three charts: one with the selected hues, a lighter one, and a darker one. The HSL code for each color is displayed below the legend.

Complementary Colors

Two complementary colors are located on opposite sides of the wheel (**Figure 15.24**). In the HSL model, the complementary hue h is h+128. The complementary hue to red (zero) is cyan (128).

Complementary colors send a message of opposition but also of balance. A chart with saturated complementary colors is an aggressively colored chart in which the colors fight (equally) for their share of attention. Apply this rule when you intend to represent very distinct variables or those that for some reason you want to show as contrasting each other. Do not use complementary colors when variables have some form of continuity or order.

Split Complementary Colors

A particularly useful scheme for data visualization is the use of split comple-mentary colors (**Figure 15.25**). In this case, direct color opposition is avoided. Instead, a less direct color opposition reduces the overall conflict while still creating distinct groups.

The example in Figure 15.25 is intended to establish an opposition between Germany, on one hand, and Spain and Greece, on the other.

UNEMPLOYMENT RATE BY SEX
United States, December of each year

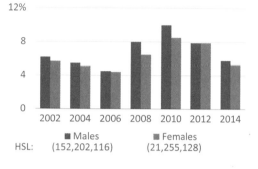

HSL: Males (152,202,116) Females (21,255,128)

UNEMPLOYMENT RATE BY COUNTRY
Germany vs. Greece and Spain

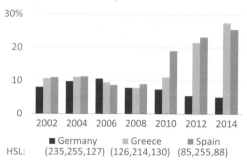

HSL: Germany (235,255,127) Greece (126,214,130) Spain (85,255,88)

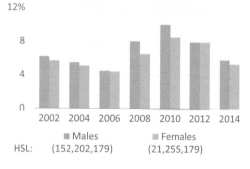

HSL: Males (152,202,179) Females (21,255,179)

HSL: Germany (235,190,192) Greece (126,214,195) Spain (85,164,165)

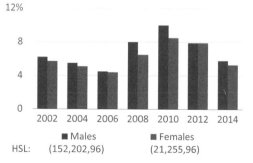

HSL: Males (152,202,96) Females (21,255,96)

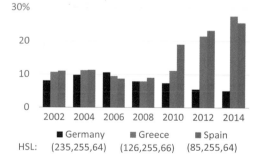

HSL: Germany (235,255,64) Greece (126,255,66) Spain (85,255,64)

Figure 15.24 Complementary colors create direct opposition.

Figure 15.25 Split complementary colors create opposition that is less direct.

Triadic Harmony

We create a triadic harmony by selecting three equidistant points on the color wheel with a gap of 85 in hue (**Figure 15.26**). The triadic principle and its use are identical to the complementary colors, although less marked. As there is no sense of continuity, triadic harmony is suitable for representing three distinct categories.

Analogous Colors

Analogous colors are those that are distant from each other by a maximum of 60 degrees (or 43 points on the scale 0–255) (**Figure 15.27**). The result is generally harmonious, but in some circumstances may suggest some continuity that does not exist. Analogous colors also suggest a content similarity where there is no reason to highlight one particular variable.

Rectangle

This is a variation of the split complementary rule in which two analogous colors are used on each side of the wheel (**Figure 15.28**). In this case, there is a clear distinction between two groups of categories.

In the chart, two groups of countries are in opposition: Germany and the U.S., on one hand, and Spain and Greece, on the other.

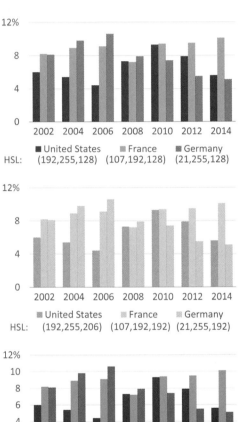

Figure 15.26 Triadic colors may represent three distinct categories.

Download the
original chart

Download the
original chart

YOUTH (<25) UNEMPLOYMENT RATE

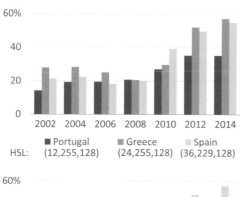

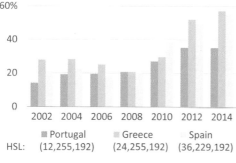

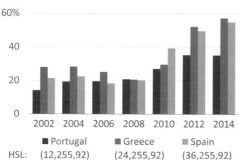

UNEMPLOYMENT RATE BY COUNTRY
Germany and U.S. vs. Greece and Spain

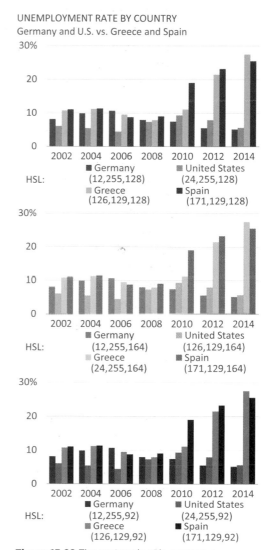

Figure 15.27 Analogous colors suggest
similarities.

Figure 15.28 The rectangle rule creates a
distinction between two groups.

Warm Colors and Cool Colors

Another color scheme is related to the concept of color temperature; that is, warm and cool (**Figure 15.29**). There is no objective way of dividing the color wheel into warm or cool colors, but generally you could consider red and the hues to the right as warm and blue and the hues to the right as cool. When you create a chart in which there is no opposition between series (or you do not want to create opposition), try choosing colors within one of the groups, warm or cool. You'll be able to choose multiple color codes and avoid a sense of continuity.

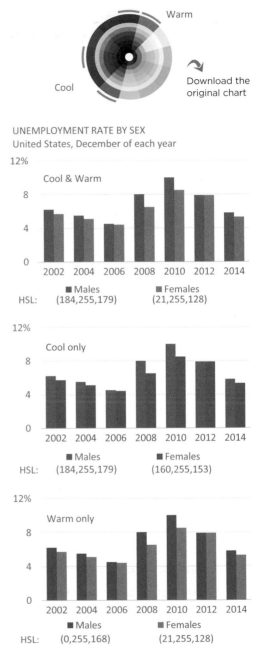

Warm

Cool

Download the original chart

UNEMPLOYMENT RATE BY SEX
United States, December of each year

Cool & Warm

HSL:
- Males (184,255,179)
- Females (21,255,128)

Cool only

HSL:
- Males (184,255,179)
- Females (160,255,153)

Warm only

HSL:
- Males (0,255,168)
- Females (21,255,128)

Figure 15.29 Warm and cool colors.

Sources for Color Palettes

The examples on the previous pages show how easy it is to reconcile the rules of color harmony to the type of message we want to convey. What they do not show is that it's more difficult to pick the color than to find the HSL codes corresponding to each rule. You can choose, say, 20 as the value for hue, which means that the complementary color will be around 148. That's easy. But you may need to do a lot of tweaking to find the "right" (subjective) color codes.

Now that you're familiar with rules of color harmony, you may want to leave the tweaking to others. Enter color palettes.

Excel

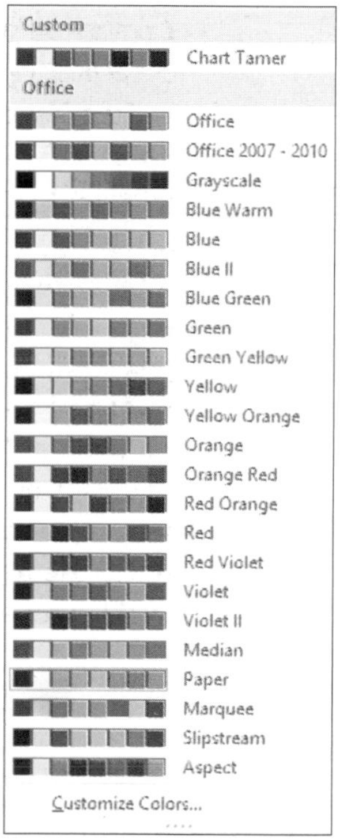

Color palettes are designed to ensure harmony and balance of chromatic stimuli. They help maintain visual coherence. Excel includes several predefined color palettes (**Figure 15.30**), and it's easy to test them and to observe the impact on the visual representation.

Unfortunately, if you inspect these predefined color palettes, you'll conclude that most are not useful for data visualization, and you may prefer to create your own palettes. Here's why the existing palettes are not useful:

Figure 15.30 Predefined color palettes in Excel (below the Chart Tamer palette shown at the top).

- **Office palettes.** If we want to avoid the "Excel look," it goes without saying that we can't use the default palette of each Excel version.

- **Hue-named palettes.** We need a palette that is flexible enough to differentiate categories using hues in multiple points of the color wheel, not in just a small section.

- **Luminance and saturation.** The palettes Median and Paper are too desaturated or too light.

- **Symbolic colors.** The palette should provide quick access to colors close to red, green, blue, and yellow, since we often need to use standard colors (think "traffic lights"). None of the other palettes offer that option.

The remaining palette, Grayscale, will be useful for testing purposes and in the unlikely event that the task actually requires it.

In an Excel color palette, there are text colors (you usually don't change that) and six accent colors. In **Figure 15.31,** these colors are displayed in the top row. I applied the accents to each slice in the pie chart below. You can compare the results for each of the chosen palettes.

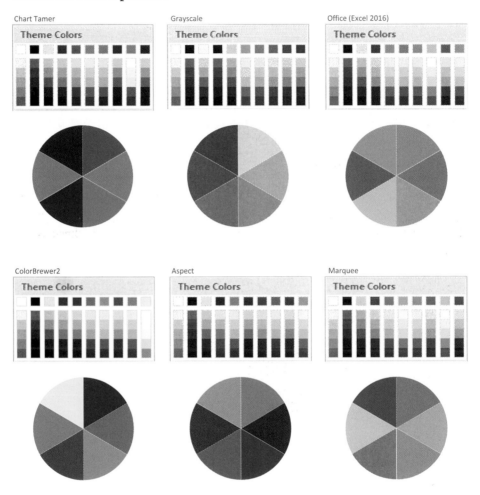

Figure 15.31 Some color palettes in Excel.

The color palette I use as my default in Excel, and the one that has been used in most charts in this book, is the Chart Tamer palette (**Figure 15.32**). This palette was designed by color expert Maureen Stone in collaboration with Stephen Few and Andreas Lipphardt for an Excel add-in.[5]

RGB COLORS FOR THE CHART TAMER PALETTE

		R	G	B
Accent 1		24	104	207
Accent 2		255	127	0
Accent 3		60	150	26
Accent 4		219	0	0
Accent 5		148	138	0
Accent 6		146	33	23

Figure 15.32 RGB colors for the Chart Tamer palette. The add-in is no longer available.

Figure 15.33 shows Excel's window for creating new palettes by editing theme colors. In general, the colors are defined as Accents 1 through 6. Once you've defined the six accent colors, Excel displays five variations for each: three lighter and two darker.

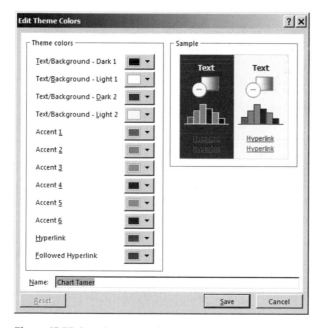

Figure 15.33 Creating new color palettes in Excel.

---

5 Another expert in data visualization, Rolf Hichert, created his own custom palette. He has a page on his website where he specifies the use of each color.

Go to the web page

Beyond Excel

In most cases, creating a new palette doesn't mean actually choosing each of the six colors, but simply importing palettes made by experts. A good source to start with is ColorBrewer (**Figure 15.34**).

Go to the
web page

Although commonly used in maps, ColorBrewer palettes are also used in charts. The website includes several useful options: number of colors, type of data (sequential, divergent, or qualitative, corresponding to three of our functional tasks of color), and conditioned to the type of use and user (such as detectable colors for color-blind people, detectable colors when printed or when photocopied).

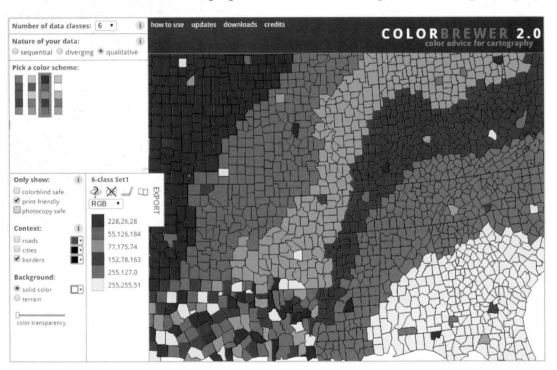

Figure 15.34 Choosing palettes in ColorBrewer 2.

To use a palette, take note of the RGB codes and create a new palette in Excel with these codes. (Search the website for information on whether using a ColorBrewer palette has any legal restrictions. You should at least mention your palette's source.)

If you're feeling creative, you might explore Adobe Color CC (**Figure 15.35**). On the website, you can interact with a color wheel, choose the rule of color harmony you wish to begin with, manipulate the values, and evaluate the results.

Go to the
web page

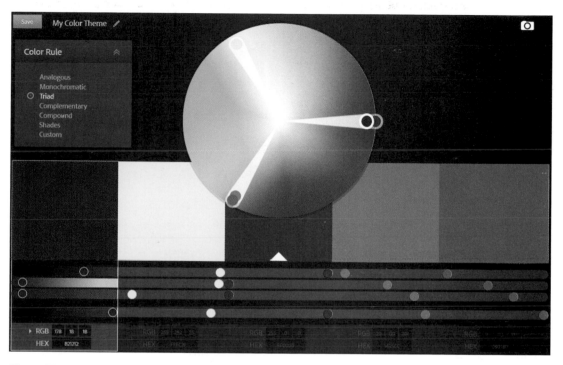

Figure 15.35 Adobe Color CC.

Another way to generate a color palette on the Adobe Color CC website is by loading an image you like and then composing the palette from there. When you're satisfied, use the bottom bar to take note of their RGB codes.

Color Blindness

Except for the grayscale palette, all other palettes in **Figure 15.36** perform poorly when using colors in the first row and testing for color blindness: Deuteranopia turns all colors into shades of green or purple.

Although color blindness is very restrictive when you want to color-code multiple categories, you can often minimize its impact by varying luminance or by skipping color-coding all together.

Go to the
web page

If you do want to use color, you can check the results using a color blindness simulator like Color Oracle and test with different levels of luminance.

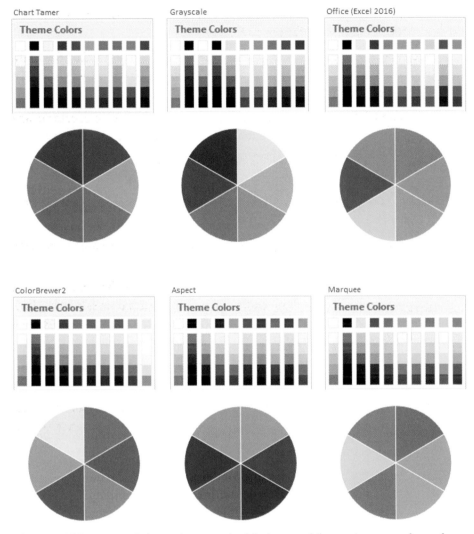

Figure 15.36 Deuteranopia is a red-green color blindness and the most common form of color blindness. This image was generated by Color Oracle, a color blindness simulator.

Takeaways

- Color use is inevitable, so we must find ways to apply it effectively to create a pleasant experience for the audience.

- We can functionalize color (that is, seek color solutions that facilitate the reading of a graphical representation and that are independent of aesthetics) in four ways:

  1. Establish the *functional tasks* of color—that is, what kind of color usage is consistent with our data and the message we want to convey.

  2. Manipulate the *intensity* of chromatic stimuli. Variations of intensity reveal levels of data relevance.

  3. Take advantage of the *symbolic nature* of color and how we should integrate it into our representations.

  4. Recognize *the role of gray*, which means utilizing the absence of color for creating context and minimizing noise.

- Once color has been made functional, we stage color—that is, we create a graphical representation in which each of these prior four elements plays a role in structuring the message, and all four support a minimum framework for using color safely.

- The aesthetic and more subjective component of color can be made less complex by rules of color harmony.

- Matching colors is difficult. Even with the help of the rules of color harmony, we need additional aids, such as the use of appropriate palettes in our graphical representations.

16

CONCLUSION

A data analyst and former coworker once asked me, with an ironic smile and half incredulously, whether data visualization was really a thing. It seemed strange to him that something as obvious as chart making could be a subject of study outside of learning how to make charts in an Excel training course.

For our business organization, trusting the numbers (the data) and having an intelligent discourse about them were essential qualities, and rightly so. As for charts, most people have never been required to present more than a few colorful slides in PowerPoint presentations. Some business organization rituals are like that.

It's All About Pragmatism, Not Aesthetics

I wrote this book thinking of those for whom charts represent the colorful moments of a presentation that can be useful for illustrating some numbers, assuming that their role ends there.

After reading this book, you must realize now that this way of looking at charts is only a cartoon-like view of the potential of data visualization. I'm sure you will not think in terms of "Your charts are prettier than mine," because none of this has to do with aesthetics, graphic design skills, or mastering the tools. Data visualization in a business organization represents a very pragmatic way of increasing the returns on investments made in the data. Furthermore, making some colorful charts just for fun means you'll be leaving money on the table.

I quoted Stephen Few several times throughout this book. He likes to say that data visualization is not difficult. Sure, it's not rocket science, nor is it one of the fine arts. Simple rules make data visualization more effective, but it cannot be left to basic automated algorithms. Data visualization makes us see, but we need to know how to design the visualizations to help us see more clearly. If we design charts well, there is a good chance they'll also be aesthetically pleasing (for a business context).

Say Goodbye to the Old Ways

We don't use "data visualization" as a fancy synonym for "making charts," just as "language" is not a synonym for "words." Understanding this difference, and the importance given to effectiveness when transmitting the message, is the first step toward changing wrong assumptions, such as thinking that charts serve only (or mostly) to illustrate. After taking this step, it's hard to go back.

I was recently flipping through a report that contained several charts. It was obvious the authors had at least taken what I see as this first step, demonstrated by the absence of pie charts and pseudo-3D effects. (Pie charts and pseudo-3D effects are certainly a couple of the worst sins against effective data visualization.) However, I remain concerned that this may be the only part of the message received outside of the data visualization community. I'm also concerned that, stripped of these two mainstays of antiquated visual representations, people now feel lost between a world that is no longer theirs and another that they're just beginning to explore.

It's likely that this has also happened to you, and that you have had the temptation to turn back. Don't do it, please. That old comfort zone is illusory and ever narrower, because the data will make you face increasingly larger challenges.

Find Your Own Data Visualization Model

It's imperative that you find an alternative visualization model. One that makes you feel comfortable and through which you're able to analyze the data and communicate your findings effectively. This is something you have to do by yourself, depending on your tasks, your skills, your organization's requirements, and the tools that it allows you to use.

You know, when people overvalue aesthetics it doesn't matter much if they're graphic designers or Excel users. The fact that one makes more aesthetically pleasing visualizations is irrelevant when the goal is to analyze data or communicate insights. Actually (and you may find it strange to read this in a data visualization book), overvaluing aesthetics is a sign of overvaluing data visualization. Whatever level of data analyst you are, your starting point is not how to select or design the most pleasing visualization for the data or the task. Your true starting point is to select a mix of tools (text, data, and visualizations) that best captures what the data have to say. For every task, for every step, there are always other options that you should consider.

In Business Visualization, Hard Work Is Not Always the Best Work

You might have smiled when I mentioned the path of least resistance in Chapter 2. That phrase is often used as a synonym for laziness, when in fact it should be a synonym for effectiveness and efficiency (better charts that use fewer cognitive resources). I see no merit at all in hard work when it stems from process inefficiencies and a lack of curiosity for finding new solutions. Constructing the visualization model should be subordinate to providing preprocessed stimuli that allow one to think and not be overwhelmed with tasks that can be simplified or outsourced.

When emphasizing effectiveness, we're also emphasizing more intelligent data management, regardless of its volume. Throughout this book, you probably correctly read hundreds of values in several charts, without all those values interfering with your reasoning. On the other hand, you might have also found it rather difficult, beginning with Chapter 1, to address some questions whose answers were hidden in a bad chart that contained only a few data points.

Organizational Literacy

The most difficult thing is not understanding or even creating your visualization style. Rather, the hardest thing is selling your style to your organization. When the organization's visualization culture is shaped by Microsoft tools, you can hardly blame managers for whom visualization is not relevant in the decision-making process.

Low graphical literacy is common and stems from a lack of awareness as well as from training that focuses much too narrowly on how to use the tools, praising the software features no matter how silly and removed from basic visualization principles these features are. This can be internalized in such a way that people refuse to recognize their low graphical literacy as a problem. Fortunately, most of the time, simple inertia is the real culprit.

By understanding the limits of the organization's visualization culture, you can initiate change by selling the benefits of your visualizations to top management, showing clearly and systematically the advantages of a model based on effectiveness rather than on models of useless effects. Changing the organizational culture is difficult and takes time, so converting one person at a time might be a reasonable goal. But the change begins with you. Design more effective versions of your charts, or practice by trying to improve some of the charts in this book. Clearly explain why the new versions are better.

Reason and Emotion

I hope it has become clear to you throughout the book that many of the issues debated by different experts in data visualization are associated with the eternal conflict between emotion and reason. Some experts claim that effectiveness should be measured by the interest that the chart awakens through its format and aesthetics (because an uninteresting chart that nobody reads is useless). Others say that emphasizing aesthetics is just fool's gold, and that any sub-optimal design choice not only endangers the effectiveness of chart reading but can lead to biases in understanding the message.

Both of these positions are legitimate, and neither has a monopoly on truth. Finding the balance between the two is always more interesting, but from a business visualization perspective, your starting point should be based in reason: Seek to make justifiable and rational design choices and, from there, move (minimally) in the opposite direction to add an emotional component that frames the visualization without distorting it (for example, in the spirit of the law of least effort, a chart title that summarizes the main conclusions is more attractive than one that merely describes its content).

Play with Constraints

To force change, impose some restrictions on yourself in the way you visualize data. Try some of these exercises:

- Avoid pie charts or pseudo-3D effects if you cannot justify them (and "My manager likes them" doesn't count).
- Reduce your chart to a minimum readable size. (It would be a good idea to test its readability on a smartphone.)
- Create small multiples when you have many series.
- Limit the number of colors in your chart to three.
- Find examples for which the logarithmic scale is useful.
- Design a dashboard.
- Create a useful chart with more than 100 series.
- Get data from your internal business intelligence (BI), and structure the data in order to create an interactive chart from a pivot table.
- Test your charts' readability for color-blind people.
- Find an article with a lot of numbers but no charts, and try to draw charts that support the text (or perhaps that contradict it).

Create more interesting challenges by combining several of these suggestions. Always compare your results with those that would have been obtained through the usual old process.

The Tools

One last word about tools. I would not have planned this book the way I did if I did not believe that access to a spreadsheet application is sufficient for understanding what data visualization is all about. I also believe that we can move from Excel charts to Excel visualizations by improving graphical literacy with only a marginal cost for the organization.

It's easy for you to use Excel for all your data analysis tasks, knowing that you can share files with colleagues, customers, and suppliers, creating a predictable information flow.

This Excel ecosystem creates a comfort zone that's hard to escape, permeating the organizational culture and thwarting alternatives that may be difficult to assess. As we discussed, tools are not neutral, and the Excel monoculture tends to force analytical perspectives of the data that are simple to apply using a spreadsheet. This does not mean that they're the most appropriate for the organization.

Ideally, a graphical representation should be designed depending only on business goals and needs. Some characteristics of the chart can be adjusted to the nature of the tool without altering the end result. Other characteristics, however, are incompatible with the software application, and the organization must decide whether it can dismiss these particular goals and needs, or whether an investment in another application is justified.

In any event, I suggest that you familiarize yourself with data visualizations made with tools other than Excel. Just search online for data visualizations done in Tableau, SAP Lumira, or QlikView, or programming languages like R, Python, or D3. If you are reluctant to leave the Microsoft umbrella, try PowerBI.

There is much to do in data visualization. There is much to research, and there is a lot of data to discover or even rediscover. I'm sure that after having read this book, you will be less tolerant of certain cartoon visualizations that distort, lie, babble with incomprehensible fragments, or merely waste your time. I'm confident that you will participate in this discovery process as a professional and as a citizen.

—Jorge Camões

INDEX